Twenty-First Century
Inequality & Capitalism

Studies in Critical Social Sciences Book Series

Haymarket Books is proud to be working with Brill Academic Publishers (www.brill.nl) to republish the *Studies in Critical Social Sciences* book series in paperback editions. This peer-reviewed book series offers insights into our current reality by exploring the content and consequences of power relationships under capitalism, and by considering the spaces of opposition and resistance to these changes that have been defining our new age. Our full catalog of *SCSS* volumes can be viewed at https://www.haymarketbooks .org/series_collections/4-studies-in-critical-social-sciences.

TWENTY-FIRST CENTURY INEQUALITY & CAPITALISM

Piketty, Marx and Beyond

EDITED BY

LAUREN LANGMAN AND DAVID A. SMITH

Haymarket Books
Chicago, IL

First published in 2017 by Brill Academic Publishers, The Netherlands.
© 2017 Koninklijke Brill NV, Leiden, The Netherlands

Published in paperback in 2018 by
Haymarket Books
P.O. Box 180165
Chicago, IL 60618
773-583-7884
www.haymarketbooks.org

ISBN: 978-1-60846-134-9

Trade distribution:
In the U.S. through Consortium Book Sales, www.cbsd.com
In the UK, Turnaround Publisher Services, www.turnaround-uk.com
In Canada, Publishers Group Canada, www.pgcbooks.ca
All other countries, Ingram Publisher Services International, ips_intlsales@ingramcontent.com

Cover design by Jamie Kerry and Ragina Johnson.

This book was published with the generous support of Lannan Foundation and the Wallace Action Fund.

Printed in United States.

10 9 8 7 6 5 4 3 2 1

Library of Congress Cataloging-in-Publication Data is available.

We dedicate this work to the great masses of humanity who have suffered under yokes of imperialism, colonialism and contemporary neo liberal, globalized capital. The underclasses of today, the victims, the displaced and expelled, the precariat, the "wretched of the earth", the surplus population of the world, suffer from poverty and indifference. We hope that efforts like ours would enable the processes of amelioration.

∴

Contents

PART 2
Inequality

PART 3
Global Inequality

Preface

Inequality in the advanced capitalist countries, especially the USA, is now greater than in the 1930 (which represented a previous peak for polarization); many would argue it has reached crisis levels. Many workers have flat or even declining incomes, as the middle class has been "hollowed out." Meanwhile, the incomes of elites have exploded, especially at lofty pinnacle of the top 1% of the top 1%. While half of Americans would have trouble coming up with $1,000 in an emergency, the elites often spend that much money on dinner. Not surprisingly, this polarization is being noticed and generating anger and discontent. Thomas Piketty' 2014 book Capital in the Twenty-First Century, may have been intended to resurrect serious discussions of political economy within economic circles and even beyond academia. It's publication came at a propitious time, as the impact of growing inequality was influencing and becoming a public issue in the way of various mass movements such as Arab spring, Occupy Wall Street, southern European austerity protests, etc. This may explain the riddle of why a relatively dense text suddenly became a best seller. Piketty and his team did extensive research to compile unprecedented historical evidence of rising inequality going back to Adam Smith and David Ricardo; he may have had nothing but good intentions in terms of reigniting "classical" debates about political economy. Despite the evocative title, Piketty claimed he had not read Marx, denying that the latter's work was of any interest. As contributors to this volume make clear: this was a rather large mistake! It's related to another: while the current crisis of capitalism may be a good time to "bring back in political economy," trying to do that but completely ignoring the "political" part is another error.

Our premise in this book is that we need to begin with an attempt to understand the dynamics of contemporary society that is embedded in capitalism as a political, economic, socio-cultural system— and, indeed, that system is now a deterritorialized, world market. Most of the authors in this collection, however critical they may be of Piketty, much appreciate the fact that his book brought so much wider attention to questions of inequality that have been largely a concern of progressive academics as well as various social justice activists. However, the narrow conceptual framework he developed greatly limited his vision, constrained his analysis and tepid suggestions for possible solutions (which, modest as they may be, Piketty himself acknowledges may be unrealistic).

The University of California, Irvine provided some funding that allowed us to include previously published work by Erik Olin Wright and Charles Reitz in this volume. We also want to acknowledge the hard work and tenacity of our authors, who drafted the chapters and graciously revised their essays in response to substantive and stylistic critiques. In some cases, the changes were quite substantial and we thank all these fellow travelers on this journey!

As we look at the world today, we can observe three major problems: growing inequality, environmental despoliation and the future of democratic governance. If we look at the levels of current inequality, it becomes ever more evident that the present state of affairs cannot continue. In the chapters that follow, there are a number of potential scenarios likely to occur. First, with the current trends for conservative, if not reactionary governments, inequality is likely to grow, as well as discontent. Second, we could see a rise of even more authoritarian state to suppress expressions of discontent and secure social stability; this can lead to an almost neo-feudal system in which the rich own almost all of the wealth, and the majority live at levels of their subsistence. Third, we could see a scenario similar to what medieval peasants experienced after allowing such a system to become normalized; the possibilities of changing the road would serve as a distraction to reforming the political economy; the medieval Carnival of Europe saw various forms of collective rituals or restricting the possibility of change and we could perhaps see privatized social media playing the same role.

There are some hints of a mobilization in response to these challenges as growing progressive, social justice movements may be emerging to fight for change. And while such change would necessarily involve major, and worldwide structural transformations, the nascent global justice movements, portend a long-term shifted attitudes, values and identities that would make a structural transformation possible; whatever else one might say about such a transformation it would involve changes in the nature of property relationships as well as the democratization of power. Finally, and not unrelated to the question of inequality, the despoliation of our environment, whether global warming, atmospheric gases, the habitat loss destroying various species, adverse weather conditions, foretell nothing but growing hardship, which of course includes malnutrition and starvation. And indeed, we could see major wars over things like water and arable land. While little touched on by Piketty, several of the authors reiterate the need for environmental sanity that would, of course, begin with the ending of a fossil fuel-based economy. What does this have to do with inequality? Given the population of the world, and its available resources, there is absolutely no question that the planet cannot sustain a population in which even one half were able to live a comfortable "middle class" lifestyle of upper-income Americans with large houses, SUVs in the driveway all indifferent to the consumption of resources and/or energy. Part and parcel of the more egalitarian world would require large, if not a massive, reduction of the intertwining of lifestyles with "conspicuous consumption." Thus, any comprehensive approach for the reduction of inequality needs to also consider the intertwining of the global economy, with the vast and often useless energy consumption, beginning with the military and, perhaps, ending with the tons of plastic bottles that are discarded every day.

Acknowledgements

This collection is the product of a number of authors whose scholarly reflections inspired and contributed to the project. We must first recognize all of those who live in chronic despair due to the nature of contemporary neoliberal capitalism: the billions of people who are on the bottom of the economic system. They are the poor, the exploited workers of the global economy, the underemployed, the disposed, the precariat and migrant, the contemporary "wretched of the earth" who bear the brunt of the sufferings of inequality, poverty from misery to sickness, often malnutrition and homelessness. Much like Piketty, we hope that our collection will stimulate further academic discussions of the nature and causes of contemporary inequality in order to ameliorate inequality and the suffering it brings.

This project came out spontaneously, after a number of online discussions among progressive sociologists who first decided we should have a special session at the American Sociological Association (ASA) meeting in San Francisco. During that online discussion, Kevin Andeson suggested that I, Lauren Langman, organize the session since I do a lot of organizing. I agreed, and at the International Sociological Association meeting in Yokohama, I ran into Saskia Sassen who was perhaps more than anyone enthusiastic and especially supportive about the idea of organizing the prospective session and quickly agreed to participate. In the next two days, I ran into Sylvia Walby and Chris Chase Dunn who were also eager to participate. David A. Smith contacted Basak Kus and Chris Chase-Dunn and asked them to also be on the panel (later he also invited some of the chapter authors to contribute to the edited volume). The next step was finding a place for the symposium and the problem was that ASA usually allocates their conference rooms long in advance. David Smith stepped in and we were able to secure a spot at a nearby Glide Memorial Church, long a bastion for San Francisco's radical organizing and social change and a counter-cultural rallying point since the 1960s; the Glide leadership was able to accommodate us.

It was springtime and too late to enter the meeting in the official ASA program, but the national organization did agree to list the session "unofficially" and we also sent a number of emails out to various ASA sections, posted signs at the meetings, etc. We expected that in the best case we might get 30 or 40 to show up. However, more than 200 people showed up—technically, we reached the maximum capacity and it was standing room only. We did not expect such an enthusiastic response! When the session was over, many in the crowd suggested that we publish the session contributions as a special issue of

Critical Sociology or a book in the *Studies in Critical Social Sciences* Series with Brill. David Fasenfest, editor of Critical Sociology as well as the book series, encouraged us to go ahead and ask other experts in the field to contribute to a book. It is very difficult to express the gratitude for all his help and cooperation. This book could not have been possible had it not been for his support. David, Thank You!

An edited collection depends entirely on the goodwill of contributors who spend enormous amounts of time preparing their papers and perhaps even more time on editing the papers: a collection like this would not exist had it not been for the cooperation of the many authors we graciously thank. In addition, we must also give special thanks to Alma Begicevic who did the final job of editing and preparing the manuscripts, and Ayala Leyser, the artist who did the cover for the book, and Steven Schmidt, a UCI doctoral student in sociology who created the index.

List of Figures and Tables

Figures

Tables

Notes on Contributors

Kevin Amidon
is an Associate Professor of World Languages and Cultures at Iowa State University. He has published a wide range of articles in critical social theory, including studies of gender, eugenics, race, evolutionary thought, the Frankfurt School, opera, and theater. He is currently writing on cultures of investigation and persuasion in German life sciences during the early twentieth century and the status of Hören (hearing, attention, obedience, and ownership) in the German opera of the 1920s.

Robert J. Antonio
teaches in the Sociology Department at the University of Kansas. His work is mainly in modern, contemporary, and critical social theory and globalization, inequality, and environment.

J. I. (Hans) Bakker
was recently the Stanley Knowles Distinguished Professor of Public Policy at Brandon University, Brandon, Manitoba. He has retired from a Professorship at the University of Guelph. His recent edited book is entitled: *The Methodology of Political Economy* (Lexington, 2015).

Roslyn Wallach Bologh
is Professor in the Department of Sociology and Anthropology at the College of Staten Island, CUNY and in the Department of Sociology at the Graduate Center, CUNY. In addition to numerous articles, she is the author of the following books: *Dialectical Phenomenology, Marx's Method and Love or Greatness, Max Weber and Masculine Thinking, A Feminist Inquiry* (Brill, 2017).

Alessandro Bonanno
is Texas State University System Regents' Professor and Distinguished Professor of Sociology at Sam Houston State University. He is the author of *The Legitimation Crisis of Neoliberalism* (Brill, 2017).

Christopher Chase-Dunn
is Distinguished Professor of Sociology and Director of the Institute for Research on World-Systems at the University of California-Riverside. His recent research focuses on the causes of empire expansion and urban growth (and decline) in the Afro-Eurasian world-system over the last 5000 years. His

studies of structural globalization and global state formation in the modern world-system have been supported by the National Science Foundation.

Harry F. Dahms

is a Professor of Sociology at the University of Tennessee-Knoxville, where he is also Co-Director of the Center for the Study of Social Justice and Co-Chair of the Committee on Social Theory. In addition, he is the editor of *Current Perspectives in Social Theory* and Director of the International Social Theory Consortium.

Eoin Flaherty

is Assistant Professor at the School of Sociology, University College Dublin. His recent work on top income inequality appears in Socio-Economic Review and he is co-editor of *The Changing Worlds and Workplaces of Capitalism* (Palgrave Macmillan, 2015).

Daniel Krier

is an associate professor of sociology at Iowa State University where he specializes in political economy and social theory. Recent books include NASCAR, *Sturgis and the New Economy of Spectacle* (2016) coauthored with William Swart and volumes co-edited with Mark Worrell entitled *Capitalism's Future: Alienation, Emancipation and Critique* (2016) and *The Social Ontology of Capitalism* (2017).

Basak Kus

is a faculty member in the sociology department at Wesleyan University. Her work focuses on neoliberal reforms, politics of economic crises, finance and society, inequality, politics of debt, and regulation.

Lauren Langman

is a professor of sociology at Loyola University Chicago. He has worked in the tradition of the Frankfurt School of Critical Theory, especially progressive global justice movements and reactionary movements, considering relationships between culture, economy and identity. He is past president of Alienation Research and Theory, Research Committee 36, of the International Sociological Association and the past president of the Marxist section of the American Sociological Association. Recent publications include *Trauma Promise and Millennium*, with Devorah Kalekin, *Alienation and Carnivalization* with Jerome Braun and a special issue of *Current Sociology* on Arab Spring the Indignados and Occupy. His latest book is on *American Character, God, Guns, Gold and*

Glory and the next is Mobilizing for Dignity. He is on several editorial boards, including *Critical Sociology*.

Dana Marie Louie

is a graduate of Wesleyan University (class of 2015). She currently works as a consultant specializing in cases relating to finance and antitrust litigation.

Peter Marcuse

is a Professor Emeritus of Urban Planning at Columbia University. He is a prolific author: among his books are *Missing Marx: A Personal and Political Journal of a Year in East Germany, 1989–1990* (1991) and *Searching for the Just City: Debates in Urban Theory and Practice* (2009).

Sandor Nagy

received his B.A. in Global Studies from the University of California, Riverside. He is a member of the Institute for Research on World-Systems, directed by Christopher Chase-Dunn. His primary research focuses on revolutions, more specifically, world revolutionary waves in the context of global social movements.

Charles Reitz

retired professor of social science and philosophy at Kansas City Kansas Community College, has published *Philosophy & Critical Pedagogy* (2016), *Crisis and Commonwealth* (2013), and *Art, Alienation and the Humanities* (2000).

William I. Robinson

is Professor of Sociology, Global and International Studies, and Latin American and Iberian Studies at the University of California at Santa Barbara, and author, among other books, of *Global Capitalism and the Crisis of Humanity* (2014, Cambridge University Press). His website is http://www.soc.ucsb.edu/faculty/robinson/ [www.soc.ucsb.edu].

Saskia Sassen

is the Robert S. Lynd Professor of Sociology and Member of The Committee on Global Thought, Columbia University (www.saskiasassen.com). Her new book is *Expulsions: Brutality and Complexity in the Global Economy* (Harvard University Press 2014) now out in 15 languages. She is the recipient of diverse awards and mentions, including multiple doctor honoris causa, named lectures. Most recently she was awarded the Principe de Asturias 2013 Prize in the Social Sciences and made a Foreign Member of the Royal Academy of the Sciences of The Netherlands.

David A. Smith

is a Professor of Sociology at the University of California at Irvine. His research focuses on global commodity chains, world cities and the political economy of the world-system. He is Editor of International Journal of Comparative Sociology and was 2015–16 President of the Society for the Study of Social Problems (his Presidential Address, "Globalizing Social Problems" is available in *Social Problems* at https://academic.oup.com/socpro/article-abstract/64/1/1/2667461/Globalizing-Social-Problems-An-Agenda-for-the.

David N. Smith

has published widely on capitalism, charisma, authoritarianism, anti-Semitism, genocide, and critical theory. Among other works, he is the author of *Marx's Capital Illustrated* (Haymarket, 2014) and the editor of *Marx's World: Asia, Africa, the Americas and Capital Accumulation in Karl Marx's Late Manuscripts* (Yale University Press, forthcoming). He teaches sociology at the University of Kansas.

Tony Smith

is a faculty member in the philosophy program at Iowa State University. He is the author of *The Logic of Marx's Capital and Globalisation: A Systematic Marxian Account*, among other works.

Michael J. Thompson

is Associate Prof. of Political Theory in the Department of Political Science at William Paterson University. His most recent book is *The Domestication of Critical Theory* (2016).

Sylvia Walby

OBE, is Distinguished Professor of Sociology, the UNESCO Chair in Gender Research, and Director of the Violence and Society UNESCO Centre, Lancaster University: http://wp.lancs.ac.uk/violence-and-society-unesco-centre/; she is the lead author of *The Concept and Measurement of Violence against Women and Men*, Bristol: Policy Press (2017).

Erik Olin Wright

is a Professor of Sociology at the University of Wisconsin–Madison. He is the author of, among others, *Interrogating Inequality* (2005) and, with Joel Rodgers, *American Society: How It Really Works* (2010). His most recent book is *Alternatives to Capitalism* (2016).

Introduction

Lauren Langman and David A. Smith

In late 2013 and early 2014 something very peculiar happened: Thomas Piketty, a relatively young and not very well-known French economist published an economic treatise with almost 600 pages of text and additional hundred pages of notes and indexes, heavily laden with both statistics and literary references about enormous—and growing—wealth and income disparities in Europe and the United States.[1] One might argue that his argument was somewhat novel and that he and his collaborators were using tax records to present empirical evidence that hadn't been previously fully explored. Although social scientists, running the gamut from economists to sociologists to psychologists, had focused a great deal of attention on issues of inequality for many years (using a variety of methods and data), most of that scholarship was consigned to the usual disciplinary oriented publications and to building scholars' *curriculum vitaes*, generating the usual narrow, esoteric debates, and drawing little wider attention in the public sphere. Piketty's work received a different reception. It was initially published in the late summer of 2013 in French and the "buzz" immediately ensued. In January 2014, the English language commentaries were published in *The Economist* and *The New York Times*. The publication of the full English translation was moved up to March 2014 and it was termed an "overnight sensation" in an anonymously written essay in *The Economist* on May 4, 2014. Interestingly, but quite problematically, Piketty was titled "A Modern Marx." By the summer of 2014, bookstores across North America were having trouble keeping hard cover copies (list price $39.95!) in stock. Whether those masses who bought the book actually *read* the book or not is debatable. A study of e-book users suggested many stopped in the first 20–30 pages[2]. Leaving aside all disclaimers, this was clearly a case of an academic book as a popular phenomenon, with the author shooting up to "rock star" fame!

By June, the listserv of the Marxist Section of the American Sociological Association (ASA) began discussing the author and the book even though,

---

1 Thomas Piketty, *Capitalism in the Twenty First Century*, (Cambridge: Harvard University Press, 2014).

2 Emily Cohen. "Not Many People Got Past Page 26 of Piketty's Book," *Huffington Post*, July 7, 2014. http://www.huffingtonpost.com/2014/07/07/piketty-book-no-one-read_n_5563629.html. Accessed October 21, 2015.

we suspect, very few of us, as yet, had read much of that imposing volume. Not surprisingly, there was excitement among this group of critical sociologists about the popularity of a hefty tome that illustrated the extreme levels of wealth inequality in contemporary core capitalist societies. But there was also a great deal of trenchant critique underlining various ways that Piketty and his arguments were hardly Marxist, and noting his many omissions and blind spots in his explanations of wealth polarization. It was an extremely engaging e-discussion—and it seemed like there would be a wonderful opportunity to discuss this at an upcoming 2014 ASA meeting. But there was a problem: the annual conference in San Francisco was coming up in August. Normally, trying to get anything like a formal "panel" organized for that in two or three months would be impossible (the slowly moving wheels of the bureaucracy usually need more than a year to do this!). We felt that "waiting" wasn't a good option, so we charged ahead and put together an "informal" session at the August conference (that was, in fact, officially listed in the ASA program). It featured four outstanding scholars, all taking a critical approach but coming from different perspectives: Christopher Chase-Dunn, Basak Kus, Saskia Sassen and Sylvia Walby. The panelists discussed the Piketty book, its central claims and arguments, and the wider debate that was opening up about global inequality. It was a somewhat raucous session, hosted by the social-justice inclined and centrally located Glide Memorial Church (we were unable to secure a room at the "regular" conference hotels). There were well over two hundred people in attendance (it was "standing room only" in the back), the presentations were relatively short, allowing a lot of time for lively discussion.

After that event, we felt that we really should try to get a publishable product out. Our idea was to include the four presenters/authors in the session, but to also invite other interested scholars in sociology and cognate fields to join in the discussion. We also believe that, while the Piketty tome itself as a sort of "phenomenon" was important—and deserved serious attention from sociologists, Marxists and other critical scholars—we wanted the scope of this volume to be broader than simply confronting that one book. Indeed, we believe that the popularity of Piketty in 2014 was, on the one hand, a product of a *zeitgeist* that was sweeping the post-"Great Recession" world, but, on the other, potentially indicative of a deep-seated structural crisis in the basic political economy of contemporary capitalism. We hope that the contents of this collection address both the popular mobilization against contemporary neoliberal capitalism and its blatant inequality, while also exposing some of those fundamental structural forces that underlie the contemporary crisis.

The Context of a Global Crisis

There is little doubt that part of the wave of the Piketty phenomenon was riding was based on a heightened sense of mass/popular anger about economic insecurity and precariousness: this led to a worldwide popular mobilization that became visible in 2011. The first stirrings were in December 2010, when the self-immolation of a Tunisian fruit peddler ignited a wave of massive protests across the Middle East initiating the "Arab Spring," massive mobilizations and protests in Egypt, Libya, Morocco and Syria. By May of that year, similar mobilizations and general strikes erupted in Southern Europe, most notably Greece, Spain and Portugal. The spark touched the United States by fall, initially as Occupy Wall Street in a small park in lower Manhattan, but Occupy camps quickly spreading across the United States in the form of hundreds of hundreds of occupations and encampments.[3] Of course, in each case local and national specific factors were cited as proximal and precipitating events (in the Middle East actions by dictatorial political regimes, in Spain and Greece grinding government austerity programs, in the US the federal bailout of the financial giants). But there were also clear commonalities: participatory democratic organizing strategies, distrust of established political channels, and a desire to fight the extreme centralization of political and economic power.

Indeed, arguably, a unifying thread to all this foment were the "legitimation crises" of the sort described by Habermas in his classical book by that name published over four decades ago.[4] A failure in the economic, political or and/or cultural systems migrate to the "life world" of motivation, emotion and identity, e.g. people become indignant, fearful, angry and despairing about hardships and the future. This typically leads to a loss of self-esteem and a dramatic withdrawal of loyalty and commitment to the institutional undergirdings of a social system.[5] Such crisis involves the economic system failing to deliver the expected wages or incomes to a significant portion of the population so that they can purchase an adequate if not slowly growing standard of living. Secondly, there

---

3 See Benjamin Tejerina, Ignacia Perugorria, Tova Benski and Lauren Langman. "From indignation to occupation: A: new wave of global mobilization," *Current Sociology*, vol. 61(4) July 2013, pp 377–561; Robert Macpherson and David A. Smith. "Occupy as a World Anti-Systemic Movement," *Peace Review*, vol. 25 (3) 2013, pp. 367–375.

4 Jürgen Habermas. *Legitimation Crisis*. (Boston: Beacon Press, 1975).

5 See Alessandro Bonnano, "Global Inequality, Competition, Uncertainty, and the Legitimation Crisis of Neoliberalism," Chapter 15 of this volume for a further discussion of legitimation crises.

is a contradiction between a government that needs to establish policies to ensure the profitability of the capitalist sector on the one hand, and the need to maintain democratic support for broad social, health, educational, environmental and other programs that may be vaguely "redistributional" and garner mass popular support, on the other. Thirdly, the system needs to provide a system of meanings, values and/or ideologies that normalize various historically arbitrary hierarchies and serve to render the nature of social relationships as normal and the prerogatives of the ruling class as serving the general interests of most people. By the time Piketty's tome appeared, the worldwide recession had weakened all three legs of the legitimacy tripod, as confidence in the economy, government, and neoliberal ideology were all fading and under broad attack. The ensuing crisis has very personal impacts on individual lives. Leaving aside the disillusionment of fading confidence in government and the growing cynicism about mythic meritocracy and promises of "upward mobility," many people are facing real economic hardships, stresses and strains of either losing a job and/or entitlements, perhaps never finding a permanent job, and/or finding one that barely enables one to survive; such experiences quite often trigger intense emotional consequences, fear, anger and hope, and especially the denial of dignity.[6] More recently we have seen what has been described as a "culture of despair" spreading among the white working classes, especially the men, who have lost jobs and face health problems, earlier deaths, drug (opioid) addictions and greater suicide rates.

Of course, as left progressive movements emerged in response to this crisis, so too did various right wing, nationalist, arguably quasi-fascist ones. Neoliberal capitalism, in its globalized moments, promised prosperity for everyone and a cosmopolitan ethos that would erode the ethnic, religious and/or cultural identities that facilitated many of the conflicts in the world. In its utopian variant it would even lead to world peace and harmony, convincing various old ethnic and national enemies to lay down their old enmities and modern weapons and beat all that into high-tech, genetically engineered, robotic "ploughshares," while singing either "we are the world" or kumbaya. But recent history is very different: instead, we continue to see seeming intractable

---

6   Donatella Della Porta et al. *Globalization from below; Transnational activists and protest networks; Social movements, Protests and Contention* (Minneapolis: University of Minnesota Press, 2016); Manuel Castells, *Networks of Outrage and Hope: Social Movements in the Internet Age,* (London: Polity, 2012); Lauren Langman "Occupy a new social movement" *Current Sociology,* vol. 61(4) 2013, pp. 510–524. See also Tova, Benski, Lauren Langman, et al., "From the Streets and Squares to Social Movement Studies: What have we learned", *Current Sociology Monograph,* vol. 61 (4) 2013, pp. 541–561.

conflicts in many parts of the world. Neoliberal globalization created vast amounts of wealth (as promised), but most of that lucre found its way into the (sometimes secret, offshore) bank accounts of a handful of elites, while the masses of workers around the world face stagnant or declining incomes at best; many face chronic underemployment, unemployment, or the unstable lives of the precariat.[7]

In this world of burgeoning inequality, increasing economic uncertainty and precariousness, massive social movements and demonstrations, and seemingly seismic shifts in various political orders, it is becoming increasingly clear that sensitivity to the "crisis of legitimacy" is no longer limited to esoteric academic debates: it is now a "front and center" concern that resonates with ordinary people (and explains the appetite for attempts to grapple with inequality, even in very long books). Recent evidence of this comes from the 2016 US Presidential campaign, where two "outsiders," Trump, a rich right-wing populist/nationalist, and Sanders, a democratic socialist, both garnered wide popular support from portions of the electorate that are, arguably, fractions of the precariat. This must be seen in the context of growing inequality where traditional working class and middle-income people are experiencing downward mobility and economic uncertainty (and many parents and youth are particularly worried about the future), while the mushrooming of elite wealth is literally, off the charts (and they have never been more content or comfortable). The political power seems to rest squarely in the hands of an increasingly disconnected plutocracy of the 1% (or more accurately the .1% or even .01%) that is better defined as a transnational capitalist class than a group that identifies with their fellow citizens[8]. Even in the US (indeed, even on Wall Street itself) we can argue that between robotics and automation, the relocation of manufacturing to low wage countries, import substitution, and the shift to financialization and globalization, there is a "hollowing out" of the middle classes and growth of a precariat.

---

7   Guy Standing. The Precariat: The New Dangerous Class. (London and New York: Bloomsbury Academic, 2011).

8   Most Americans accept an inegalitarian distribution of wealth and believe that it is fair that the highly trained professionals and successful businesspeople make far higher than average incomes. When asked how they imagine the actual income distribution was, they clearly saw the growing inequality of wealth. Then when we look at the actual distribution of wealth, it shows how the top 1% of the 1% are off the charts. There is an excellent You Tube showing the desired, imagined and actual distributions. See: https://www.youtube.com/watch?v=dttG9aIa9RQ&t=197s. Accessed January, 12, 2017.

A Brief History of Neoliberal Capitalism

What are the origins of all this? Clearly, part of the source lies in globalization and with it the emergence of increasingly powerful transnational capitalist class of elites. One can argue that today the world economy is governed
by an unholy transnational regulatory trinity of agencies: the World Bank,
IMF and WTO which generally dictate state policies in a world in which most
political leaders are either themselves members of the transnational capitalist class or beholden to that class for various forms of political contributions,
investments, technical and economic expertise, etc.[9] Moreover, the realities
of the contemporary world are such that most national elites, regardless of
their political party identification and/or stated ideologies, are committed to
the growth imperative of global capitalism and as a result, the operations of
the global economy. So while, on the one hand, the proponents of capitalist
globalization can herald apparent successes like economic benefits to vast
numbers of poor peasants in India and China, in other parts of the under-
developed world there are growing hardships, stress and strains, and relative
economic stagnation.[10] Furthermore, in many poor countries it is clear that
the overwhelming power of global capital undermines any semblance of
popular democracy that might act as an expression of resistance or act like
a countervailing force. So throughout the poverty-stricken underdeveloped
world we see various forms of "structural adjustment" offered (often under
the aegis of the IMF and World Bank) that require "belt tightening" that involves currency devaluation, public spending retrenchment necessitating
massive cuts to benefits and public programs (including those supporting
mass education, health, subsidies for basic subsistence), privatization of basic services such as sanitation, waste removal and water supplies, etc. All this
leads to burgeoning inequality and increasing hardships faced by growing
numbers of people in our contemporary "planet of slums."[11] So the "legitimation crisis" described above, while most familiar in various "first world"

---

9   William I. Robinson, "Capitalism in the Twenty-First Century: Global Inequality, Piketty,
        and the Transnational Capitalist Class," Chapter 13 this volume, also the work of Leslie
        Sklair, *The Transnational Capitalist Class*. (Oxford: Blackwell, 2001) and Jerry Harris, *Glob-
        al Capitalism and the Crisis of Democracy*. (Atlanta: Clarity Press, 2016).

10   Branko Milanovic. *Worlds Apart: Measuring International and Global Inequality*. (Prince-
        ton: Princeton University Press, 2005); Ho-Fung Hung and Jamie Kucinkas. "Globalization
        and Global Inequality: Assessing the Impact of the Rise of China and India, 1980–2005,"
        American Journal of Sociology Vol. 116 (5) 2011, pp. 1478–1513.

11   Mike Davis. *Planet of Slums*. (New York: Verso, 2006).

contexts, has, indeed "gone global"! The sheer magnitude of humanity suffering absolute immiseration, coupled with the abject failures of various governments to address the suffering, challenges the legitimacy not only of myriad supposedly sovereign states, but of the global economic system itself, raising questions about the viability of the neoliberal vision that is now the hegemonic ideology of globalization, especially its dominant sector, financialization. These events were reflected in the overthrow of Ben Ali in Tunisia Mubarak in Egypt. In Europe, E Syriza and Podemos, left parties have emerged, as well as growing right wing movements-seen for example in various anti-immigrant movements championed by folks like Geert Wilders or Marine Le Pen.

Although little discussed in the mass media, save in a few business journals or pages in financial news, after the Bretton Woods conference of 1944, the intact industrial capacity of America and the combination of pent-up demand and available cash led to a growing civilian economy and rising prosperity in the United States and eventually many other wealth "core" economies (in Europe, but also Japan, Canada, Australia, etc.). But one consequence of the Bretton Woods arrangement which promulgated a set of international economic policies (involving currencies, trade, and so forth) and led to rapid recovery in formerly industrialized economies in Europe and Japan, was that foreign-made goods, often of very high quality, began to enter the American market. And this was a harbinger of a much more basic transformation. By the late 1960s, there were signs of major changes, the beginning of a worldwide economic restructuring. This was described in various terms: the shift from Fordism to Post-Fordism.[12] This marked the emergence of a new "global assembly line."[13] Thus emerged a "new international division of labor."[14] But the contours of the basic argument were the same: the world economy was rapidly changing to one based on globalized production processes in which economic activities, especially manufacturing, tended to gravitate away from higher wage nations and regions and toward low-wage ones, so that capitalists could cut their labor costs. This implied the "de-industrialization" of high-wage

---

12   See Michel Aglietta. *A Theory of Capitalist Regulation: The US Experience.* (New York: Verso, 1979) and Alain Lipietz. *Mirages and Miracles: Crisis in Global Fordism.* (New York: Verso, 1987).

13   Anna Fuentes and Barbara Ehrenreich. *Women in the Global Factory.* (Boston: South End Press, 1983).

14   Folker Fröbel, Jürgen Heinrichs and Otto Kreye. *The New International Division of Labour.* (Cambridge: Cambridge University Press, 1980).

wealthy "core" nations (like the United States)[15] through capital flight to low-wage "peripheral" areas.[16]

Of course, in the US this meant that many factories, steel mills, textile mills, etc., began to close in the industrialized and unionized regions (which now are referred to as "the Rust Belt") to first, move to "right to work" states in the US South, and later move completely "south of the border" to places like Mexico (post-NAFTA in the late 1990s) or, more recently in the young 21st century, to various poor regions in Asia. The reality today is that the prices of imports from developing countries cost far less than American-made products for a wide range of consumer goods and industrial inputs ranging from steel ingots, beams or rolled sheets to shoes, shirts and underwear. At the same time, a longer term rise in capital-intensive agribusiness in North America that displaced so many family farmers across the US heartland[17] over several decades, was also spilling "offshore" as the farms of northern Mexico, began to produce more and more strawberries, tomatoes, avocados watermelons etc. for export to the United States, while it became much cheaper for Mexicans to purchase the mass produced (and subsidized) corn grown in the United States. Millions of Mexican peasants were displaced. As these trends continued, many observers noted a fundamental change in the nature of the global economy as more and more multinational companies slowly morphed into transnational corporations with various plans, offices, warehouses, assembly and distribution locations throughout the world. As these trends continued to develop, we began to call it globalization.[18] We might parenthetically note that at this time, the seventies, following the diplomatic recognition of the People's Republic of China, a nation with a massive supply of cheap labor began produce more and more goods destined for global markets; eventually the PRC became the "factory" for the world and today its number two economy.[19]

As globalization proceeded to establish a deterritorialized, seamless, transnational capitalist world market, two other trends were evident, 1) namely

---

15   Barry Bluestone and Bennett Harrison. *The Deindustrialization of America.* (New York: Basic Books, 1982).

16   Robert Ross and Kent Trachte. *Global Capitalism: The New Leviathan.* Albany, (New York: State University of New York Press, 1990).

17   See chart and table in Roberto Ferdman. "The Decline of the Small American Family Farm in One Chart," *The Washington Post,* September 16, 2014.

18   Cf. William I. Robinson. *A Theory of Global Capitalism: Production, Class, and State in a Transnational World.* (Baltimore: Johns Hopkins University Press, 2004).

19   Ho-fung Hung. *China and the Transformation of Global Capitalism.* (Baltimore: Johns Hopkins University Press, 2009).

the rapid expansion of financial markets in which more and more commerce consisted of financial speculation, what was called "casino capitalism"[20] in which certain "global cities" became central nodes for these financial markets.[21] Various forms of financial speculation and investment began to have more and more impact on global and national economies. Today, finance, insurance and real estate (known by the acronym FIRE), produce about 30 % of the profits of the American economy, despite producing a much smaller percentage (less than 10%) of the actual "value added,"[22] By and large most such activities from currency speculation, mergers and acquisitions, hedge fund management produce vast profits, but unlike the old Fordist economic regime jobs (typical of the industrial era at least from the late 1800s until roughly 1970 or so) this sector produced great profits but employed relatively few people. One consequence of the financialization of the world economy has been the displacement, indeed expulsion, of vast numbers of workers into the precarious ranks of the extremely poor. This has taken place in the gentrified parts of cities as well as the displacement of indigenous peoples from ancestral lands.[23]

In addition to this fundamental international economic restructuring, a second major transformation swept across the world in the late 20th century—and may pose a different but equally dramatic structural challenge to global capitalism. This trend might data to the wholesale movement of computers into laboratories, universities and research centers, and some large corporations, the rise of the internet and the ubiquity of e-mail as crucial communication, the era of nerdy geeks who played with computers, the invention of the semiconductor and the subsequent rise of Silicon Valley. We could focus on how this revolution in computing or artificial intelligence got its start, the role of small start-ups and garage-based innovators, whether Al Gore did, in fact, "invent the internet," etc. However, the key insight here is that when we fast-forward to the present now billions of people have smartphones with more capacity than the Apollo rocket that went to the moon in the 1969. As part of the global restructuring explained above, of course, we know that more and

20   Susan Strange. *Casino Capitalism*. (New York: Basil Blackwell, 1986).

21   Saskia Sassen. *The Global City: New York, London, Tokyo*. (Princeton: Princeton University Press, 1991).

22   Monica, Strachan. U.S. Economy Lost Nearly 700,000 Jobs Because Of NAFTA, Huffington Post, http://www.huffingtonpost.com/2011/05/12/nafta-job-loss-trade-deficit -epi_n_859983.html. Accessed July 18, 2016.

23   Saskia Sassen. *Explusions: Brutality and Complexity in the Global Economy*. (Cambridge: Harvard University Press, 2014).

more high tech computer components are now are manufactured abroad, and while many software companies emerged (Microsoft, Oracle) such enterprises do not employ the vast workforces more typical of previous eras of industrial production. But perhaps more critically, we are also seeing more and more applications of computers to design almost everything from roads and bridges to cars, planes and boats; increasingly design was integrated into production such that Cad-Cam meant that far fewer workers had unprecedented growth in their levels of productivity which eliminated a great number of other workers. As a result of computerization, integrated with robotics and increasingly artificial intelligence (AI), we see more black factories (most of the work being done by robots working 24/7 for no pay, no benefits, no unions and no complaints). This shift fits in with the notion of "lean and mean" reorganizations of work into more "flexible" and also "flatter" and more horizontal companies.[24] At first, this seems to be a class-based phenomena: increased overall productivity promoted by AI led to a loss of work, jobs and pay for blue collar laborers, but not only larger corporate profits but also rising white collar incomes. However, some are now suggesting that the Luddites of two centuries ago were not so much "wrong" as premature in their apocryphal pessimism about technological change.[25] Sociologist Randall Collins recently argued that AI may hasten a final crisis of capitalism itself, noting that "Until the 1980s or 1990s, mechanization chiefly displaced manual labor. In the most recent wave of technology, we now have the displacement of administrative labor, the downsizing of the middle class."[26] Now the robots are threatening to, essentially take *all* the jobs: "The real threat of the future is not some Frankensteinian revolt of the robots, but the last stage of technological displacement of labor on behalf of a tiny capitalist class of robot owners"[27]: not a happy outcome for the rest of us! As we

---

24   Bennett Harrison. *Lean and Mean: The Changing Landscape of Corporate Power in the Age of Flexibility.* (New York: Basic Books, 1994).

25   Randall Collins. "The End of Middle-Class Work: No More Escapes," Chapter 2, pp. 37–69 in Immanuel Wallerstein, Randall Collins, Michael Mann, Georgi Derluguian and Craig Calhoun, *Does Capitalism Have a Future?* (New York: Oxford University Press, 2013). Quotation from Kevin Drum, p. 39. See also "Welcome, Robot Overlords. Please Don't Fire," *Mother Jones* May/June 2013.

26   Randall Collins, "The End of Middle Class Work: No More Escapes". In Immanuel. Wallerstein, Randall Collins, Micheal Mann, Georgy. Derluguian, C. Caljhoun, *Does Capitalism Have a Future?* (Oxford: Oxford University Press, 2013), p. 39.

27   Randall Collins, "The End of Middle Class Work: No More Escapes". In Immanuel. Wallerstein, Randall Collins, Michael Mann, Georgy. Derluguian, C. Calhoun, *Does Capitalism Have a Future?* (Oxford: Oxford University Press, 2013), p. 68.

were finishing this volume, there was more and more notice of driverless cars (Uber/Lyft) and long haul trucks. And another few million jobs lost.[28]

As globalization spread throughout the world, a new ideological framework emerged, neoliberalism, a revival of the ideas of Smith and Ricardo, advocated by Frederick Hayek and Milton Friedman that idealized market freedom, disdained regulations and/or any trade barriers.[29] Neoliberalism displaced the Fordist neo-Keynesianism that not only a initiated a major recovery after the Great Depression, but further enabled the growing prosperity after World War II.[30] But with the elections of Reagan and Thatcher in the US and UK, there came a wider embrace of neoliberalism which attempted to valorize the free market and claim that an unfettered market provides solutions to most problems such as poverty and economic stagnation could be quickly solved by freeing markets of regulations and constraints.[31] The ideological belief that a market economy functions much better than does a planned or interventionist economy, that a rising tide would raise all boats, became quite similar to a religious belief that suffering will be rewarded in the future. Indeed it was often called "market fundamentalism."[32] While this myth of a "flat world" that was suddenly equalized by technology and markets was patently false, it was a powerful elixir to continued stagnation and desperate poverty in most of the

---

28   Ryan Petersen, The driverless truck is coming, and it's going to automate millions of jobs. https://techcrunch.com/2016/04/25/the-driverless-truck-is-coming-and-its-going-to -automate-millions-of-jobs/ Accessed November 12, 2016.

29   As will be noted in a number of the papers below, as was noted by O'Connor (1979) and Offe (1984), in order to sustain the legitimacy of the capitalist system, the capitalist state needed to provide various entitlements and benefits as well as ensure economic growth, but in order to do so, it required greater taxation which both adversely impacted corporate profits and the disposable income of individuals creating an unstable situation. In more Marxist terms, the falling greater profit required a restructuring of capitalism and a reduction in state expenses that on the one hand would lead to greater prosperity for the corporations, but greater hardships for the workers. See D.N. Smith, Chapter 16, below.

30   As will be seen however, for Piketty, low growth rates are typically the norm and while postwar periods may show rapid growth spikes, such growth rates are not typical and generally don't last very long. NB! As several of the authors will point out, the explosion of symbolic wealth, a.k.a. the zombie capital of financialization, held by only a minority of the transnational capitalist class, creates an illusory appearance of general prosperity.

31   David Harvey. *The New Imperialism*. (New York: Oxford University Press, 2003).

32   Richard Kozul-Wright and Paul Rayment. *The Resistible Rise of Market Fundamentalism: Rethinking Development Policy*. (New York: Zed Books, 2007); Ha-Joon Chang. *Bad Samaritans: The Myth of Free Trade and the Secret History of Capitalism*. (New York: Bloomsbury Press, 2008).

underdeveloped world: don't worry: things will get better if you just adapt the market policies and reduce state spending and regulation: "disaster capitalism" may seem terrible, but eventually it will lead to prosperity.[33] In the more prosperous regions of the world, where workers had enjoyed as much as 200 years of rising productivity translating into more money and comfort, the message was just as profound: first, as Margaret Thatcher famously declared, "there is no alternative" to globalization, and, second, in the long run it will all lead to a very sweet hereafter.

Notes on a Crisis in the United States

Many of the readers of this volume—and, many of the authors of the essays in this book—are particularly concerned with issues in the United States. So it is important to attempt to "situate" our own society in the crisis of global capitalism in the 21st century. In world-system theory parlance, the US enjoyed a long period of global capitalist hegemony in the period after World War II.[34] The national economy was extremely prosperous for two or three decades, the US military might was so overwhelming that the period was described as "Pax Americana."[35] Our leaders ruled the world and our economy boomed. This country epitomized what economic John Galbraith called "the affluent society" in a 1958 book, with boundless upward mobility. By the time of Barack Obama's 2009 inaugural address, the president felt compelled to address the he "nagging fear that America's decline is inevitable, and that the next generation must lower its sights."

As noted above, the late 20th century was, in fact, a time of economic growth and the perception of progress in many of the richer "core" regions of the world. But US economic dynamism was exceptional. The very notion of Fordism, as a manufacturing regime inextricably linked to rising wages, unionization and the creation of a large consumer economy emerged from the auto factories of Detroit. For several decades the economy boomed, with a long, slow rise in worker productivity (and factory workers becoming more

---

33   Naomi Klein. *Shock Doctrine: The Role of Disaster Capitalism.* (New York: Henry Holt and Company, 2007).

34   Immanuel Wallerstein. *The Capitalist World-Economy.* (New York: Cambridge University Press, 1979); Giovanni Arrighi. *The Long Twentieth Century: Money, Power and the Origins of Our Times.* (New York: Verso, 1994).

35   Immanuel Wallerstein. "The World-System After the Cold War." *Peace Review* Vol. 30 (1) 1993, pp. 1–6.

productive due to greater investments in more advanced machinery and ratio-nalized processes) linked to workers making more and more money, with both annual raises and even better jobs for the next generation both solid expecta-tions. But by the 1970s and 1980s this was no longer the case. Now the impacts of union busting, the movement of factories to "right to work" states, then over-seas in "race to the bottom" wages, the increasingly threat of technological dis-placement, were linked to the scourges of neoliberalism, the privatization of various aspects of the welfare state and the retrenchments of various benefits. So the incomes of most people became stagnant. But, not surprisingly, families wanted to maintain patterns of consumption. This meant that in many cas-es, married women enter the labor force to supplement the husband's wages. Moreover, at the same time, the proliferation of credit cards enabled people to buy things they might not otherwise be able to afford. As Wolff has put it, with the growing profits of the capitalist class, they now made more profits by lending money to the evermore cash starved workers.[36] Indeed, as time passed it became increasingly plain that investing in "debt" was probably more prof-itable than putting money into making things. The cumulative effect of these trends was the slow but steady growth of inequality and the wealth of the very rich became proportionally greater. The six Walton heirs have as much wealth as about 30% of the US, while the 20 richest men in America (about the num-ber that could fit in a large Gulfstream jet) own about half the wealth. Globally, about 80 some families control the vast majority of the world's wealth.

For much of recent United States history, the dominant legitimating ide-ology has relied disproportionately on the nebulous notion of the "American dream" in which everybody who works hard will eventually succeed and grow more prosperous and, even if he or she might not, then surely their children will find upward mobility. For reasons that may be exceptional in United States history, including the lack of any genuine socialist politics in this country, the rich have always been idealized and quite often "seen" as better people and exemplars of the American dream and suspects of the work ethic. Perhaps this underlies some of the support for a Trump candidacy in 2016.

But even in the US—indeed, even on Wall Street itself!—the implosion of the finance-led "late capitalism" was becoming starkly obvious to more and more people. This may lead to support for democratic socialism, but it also no doubt also underlies the current appeal various right-wing, nationalist, argu-ably quasi-fascist social movements, as well.

---

36   Richard Wolff. "Economic Crisis from a Socialist Perspective." *Socialism and Democracy*, vol. 18 (3) 1997, pp. 393–422.

While life is much more stark for the billions of people in the mega-cities of the poor regions of the world, there is also a tendency for workers here in the US to "fall down" into an existence characterized by stagnant or declining incomes, underemployment, unemployment, and instability: in short a US pre-cariat.[37]

Although these trends were charted by many sociologists and political scientists, some left-wing economic historians and a few, or should we say very few economists, when the economy imploded in 2007–08, businesses went into a downward tailspin, thousands and thousands of companies went bankrupt, millions of workers lost jobs, many lost homes, especially those who had purchased the "subprime mortgages." While the federal government, beginning with George W. Bush and then fully implemented by Obama bailed out the major banks, investment houses and even some manufacturers, e.g. GM, there was very little aid forthcoming to the very people whose taxes had been used to bailout the major financial houses. And for young people, life became more precarious. The demographic profile of the supporters of the nationwide "Occupy" movement in 2011–12—and the very strong millennial support for the candidacy of Bernie Sanders in 2016—illustrate the dwindling life chances for many younger US citizens who are increasingly turning to the "grey" or "gig" economy where they might work several jobs in "off the books" low paid service work, but did little more than simply survive. This heavily impacted age-cohort also are the students sitting in our university classes and lecture halls—eager to understand the causes of the plight of their generation. In light of all this, surprisingly, most of our scholarly comrades in sociology (and for that matter, across the wide spectrum of the social sciences) are strangely silent about this crisis of inequality of contemporary capitalism.

The Goal of This Volume

Obviously, we see our role as editors of this collection as addressing a critical need for serious inquiry, research and debates about precisely this question of inequality. We do intend to use the Piketty book at as launching point. While a number of people have offered critiques and reviews of his work, some published some not, some privately circulated, some appeared in major newspapers and/or online websites, the vast majority of treatments were largely limited to various narrow issues about his economic analysis. We know from

---

37   Guy Standing. *The Precariat*. (London: Bloomsbury, 2011).

our experiences that the Piketty volume opened up discussion and debate on a wide range of sociological, political and historical issues. To our knowledge, there exists no single source where a number of leading critical social scientists can be found together. In view of the efforts that went to organizing the special session, many people were consulted. The ASA presentation includes four very well known to highly respected scholars whose work on political economy has been widely recognized even beyond the discipline of sociology. Given the centrality of the question of growing inequality, its impact on politics and culture, life and health it seems that the various critiques of Piketty and discussions of inequality should be gathered together for wider audiences. But we also knew that we would need to cast a wider net, both in terms of the sorts of scholarly expertise we sought and the issues we would explore in this book.

This is indeed an exciting time in the economic, political and cultural realities of the contemporary world. And while much of the public debates over political economy tend to be ideological arguments and polemics for or against certain policies, what is surely needed this time is set of clearly reasoned views and arguments, not polemics and tirades regarding inequality and the contributions of Piketty. Regardless where individuals may stand in the debates, we are all grateful for making inequality a central concern.

An Overview of the Contents

When we surveyed the contributions to this edited collection, we decided that we needed to begin with reviews and critiques of the Piketty book that were relatively broad and/or based on alternative conceptual understandings, move on to essays that were particularly focused on inequalities, both of the national and global generas, and conclude with some chapters that provided particular angles on the contemporary twenty-first century crisis of capitalism with some thoughts about how to respond.

The initial section of the volume is the longest and includes the most contributions: it begins with an appreciative, but also critical review of the Piketty volume that initially appeared in *Contexts* (the quarterly magazine published by the ASA) by iconic Marxist sociologist Erik Olin Wright. He credits the book for creating a great deal of attention for a surprisingly neglected topic in sociological research: inequality (in terms of both income and wealth), noting that the Occupy movement that was the backdrop for its publication, with its "1 percent versus 99 percent" logic underlines the deep underlying antagonism inherent in this discussion. Wright summarizes the U-shaped graphs Piketty presents that show high income inequality early in the twentieth century, decreases in mid-century, and rapid rises in inequality in the last three decades. Then, he turns to wealth and highlights Piketty's two key arguments: 1) that concentrations of wealth are always greater than those of income, but also 2) that measures of the value of capital relative to total income is tending to increase as economic growth slows, which also increases the weight of inherited wealth, leading to unprecedented levels of wealth inequality in the twenty-first century (that Piketty worries will continue unabated unless there is some political intervention). While Wright is impressed with this empirical depth of the research and the perceptive focus on increasing income and wealth concentration across rich capitalist societies, he is disappointed that Piketty essentially ignores the dynamics of real-life class relations. Only by fully understanding the way CEO power is embedded in class relations—or the importance of household mortgages and debt in contemporary society—can we fully comprehend the true forces working to generate the escalating economic inequality Piketty's study reveals. The failure to diagnose the range of critical social mechanisms at work is a key reason that Piketty's main proposal to addressing rising inequality (a global tax on capital) is so partial and inadequate.

The next three chapters are all by participants in the original panel discussion of the Piketty book at Glide Memorial Church in the summer of 2014. Basak Kus (writing here with Dana Louie) also provides a broad overview the French economist's arguments in comparative and historical perspective. The essay opens on a literary note recounting a story Piketty excerpts from a novel by Honoré de Balzac where an old man explains that it is almost impossible to become truly rich through hard work and income from labor: the idea of a "meritocracy" is simply naïve and the real key to wealth, he tells a protégé, is inheritance. Indeed Vautrin's lesson proves to be an apt one, borne out by the elaborate longitudinal data analysis across various countries, indeed, it may be the most pithy précis for the hundreds of pages of *Capital*. Kus and Louie describe and discuss the key $r > g$ hypothesis, where r is the rate of return on capital and g is the growth of national income: this is the mechanism that Piketty identifies as the motor of wealth concentration. They also provide a concise summary of the various historical trends of wealth inequality for the United States and various European countries from the book. While there is a tendency to follow the U-shaped pattern reported in the graph in Wright's chapter (above), it is interesting to note that US wealth concentration, historically, was markedly lower than European countries due to factors like immigration and cheap land on the frontier, and the absence of a "patrimonial middle class" characteristic of Europe (Piketty thinks this may be "why Americans seem to take a more benign view of capitalism than Europeans").

However, there is also a strong tendency, documented in *Capital*, for wealth to concentrate—especially, among the hyper-rich (not the 1 percent, but the .1 percent or an even smaller fraction of the world's billionaires). Piketty's empirical analysis suggests that only in the inter-war years of the mid-twentieth century do we see some attenuation of these trends (and he hints that this may have been anomalous). As we enter the twenty-first century he argues that economic inequality, with massive proportions of assets controlled by a tiny elite, may reach record levels soon—and that this leads to various economic, social and political crises, including foundational threats to democracy. This prompts him to suggest the need for a new, and global, policy approach involving a global tax on capital. The chapter authors note various practical difficulties with his approach—and warn, in their final remarks that without some dramatic economic and political transformation, we may be facing an impending patrimonial system in the new millennium. They credit Piketty's work on wealth inequality with putting this squarely on the agenda for both academic but also (more importantly) political debates.

Sylvia Walby's chapter that follows, opens echoing this appreciation. She also defends his analysis from a critique that he is wrong about British data (concluding maybe "sloppy" but generally correct). But she then turns a more critical eye on his arguments, highlighting the lack of any real analysis of power, political change/transformation, and/or geopolitical events. Walby reiterates the key role that Piketty grants to the world wars in reducing wealth inequality in the mid-twentieth century. But here she argues that war is treated as an exogenous event rather than part of the social system. She's unequivocally calls this "a mistake." Violence should rather be treated as interconnected with wider social systems and has varied but important impacts on inequality. War impacts it in a variety of ways including bankruptcies, the destruction of factories, or by sowing political "chaos" or changing broad public policies trajectories.[38] Apropos the political, Walby also notes a curious lack of attention to or interest in democracy or political mobilization in the pages of *Capital*. She also critiques his failure to distinguish between financial and industrial "capital" (very different, with the financial sort being notorious volatile). Also absent is any attention to gender (women's historically increasingly labor force participation seems to escape Piketty's notice, he is silent about gendered inequality)

---

38   We would note that this is especially clear in the United States where the combination of government spending on wages and pent-up demand, together with massive government spending on housing, infrastructure, education, etc., enabled millions of GIs to pursue higher education, buy homes—accessible on the newly built highways, and either find corporate careers or gain SBA loans to begin businesses.

and changing fertility across societies (at a time when many countries were experiencing dramatic demographic transitions, with enormous political/ economic impacts). She concludes, "Piketty makes a major contribution to social science and public debate" but needs a theory of society that considers the central salience of "violence, democracy, finance and gender." In short, she claims that Piketty should be turned into a sociologist—or, minimally, needs to recognize that economic systems and actors are located in much broader social systems and contexts.

The next two chapters focus on that particularly important, but inherently unstable sector of capital linked to *financialization*. Both critique Piketty for failing to conceptualize this sector as a dynamic (and relatively new/evolving) structural characteristic of global capitalism that is a systemic source of inequality. They engage the debate on inequalities from earlier essays, but also exemplify different strands of a growing focus in social science and political economy that emphasizes the disproportionate role finance plays in twenty-first century capitalism.

Saskia Sassen's chapter begins with some broad conceptual ideas derived from her recent work on "assemblages" and "exclusion" about the workings of the contemporary global economy. Her premise is that capitalism incorporates an array of dynamics today that are essentially transformative in a "predatory" way that depends essentially on "extraction" of value from some people[39] to the enormous benefit of others—and she claims that the underlying financialization logic is progressively expanding. Unlike "traditional banking", this sector relies on various forms of innovation of new forms of value-extraction involving various "products" linked, most prominently, to various forms of debt (assessed to households in consumer economies, but also to nation states in a globalized financial system). Sassen's essay is wide-ranging, ranging from the reformulation of the Bretton Woods world in the late twentieth century to recent reformulation of norms about the commodification of debt that makes a "global economy" possible based on various sorts of speculative financial instruments. A central focus is how local housing became a global financial instrument via the securitization of mortgages. She spends much of the latter portion of her discussion explaining just how this process took place over the past two decades in the U.S. Basically, there is a delinking between mortgages and their key purpose: facilitating home-ownership for ordinary citizens of modest to moderate means. Mortgages were "sliced up" into small pieces, the

---

39   Or indeed, even from nature itself: Saskia Sassen, *Expulsions: Brutality and Complexity in the Global Economy*. (Cambridge: Harvard University Press, 2014). See particularly Chapters 1 and 3; Robert Antonio in Chapter 14 below also addresses some of these issues.

creditworthiness of the holders became irrelevant, and perverse incentives grew to over-sell the riskiest (sub-prime, adjustable rate) mortgages. This inexorably led to a "housing bubble" and the foreclosure crisis in the u.s in 2007 that precipitated a worldwide financial disaster soon thereafter. Sassen's emphasis here is how this new form of debt (created by "brilliant mathematicians that generated wealth for savvy investors") was designed to "extract" and profiteer on the backs of poor and modest-income families; the instruments were aggressively marketed to people who would ultimately be unable to pay (and lose their homes and savings as a result) in order to maximize financial profits. She shows that people of color "paid" the highest price in all this—and she warns that this financialization of household debt was so "successful" in places like the United States that it is now becoming a worldwide phenomenon with highly concentrated global banks controlling most of the debt and, therefore, reaping the mega-profits. In addition to deepening our understanding of the generation of wealth, poverty and inequality, this analysis also points to a glaring irrationality in contemporary global capitalism.

The next chapter by Eoin Flaherty also contributes to the discussion of financialization as a generator of inequality (comparing it to other factors like globalization, welfare retrenchment, and the rise of skill-biased technological employment). He points out recent research (particularly post-2008) that fleshed out how the institutional and regulatory characteristics of global finance are specifically tied to growing disparities in wealth and income (and, of course, Sassen's exposition of the mortgage securitization is an example). So he believes Piketty's gloomy prognosis about growing inequality is warranted. However, he urges us not to simply see this as the result of "misguided policy": we need to understand it all in an institutional context of a larger neoliberal assault on the labor movement and the welfare state which, in turn, is inherent to a particular new regime of capital accumulation. Flaherty provides a plethora of data on recent trends in economic inequality, takes great care to differentiate various components of income inequality, and shows how they empirical align with each other and with key variables that might "explain" the institutional drivers of rising polarization. He critically analyses a great deal of very recent scholarship, arguing that the consolidation of what he calls "shareholder managerialism" provides a direct link from the profit-seeking of corporate shareholders to the lived experience of employment precarity. So, while the "very rich" may rely almost exclusively on investment and rent-generating income streams, "the rest" now depend on debt, falling social transfers, and stagnant wages to subsist. This is a deeply "class-based" dynamic. There is now a very strong (predatory) relationship between broad class groups. So, while the share of GDP accruing to labor has fallen as a result of de-unionization and globalization, a greater share of productivity is being captured by an ever-shrinking pool of rentiers. Similarly, the monopolization of financial instruments linked to securitization by resource-endowed individuals is implicated in the changing shape of the Gini income distribution, as those at the bottom assume the debt, which is subsequently leveraged by those at the top. Flaherty argues that Piketty's work can contribute "to normative criticism of the basic inequality of capitalism." But he also believes that a full accounting of how today's economic inequality emerged, as well as a useful exposition of what can be done about it, is more likely to come from a Marxist analysis of "the fundamental institutions of capitalism" and "the very logic of a deregulation-driven social structures of accumulation analysis of financialization" rather than a reductionist approach stressing $r > g$.

The final three chapters of the first section of the volume all engage critical theory and ideas from the Frankfurt School in various ways; all three of these chapters also seek to contextualize Piketty's arguments in historical terms. Hans Bakker sets out to critique his assumptions based, not only on a neo-Marxist/neo-Weberian perspective, but also drawing more attention to the early stages of capitalist imperialism and colonialism, as well as the shift from inequalities in pre-capitalist societies to those of finance capitalism (see above). He notes that in *Capital* Piketty uses the word "patrimonialism" and even "hyper-patrimonialism": some might dismiss this as unimportant, the use of colorful descriptive language. But Bakker argues that, in fact, Max Weber's idea of "patrimonial prebendalism" could be extremely instructive applied the sorts of "neo-patrimonial" contemporary inequalities outlined by Piketty—but notes that he never cites Weber even once in his very long book! Like many critical theorists, Bakker argues that we need to understand Weber in dialogue with Marx (not in opposition to him), building a sociological political economy/historical materialism. He believes that neo-patrimonialism is a very illuminating way to think about the top one percent or one-tenth of one percent in today's society. Bakker develops a detailed historical argument (that also reflects on contributions of various Frankfurt School luminaries) and sees in Piketty, for all the empirical riches, a relative theoretical poverty, with the lack of attention to imperialism/colonialism, plus his failure to link the "baronial" influence of the modern day patrimonial elites to any form of class analysis.

In the essay that follows, Roselyn Bologh continues this line of argument, showing how Piketty's "misses" much in terms of understanding and explaining the dynamics of today's extreme inequality, by ignoring classical and critical theoretical insights into the nature of society (and his apparent ignorance of Weber). Like Bakker, she notes that Piketty tantalizingly hints at the dangerous return to an early form of "patrimonial capitalism" (based on inheritance and "unearned income"), but fails to understand the relational and power dimensions all this entails. His statistical analysis captures the quantitative material differences between groups in terms of income and especially wealth, but he fails to capture the extent to which capitalist wealth is combined with power that allows the rich to shape the political and economic agendas that preserve, and indeed increase, their largesse by limiting the social-political clout of subordinate groups (so the problem is all about "distribution" rather than production, exchange and the associated social relations—and his "policy recommendation" of a global tax on wealth rings hollow). Bologh also draws on Weberian insights about the differentiation in types of property ownership to critique Piketty's blindness to distinct types of *rentiers*: some do indeed, rent land, but others profit from ownership in other assets like warehouses, factories, transportation systems, other services, and finance. Ultimately, she suggests that the most powerful and potentially pernicious "patrimonial capitalists" are those who primarily rely on finance and debt as an instrument not only of enrichment but also of control. They feed off progressively widening inequality and profit enormously from economic stagnation, policies of austerity and periodic crises; this is very different from the dynamics of the benefitted older generations of industrial capitalists and illustrates how these powerful contemporary *rentiers* are, in fact, a fetter on economic dynamism in the twenty-first century. This helps to explain the current expressions of wide-spread discontent in capitalist societies in which many ordinary citizens are very angry at the Wall Street elite and "the 1 percent" instead of the old targets of class conflict, which were the giant industrial corporations. Bologh nicely connects her rich historical/theoretical essay to the present noting that "the unexpected surge in support for Trump and Sanders in 2016" shows that a large portion of the U.S. population is beginning to understand how this dynamic is shutting them out and leaving them behind. Piketty's analysis only begins to suggest this: we need a much deeper critical sociological view to probe the depths and diagnose the real causes the terrifying "new dark age" we may be entering.

This theme echoes again in Harry Dahms' chapter in which he attempts to fashion a "planetary sociology" that can point to radical reform leading out of that dismal crisis. He spends some time appreciating one of Piketty's insights: the manner in which the focus on "the threat of a rising China" is a distraction in the face of "oligarchic divergence" in rich western nations, and applauds his ability to "phase into and out of sociological concerns and questions," but also notes the limits of his thinking as "a professional economist." Dahms argues that the logic of capitalism in inimically tied to growing economic inequality (providing an overview of this dynamic during a period of "seventy-year peace" in the post-World War II era) and develops a Frankfurt School lens to scope out how to move beyond Piketty. He is convinced that we must see this in terms of a *global* rather than a national dynamic—and begins to bring in the natural world and the environment.[40] Dahms claims sociology is uniquely suited "to confront the vicissitudes of globalization" because our discipline takes a skeptical stance toward the inevitability of evolution and "progress," the costs and benefits of social change, and whether that is sustainable, productive ... or destructive. In this light, he views Piketty's idea of a global tax on profits as a "solution" in a very critical way, concluding his essay with the observation that while "inequality is supposed to be incompatible with modern western democratic societies" it is also undeniably the "motivational infrastructure" upon which individuals and institutions rely. This tension between "the impossible" and "the inevitable" is the space in which some sort of a new sociological imagination for the twenty-first century must insert itself, with the hope that radical reform is possible.

The next three chapters are grouped under a new heading, "Inequality", and each centers on some specific elements of Piketty's empirical argument about inequality. All three essays argue in different ways that his narrow vision as an economist blinds him to key insights, and, interestingly, each uses data, graphs and the logic of equations to deconstruct particularly pieces of Piketty's tome. While these arguments are more focused, the authors in the section of the book continue a theme from the last three contributions: all are working in the theoretical and philosophical traditions of critical theory.

Daniel Krier and Kevin Amidon emphasize Piketty's adherence to a reductionist, economist framework that downplays (if it doesn't completely ignore) social, cultural and historical dynamics. They see his view of capital (and his rather dismissive rejection of Marx's work), based solely on market and exchange value of things, as missing how "value, the labor process, the working day, the extraction of surplus value" and the exploitative nature between classes are foundational. They underline the limitation of that view with a discussion of how the Frenchman views slavery in the antebellum American South: it is simply about the money-value of the slaves as property: "The social ontology and historical determinants of workplace inequality, even slavery, remain unanalyzed" since "domination and exploitation is economic rather than political, as though the primary problem with slavery was reducible to low income and meagre possessions" rather than a brutal labor relation based on a particular cultural-historical context. In terms of today's inequality, Piketty

---

40   For a fuller development of these themes, see Robert Antonio, Chapter 16 this volume.

sees potential forces of economic "convergence" operating via "the diffusion of knowledge and the acquisition of skills"—and seems to assume that these cascade freely to poorer or disadvantaged people and places, with no understanding of how "immaterial capital" (patents, intellectual property, brands and trademarks), in effect, legally "enclose" these advantages. Similarly, he sees excessive executive compensation as a testament to exceptional bargaining power (what new US President might call superior "deal making") while discounting the politicized financial deregulation that recent led to an ever more "powerful corporate control center." Near the end of their essay, Krier and Amidon bring in the familiar "varieties of capitalism" approach and (recoding Piketty's data) plot a time-line graph showing how these culturally inflected societal types diverge in terms of top compensation; they also suggest that, had he paid attention to sub-national regional cultures and identities (in either France or the United States), he would have seen more evidence for the key role of cultural contexts and folkways in determining distributive patterns. Finally, they find most "dispiriting" his "almost total resignation to disciplinary conformity" as an economist lead Piketty to consign politics to the realm of utopian thinking: he is even nihilistic about *his own* "solution" of a wealth tax, acknowledging it, too, may be an unrealistic dream.

Chapter 10 that follows is a reprint of an article from *Review of Radical Political Economy* in which Charles Reitz uses data from the *Statistical Abstract of the United States 2011* to re-examine Piketty's assumption that there are "typical" splits in national income between labor (two-thirds) and capital (one third). In *Capital* he assumes that a portion of what many would consider "the income of capital" is actually "remuneration for entrepreneurial labor"—which leads him to the rather strained claim that some of the unprecedented rises in executive pay should be consider "wages" perhaps linked in some extenuated way to productivity (Piketty admits there are limits on how "deserved" these top incomes really might be, but still argues that they are "pay" for managerial labor). For Reitz this logical dance constitutes a major obfuscation in the Piketty argument. Instead, he argues that top management compensation is the result of structural power in which the organizational structure and culture of giant capitalist firms: instead of ascribing this to "executive wages," Reitz (more conventionally) labels it "rent, interest, dividends and profit." And he presents data estimates that show a very large asymmetry between capital income in manufacturing (the total value-added produced minus the wages to workers in that sector) in magnitude of a 3:1 split that favors capital over labor in the this broad sector (and even higher ratios in subsectors of industry, like the garment and apparel production). Reitz data and estimates are very simple and lack the detail and sophistication of Piketty's book. But his critique of *Capital* is really conceptual: the economist sees societies like the US as dominated by "supermanagers" when, in fact, the reality is capitalism, tightly controlled by "a parasitic rentier class" with almost boundless power. Clearly, this leads to a much different view of the future and need for a radical political economy that stresses transformation over Piketty's meek policy prescriptions to address widening material gaps (which seem anything but utopian!).

The last offering in this section is, in effect, a re-imaging of the meaning of inequality/equality and what constitutes a just society. Michael Thompson praises Piketty's ability to chart the empirical contours of inequality in contemporary societies. His primary concern it the fundamental question of the morality of equality/inequality: the latter can be seen as the extent to which only certain members of the community are able to control the common resources—and to redefine the purposes and ends of society itself. Today we live in a society dominated by "liberal" views that claim existing inequalities are justified based on market principles and individualistic accounts of welfare and utility. Thompson develops a different view (he calls this "republicanism," but not to be confused with the very "liberal" view of today's US Republican political party) and argues that it is based on radical democratization (it is, quintessentially, a political idea—which the author explicitly links to the Progressive movement of a century ago) that maximizes public goods rather than private advantages. So, ultimately, Thompson wants to fundamentally re-orient the way we view inequality—he argues that it should be seen as the advancement of private ends over public ones, and as something that only comes about when "unequal exchanges" between people and groups. These unequal exchanges are based on three different types of mechanism: *extraction, asymmetrical information* and *exclusion*—and the essay provides examples of how each works in today's neo-liberal society. A crucial point is that "markets are not simply relations of exchange, but also mechanism of social power," belying Piketty's ideological obfuscation that, in the end, all market relations are actually based on some sort of "equal" exchange (which could not be further from the truth). Not only is this arguing that politics (and the on-the-ground reality of state policies) leads to high/escalating levels of economic inequality, but, growing inequality, in turn, provides feedback into the polity that creates "anti-democratic pathologies within society" (a vicious cycle if there ever was one!), with oligarchic inequality eroding democratic practice. This degradation is both "structural" and ideological as the culture and attitudes become more obsequient ... and the downward spiral continues. Thompson proposes an alternative possible world in which distributive justice is valued, widespread participation occurs, active citizenship is promoted, and progressive social movements "infect the state and its ability to defend common purposes."

The next section of the volume shifts the focus to global inequality, with three chapters that either confront Piketty about the limits of his vision, and/or attempt to move beyond his insights by bringing in dimensions of world inequality he doesn't fully explore. Tony Smith's succinct essay (Chapter 12) offers an appreciation of Piketty's depiction of growing within nation inequality—but bemoans his lack of attention to the world market and complete lack of attention to the dynamic of capitalist over-accumulation and the rise of neoliberalism in the late twentieth century. William Robinson (Chapter 13) offers an even more scathing and comprehensive critique, arguing that Piketty, while drawing attention to savage inequalities, essentially provides a "safe" mildly reformist diagnosis that fits into the current neoliberal agenda of today's transnational capitalist class. Finally, although Chase-Dunn and Nagy (Chapter 14) laud Piketty's "path-breaking research," they develop a political economy of the world-system approach that argues that a key dynamic (ignored by Piketty) is the role of social movements, some of which might even be able to become genuine "anti-systemic" forces that could challenge—and perhaps fundamentally transform—the neoliberal capitalist *status quo*.

Smith's essay is the most succinct of these: His initial observation is that Piketty (surprisingly) pays virtually no attention the world market or global inequality in *Capital*. To the extent he considers this at all, he seems to assume that "knowledge diffusion" is the key to national development in poorer regions (so a key factor in "developmental states" is good governing institutions that can create an institutional framework for increasing local technological sophistication). In the face of this quite "optimistic" view, Smith reminds us that the "in global capitalism the 'default setting,' so to speak, is for knowledge and technological know-how to serve as means enabling wealthy regions to reproduce and extend their relative advantage over time." This sort of "technological dependence"[41] is hard to overcome: R&D is very costly, intellectual property rights limit seamless technology transfer (and make it costly), and there is a danger that poor countries borrowing to promote development will end up "falling into the 'debt trap.'" Another problem is getting a wealthy region to accept your exported products. The iconic example of "successful" development via export manufacturing are the East Asian countries in post-World War II era. But Smith persuasively argues that, while economists like Piketty are often

---

41   This term isn't used in Chapter 12, but one of the book co-editors uses it to discuss the same process the author argues for, illustrated by the case of high tech industry in South Korea in the 1990s, see David A. Smith. "Technology, Commodity Chains and Global Inequality: The South Korean Case in the 1990s." *Review of International Political Economy*, vol. 4 (4) 1997, pp. 734–762.

quick to argue these cases show how "development" can occur even in very poor countries, the historical conjuncture, in fact, was rather unique—and the technological production gap remains a major weapon of the wealthy states to perpetuate global inequality and poverty. In the chapter, Smith proceeds to discuss mechanisms of inequality within nations and develops a historical perspective summarizing comparative patterns of capitalist development in some leading countries in the second half of the twentieth century. Piketty and left liberals tend to view the past few decades as a time of economic growth coupled with some (not well comprehended) failure of political will to tax, redistribute and regulate (perhaps the cause is the greed of the rich?). Smith's argument is different. He points to the rapid growth in the post-World War II era of Japanese and European economies, which created a boom and excess productive capacity by the 1970s. This lead to an *"overaccumulation crisis"* and a falling rate of profit—which, in turn, gave rise to global neoliberalism, which, in effect, restores capitalist profitability via a relentless attack on labor and state social reproduction, capital flight to parts of the world where wages are low, and the explosion of credit, debt and financialization. For Smith, the extreme rises in inequality that Piketty documents in his book inexorably follow: they are a function of this current capitalist conjuncture.

William Robinson opens his chapter with a quick review of the yawning gap between the world's super-rich and the poorest half of humanity, and how dramatically that discrepancy grew just since 2010. But he dismisses the idea that outrage over these inequalities explains Piketty's star treatment; rather, he sees the Frenchman as a favorite of transnational elites in search of an eloquent voice for moderate reform. After all, with Piketty the problem isn't capitalism, but some institutional features that can be addressed with minor "tweaks" that fix "bad policies." Instead, Robinson wants us to focus squarely on the global capitalist economy and the class warfare of the transnational capitalist elites. The basic claims here resonates with the previous chapter: he explicitly discusses how the overaccumulation crisis in the 1970s led the transnational capitalist class to see popular and working class demands as a serious fetter on profits, sparking a shift from a Fordist-Keynesian production regime to one that "went global" and congealed on a neoliberal "Washington consensus." This new regime emphasizes privatization of state functions, "liberalization" of trade and investment, a push for "flexible" labor, and promotion of a new global "precariat." He goes a bit farther by arguing that the transnational capitalists more recently moved into a project of *"hyper-accumulation"* that involves applying new technologies (like computing and informatics), conquering new global markets (middle class consumers in places like India and China), "social cleansing" and organized violence (the "war on drugs/on terror") that are leading primitive accumulation through massive migrations and land grabs akin to a "a new round of global enclosures." Robinson sees financial institutions and various aspects of a new "militarized accumulation" as additional elements of all this. It's a rather horrific situation! Particularly, given the recent period of stagnation, the 2008 global financial collapse, etc. In light of all this, various elite commentators and reformist economists have written about escalating inequalities and the attendant rising disillusionment with capitalism; Robinson casts Piketty as part of this new elite readiness to accept a critique of unfettered neoliberal global capitalism. But he warns us not to be fooled: Piketty is accommodating to capital, not radical in any way: he tells us Piketty is an icon of an "emerging post-neo-liberal era in which states are to play a limited role in a mild reregulation of capital and effect of limited redistribution through transfer payments, more progressive income tax, and a tax on capital." Then he turns up his critique: Part of this involves the definition of "capital" as anything a person owns: this would include a "can of beans or the shirt on one's back"—but, obviously, only certain (very different) types of property generate income. More basically, Piketty assiduously avoids any mention of either *power* or *exploitation*, so he cannot "explain" inequality within the capitalist system; instead he only offers neo-classical circular reasoning (involving inequality and slow growth) and unrealistic economic assumptions. Robinson note also two glaring omissions: 1) no serious historical or analytic treatment of the global North-South divide created by imperialism (poor countries are seen as "catching up"), and 2) no mention of the astounding gap in terms of global inequality in which the tiny fraction of billionaires are obscenely rich, while "80 percent of humanity has to make do with just 5.5 percent of global wealth" (he equates this with "global apartheid"). The chapter concludes, "A necessary step in overthrowing global apartheid is a critique of its elite critics."

Chapter 14 (by Chase-Dunn and Nagy) is less focused on critique of *Capital* (they use Piketty's research on growing inequalities mainly as a context) and more centered on understanding the role of social movements (including revolutionary ones) in shaping society and inequality over time. Their interest in this isn't purely "academic," since they also want to assess the possibilities for popular mobilization to challenge the current polarization trend. This chapter provides a succinct summary of the "world-systems perspective," including some discussion of how historical hegemonic cycles impacted societal rise and fall—and help us to understand the current conjuncture in which we are seeing another "Age of Extremes" which not only involves poverty and dispossession, but also a full-blown ecological crisis. A brief review of "world revolutions" of the past leads to speculation about the global "antisystemic movements" of today (for example, recent ones like the Arab Spring, anti-austerity protests in Greece and Spain, the global Occupy wave)—and, ultimately, to an analysis of the current state of the global justice movement (with extended attention to the World Social Forum). This leads them back to Piketty, who they see as shining light on global inequalities. But Chase-Dunn and Nagy ignore his mild policy suggestions: they insist that the only "solution" is transnational activism that leads to some form of true global democracy. One particular insight they promote is that this can only succeed with a movement that can organize worldwide, in particular, overcoming the splits between the collective interests between progressive forces in the Global North and South (or, in world system parlance, the core and the non-core countries). There is some hope: the rise of notions like universal human rights, widespread realization that anti-austerity is a global assault on citizens everywhere, and transnational labor solidarity, all suggest the possibility of unifying around a progressive alternative to neoliberal capitalist globalization. These authors insist on guarded optimism since the alternative is an apocalyptic perfect storm of disaster and chaos.

The final section of the book takes up this theme of crisis and possible transformation. Alessandro Bonanno (Chapter 15) retains the theme of global inequality and limits of the worldwide neoliberal project, pointing to an impending legitimation crisis; Robert Antonio's essay (Chapter 16) delves more deeply into the depths of the ecological catastrophe, primarily focusing on human caused climate change, and suggests a stark choice between contemporary capitalism and planetary survival. The next chapter (17), by David N. Smith, argues by ignoring Marx Piketty cannot interpret his own findings—and goes on to develop a clear cogent explication of Marx's theory of profit and the crisis of capitalism. The final essay by Peter Marcuse (Chapter 18) is a broad rumination on possible routes out of this same crisis.

Bonnano begins with the observation that while Piketty is no Marxist, he does make an argument about the structural proclivities for capital to generate extreme levels of unsustainable inequality. Piketty is suggesting a return to some sort of "regulated capitalism." Borrowing from Habermas, Bonnano sees the problem as a major "legitimation crisis" for an economy that recently transitioned from Fordism to neoliberalism. The old buffers on the savagery of capitalism present in the mid-twentieth century (effective labor unions, welfare state programs that "de-commodified" education, health, social services, etc.) gave way a few decades ago to a Post-Fordist era of state privatization and austerity and a governance regime that views labor unions as "distortions" that hurt economic competition and growth. Following a Foucauldian understanding, the author makes it clear that this transition to neoliberalism was partly an intellectual project (discussing the crucial roles played by scholars like Milton Friedman and F.A. Hayek in justifying the erosion of the state and destruction of union power). The neoliberal worldview emphasizes the inevitability of both inequality and uncertainty (both seen as *desirable* outcomes of markets and unfetter competition). But this form of capitalism brings about extreme poverty and wealth concentration, economic volatility and instability, precarious and tenuous labor markets for many people, etc.—so, however much economists may favor it, it tends to engender a great deal of mass resistance. That building opposition and anger leads to demands for change—but there is a contradiction: there is a demand for the state to intervene to "fix" the problems, yet neoliberalism ideology itself is deeply anti-statist. This is the paradox of Piketty's proposal to use state-sponsored strategies to address inequality (and perhaps part of the reason is sees this as "utopian"): his own analysis "implies anti-neoliberal strategies that require state forms that transcend the nation state." Bonnano adds two other considerations about the current situation: first, we need to consider the global aspect of today's capitalism (corporate players can by-pass state measures because they are transnational entities); second, the potential oppositional political parties and movements are also limited, reformist, and also grounded in nations.

Piketty does mention that a looming ecological/climate change disaster is a major long-term concern for humanity. Robert Antonio (Chapter 16) opens acknowledging this, and gives the Frenchman credit where it is due. But there is a problem, again, with under-theorization. In *Capital* environmental cataclysm is seen as another possible "shock" to the economic system—and Piketty wades into internecine debates within contemporary economics about how serious the ecological threat is, and how broad a response is needed. In fact, he is rather enlightened, siding with the other economists who argue that big changes that would lead to a more democratic control of capital are necessary (a view that Antonio argues would be seconded by climate scientists). The chapter provides some dire data on the danger of global warming, the impending "tipping points" and the devastating impact that runaway climate change would have in terms of global conflict/chaos, refugees' flows, extremist ideologies, etc. Not surprisingly, *Capital* ignores how the current neoliberal regime of capitalist accumulation is implicated in ecological destruction; to formulate any real pathway out of this planet threatening conundrum we must confront precisely this reality. Despite genuine concerns about environmental crisis, Piketty is reluctant to abandon the key notion of the "*growth imperative*" (so integral to capitalism) or recognize that the neoliberal ethos of deregulation will effectively block the emergence of a "comprehensive, mandatory, global regulatory regime needed to deal seriously with climate change." Antonio is sympathetic with Piketty's broad call for a democracy that can "regain control of capitalism" and his specific proposals about a progressive carbon tax to fund climate change measures.[42] But reiterating a theme running through this collection, he concludes that we need to more much farther and understand how the "de-democratizing force of income divergence and dispossession" inherent in today's global capitalism underpin the impending ecological catastrophe. Radical fundamental change that builds the cultural and political resources needed to create a more just society based on both collective well-being and a sustainable just society are imperatives if we want to preserve life on the planet. The choice seems to be to either transcend capitalism or risk planetary survival.

"Piketty is free, if he wishes, to ignore Marx, but he does at the risk of failing to grasp his own findings." David N. Smith makes this bald statement early in his essay: he does not find the economist's claim that Marx is too hard to understand very satisfactory—and he also points out that, contrary to the Frenchman's claim, Marx has a great deal to say about the increasing productivity at the core of modern capitalism. Smith points out that, based on the surplus theory of value, Marx believe growing capitalist accumulation or "the rising organic composition of capital" would lead to a fall in the rate of profit (and, essentially, be "the Achilles' heel" of capitalism). Indeed, recent empirical evidence shows that this is happening in places like the United States today. As Piketty shows, there is a lot of concentrated money and wealth—but the "problem" is that rates of return on investment in production are shrinking, so more and more big money is flowing into purely speculative investments (and even the profit rates seem to be in decline): Smith calls this sort of money "pseudocapital." But Piketty fails to understand that we are simultaneously seeing vast wealth along with increasing economic paralysis and impending stagnation. The author notes that he is not alone in misunderstanding this tendency—indeed, quite a few avowed Marxists (Rosa Luxemburg and Theodor Adorno, among others) who fixated on the early volumes of Das Kapital ignored Marx's argument about this in Volume 3 (which Engels did not publish until almost two decades after his collaborator's death). Smith tells us that concentration and rising mass production are the only ways that large industrial capital can counteract the fall rate of profit (smaller firms presumably perish), and capital finds itself "superabundant" in relation to the opportunities for profitable investment. While he did not predict automatic collapse, Marx saw this as leading to crisis in terms of stagnation and declining employment and

---

42   This recommendation is not found in *Capital* but in a more recent journal article Piketty
      co-authored that Antonio discusses in Chapter 16.

demand. As a result the current reality in the twenty-first century can be summarized: "'Awash' in money (in the favored idiom of *The Wall Street Journal*) corporations, sovereign wealth funds, and other bastions of overflow wealth increasingly see capital investment as folly. Capitalist verge, quite literally, on social suicide, as they shed their capitalist skins to reinvent themselves as swindlers and swashbucklers" This is the dynamic underlying the exploding inequality Piketty documents so clearly—but even if they were feasible and less modest his book's proposals for some redistribution from the rich to the masses won't "solve" the real crisis. Smith concludes that the problem is *not* money and who has it, but the inherent contradictions in the capitalist system itself, ending with a clarion call for better theory and more meaningful study to inform much needed *praxis*.

The final contribution to the volume (Chapter 18) is a philosophical reflection by Peter Marcuse on the nature of inequality and social justice, provoked by Piketty's book, which leads into a thoughtful overview of various potential political responses to unjust inequality. Marcuse begins with the observation that not all inequality is unjust: he argues that sometimes there are differential rewards based on "differences" in skills or competencies—and we also tend to support greater economic support for people with certain disabilities. Instead, the degree of acceptable inequalities in wealth and power can only be determined through some sort of democratic processes (which, for example, lead to decisions about how progressive taxes should be). For Marcuse, "unjust inequality derives from the exercise of power used for exploitation or oppression of one person or group by another"—and this can only be addressed/ameliorated by dealing the distribution of power via the political process. This leads him into an informative inventory of potential political responses to inequality: the standard ones are conservative, liberal, progressive, and radical, and he illustrates those with examples from the recent 2016 US political campaigns. Conservatives generally accept inequality (and indeed may even see as desirable) since it is the result of individual differences in ability and motivation (and also imbues all this with vague "moral propriety"). It's not surprising that native born economically well-off whites are attracted to this view: it is a legitimating ideology that tends to obscure various types of privilege over women, racial/ethnic minorities, LGBT people, foreigners and other "non-conformists." Liberals are exemplified here by moderate Democrats like Hillary Clinton: they are concerned more with non-economic inequalities and very gross economic ones, (implicitly this is where Piketty "fits" on the spectrum). Liberals don't address the underlying causes of inequality (or acknowledge that some benefit greatly from exploitation of others); the main focus is on making sure the poor are adequately supported (the rich should help via charity, but there is little recognition that wealth for some may come at the expensive of others). Taxes on the rich need to be kept moderate since they are the job creators for everyone else; "the liberal response to inequality is to address it only at the bottom and the middle" leaving the political-economic structures unchanged. Bernie Sanders' "democratic socialism" epitomizes the progressive agenda, sharing many values with liberals, but offering a more "confrontational" politics that appeal to "a younger and more populist base." While progressives are willing to directly attack the holders of power to reduce inequality (and more willing to impose higher taxes on the wealthy), Sanders calls for "revolution" are through the existing electoral processes and not intended to radical transform structural relationships, namely property owners, in society (the progressive purpose seems to be to push for some redistribution in the existing economy, not fundamentally transform it). Radicals, on the other hand, take a very different view: it is rooted in a Marxist/socialist vision and would attempt to foster fundamental changes in the nature of capitalism (redistribution without structural changes is not enough)—this is the only path to ending class exploitation. Marcuse lists possible radical polices: guaranteed annual income for everyone, government or non-profit control of production of basic goods and services, nationalization of all major productive enterprises, sharply progressive/confiscatory taxes on income/wealth, free education at every level, the cessation of military production, participatory democratic decision-making, strong/sustainable environmental standards, etc. While he sees this as "obviously utopian" this agenda does provide a glimpse of what a just society might be—and also suggests some policies that liberals and progressives might consider (if only partially). In the end, Marcuse aspires to an approach that might combine and blend the three critical ideologies, which he calls a "transformative" response. He concludes that "unjust inequality is really a major problem of our times ... emphasizing justice as an essential characteristic of what is desired is the answer, and recognizing that only justice can ultimately end the inequalities that plague society."

It is fitting that the final chapter of the edited collection be a clarion call for justice from a wise old urban planner steeped in critical theory. The co-editors intend this book to be read by scholars and member of the educated and enlighten public who are interested in Thomas Piketty's *Capital in the Twenty-First Century* and are eager to more intensively examine and debate its arguments. Our authors are scholars, mostly from the disciplinary tradition of sociology who tend to be grounded in either global political economy or critical theory—and most are at least broadly sympathetic with the Marxist/socialist strand of social thought. Analyzing and presenting arguments is, of course, the essence of academia; it is what many of us do "for a living." So many books like this are published as a matter of course, for very small audiences of "experts" who engage each other, publish some more, etc. But we aspire to grander goals in producing this collection. We believe that exploding inequality is one of the most telling (and unjust) manifestations of a global and national economy in profound crisis (along with some other impending capitalist cataclysms like global war or environmental catastrophe). While many of our academic colleagues "go about their business" teaching and studying in very narrow esoteric fields in which they are, undoubtedly, world leading experts, we feel that current conjuncture creates a sense of urgency, a need to find ways forward out of impending crisis. To do this we need to attempt to understand how our current understanding of contemporary society, culture and world political economy can help us not only to interpret the world, but to provide advice on changing it. So we are offering a "public sociology" that we hope might include guidance to politically informed and active citizens who do care about unjust inequality—and are looking for guidance about what is to be done about it. Very recently, an online article appeared in *The New York Times* that posed the question, "What if Sociologists had as much Influence as Economists?"[43] Indeed! We appreciate his empirical contribution to the debate, but we believe the analysis offer here, which goes far beyond Piketty, offers more guidance about the real world issue of inequality—and what people can do about it.

---

43   Neil Irwin, "What if Sociologists Had as Much Influence as Sociologists?" In "Economic View: The Upshot" *The New York Times* March 17, 2017. https://www.nytimes .com/2017/03/17/upshot/what-if-sociologists-had-as-much-influence-as-economists .html?_r=0. Accessed April 25, 2017.

PART 1

Broad Reviews and Critiques

∴

CHAPTER 1

Class and Inequality in Piketty[1]

Eric Olin Wright

Introduction

Until recently, the only context in which inequality was treated as a problem was in discussions of opportunities and rights. Equal opportunity and equal rights are deeply held American values, and certain kinds of inequalities were seen as violating these ideals. Racial and gender discrimination, for example, are viewed as problems because they create unfair competitive advantages for some people. They violate the ideal of a level playing field. Likewise, poverty is viewed as an important problem, but the main issue has not generally been the *distance* between the poor and the rich. Rather, it has been the absolute material deprivations of people living in poverty and how their unmet needs harm them. Not surprisingly, then, the LBJ-era "War on Poverty" led to the creation of an office of economic opportunity, not an office for the reduction of inequality. The way poverty constitutes a disadvantage was of great concern, but almost no public attention was given to the degree of inequality of resources or conditions of life across the income distribution as a whole. Inequality was not an important publicly recognized problem.

Even among scholars, discussions of inequality have historically focused on social mobility and the social production of advantages and disadvantages. There was a great deal of concern about inequalities in the way people got access to social positions and certainly much study of how hard life was for people living below the poverty line, but almost no concern with the magnitude of inequalities among the positions themselves. Inequality was not an important academically recognized problem.

Conservatives and liberals shared this inattention. To be concerned with the distance between the rich, the poor, and the middle class was seen as a thin veil for envy and resentment. So long as fortunes and high income were acquired legally, the degree of inequality generated was unobjectionable. And what's more, as many argue even today, in the long run, the high incomes of

---

1   This essay originally appeared in *Contexts* vol. 14(1) 2015, pp. 58–61. Used by permission of author, Sage Publications and American Sociological Association.

the wealthy were said to benefit everyone. Out of this high income, people said, new investments were made, and these filled a necessary condition for proverbial "rising tide" that lifts all boats. Inequality was not an important politically recognized problem, either.

This situation has changed dramatically: today, talk about inequality is everywhere. The media, the academy, and politicians all speak to the problem of inequality in its own right. The slogan of the Occupy Movement is exemplary: We are the 99%. The 1% versus the 99% logic indicates an antagonism between those at the very top of the income distribution and everyone else. Now politicians and pundits speak of the dangers of increasing inequality. Scholars have begun to study it systematically.

It is in this context that Thomas Piketty's book *Capital in the Twentieth Century* appeared. Nearly 600 pages long and published by an academic press, it is a serious, scholarly work (some lively bits notwithstanding)—not the sort of book anyone expects to be a bestseller. And yet, it is. This reflects the salience of inequality as an issue of broad concern.

Piketty's book is built around the detailed analysis of the trajectory of two dimensions of economic inequality: income and wealth. Previous research on these issues has been severely hampered by lack of data on the richest people. The people at the very top are not selected in survey samples, so it has been impossible to systematically study the historical trajectory of inequality for more than a few decades because of a lack of good data before the mid-20th century. Piketty has solved these problems, to a significant extent, by assembling a massive dataset that goes back to the early 1900s and is based on tax and estate data.

The Trajectory of Income Inequality

The central observation of Piketty's analysis seen in the now-familiar U-shaped graph of the share of national income going to the top layers of the income distribution. A version is reproduced below, showing the percentage of national income in the United States going to the richest 10% and 1% from 1913 to 2012. The share of the top decile in total national income reached an early peak of 49% in 1928, and then hovered around 45% until WWII, when it dropped precipitously to around 35%. There it remained for four decades, until it began to rise rapidly in the 1980s, reaching a new high of just over 50% in 2012. That is, in 2012 the richest 10% of the population received just over half of *all* income generated in the American economy.

This graph has undoubtedly received the most widespread publicity of any of the findings reported in Piketty's book. But there is a second finding that is of almost equal importance: The sharp rise in income share of the top income decile (see Figure 1.1) is largely the result of the dramatic rise in income share of the top 1%. Of the 17-percentage point increase in the share of income going to the top decile between 1975 and 2012, 13.6 percentage points (80% of the increase) went to "the 1%." The share going to the next richest 9% of the population only increased by 3.4 percentage points. Income is not merely becoming more concentrated at the top; it is being much more concentrated at the top of the top.

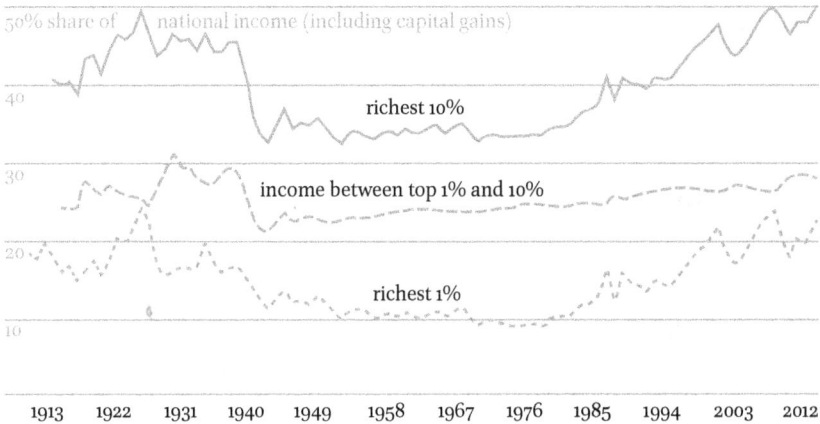

Share of Total National Income going to different high income categories

FIGURE 1.1   *Share of total national income going to different high income categories.* (SOURCE: http://topincomes.g-mond.parisschoolofeconomics.eu)

A third finding on the trajectory of income inequality is significant: While in every country studied, income concentration at the top of the distribution declined sharply in the first half of the 20th century, there is considerable variation across countries in the degree to which concentration increased by the century's end. These trends are much more pronounced in the United States than in other countries, and are quite muted in some.

How does Piketty explain these broad patterns? The crux of Piketty's analysis boils down to two main points. First, the rapid increase in concentration of income since the early 1980s is mainly the result of increases in super-salaries, rather than dramatic increases in income from capital ownership. This reflects the fact that the high income concentration in the early 20th century had a very different underlying basis than in the present day: In the earlier period, "income from capital (essentially dividends and capital gains) was the primary resource for the top 1 percent of the income hierarchy ... In 2007 one has to climb to the 0.1 percent level before this is true" (p. 301).

Second, the universal decline in income inequality in the middle of the 20th century and the variations across countries in the extent of its increase by the end of the century are largely the result of the exercise of power, not the natural workings of the market. Power exercised by the state is especially important in counteracting the inegalitarian forces of the market through taxation, income transfers, and a range of regulations. But also important is the power of what Piketty terms "supermanagers": "these top managers by and large have the power to set their own remuneration, in some cases without limit and in many case without any clear relation to their individual productivity" (p. 24). The exercise of power is constrained by social norms, which vary across countries, but is very weakly constrained by ordinary market processes.

The Trajectory of Wealth Inequality

Piketty uses the terms wealth and capital interchangeably. He defines capital in a comprehensive manner as "the sum total of nonhuman assets that can be owned and exchanged on some market. Capital includes all forms of real property (including residential real estate) as well as financial and professional capital (plants, infrastructure, machinery, patents, and so on) used by firms and government agencies" (p. 46). Ownership of such assets is important to people for a variety of reasons, but especially because it generates a flow of income, which Piketty refers to as the return on capital. A fundamental feature of any market economy, then, is the division of the national income into the portion that goes to owners of capital and the portion that goes to sellers of labor.

The story Piketty tells about wealth inequality revolves around two basic observations: First, levels of concentration of wealth are always greater than concentrations of income, and second, the key to understanding the long-term trajectory of wealth concentration is what Piketty calls the capital/income ratio. The first of these observations is familiar: In the U.S. in 2010, the top decile of wealth holders owned 70% of all wealth and the bottom half of wealth holders owned virtually nothing. As with the income distribution, during the middle of the 20th century this concentration at the top declined from considerably higher earlier levels (in 1910 the top decile of wealth holders in the US owned 80% of all wealth), but the

rise in wealth concentration has been more muted than the rise in income in recent decades. Still, the main point is that *wealth concentration is always very high.*

The second element of Piketty's analysis of wealth, the capital/income ratio,
is less familiar. It is a way of measuring the value of capital relative to the total
income generated by an economy. In developed capitalist economies today,
this ratio for privately owned capital is between 4:1 and 7:1, meaning that the
value of capital is typically 4 to 7 times greater than the annual total income
in the economy. Piketty argues that this ratio is the structural basis for the distribution of income: All other things being equal, for a given return on capital,
the higher the capital/income ratio, the higher the proportion of national income going to wealth holders.

A substantial part of Piketty's book is devoted to exploring the trajectory of
the capital/income ratio and its ramifications. These analyses are undoubtedly
the most difficult in the book. They involve discussions of the interconnections
among economic growth rates, population growth, productivity, savings rates,
taxation, and other things. Without going into details, a number of Piketty's
conclusions are worth noting:

- As economic growth in rich countries declines, the capital/income ratio is almost certain to rise unless counteracting political measures are
  taken.
- Over time, the rise in the capital/income ratio will increase the weight
  of inherited wealth, so concentrations of wealth should begin to rise
  more sharply in the course of the 21st century.
- Given the presence of unprecedented high concentrations of earnings among people who also receive considerable income from capital
  ownership, concentrations of income are likely to exceed levels observed in the 19th century.

The implication of these arguments is sobering: "The world to come may well
combine the worst of the two past worlds: both very large inequality of inherited wealth and very high wage inequalities justified in terms of merit and
productivity (claims with very little factual basis, as noted). Meritocratic ex-
tremism can thus lead to a race between supermanagers and rentiers to the
detriment of those who are neither" (p. 417). The only remedy, Piketty argues,
is political intervention: "there is no natural, spontaneous process to prevent
destabilizing inegalitarian forces from prevailing permanently" (p. 21).

His preferred policy solution is the introduction of a global tax on capital.
Even if one is skeptical about that specific proposal, the basic message remains convincing: so long as market dynamics are left largely unhindered, the

polarization of the extreme concentration of income and wealth is likely to deepen.

The Problematic Role of Class

On the first page of Chapter One, Piketty recounts a vivid example of the salience of capital ownership in a bitter class conflict in South Africa in 2012: the strike of workers at the Marikana platinum mine which resulted in the massacre of 34 miners by police. He writes:

> For those who own nothing but their labor power and who often live in humble conditions (not to say wretched conditions in the case of eighteenth-century peasants or the Marikana miners), it is difficult to accept that the owners of capital—some of whom have inherited at least part of their wealth—are able to appropriate so much of the wealth produced by their labor (p. 49).

This is a potent class analysis. In this account, classes are not arbitrary divisions within some distribution of income or wealth—a top, middle, and bottom—but real social categories constituted through social relations. The owners of capital do not simply receive a return on capital; they *exploit* the miners by appropriating "wealth produced by their labor." Rather than a division of the national income pie into shares, it is a transfer.

Though the terms "capital" and "labor" continue throughout the book, with very few exceptions, this relational concept of class largely disappears after the first salvo. I do not think that this undermines the value of Piketty's empirical research or the interest in his theoretical arguments. But it does obscure some of the critical social mechanisms at work in the processes he studies.

Let me elaborate with two examples, one from the analysis of income inequality, and one from the analysis of returns on capital.

One of Piketty's important arguments is that the sharply rising income inequality in the u.s. since the early 1980s "was largely the result of an unprecedented increase in wage inequality and in particular the emergence of extremely high remunerations at the summit of the wage hierarchy, particularly among top managers of large firms" (p. 298). This conclusion depends, in part, on what, precisely, is considered a "wage" and what is "capital income." Piketty adopts the conventional classification of economics and includes stock options and bonuses as part of top managers' "wages". This is obviously correct for purposes of tax law and the theories of conventional economics, in which a CEO is just a particularly well-paid employee. But this accounting becomes less obvious when we think of the position of CEO as embedded in class relations. As Piketty himself points out, to a significant extent, the top managers of corporations have the power to set their own remuneration. This power can be viewed as an aspect of ownership. Because of this, rather than a wage, in the ordinary sense, a significant part of the earnings of top managers should be thought of as an allocation of the firm's profits to their personal accounts. Although different from stock holding, CEOs' earnings and other compensation should thus be thought of as, in part, a return on capital.

It would, of course, be extremely difficult in a relational class analysis of corporate cash flow to figure out how to divide the earnings of top managers into one component that is functionally a return on capital and another that is functionally a wage. The problem is quite similar to dividing self-employment income into a wage component and a capital component, since (as Piketty notes) the income generated by sole proprietors' economic activity inherently mixes capital and labor.

The absence of a relational class analysis is also reflected in the way Piketty combines different kinds of assets into the category "capital" and then talks about "returns" to this heterogeneous aggregate. In particular, he folds residential real estate and capitalist property into capital. This is important because residential real estate comprises somewhere between 40 and 60 percent of the value of all capital in the countries for which Piketty provides data on real estate. Combining all income-generating assets into a single category is perfectly reasonable from the point of view of standard economic theory, in which these are simply alternative investments, but combining them makes much less sense if we want to identify the social mechanisms through which returns are generated.

Owner-occupied housing, for instance, generates a return to the owner in two ways: as housing services, which are valued as a form of imputed rent, and as capital gains, when the value of the real estate appreciates over time. In the U.S. in 2012, about two-thirds of the population was homeowners; roughly, 30% owned their homes outright, while another 51% had positive equity but were still paying off mortgages. The social relations in which these returns are earned are completely different from those depicted in Piketty's story about London owners and South African miners. Furthermore, the social struggles unleashed by these different forms of wealth inequality are completely different, as are the public policies needed to respond to the harms generated by different kinds of returns to capital.

The growing attention to inequality is good, and Piketty deserves credit for contributing to that. But Piketty gets it wrong by treating capital and labor exclusively as factors of production each earning a return. If we want to really understand—and even alter—what's going on as inequality creates social and economic distance, we must go beyond income and wealth trends to identify the class relations that generate escalating economic inequality.

CHAPTER 2

Vautrin's Lesson: Historical Trends, Universal Challenges, and Policy Responses

Basak Kus and Dana Louie

Introduction

Early on in *Capital in the Twenty-First Century* Thomas Piketty[1] recounts a piece of advice voiced by Vautrin—a character in Honoré de Balzac's novel *Père Goriot*. This advice, what he terms "Vautrin's lesson," suggests that it is nearly impossible to become truly wealthy through hard work and labor income. The truly rich inherit wealth. Piketty shows in *Capital* the gravity and reality of this lesson with a masterful exploration of the architecture and dynamics of wealth inequality throughout history, at the present moment, and projected forward. In an empirical study that is at once informed by economic theory and historical evidence, he first sketches the larger dynamics that shape the creation and distribution of private capital—what he terms the laws of capitalism—then zooms into the experience of specific countries with a historical lens and discusses how these dynamics played out in different nations. An important outcome of this dual lens is an understanding of economic inequality as a political phenomenon whose patterns, degree, and impact depend a lot on the specific institutions and policies that are in place. In fact, one of the more important contributions of the book is its attempt to theorize how it is that modern capitalism leads to and has led to quite skewed patterns of wealth accumulation and concentration, while at the same time opening a discussion as to how these trends can be mitigated, and have been mitigated in the past, intentionally or unintentionally, as a result of specific policy choices or larger political events such as crises or world wars.

Our chapter places Vautrin's lesson in a comparative and historical light. We first provide an overview of Piketty's analysis of the transformation and distribution of wealth. Then, we discuss the challenges the existing disparity in wealth ownership poses to advanced nations in the twenty-first century,

---

1 Thomas Piketty, *Capital in the Twenty-First Century* (Cambridge: Harvard University Press, 2014). As this work is referenced extensively in this chapter, for ease of navigation page numbers are given in parentheses in the text rather than in footnotes.

and discuss how these challenges have been tackled in the past and might be tackled in the future.

Capital and Its Distribution[2]

Piketty uses the term 'capital' interchangeably with 'wealth' to refer to "non-human assets that can be owned and exchanged on some market" (p. 46). This definition includes property, financial assets, and professional capital (i.e., plant, property, and equipment), but leaves out human capital, as it cannot be traded. In *Capital*, he provides longitudinal data on how much wealth/capital Western nations have come to own since the eighteenth century, how the composition of this wealth has changed over time, and how this wealth has been distributed.

One of the key concepts that form *Capital*'s technical foundations is the capital/income ratio, β—the total stock of capital owned by a nation over the yearly national income. Using this measure to trace the accumulation of private wealth over time and across nations, Piketty finds a historical difference between the US and Europe in the pattern of change. In most of the European countries, the trajectory of β follows a u-curve whereby the high levels of wealth relative to national income that characterized the eighteenth and nineteenth centuries dropped off sharply during war years, only to show a steady increase in subsequent decades. In France and Britain, the β ratio remained around 7 until the end of the nineteenth century, fell to 2–3 between the wars, and has since risen to 5–6 (pp. 216–217). The trajectory in Germany was similar, although the levels of private wealth in that country have been less than in Britain and France (p. 144). Turning to the US, then, Piketty observes a much more stable trajectory that he attributes to two main causes. One is lower aggregate wealth. The immigrants who settled in America did not bring large amounts of capital, and from this base wealth accumulated relatively slowly, such that the aggregate value of wealth in the eighteenth and nineteenth centuries was much smaller in the US than in Europe. Moreover, the land in the new nation, being available in such great quantities, had a very small market value (p. 155). Two, although the two world wars had an impact on aggregate wealth in the US, this impact was much less than in Europe, and overall the United States enjoyed a much more stable capital/income ratio than Europe

---

2 Piketty's analysis of capital accumulation and distribution is discussed extensively in Basak Kus, "Wealth Inequality; Historical Trends and Cross-National Differences," *Sociology Compass*, vol. 10 (6) 2016, pp. 518–529.

in the twentieth century. Piketty suggests that this less volatile trajectory may in fact explain "why Americans seem to take a more benign view of capitalism than Europeans" (p. 155).

With respect to the composition of wealth in Western nations, Piketty's analysis reveals several trends. The first one concerns the changing value of farmland over time. While agricultural land represented a large chunk of the total national wealth at the beginning of the eighteenth century, its share in total national wealth was significantly diminished by the end of the nineteenth. The same period saw the value of housing, industrial, and financial assets increase. This transition happened more quickly Britain than in continental Europe where farmland retained its value for a few more decades (pp. 119–20).

Second, the role of foreign capital changed over time. Foreign assets began to gain importance in some European nations in the late eighteenth and nineteenth centuries. The value of foreign assets owned by colonial Britain in the early twentieth century amounted to almost twice its yearly income, and France was in a similar position (p. 120). In the second half of the twentieth century, however, foreign assets evaporated in both of these nations as a result of two world wars, economic crises, and decolonization (p. 121). In Germany, foreign assets historically made up a much smaller share of total wealth since it was never a colonial empire. It is only in the last few decades that Germany has amassed significant foreign assets thanks to trade surpluses (p. 142). In the US, by contrast, foreign capital did not contribute much to aggregate wealth. Slavery, however, was an important factor. Slaves represented one fifth of the population in nineteenth century America; measured in capital, they represented one and a half times the national income (p. 159). Piketty notes that "southern slave owners in the New World controlled more wealth than the landlords of old Europe" (p. 160). The US embodied "two diametrically opposed realities" as such: the South, with high capital due to slaves and slave plantations, and the North with relatively little capital due to a higher population of immigrants (p. 161).

How has private wealth been distributed in Western societies? This is the third key question that Piketty answers in *Capital*. He shows that during the nineteenth century and up to World War I, Europe was a land of patrimonial societies characterized by a hyper-concentration of wealth. The top 10 percent of the population owned 80–90 percent of total wealth, and the top 1 percent owned 50–60 percent of total wealth (p. 345). Inheritance and marriage played a key role in ensuring someone's wellbeing and standing in society, much more so than work or study. Moreover, these societies showed no sign of decreasing wealth inequality (p. 339). Wealth ownership in European nations began to disperse only after the war (p. 343). According to Piketty, the dispersion in capital did not benefit the poorest half of the population but to those in the 50th–90th percentiles of the wealth distribution—what he calls the "patrimonial middle class" (p. 346). This trajectory has been similar across European nations: "the major structural transformation was the emergence of a middle group" (p. 347). Since the 1970s, wealth inequality has once again begun to increase.

In terms of distribution of wealth, some important differences stand out in the US case. First, early in the nineteenth century inequality of wealth in the US was much less pronounced than it was in Europe. The US was "a new country whose population largely consisted of immigrants who came to the New World with little or no wealth" (p. 347). In the second half of the twentieth century, however, the American wealth ownership became increasingly concentrated and it eventually surpassed the European levels.

What drives wealth inequality? According to Piketty, what has been the driving force of capital inequality in the past and will continue to cause greater inequality in the future is the fact that $r > g$, where r is the rate of return on capital and g is the growth rate of national income. Where the rate of return on capital is "markedly and durably higher than the rate of growth" (p. 351), as for instance in the agrarian societies of the nineteenth century, recapitalization of accumulated wealth outpaces the growth of the economy. In such scenarios, wealth can become hyper-concentrated.

The period when we observed a decline in inequality in the twentieth century was an exceptional period in this regard. Technological progress and the expansion in labor force had created rapid growth. And at the same time, the shocks of the world wars—the physical destruction, but more importantly the socio-political landscape and the progressive tax policies that came after the war—had reduced the rate of return on capital, creating an environment where g was greater than r. Maybe for the first time in history, this was a time when Vautrin's lesson did not apply—labor and hard work could make one truly wealthy (p. 419).

Many of Piketty's predictions about capital in the future hinge on historical understanding of the relationship between r and g. Growth comes from two factors, Piketty explains: population growth and per capita income growth, with about half of growth derived from each factor (pp. 72–73). Although population growth has fluctuated, with low growth in the 1700s and times of high growth in the 1900s, over the long run it has been about .8 percent (p. 77). This rate, however, is not sustainable. Similarly, per capita income growth is also expected to be low. As with population growth, income growth holds a long-run value of about .8 percent when examining data from 1700 to the present, with lower growth in the earlier years and the highest growth (around 1.6 percent) in the most recent century (p. 93). Though Piketty does not himself make a definitive claim about what the income growth rate will be in the future, he points to some economic forecasts and lands at a median rate of 1.2 percent (p. 95). The implications of these low rates can be understood in a few ways. When population growth is high, family wealth becomes diluted more quickly as inheritance will go to several children. Additionally, if the high population growth is due to immigration, inherited wealth will be less as immigrants often arrive with little capital. Income growth works in the same direction: when income growth is high, accumulated capital is less important as future generations will make greater amounts of income, rendering the accumulated wealth of lesser real value (p. 83). Finally, with a lower g, the capital/income ratio increases. Thus, the result of lower population and income growth is clearly one of increasing disparity in wealth ownership. Moreover, Piketty asserts that inflation, which acts as an equalizing force in the same way that growth does, was likely a twentieth-century phenomenon (pp. 106–109). Inflation lessens capital's value for future generations, rendering real wealth less valuable. If inflation was truly a twentieth-century phenomenon, this force of convergence is also lost.

Although Piketty's analysis suggests that with low rates on both accounts (income and growth) the future is likely to hold even higher levels of wealth concentration, this is not an inevitable trend. It may be the case that the steepest increases in wealth inequality were observed in societies characterized by low growth and high return on capital, but at the end both of these factors and the overall level of wealth inequality remain shaped by the existing institutions and policies. Piketty does not dismiss this possibility. He argues that while several forces such as the slowdown of population growth and global competition to attract capital might lead to a higher r–g gap and higher inequality in the future, the outcome will ultimately depend on the institutions and policies that are adopted.

Vautrin's Lesson for the 21st Century: Inheritance, Labor, and Capital

One of *Capital*'s most important sections is where Piketty discusses the role of inheritance in society. It is not only that the level of national wealth is about to reach its eighteenth-century levels, or the fact that the distribution of wealth has become more unequal in the past few decades that makes the question of wealth ownership a pressing issue. It is also that wealth accumulates at increasing rates in the hands of those who started life with significant amounts of capital to begin with. In other words, we are fast approaching a time when Vautrin's words will be as relevant as they were in the nineteenth century.

In Balzac's brilliant novel *Père Goriot*, Vautrin tells Eugene de Rastignac, a penniless young noble who is trying to find his way in the Parisian society, to quit having illusory thoughts about attaining socio-economic status by investing in a professional career. According to Vautrin, even if Rastignac received the best education he could, and achieved a brilliant career in law, he would still be living on a mediocre income. A better course of action would be to marry a wealthy woman. Marriage and inheritance define one's place in society more than education, hard work, or professional competence.

Piketty shows that the share of inheritance in total wealth[3] of Western nations remained high in nineteenth-century Europe began to decline early in the twentieth century, only to rise again since the 1980s (p. 425). Looking at Forbes' billionaire list, we realize that bountiful inherited wealth grows just as fast if not faster than earned wealth due to its initial size. Overall, inheritance keeps wealth concentrated and allows wealthy individuals to accumulate more wealth by having a large stock of capital. Looking just at the fortunes of Microsoft's founder, Bill Gates, and the heir to L'Oréal, Liliane Bettencourt, we learn that Bettencourt's fortune has grown at the same rate as Gates's even though Bettencourt has "never worked a day in her life" (p. 440), while Gates can be credited with creating the world's most used operating system. The glaring reality is that "wealth is not just a matter of merit" (p. 441) and as Vautrin's lesson suggests, labor will never be comparable to the power of inheritance.

In this context, Piketty argues, the idea that "unrestricted competition will put an end to inheritance and move toward a more meritocratic world is a dangerous illusion" (p. 424). At a global level, wealth inequality is currently similar in magnitude to the inequality that existed in Europe during the Belle Époque. The top .1 percent owns nearly 20 percent of global wealth, the top 1 percent owns about 50 percent, and the top 10 percent owns 80–90 percent (p. 345). What this means for the other 90 percent of the world is truly daunting.

What we can ultimately conclude from Piketty's brilliant analysis of capital is that not only is capital inequality at present tremendous, but that the intrinsic nature of wealth is such that wealth reproduces itself, leading to a higher and higher concentration of capital. Moreover, the rate of return on capital r remains typically larger for larger investments in part because individuals or institutions can employ better wealth management if they have large funds to

---

3   Specifically, Piketty examines the share of inheritance in the total resources of cohorts born in 1790–2030.

spare, and in part simply because of the palpability of economies of scale. The primary implication of this tendency is that large fortunes, by generating large incomes from capital, reproduce themselves. American university endowments provide a perfect example of how the increase in income from capital depends on the size of the initial wealth. Piketty shows that while university endowments greater than $1 billion make an 8.8 percent return, those with less than $100 million make a 6.2 percent return (p. 449). With a $30 billion endowment, Harvard, for instance, is able to pay nearly $100 million annually for the best investing management in order to achieve a return on capital of about 10 percent. That is, Harvard's endowment earns nearly $3 billion a year as just capital income simply because the endowment was so immense to begin with (p. 450).

Can Vautrin's Lesson be Countered?

Looking forward, there are several predictions Piketty makes in *Capital*. First, he expects that savings will stabilize at around 10 percent, and growth is poised to slow. With a stable savings rate and a shrinking growth rate, the capital income ratio, β, which has been on a steady increase since the 1950s, will continue to rise. In fact, Piketty warns us that without intervention, β could surpass the high levels that existed in the 1700s and we could witness a capital/income ratio of 700 percent by the end of the twenty-first century (p. 195).

Second, in the absence of policy change, the income from capital will become a greater portion of total income (p. 222). Labor will become less powerful as its income will be a smaller share, with implications for the possibility, or lack thereof, for mobility and the likelihood of greater capital concentration.

This kind of extreme concentration of income and wealth is worrying. One of the warnings that we can take away from Piketty is that the patrimonial system is coming back, and policy reform is necessary to counter it. A number of recent studies point to possible economic, social, and political consequences of increasing wealth disparity.[4] Worrying impacts on the economy include

---

4　See for instance Daron Acemoglu and James A. Robinson, "The Rise and Decline of General Laws of Capitalism" *Journal of Economic Perspectives* vol. 29 (1) 2015, pp. 3–28; Larry M. Bartels, *Unequal Democracy: The Political Economy of the New Gilded Age* (Princeton: Princeton University Press, 2009); Oded Galor and Omer Moav, "From Physical to Human Capital Accumulation: Inequality and the Process of Development," *Review of Economic Studies* vol. 7(1) 2004, pp. 1001–26; Paul Pierson and Jacob S. Hacker, *Winner-Take-All Politics: How Washington Made the Rich Richer—and Turned its Back on the Middle Class*

an ultimate decrease in labor productivity and growth due to the decreased ability of poorer households to accumulate physical and human capital.[5] Socially, meanwhile, the 'uneven playing field' created by persistent and rising inequality erodes the equality of opportunity sought by meritocratic societies.[6] In addition, politically, participatory democracy itself may be at risk from sustained high levels of wealth inequality and income inequality. A report issued by the American Political Science Organization warns that over-concentration of wealth and income can affect the participation of citizens, the responsiveness of their government, and patterns of policymaking.[7] The report shows that public officials and policies tend to be much more responsive to the economically privileged than those who are less affluent, and policies tend to reflect the preferences of the wealthy and high-income. The report also shows that wealth and income are directly associated with voting, campaign contributions, affiliation with political groups, and involvement with community life (p. 6).

So can Vautrin's lesson be countered? History shows us some footprints with respect to this question. During and following the world wars was a time, maybe the first in history, when Vautrin's lesson was not necessarily true; labor and hard work became in fact mechanisms to rise in society. Since the world wars, "[a] society structured by the hierarchy of wealth has been replaced by a society whose structure depends almost entirely on the hierarchy of labor and human capital" (p. 449). This has come about due to a complex interplay of several forces. Piketty points out that physical destruction

---

(New York: Simon & Schuster, 2011); Theda Skocpol, "Voice and Inequality: The Transformation of American Civic Democracy," *Perspectives on Politics* vol. 2 (1) 2004, pp. 3–20; Timothy M. Smeeding, "Public Policy, Economic Inequality, and Poverty: The United States in Comparative Perspective," *Social Sciene Quarterly* vol. 86 (1) 2005, pp. 955–983; Joseph E. Stiglitz, *The Price of Inequality: How Today's Divided Society Engineers Our Future* (New York: W. W. Norton and Company, 2012).

5   See Joseph E. Stiglitz, The Price of Inequality: How Today's Divided Society Engineers Our Future (New York: W. W. Norton, 2012); Oded Galor and Omer Moav, "From Physical to Human Capital Accumulation." *The Review of Economic Studies* Vol. 71 (4) 2004, pp. 1001–1026.

6   Daron Acemoglu, Suresh Naidu, Pascual Restrepo and James A. Robinson. "Democracy, Redistribution, and Inequality" National Bureau of Economic Research, Working *Paper No. 19746*. December 2013. http://www.nber.org/papers/w19746. Accessed January 24, 2017.

7   'American Democracy in an Age of Rising Inequality. Task Force on Inequality and American Democracy.' American Political Science Association, Washington, D.C. http://www .apsanet.org/PUBLICATIONS/Reports/Task-Force-on-Inequality-and-American-Democracy Last. Accessed March 9, 2016.

of capital because of the wars had a small but not inconsequential result. However, it was more the policies and lifestyles that contributed to the compression of inequality. The years after the world wars were marked by a redistribution of wealth that disproportionately hurt the wealthiest. Along with a slew of nationalization, industrialized western countries witnessed a growth of progressive taxes. Additionally, the "patrimonial middle class" took a portion out of the wealth of the top 10 percent (p. 373), and Finally, foreign assets that had made up a substantial portion of wealth before the wars essentially disappeared after them (p. 370). However, despite the substantial contraction in their wealth, the wealthy elite did not reduce their spending in tandem with the reduction in their fortunes (p. 369). Thus, fortunes diminished and inheritance declined. With a high growth rate, g was greater than r, and thus inequality fell. Piketty makes it clear, though, that this falling inequality was an unusual occurrence and that the world wars had only "wiped away the past to create the illusion that capitalism had been structurally transformed" (p. 118).

The point is, nations tackled economic inequality in a variety of ways in the past—some more effective than others—and will continue tackling it in the future—again, some more effectively than others.

In the final section of his book, Piketty calls the progressive global tax on capital his ideal policy for the new global economy. He first distinguishes between four different taxes: those on income, capital, consumption, and contributions to government-sponsored social insurance programs. Piketty focuses his argument specifically on capital taxes, which "generally include any levy on the flow of income from capital (such as corporate income tax), as well as any tax on the value of the capital stock (such as a real estate tax, an estate tax, or a wealth tax)" (p. 494). While a high marginal tax rate on the highest incomes is necessary, he argues, it is hardly enough and should be supplemented with a progressive tax on capital. Rather than transferring funds from the wealthy to the poor, the current redistributive model is hung up on income levels, which are not the most accurate measure of economic equality, especially given the low levels of mobility.

The United States and Britain were the founders and supporters of the progressive tax. In fact, "the u.s. was the first country to try rates above 70 percent, first on income and then on estates" (p. 505) Moreover, one of the major motivations for the progressive tax dates back to the Gilded Age, when America's fear of resembling Old Europe, between taxes and inequality of wealth, led to many tax laws being passed during the twentieth century.

Since the 1980s, there has been a large decrease in the progressivity of the income tax, however, while calls for a progressive capital tax have routinely been ignored. This is time for reform, according to Piketty. A progressive glob-al capital tax coupled with a very high level of international financial trans-parency is the reform that governments must undertake (p. 667). Rather than attempting to finance the social state, the goal of the capital tax would be to regulate capitalism—"to stop the indefinite increase of inequality of wealth, and second to impose effective regulation on the financial and banking system in order to avoid crisis" (p. 518).

The capital tax would be beneficial in many ways, according to Piketty: it would be a cadastral financial survey of the entire world, define norms, impose a legal framework on economic activity, refine the various asset types, set rules for valuing assets, liabilities, and net wealth, and force governments to clarify and broaden international agreements (p. 520).

Furthermore, a progressive capital tax would provide contributive and incentive justifications. The contributive logic is that, income is not repre-sentative of the wealthiest individuals, since many have inherited fortunes (p.676). Therefore, a direct income tax, even an extremely progressive one, is not enough to access their contribution. "Only a direct tax on capital," Piketty argues, "can correctly gauge the contributive capacity of the wealthy" (p. 676). This direct tax would stifle tax evasion, and global transparency would pre-vent the wealthy individuals from investing in foreign banks to safeguard their funds. On the other hand, the logic of incentive explains the way in which a capital tax acts as incentive to seek the best possible return on one's capital stock. However, neither justification alone seems to be complete, thus, Piketty reconstructs his ideal tax system as a compromise between incentive logic (fa-voring tax on capital stock) and insurance logic (favoring tax on the revenue stream stemming from capital) (p. 680). This is not an easily applicable idea, however. It would require not only that all individuals be willing to partake in such a large-scale taxation program, but also that all countries be cooperative and supportive.

To conclude, the question of wealth ownership encapsulates some of the major philosophical and moral conundrums that modern capitalism embod-ies concerning equality, liberty, property rights, and meritocracy.[8] Whereas the modern democracies subscribe to the principle of meritocracy—the under-standing that social inequality, inasmuch as it exists, should be the result of the achievements and contributions of individuals—this principle does not in fact justify existing levels of wealth disparity. One of the warnings we can take

---

8 Jens Beckert, *Inherited Wealth*, translated by Thomas Dunlap (Princeton: Princeton University Press, 2007).

away from Piketty is that, without any economic or political transformation, the patrimonial system is coming back. This trend would have devastating consequences for the future of democracy and social welfare. Piketty's work is important not only because it has made a huge contribution to the academic literature on wealth inequality, but also because it has put the question at the center of contemporary political debates.

CHAPTER 3

Turning Piketty into a Sociologist?

Sylvia Walby

Introduction

Piketty has made a major contribution to social science and to public debate in his book, *Capital in the Twenty-First Century*.[1] Most importantly, he demonstrated the relevance of wealth, of capital, not only of income, when discussing the economy and in particular when discussing economic inequalities. Some criticisms of his work are unjustified, such as his use of statistics. However, there are gaps if this work is to become a comprehensive framework for the analysis of economy and society.

Areas where further development of the analytical framework is not yet sufficient include: treating war as an exogenous shock and outside his theorization of societal dynamics, when violence and economy are interconnected; neglect of democracy and political mobilization; underestimating the distinctiveness and significance of finance capital; neglecting gender, in particular, insufficient treatment of fertility and demographic changes concerning married/ partnered women.

The Importance of Wealth

The strength of Piketty's book lies in its demonstration that capital (wealth) matters and drives inequalities. He creates significant, substantial, and rigorous new data sets on wealth over time and comparative between countries, created from data from tax authorities. This data is used to test and support his arguments.

Piketty sets up a debate between two schools of thought on the relationship between inequality and wealth: the 'trickle down' (Kuznets) and 'increasing inequality' (Marx) theses. He demonstrates that 'trickle down' is incorrect and that 'increasing inequality' is the correct account. He argues that there is

---

1 Thomas Piketty, *Capital in the Twenty-First Century* (Cambridge, MA: Harvard University Press, 2014).

an inevitable concentration of capital when the growth rate is less than the savings rate, which is usually the case when the growth rate is low.

Piketty finds that inequality is increasing. While there have been some historical moments when inequality declines, this is not inevitable.

The implication of the analysis is that social science and public policy should not restrict the analysis of inequality to differences in earned income. Rather Piketty successfully demonstrates the importance of capital for economy and society.

Contested Data and Trends

The data collected and presented by Piketty have been contested. In particular, there are contestations over the interpolations that are used to address missing data, with implications for the summary trends that can be drawn from the data.

Giles[2] contests the interpretation of the data concerning especially increases in wealth inequality in recent years. Giles argues that: the way that Piketty fills in the missing gaps in data exaggerates the rise in wealth inequality in recent years; and that a number of other adjustments are ad hoc, and made to suit his argument. In particular, Giles uses alternative sources of data on the UK to argue that Piketty is sloppy and wrong. See Figure 3.1 below. The Economist[3] reviews the debate between Giles and Piketty, concluding that the critique is over-stated and that most of the interpolation of trends where there is missing data is reasonable. The biggest differences between Giles and Piketty concern UK data, where the UK Office for National Statistics has created a data set on wealth distribution, gathered in a recent survey in which respondents self-report their wealth. The ONS survey finds a lower concentration of wealth than does Piketty from his data set that is derived from tax statistics. (Giles does not dispute Piketty's analysis of trends in France and Sweden.) As The Economist notes, time trends will always have missing data that require interpolation of estimates and self-reports of wealth are always likely to be under-reports of the amount of wealth. Hence the conclusion of The Economist is that while

---

2 Chris Giles, 'Piketty findings undercut by errors' Financial Times, 23 May 2014. An on-line video is available at: http://www.ft.com/cms/s/2/e1f343ca-e281-11e3-89fd-00144feabdco .html#axzz34tqe4Asv. Accessed December 8, 2016.

3 Economist, The (2014) 'Picking holes in Piketty'. Available on-line on 15/8/2014 at: http://www.economist.com/news/finance-and-economics/21603022-latest-controversy -around-thomas-pikettys-blockbuster-book-concerns-its. Accessed August 2, 2016.

some of Giles' complaint of 'sloppiness' is up-held, the more substantial charge that Piketty is cherry-picking his statistics to suit his argument is not, and that Piketty's book remains a substantial piece of scholarship.

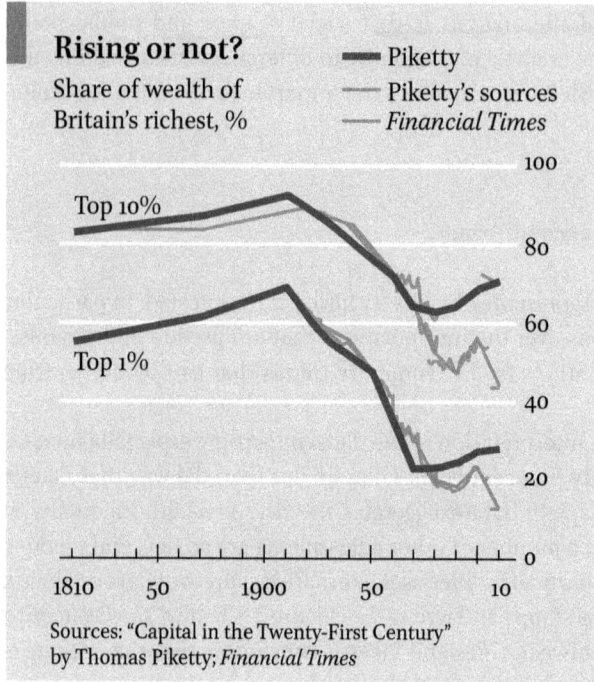

Rising or not?
Share of wealth of
Britain's richest, %

— Piketty
— Piketty's sources
— *Financial Times*

FIGURE 3.1   *Rising or not? Share of wealth of Britain's richest.* SOURCE: CHRIS GILES (2014) *THE ECONOMIST*, 23 MAY 2014

Assembling these data is a huge challenge, which Piketty has met better than anyone else. It is unavoidable that historical data will have some gaps. The conclusion drawn here is that the trends in inequality produced by Piketty were the best estimates available at the time of publication.

Violence

Piketty is interested in what reduces wealth inequality as well as what increases it. He ends his book with a call for a wealth tax; noting that variations in the rate of taxation have been common in US/European history.

But his analysis as to how and why wealth inequalities were reduced historically centers not so much on taxation, but on war. It is war that produces the circumstances in which wealth inequality is reduced. Piketty argues that it is not only that fixed capital is destroyed in war, though it is, but also that war creates 'chaos', during the course of which wealth inequalities decline. In particular, the 1914–1918 war created the circumstances for the decline of inequality.

> It is quite difficult to say where this trajectory would have led without the major economic and political shocks initiated by the war. With the aid of historical analysis and a little perspective, we can see those shocks as the only forces since the Industrial Revolution powerful enough to reduce inequality[4]

The mechanisms vary a little in different parts of the text. Sometimes it is a focus on 'chaos' as in 'the history of inequality: a chaotic political history'[5] and 'the chaos of the interwar years'[6]. Sometimes it is more nuanced: 'destruction caused by two world wars, bankruptcies caused by the Great Depression, and above all new public policies enacted in this period (from rent control to nationalizations and ... inflation).

Piketty analyses war as if it were an exogenous shock. This is a mistake. While he has a unified system of political economy that ranges widely, he excludes war as if it is not part of the social system. If war and other forms of violence are treated as part of the system, then the system is different, and the interventions are different.

There are significant correlations between violence and economic inequality. This has been well documented through comparisons between countries in their homicide rates, which correlate with income inequality, and correlations between inequality and violence within a country.[7] Rummell[8] has long argued that power kills. We can go beyond this to encompass both inter-personal and

---

4 Thomas Piketty, *Capital in the Twenty-First Century* (Cambridge, MA: Harvard University Press, 2014), p. 8.

5 Thomas Piketty, *Capital in the Twenty-First Century* (Cambridge, MA: Harvard University Press, 2014), p. 274.

6 Thomas Piketty, *Capital in the Twenty-First Century* (Cambridge, MA: Harvard University Press, 2014), p. 284.

7 See a meta-analysis of over 200 studies in Travis C. Pratt and Francis T. Cullen, "Assessing Macro-Level Predictors and Theories of Crime: A Meta-Analysis," *Crime and Justice: A Review of Research*, Vol. 32 Michael Tonry (ed). (Chicago: University of Chicago Press, 2005), pp. 373–450.

8 Rudolph J Rummel, *Power Kills: Democracy as a Method of Nonviolence.* (New Brunswick: Transaction, 1997).

inter-state violence, including the varied forms that violence can take, from wars and the military to inter-personal violence, with genocide and irregular militias. In *Globalisation and Inequalites*,[9] I show that different forms of violence correlate sufficiently for this to be conceptualized as a single system or institutional domain.

My argument here is that violence should not be treated as an exogenous shock, but is interconnected with inequality as part of a wider social system.

Democracy

Democracy and political mobilization are curiously absent in Piketty's book. Even though many countries saw a radical deepening of democracy in 1918, there is little discussion of its significance, except for a brief mention in relation to welfare state expenditures. Similarly there is little about trade unions apart from brief references to collective bargaining.

There is little discussion of the capacity of the state to act. This is despite the significantly enhanced capacity of the state during the major wars 1914–8 and 1939–45. Instead, Piketty refers to the immediate post-war period as "chaos."

The solution, taxing capital, requires Piketty to address the issue of the capacity of the state, and he dips into the debates on the EU, and its capacity to act, in ways that are under-developed in the rest of the book. In short, at this point Piketty needs a theory of the state and of political action, but he has spent very little time building this in the rest of the book. In consequence it appears voluntarist, rather than realistic.

Despite his interest in the state and in politics, which is core to his solution to the issue, which is wealth tax, Piketty has a rather under-developed theory in this area. In particular it is missing an account of democracy and of the variations in the depth of democracy.

Finance Capital

While Piketty addresses capital, he makes little distinction between financial and industrial capital. Yet finance is importantly and differently implicated in economic growth than industrial capital.

---

9   Sylvia Walby, *Globalization and Inequalities: Complexity and Contested Modernities.* (London: Sage, 2009).

As Keynes[10] and Minsky[11] showed, finance capital is intrinsically unstable. Its volatility can drive both economic growth and economic recession. Changes in the value of money have massive implications for wealth and for inequality. Financial crisis destroys value and changes inequalities.[12]

This nuancing of the conceptualization of capital so as to separately and additionally address finance is necessary for a comprehensive approach to capital.

Gender, Fertility and Demography

Piketty's neglect of gender is an important issue, but not in the way suggested by his critics, which is usually focused on his neglect of gendered inequalities in earned income.[13] Rather the problem is because his theorization of changes in fertility (which intersect the relation between wealth and growth) does not take account of differences in gender regimes that shape fertility levels (social democratic gender regimes in Europe have higher fertility rates than neoliberal ones).

Gender is absent where it should be present. The value of unpaid domestic labor, largely though not entirely performed by women, is omitted. This means that the increasing incorporation of women's labor into waged labor is omitted. This is a mistake for his model, let alone for the changing shape of inequality.

Piketty sidelines human capital, and therefore underestimates the significance of issues where gender intersects with inequality and with capital. There is ambivalence in the argument over not wanting to conceptualize education and skill as human capital, while simultaneously wanting to argue that education is a potential force for equality. This is gendered terrain, because of the narrowing of gendered differences in those aspects of human capital that are acquired through schools and colleges.

---

10   John M. Keynes, *The General theory of Employment, Interest and Money*. (London: Macmillan, 1936).

11   Hyman Minksy. *Stabilizing an Unstable Economy*. (New York: McGraw-Hill, 2008).

12   See Sylvia Walby 'Finance versus democracy: theorizing finance in society' *Work, Employment and Society*, vol. 27(3) 2013, pp. 489–507; and Sylvia Walby, *Crisis*. (Cambridge: Polity Press, 2015).

13   Kate Bahn, Joelle Gamble, Zillah Eisenstein and Heather Boushey "How Gender Changes Piketty's 'Capital in the Twenty-First Century'", *The Nation* (August 6, 2014) https://www.thenation.com/article/how-gender-changes-pikettys-capital-twenty-first-century/ Accessed December 9, 2016.

Piketty treats changes in demography as somewhere between a natural consequence of economic development and random or inexplicable. This is because he does not have a concept of gender, let alone a theory of different gender regimes. The fertility rate within Europe varies, not with the level of economic development, but rather with the extent to which the gender regime is neoliberal or social democratic, being lower in the former than the latter. Where there is greater depth of gendered democracy, there is greater provision of the welfare provision (such as nurseries) and the regulation of working time in employment (such as maternity and paternity leaves) to ensure compatibility between employment and care-work and thus facilitates higher fertility rates.[14] This can be seen in the replacement rates of fertility in the Nordic countries and the low rates in eastern Europe which have neoliberal regimes: both have high rates of female employment, but only the former have nurseries and extended leaves for childbearing and childcare.

Conclusion

Piketty has made major contributions to social science and public debate. Nevertheless, there are remaining gaps that need to be addressed before this can become a framework for a comprehensive analysis of economy and society.

The most important contributions of Piketty's work are: demonstrating the relevance of capital, not only of income; assembling the data sets needed to test and establish this thesis; original analysis of large scale change, using both theory and data; convincing account of significant variations in wealth inequality over time; and demonstrating the non-inevitability of wealth inequality.

The data used to underpin Piketty's argument has rightly been subject to scrutiny, since the nuances of the data on levels of wealth are central to Piketty's claims. In the debate about data assessed here, in particular the debate with Giles, Piketty's data derived from tax receipts are more reliable than data from self-report surveys for information on wealth.

There are four remaining gaps concerning: violence, democracy, finance and gender. Theories of society can and should include violence and not treat it as exogenous to the social system. Violence is not reducible to the economy but it is interconnected with the economy. War not exogenous to society, even

---

14   See Sylvia Walby, *Globalization and Inequalities: Complexity and Contested Modernities*, (London: Sage Press, 2009), and Sylvia Walby *The Future of Feminism*. (Cambridge: Polity Press, 2011).

if it is to the economy: there are significant interconnections between economic inequality and violence, which should be brought back in. Better theorizing of state, politics and democracy is needed. Finance is underestimated. Better gender analysis needed, not least for analysis of fertility.

Piketty makes a major contribution to social science, but he needs a theory of society, within which to insert his analysis about capital in order to make sense of it. Piketty remains an economist; he needs to become a sociologist.

CHAPTER 4

Predatory Logics: Going Well beyond Inequality

Saskia Sassen

Introduction

Much of the research on inequality focuses on income distributions. This is crucial information to understand key features of the social, economic and political dynamics of a place, a country, a sovereign nation, or an international system. We know from existing data, especially for the West, that the vectors that produced those distributions can vary across space and across time. The sources of inequality cannot be derived simply from income distributions. There are major constitutive elements in complex social systems that contribute to inequalities that cannot be captured through an analysis of income distributions.

Measuring inequality is not enough. Humankind has lived with it since the start. No complex politico-economic system that we know of lacks inequality. For instance, focusing on a narrow but familiar space-time, the data show that the post-WWII capitalist period in the West was quite different from the post 1980s, but inequality is present in both. Further, no two 'Western' countries were and are the same in terms of economic structure, yet all are marked by inequality. Much effort to study inequality in the current period limits itself to measuring that which can be shown to be a distribution, such as income. We need to interpellate inequality, uncover its sources, detect major breaks in a system's evolution, and more, in order to understand inequality and in order to decide at what point and under what conditions it becomes too unjust, or risks destroying the system within which it happens. In order to establish this we need to develop a logic that enables us to understand what it is we find unacceptable. Simply focusing on the distribution is not enough.

Piketty takes us well beyond measuring inequality and showing the features of the distribution. He contributes that larger setting and shows us how it evolved across time, and what contributed to inequality. He depends to a good extent on measuring distributions, but he also brings in larger contexts across the diverse periods in the century that is his focus. Thereby he goes much farther than much current work on inequality, which seems to be satisfied with documenting distributions.

And yet, Piketty's work does leave me with a concern about absences. In this brief text I focus on one such absence that cannot be simply understood as a distribution. It has to do with predatory logics—active actors. Even though Piketty does focus on larger dynamics, such as the taxation system, he does seem to stay away from major predatory logics. Elsewhere[1] I have developed an interpretation of diverse conditions and dynamics in our current period that can be conceived of as predatory. A familiar example that illustrates the point is mining. In my work, I have focused especially on finance, and conceptualized it as marked by a predatory logic in our current period. This logic cannot simply be studied as a distribution, even though it is marked by enormous differences in outcomes between winners and losers. Nor can it simply be explained as marked by inequality. It is a distinct domain, with a distinct operational space that feeds into that distribution. Thus, here is a difference with taxation, which does explicitly contribute to shaping the income distribution.

The general background proposition for this paper is that the difference between periods over time is only minimally accidental: such differences are the outcome of a mix of identifiable transformative processes. For instance, as with all major epochs, the differences between the post-war decades in the West and the period that took off in the 1980s cannot be seen simply as an evolution or more of the same, even if much did not change. Specific conditions, actors and interests were in play, and there were sharp disruptions of what had been established modus operandi. Nor can the differences be reduced to changed outcomes, as in changing distributions.

The focus here is on a specific, complex, re-assembling of key elements that I see as one of the transformative dynamics of our current (Western) period—the post-1980s. It is the re-making of high-finance, henceforth simply referred to as finance. I find that Piketty did not consider high finance sufficiently in his analysis as one of the forces generating massive distributional shifts. Finance is not the only key transformer of the post-1980s, nor will it have the capabilities it has today in near futures. Finance is an old actor that has undergone many transformations across time and space, and this will continue. I will focus on particular features of its post 1980s instantiation or re-invention. The second half of the paper then takes one specific case to illustrate its predatory features, specifically starting in the 2000s. Generally, this is an analysis that posits that we need to go well beyond the notion of inequality to get at some of the major logics in play in our current period.

1   Saskia Sassen, *Expulsions: Brutality and Complexity in the Global Economy*. (Cambridge: Harvard University Press, 2014).

Finance: An Assemblage of Capabilities

Critical to my argument is the distinction between finance and traditional banking. I emphasize[2] that the traditional bank is in the business of selling money. In the post-WWII decades, such banking benefitted from an economic logic that enabled the making of large prosperous working and middle classes, and from the fact that each generation did a bit better than the preceding one, partly thanks to diverse government programs. Banking was part of the larger logic of mass consumption. What takes off in the late 1980s is very different: it is marked by a proliferation of innovations that enable the making of powerful capabilities for the 'financializing' of a growing range of entities—from complex forms of debt to modest housing. I characterize finance as marked by a logic of extraction[3] rather than mass consumption, a conceptualization I explain briefly here. But for now let me add that one consequence is that finance constructs a distinct operational space that has nothing to do with mass consumption and everything with extraction of gains from diverse parties and settings. It uses brilliant minds and algorithmic math to financialize domains that in the past might have been seen simply as assets or beyond finance, or of not interest to finance.

This angle into the question of inequality, and, especially, the specific modes that inequality takes on in the current period, take us beyond income distributions and unequal power. It invites us to see that there is a brilliant, powerful, and very dangerous actor that is transforming the rules of the game.

Even if inequality has always existed in complex systems, in part, it is repeatedly made via specific conditions, decisions, and systemic arrangements. One big difference in the West between the post-WWII period and the post-1980s period is, in my reading, that in the former, all major classes (even if not all members of these classes) experienced betterment in their conditions, while in the post-1980s, the rich got richer and the lower 60% or more began to lose ground. Though it varies by country, up to the 1980s, the working and middle classes gained income, access to diverse services, and experienced the fact that each new generation generally did better than the preceding one. When privatization and deregulation begin to mark the new rules of the game in the late 1980s, the working and modest middle classes begin to lose ground. In the Global South, the so-called economic restructuring programs of the IMF

---

2   Saskia Sassen, *Expulsions: Brutality and Complexity in the Global Economy.* (Cambridge: Harvard University Press, 2014). See more specifically Chapters 1 and 3.

3   Saskia Sassen, *Expulsions: Brutality and Complexity in the Global Economy.* (Cambridge: Harvard University Press, 2014). See Chapter 3.

and the World Bank take on the roles that national governments and powerful business sectors take on in the North. Even if with diverse dynamics, both regions saw a significant sector get richer than might have been expected and the rest become poorer than they had expected.

There is a rapidly growing scholarship on financial institutions and markets that has made a critical contribution to our understanding of high finance—in good part because it is written by social scientists rather than "financial experts."[4] Nevertheless, my effort here goes in a somewhat different direction: the focus is on the financializing of more and more components of our economies. My argument is that this has been a major source for the growth in inequality in the post-1980s period across more and more parts of the world. Given limited space I will focus primarily on the US, but clearly, the financial system is global and so is its impact.[5]

A first critical point in my analysis is that global finance has debordered the narrowly defined notion of financial firms and markets, and financial institutions generally. It is not so much about institutions as about a larger assemblage of institutional, technical, and geographical components that function as capabilities for the financializing of more and more material and non-material elements[6] (Sassen 2008a: Chs 4, 5, 7: 348–65; 2013). These components include, among others, a broad range of financial and nonfinancial institutions, different types of jurisdictions, technical infrastructures, and public and private domains. It is precisely this larger assemblage that has

---

4 Representative of diverse approaches are, for example: Donald *MacKenzie,* Fabian *Muniesa* and Lucia *Siu* (eds.) *Do Economists Make Markets? On the Performativity of Economics.* (Princeton: Princeton University Press, 2007); Karin Knorr Cetina and Alex Preda, (eds.). *The Sociology of Financial Markets.* (Oxford: Oxford University Press, 2004); Barry Eichengreen, *Capital Flows and Crises.* (Cambridge: MIT Press, 2004); Caitlin Zaloom, *Out of the Pits: Traders and Technology from Chicago to London.* (Chicago: University of Chicago Press, 2006); Melissa S. Fisher, Greg Downey (eds.) *Frontiers of Capital: Ethnographic Reflections on the New Economy.* (Durham: Duke University Press, 2006). Greta R. Krippner, *Capitalizing on Crisis: The Political Origins of the Rise of Finance.* (Cambridge: Harvard University Press, 2011); *Globalization and Crisis* Special issue 7/1–2, February/April, 2010 cited in Tom Reifer (ed.) *Global Crises and the Challenges of the 21st Century,* (New York: Routledge 2010).

5 I have made a detailed analysis of how the financial system has constructed an operational space that is, yes, global but marked by very specific insertions in diverse locations across the world. See Saskia Sassen, "The Global City: Enabling Economic Intermediation and Bearing Its Costs." *City & Community* vol. 15 (2) 2016, pp. 97–108.

6 Saskia Sassen, *Territory, Authority, Rights: From Medieval to Global Assemblages.* (Princeton: Princeton University Press, 2008). See Chapters 4, 5 and 7, pp. 348–65.

enabled finance to shake up so much of the established order that arose in the post-WWII era.[7]

These features of today's financial system also explain why I posit[8] that finance today is basically an extractive industry—a term usually confined to mining and other material sectors. The distinctive growth patterns and conditions *for* growth of the global financial system are quite different from those of other economic sectors. It can extract value from even from very modest material and immaterial elements because it re-positions them in a larger financial space where they can function in modes that are quite different from what is the case in most other sectors, including traditional banking. A straightforward way in which I like to describe this difference is that the traditional bank sells something it has—money—and therein lies its source of profits. Finance, in contrast, sells something it does not have and therein lies its need to develop instruments that allow it to invade other sectors; that invasion is usually described in a far more abstract way with the term "financialization."

This kind of analytics brings to the fore the fact that finance has properties that differentiate it from the rest of the market economy: the financializing of other economic sectors functions as the grist for its mill. It financializes mining products, housing, traditional loans, bankruptcies, commodities, currencies, and much more. This contributes to the networked format of finance; a feature that enables finance to incorporate diverse elements and develop innovative formats, such as alliances of exchanges. These contrasts with the old-style format of the corporation and traditional bank, both marked by closure and vertical integration

It is against this background that I want to examine the question of inequality. It means expanding the more traditional sociological quantitative analysis

---

7   This analytical perspective helps explain why the Bretton Woods (BW) internationalism was not enough to generate the global financial system that emerged in the 1980s. Many of the components that became important in the 1980s were in place in the postwar period, as they were at the end of the 1800s. But the organizing logic of the whole assemblage of elements in each of those earlier periods was not conducive to the formation of a global, as distinct from an international, capital market, and even less for the type of financializing capability that distinguishes today financial system from earlier so-called financial regimes even though they should be described as more akin to traditional banking than finance (see Saskia Sassen *Territory, Authority, Rights: From Medieval to Global Assemblages* (Princeton: Princeton University Press, 2008) and Saskia Sassen, *Expulsions: Brutality and Complexity in the Global Economy.* (Cambridge, MA: Harvard University Press, 2014). See Chapter 30.

8   Saskia Sassen, *Expulsions: Brutality and Complexity in the Global Economy.* (Cambridge: Harvard University Press, 2014), Chapter 3.

of inequality—notably income distributions—in order to include elements such as the destruction of traditional economies and of traditional household growth strategies. It is a radically different organizing logic from that of, for instance, the typical mass consumer oriented corporation. The latter needs and thrives on households doing well, and on the sons and daughters doing better than their parents, on governments supporting households via health subsidies so they can use private hospitals and buy prescribed medications, and so on. Finance, like mining, wants to extract value it can immediately put to work (that is, financialize) for specific aims, and once it has executed that operation, it leaves behind destruction and moves on to the next target.

One indicator of this constitutive difference is the sharp policy changes that took off in the 1980s, from protectionisms of all sorts to deregulations of all sorts. It points to the specificity of the larger assemblage of elements that constitutes today's global financial system. It is not simply the power of finance and multinational corporations that reconfigure the system. Significant for finance are the new forms of private authority, actually enabled by the growing power of the executive branch of government, which in turn further feed executive branch power.[9] Present in this dynamic is the possibility of an articulation between the executive branch and the financial system that cannot be simplified as either "the decline of the state" or the dominance of finance over the state. Nor can it be seen as a mere continuation of Bretton Woods' multilateralism.

Two framing features radically distinguish the postwar Bretton Woods financial system, especially in its first decade, from the current global system, even if the latter incorporates some Bretton Woods rules. One is the role of financial markets. Until the 1950s financial policy was cautionary, regulatory controls were in place, and the stock market was relatively inactive. The central policy issue was unemployment, not free trade or global finance, as it became in the 1980s.[10] In fact, unemployment was seen as resulting from free trade.[11] The early phase of the Bretton Woods project involved the making of a global system to protect against major crises. While it is not easy to disentangle the

---

9   Saskia Sassen, *Territory, Authority,Rights: From Medieval to Global Assemblages* (Princeton: Princeton University Press, 2008). Chapter 4.

10   William K. Tabb, *Economic Governance in the Age of Globalization.* (New York: Columbia University Press, 2004).

11   There was neither strong opposition to free trade nor much serious consideration of it. Jacob Viner notes at that time that no one was addressing the question of free trade or, indeed, even talking about it. See Jacob Viner, *The Long View and the Short: Studies in Economic Theory* (Glencoe, Ill: The Free Press, 1958).

causal interactions between policy and stock markets, governments generally kept these policies in place even as growth resumed and stock markets revived in the 1950s. This became unacceptable in the 1980s.

The second major framing condition was the use of managed exchange rates and controls on international capital flows to protect the financial system from international competitive and exchange rate pressures. This insulation was the norm in the world economy of that time.[12] All the major powers supported systems for domestic economic management—including the United States. The most familiar of these policy systems are Britain's Keynesian welfare state, West Germany's "social market," France's "indicative planning," and Japan's Ministry of International Trade and Industry (MITI) model of systematic promotion of export industries. There was a trade-off in the early Bretton Woods phase between embedded liberalism in the international trading and production order and increased domestic economic management aimed at protecting national economies from external disruptions and shocks. Underlying this policy stance was a concern with the redistributive effects of capitalist economies. Keynes proposed making debtor and surplus countries work at returning the international system to balance—which the United States, then the leading surplus country, rejected.[13] Keynes wanted easier borrowing for debtor nations (by then Britain was a debtor nation) and

---

12   Barry Eichengreen, "The Great Depression as a Credit Boom Gone Wrong" *Bank for International Settlements Working paper;* Paper 137, 25.09. 2003; David A. Smith, Dorothy J. Solinger and Steven C. Topik (eds.), "Sovereignty, Territoriality, and the Globalization of Finance," *States and Sovereignty in the Global Economy.* (London: Routledge, 1999). pp. 138–157. See also Eric N. Helleiner, *The Status Quo Crisis: Global Financial Governance After the 2008 Meltdown.* (New York: Oxford University Press, 2014).

13   The United States insisted that surplus countries not be penalized. Eventually the United States became far less competitive and a massive debtor; nonetheless its hegemonic position allowed it to escape the disciplining of the supranational system and market dynamics that other debtor countries were subjected to. See Saskia Sassen, *Losing control?:Sovereignty in the age of globalization* (New York: Columbia University: 1996). Chapter 2; Saskia Sassen, *Globalization and its Discontents* (New York: W. W. Norton, 1998). Chapter 4. Much like Britain at its time of world dominance, in the postwar period the United States sought an open trading system, while most other countries sought protections under national developmentalist regimes. There is a vast scholarship on the postwar asymmetry between the United States and most other countries that traces in enormous detail the consequences for different actors of having an open trading system under US dominance versus the advantages for development of nationally protected economies; it is quite different from the scholarship that emerges in the 1980s and 1990s. It is impossible to do justice here to that postwar scholarship.

prevention of capital flight.[14] The actual regime adopted was not quite what Keynes had proposed.[15]

Bretton Woods delivered multiple capabilities for globalizing finance. However, these framing aims amounted to a different organizing logic from what was to become necessary for the current global financial system.

The Global Capital Market: Power and Norm-Making

The many negotiations between national states and global economic actors that led to our current global financial system generated a *de facto* normativity. Among familiar components are privileging low inflation over employment growth, exchange rate parity, and the variety of items found in IMF conditionality.[16] The claims and criteria for policymaking that emerge as legitimate overrode older norms that privileged expenditures to ensure the well-being of people at large; the latter type norms are now seen as making states "less competitive" in a normative context where states are expected to become more so.

In my reading,[17] this normative transformation entails a privatizing of capacities for making norms, capacities we have associated with the state in our recent history. This brings with it strengthened possibilities of norm-making in the interests of the few rather than the majority. In itself, this is not new. New is the formalization of these privatized norm-making capacities and the sharper restricting of the beneficiaries. This privatizing also brings with it a weakening and even elimination of public accountability. In practice, this might not appear to be much of a change given multiple corruptions of the political

---

14   William Tabb, among others, finds that there is a strong case to be made that the high costs borne by the more vulnerable components of the world community could have been avoided if Keynes's position that surplus countries had as much responsibility as debtor ones to reestablish equilibrium had prevailed. See William Tabb, *Economic Governance in the Age of Globalization*. (New York: Columbia University Press, 2004). Ch. 5.

15   John Ruggie. "Territoriality and Beyond: Problematizing Modernity in International Relations." *International Organization*, vol. 47 (1), 1993, pp. 139–74; William Tabb, *Economic Governance in the Age of Globalization*. (New York: Columbia University Press, 2004); Ethan Kapstein, *Governing the Global Economy: International Finance and the State*. (Cambridge: Harvard University Press, 1994). More specifically see pp. 93, 112.

16   Since the Southeast Asian financial crisis, there has been a revision of some of the specifics of these standards. For instance, exchange rate parity is now evaluated in less strict terms.

17   Saskia Sassen. *Globalization and its Discontents* (New York: W. W. Norton, 1998). Chapter 5.

process. However, the formalizing of this weakened public accountability is consequential.

This was the setting for the ascendance of the post-1980s global financial system. The global capital market represents a concentration of power capable of systemically, not just through influence, shaping elements of national government economic policy and, by extension, other policies. The powerful have long been able to influence government policy.[18] Today, the operational logic of the global financial system has become a norm for "proper" economic policy.[19] These markets can now exercise the accountability functions formally associated with citizenship in liberal democracies: they can vote governments' economic policies out or in; they can force governments to take certain measures and not others. Given the properties of the systems through which these markets operate—speed, simultaneity, and interconnectivity—the resulting orders of magnitude give them real weight in the economies of countries and their policymaking.

There has long been a market for capital and it has long consisted of multiple, variously specialized, financial markets.[20] It has also long had global components.[21] Indeed, a strong line of interpretation in the literature of the 1990s[22] is that the post-1980s market for capital is nothing new and represents a return to an earlier global era—the turn of the century and, then again, the interwar period. However, all of this holds only at a high level of generality. When we factor in the specifics of today's capital market some significant differences emerge with those past phases. I emphasize two major ones here. One concerns today's far higher level of formalization and institutionalization of the global market for capital, partly an outcome of the interaction with national regulatory systems that themselves gradually became far more elaborate over the last hundred years.[23] The second concerns the transformative impact of the

---

18 Giovanni Arrighi, *The Long Twentieth Century: Money, Power, and the Origins of Our Times*. (London: Verso, 1994).

19 Saskia Sassen. *Globalization and its Discontents* (New York: W. W. Norton, 1998). Chapter 5.

20 E.g. Berry Eichengreen, *Global Imbalances and the Lessons of Bretton Woods*, (Cambridge, Massachussets: MIT Press, 2004); Eric N. Helleiner, *The status quo crisis: Global financial governance after the 2008 meltdown*. (New York: Oxford University Press, 2014).

21 Giovanni Arrighi, The Long Twentieth Century: Money, Power, and the Origins of Our Times. (London: Verso, 1994); See above, Berry Eichengreen, *Global Imbalances and the Lessons of Bretton Woods*, (Cambridge, Massachussets: MIT Press, 2004).

22 Paul Hirst, Grahame Thompson and Simon Bromley Eds. *Globalization in Question*. (Cambridge: Polity Press, 1996).

23 Saskia Sassen, *The Global City* (Princeton: Princeton University Press, 2001).

new information and communication technologies, particularly computer-based technologies (henceforth referred to as digitization). In combination with the mix of dynamics and policies, we usually refer to as globalization they have constituted the capital market as a distinct institutional order, to be differentiated from other major markets and circulation systems such as global trade.

One outcome of these processes is the formation of a strategic cross-border operational field constituted through the partial disembedding of specific state operations from the broader institutional frame of the state; this entailed a shift from national agendas to a series of new global agendas. The transactions are strategic, cut across borders, and entail specific interactions among government agencies and business sectors, addressing the new conditions produced and required by corporate economic globalization. They do not engage the state as such, as in international treaties, or intergovernmental networks. Rather, these transactions consist of the operations and policies of specific subcomponents of diverse institutional orders, prominently including the state (for instance, technical regulatory agencies, specialized sections of central banks and ministries of finance, special commissions within the executive branch of government, etc.), the supranational system linked to the economy (IMF, World Trade Organization (WTO)), and private non-state sectors. In this process, these transactions push toward convergence across countries in order to create the requisite conditions for a workable global financial system. This global financial system, in turn, is embedded in a vast array of specific, often highly specialized, bits of state and supranational institutions; it does not only consist of its firms, exchanges, and electronic networks.[24]

There are two distinct features about this field of transactions that lead me to posit that we can conceive of it as a disembedded space in the process of becoming structured. The transactions take place in familiar settings: the state, the interstate system, and the "private sector." However, the practices of the agents involved are constructing a distinct assemblage of bits of territory, authority, and rights that function as a new type of operational field. In this regard, it is a field that exceeds the institutional world of the interstate system and of "the global economy." Insofar as interactions between these specific state actors and specific private corporate actors provide substantive public rationales for developing national and international policy, it is an operational field that denationalizes state agendas. That is to say, the rationales for global

---

24   Saskia Sassen, *Territory, Authority, Rights: From Medieval to Global Assemblages* (Princeton: Princeton University Press, 2008), pp. 348–65, Chapter 5.

action of those specific state and corporate actors run through national formal law and policy, but are in fact rationales that denationalize state policy.[25]
This can bring with it a proliferation of rules that begin to assemble into partial, specialized systems of law only partly embedded in national systems, if at
all. Here we enter a whole new domain of private authorities—fragmented,
specialized, and increasingly formalized but not running through national
law *per se*.

Two sets of interrelated empirical features of these markets signal the rapid
transformation since the mid-1980s.[26] One is accelerated growth, partly due to
electronic linking of markets—both nationally and globally—and the sharp rise
in innovations enabled by both financial economics and digitization. The second is the sharp growth of a particular type of financial instrument—the derivative—a growth evident both in the proliferation of different types of derivatives
and in its becoming the leading instrument in financial markets.[27] This diversification and dominance of derivatives has made finance more complex and
enabled growth rates that diverge sharply from those of other globalized sectors.

When Local Housing Becomes a Global Financial Instrument

Beyond its social and political role, housing has long been a critical economic sector in all developed societies and has made major contributions
to economic growth. There have historically been three ways in which it

---

25   Saskia Sassen, *Territory, Authority,Rights: From Medieval to Global Assemblages* (Prince-
     ton: Princeton University Press, 2008). See Chapter 4.

26   There are other factors that are significant, particularly institutional changes, such as the
     bundle of policies usually grouped under the term deregulation and, on a more theoret-
     ical level, the changing scales for capital accumulation. For a full analysis of these issues.
     See Barry Eichengreen, *Global Imbalances and the Lessons of Bretton Woods*, (Cambridge:
     MIT Press, 2004); Barry Eichengreen and Albert Fishlow, *Contending with Capital Flows:
     What is Different about the 1990s? Occasional paper.* (New York: Council of Foreign Re-
     lations 1996); and Greta Krippner, *Capitalizing on Crisis; The Political Origins of the Rise
     of Finance.* (Cambridge: Harvard University Press, 2012). To more fully understand new
     scales for capital accumulation including deregulation, re-regulation and recent develop-
     ments in the financial markets, see the special issue on *Globalization and Crisis*, in *Glo-
     balizations* vol. 7, 2010. For a state of the art examination of the full array of specialized
     corporate services, see John R. Bryson and Peter W. Daniels (eds.) *The Service Industries
     Handbook*. (Cheltenham: Edward Elgar, 2009)

27   Saskia Sassen *Territory, Authority, Rights: From Medieval to Global Assemblages* (Prince-
     ton: Princeton University Press, 2008) p. 350.

played this economic role: as part of the construction sector, as part of the real estate market, and as part of the banking sector in the form of mortgages. In all three sectors it has at times been a vector for innovations. For instance, solar energy has largely been applied to housing rather than to offices or factories. Mass construction has used housing as a key channel to develop new techniques and formats, and the industrial production of prefabricated buildings has similarly focused on housing to work out the kinks.

Mortgages have also been one of the key sources of income and innovations for traditional-style banking. The thirty-year mortgage, now a worldwide standard, was actually a major innovation for credit markets. Japan and then China instituted, respectively, ninety- and seventy-year mortgages to deal with a rapidly growing demand for housing finance in a context where three generations were necessary to cover the cost of housing in a boom period—the 1980s in Japan and the 2000s in China.

The securitizing of mortgages, which took off in the 1980s, added yet another role for housing in the economy. Securitizing home mortgages can create growth in an economy. Nevertheless, it also opens up the mortgage market to speculation, making it vulnerable to risk and loss. This is acceptable if the owner of the mortgaged property decides to speculate and is fully informed of the risks. However, it is not acceptable if the decision to enter a risky arrangement is made without such knowing consent. Even knowing consent may not be enough at a time when contracts are long and impenetrable and the culture pervading the financial and investment industry is not characterized by openness and transparency. It is worth recalling the notorious bankruptcy of Orange County, a municipal government in California: what the local government thought was a loan turned out to be a highly speculative investment, bankrupting the county and its pension funds. A similar crisis happened late in 2012 when dozens of municipal governments in Italy confronted a bud- get crisis because what they thought were straightforward bank loans turned out to be credit default swaps—one of the riskiest and most speculative types of investment.

The securitizing of home mortgages has a similar effect: on one hand it transforms what might look like a traditional mortgage into part of a speculative investment instrument to be sold and bought in speculative markets and on the other, it follows a different pathway and represents yet another financial innovation capable of extreme destruction. It inserts a new channel for using housing as an asset that is to be represented by a contract (the mortgage) and can be sliced into smaller components and mixed with other types of debt for sale in the high- finance circuit.

Below I develop this in some detail.[28] I focus on the United States because it was ground zero for this innovation and its application. The case serves to illustrate some of the features of financialization, specifically the use of complex instruments in the making of a short, highly profitable investment cycle for some and enormous losses for the many millions of households that were *used* for a financial, not housing, project.

Furthermore, within the logic of finance, it is also possible to make a good profit by betting against the success of an innovation—that is, to profit by predicting failure. This type of profit making happened as well with subprime mortgages and a series of other financial innovations, notably credit default swaps. In fact, it was the far larger market of swaps that sparked the September 2008 financial crisis: anxious investors trying to cash in their credit default swaps beginning in 2007 made visible the fact that this $60 trillion market lacked the actual funds to meet its obligations. In short, the so-called sub-prime crisis was not due to irresponsible households taking on mortgages they could not afford, as is still commonly asserted in the United States and the rest of the world. Rather, the mounting foreclosures signaled to those investors who had bought credit default swaps, that it was time to cash in their "insurance," but the money was not there, because the foreclosures had also devalued the swaps, and, further, the swaps were not an insurance, but a derivative based instrument.[29]

The Search for Actual Assets

By the early 2000s, the sharp acceleration of financial value compared to actual GDP was generating an acute demand for securities backed by actual assets. It is in this context that even low-grade mortgages on modest homes became grist for the financial mill in the U.S. Mortgages on modest homes were basically unattractive to traditional banks, and, importantly, they were one of the few under-financialized items in the US economy. The financializing of regular mortgages and of consumer loans had already been in place for two decades, so what was left was at the margins—low grade mortgages, student loans, and such.

---

28   Saskia Sassen, *Expulsions; Brutality and Complexity in the Global Economy* (Cambridge: The Belknap Press of Harvard University Press, 2014). See Chapter 3.

29   For a more detailed description see Saskia Sassen, *Expulsions; Brutality and Complexity in the Global Economy* (Cambridge: The Belknap Press of Harvard University Press, 2014). Chapter 3.

This delinking made the creditworthiness of mortgage holders irrelevant to the potential for profit. The result was to put modest households in a high-risk situation, with salespeople pushing to get the contract signed. The desirable level was for each salesperson to get 500 contracts signed per week.

Each mortgage represented the "asset" in the newly invented financial instrument. The asset was not necessarily the whole house—there was much splicing to multiply the number of fragments of a house that could provide a piece of asset for those asset-backed securities. These fragments were bundled up with high-grade debt (that was not asset backed), and so generate an "investment product" that could be sold as an *asset*-backed security to investors—and thereby the mission was accomplished. This was clearly a bit deceptive, to put it kindly. But many investors bought and speculated on the instrument and made good profits, given the growing demand for actual asset-backed securities.

It took a complex set of innovations to make possible this de-linking of the source of profits from the actual value of the asset. Such delinking made the creditworthiness of mortgage holders irrelevant to the potential for profit in the financial sector. The result was to put modest households in a high-risk situation, with salespeople pushing to get the contract signed. What mattered was that signature on the contract. Whether the buyer of the mortgage could pay, the monthly installments mattered less than signing the contract. Eventually by the mid-2000s, it was clear to the financiers that all they needed to secure was the signature on the contract and it did not really matter whether the signing households paid or not. The source of profit was not the mortgage. It was the complex instrument with a bit of asset and lot of high-grade debt to camouflage the minimal and low-value asset. For it to work, at least 500 such mortgage contracts had to be signed per week for each mortgage sales agent.

14 Million Households Pay the Price for Financial Abuse

As the demand for asset-backed securities grew, so did the selling, often pushy selling, of sub-prime mortgages. Eventually mortgage buyers were not asked for any payment for five years, since the source of profit was not the (very modest) mortgage payments. It generated high profits to those investors who sold the resulting asset backed securities. Institutions that kept these securities lost quite a bit of capital when the crisis hit. Thus, the foreclosure crisis that exploded in 2007 was not a crisis generated by irresponsible mortgage buyers. It was a crisis generated by abusive, aggressive, and speculative financial firms and banks.

And it was a major, life-changing crisis for the millions of middle- and work-ing class families most of whom we now know had been signed on under false pretenses. They could not pay their mortgages and lost everything, including the little they had had before they took on the mortgage (see Table 4.1). Ac-cording to Bernanke, former head of the Federal Reserve, when he stepped down one of the issues he raised in his final speech, was the fact that four-teen million households had lost their homes to foreclosures. Fourteen million households can be up to 30, 40, or more million individuals. This is more than the total population of many countries. Millions of them now live in tent cities.

TABLE 4.1 *Foreclosures filed in the USA, 2006–2014*[30]

· 2006: 1.2 million foreclosures
(One for every 92 households)
 · 2007: 2.2 million foreclosures
 · 2008: 3.1 million
 · 2009: 3.9 million
(1 in 45 US households)
 · 2010: 2.9 mill foreclosures
 · **2011:** 2,698,967
 · **2012:** 2,304,941
 · **2013:** foreclosures filed on 1,361,795 properties
 · **2014:** foreclosure filed on 1,117,426 properties

SOURCE: REALTYTRAC BASED ON FEDERAL RESERVE BANK DATA

Did Foreclosures Create the Crisis?

A common notion regarding the financial crisis was that it resulted from irre-sponsible buyers of these mortgages who should have known that they could not pay for them. It overlooks the fact that the instrument was designed so as to de-link the potential profits for the mortgage-sellers and investors from the consumer's capacity to pay the mortgage. This was, then, also what made it dangerous and dodgy for the buyers of the mortgage, who were mostly of modest income—those who thought they could not afford to buy a house. In addition, this is also critical for its potential spread to the global market of 2 billion middle and lower income households.

---

30   A particular property may have more than one foreclosure.

It is also a feature often overlooked in explanations of the crisis, and in analyses of inequality. This was an instrument designed by brilliant mathematicians that generated wealth for well informed investors and rendered very modest households even poorer than they were; it took the little they had, and many of them became homeless.

In all of this, there is a little tail that wagged the big financial firms. For high-finance, these millions of modest foreclosures in 2006 and 2007 created a crisis of confidence: The foreclosures were a sort of 'larger world' signal that something was wrong. However, given the complexity of the bundled instruments, it had become impossible to identify the toxic component. The value involved in the mortgages, a mere US$ 300 billion, could not have brought down the financial system.

There is a profound irony in this crisis of confidence: the brilliance of those who make these financial instruments became the undoing of a large number of investors (besides the tragic undoing of the modest-income families who had been sold these mortgages). The toxic link was that for these mortgages to work as assets for investors, vast numbers of mortgages were sold regardless of whether these homebuyers could pay their monthly fee. The faster these mortgages could be sold, the faster they could be bundled into investment instruments and sold off to investors. Overall, subprime mortgages more than tripled from 2000 to 2006, and accounted for 20% of all mortgages in the US in 2006. This premium on speed also secured the fees for the sub-prime mortgage sellers and reduced the effects of mortgage default on the profits of the sub-prime sellers. In fact, those sub-prime sellers that sold off the contracts did fine. It was those who did not sell off these mortgages as part of investment instruments who went bankrupt eventually, but not before having secured some profits from mortgage buyers and at least some selling of asset-backed securities.

Sub-prime mortgages can be valuable instruments to enable modest-income households to buy a house. But what happened in the US over the past decade was an extreme abuse that had little to do with securing housing for modest families. In an increasingly globalized world the good and, perhaps mostly, the abusive uses of this instrument can easily proliferate.

Who Paid the Biggest Price?

The aggressive sale of subprime mortgages to those unable to pay for them becomes clear in the microcosm that is New York City. If we consider the key years when this takes off, from 2002 to 2006, it is clear that Whites, who have a far higher average income than all the other groups in New York City, were far less likely to have subprime mortgages than all other groups (See Table 4.2). Thus, 9.1 percent of all mortgages taken by Whites were subprime mortgages in 2006 compared with 13.6 percent among Asians, 28.6 percent among Hispanics, and 40.7 percent among Blacks. While all groups had high growth rates in sub-prime borrowing, if we consider the most acute period, 2003 to 2005, it more than doubled for Whites, but tripled for Asians and Hispanics and quadrupled for blacks.[31] Most of these households have lost their homes to foreclosure, and many of the neighborhoods have become devastated urban spaces. A further breakdown by neighborhood in New York City shows that the ten worst hit neighborhoods were poor: between 34 and 47 percent of residents in these neighborhoods who took mortgages got subprime mortgages.

TABLE 4.2 *Rate of conventional subprime lending by race, New York City 2002–06*

	2002	2003	2004	2005	2006
White	4.6%	6.2%	7.2%	11.2%	9.1%
Black	13.4%	20.5%	35.2%	47.1%	40.7%
Hispanic	11.9%	18.1%	27.6%	39.3%	28.6%
Asian	4.2%	6.2%	9.4%	18.3%	13.6%

SOURCE: FURMAN CENTER FOR REAL ESTATE & URBAN POLICY, 2007

The costs extend to whole metropolitan areas through the loss of property tax income for municipal governments. Table 3 shows the ten U.S. metro areas with the largest estimated losses of real gross municipal product (GMP) for 2008 due to the mortgage crisis and associated consequences, as measured by Global Insight. The total economic loss of these ten metro areas is estimated at over $45 billion for the year 2008. In that year, New York lost more than $10 billion in GMP, Los Angeles $8.3 billion, and Dallas, Washington, and Chicago each about $4 billion.

---

31   It is worth noting that a federal lawsuit filed in New York in 2016 claims that private investors who have taken ownership of federally insured mortgages are putting black homeowners at higher risk of foreclosure. See http://www.nytimes.com/2016/08/15/nyregion/sale-of-federal-mortgages-to-investors-puts-greater-burden-on-blacks-suit-says.html?em_pos=small&emc=edit_ur_20160815&nl=nytoday&nlid=54151248&ref=headline&_r=0. Accessed December 16, 2016.

When It All Goes Global

The subprime mortgage instrument developed in these years is just one example of how financial institutions can achieve major additions to financial value while disregarding negative social out- comes and even negative outcomes for the national economy. This disregard is entirely legal, notwithstanding its pernicious effects. If we consider the first half of the 2000's when this innovation took off and bring into the picture global information about housing and household debt (see Figure 4.1), several strong patterns emerge. Critical here is household debt and residential mortgage debt. These can easily function as a source of cash for banks and financial institutions that can use these mortgages and cash to develop diverse investments, as we have seen in the US with the subprime mortgage. Table 4.3 and Figure 4.2 below show residential mortgage debt in several Western countries and in several Asian countries in 2006, right before the crisis explodes.[32]

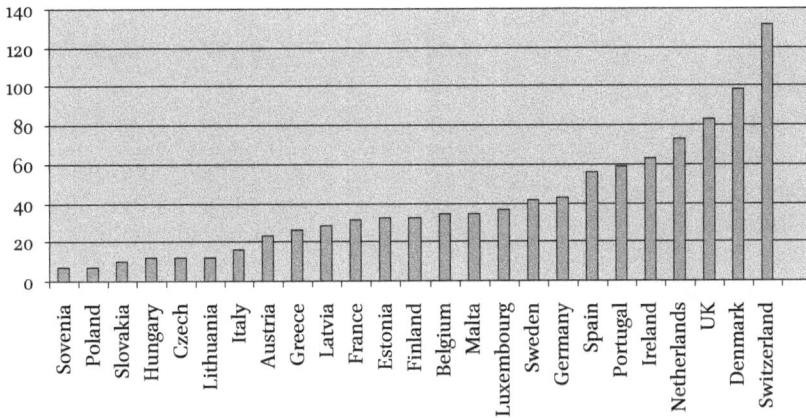

FIGURE 4.1   *Ratio of residential mortgage debt to GDP (Select countries/end 2006).*
SOURCE: http://www.germany-re.com/files/00034800/MS%20Housing%20
Report%202007.pdf

The larger question of debt includes a whole range of instantiations. Perhaps in this context it is worth noting a key feature of household debt. The ratio of household debt to personal disposable income has grown rapidly over a very

---

32   I develop this at length in Saskia Sassen, *Expulsions; Brutality and Complexity in the Global Economy* (Cambridge: The Belknap Press of Harvard University Press, 2014).

short period of time in a fairly diverse set of Global North countries. The period from 2000 to 2005, also the period when the sub-prime mortgage took off, is one were debt household seems to have grown sharply in a broad range of countries. For instance, to take cases with high increases, in the Czech Republic this ratio jumped from 8% in 2000 to 27% by 2005, in Hungary from 11% to 39%, in South Korea from 33% to 68%; in mature markets these ratios went from 83% to 124% in Australia, from 65% to 113% in Spain, and from 104% to 133% in the US. These are high growth rates and they indicate the potential for further growth in household debt.

TABLE 4.3 *Ratio of household credit to personal disposable income (2000–05)*

	2000	2001	2002	2003	2004	2005
Emerging markets						
Czech Republic	8.5	10.1	12.9	16.4	21.3	27.1
Hungary	11.2	14.4	20.9	29.5	33.9	39.3
Poland	10.1	10.3	10.9	12.6	14.5	18.2
India	4.7	5.4	6.4	7.4	9.7	...
Korea	33.0	43.9	57.3	62.6	64.5	68.9
Philippines	1.7	4.6	5.5	5.5	5.6	...
Taiwan	75.1	72.7	76.0	83.0	95.5	...
Thailand	26.0	25.6	28.6	34.3	36.4	...
Mature markets						
Australia	83.3	86.7	95.6	109.0	119.0	124.5
France	57.8	57.5	58.2	59.8	64.2	69.2
Germany	70.4	70.1	69.1	70.3	70.5	70.0
Italy	25.0	25.8	27.0	28.7	31.8	34.8
Japan	73.6	75.7	77.6	77.3	77.9	77.8
Spain	65.2	70.4	76.9	86.4	98.8	112.7
United States	104.0	105.1	110.8	118.2	126.0	132.7

SOURCE: IMF STAFF ESTIMATES BASED ON DATA FROM COUNTRY AUTHORITIES, CEIC, OECD, AND BLOOMBERG

Further, this larger international landscape shows us something of interest in the light of the financial system's abuse of modest households via the sub-prime mortgage. Thus, it is worth noting that even in fairly modest income countries a good share of new household debt is held or controlled by

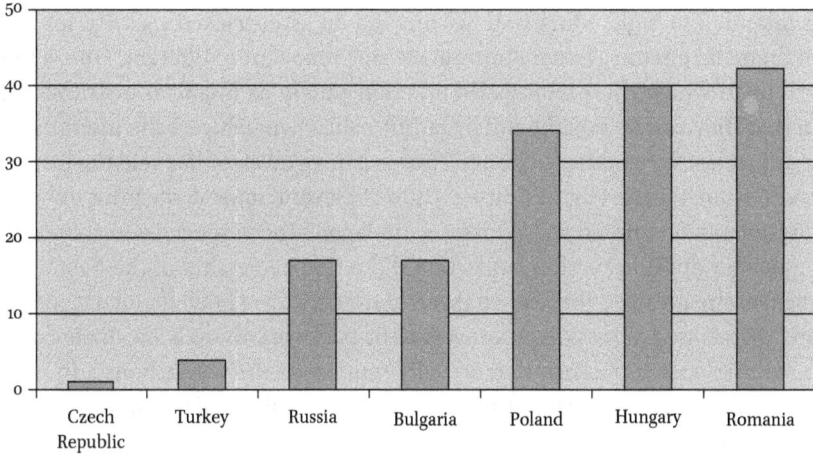

FIGURE 4.2   *Share of foreign-currency-denominated household credit, end-2005 (in percent of*
total household credit). SOURCE: IMF 2006. "GLOBAL FINANCIAL STABILITY
REPORT: MARKET DEVELOPMENTS AND ISSUES." IMF: WORLD ECONOMIC
AND FINANCIAL SURVEYS. SEPTEMBER, 2006. RETRIEVED AUGUST 26, 2008.
[http://www.imf.org/external/pubs/ft/GFSR/2006/02/pdf/chap2.pdf] P. 54

international financial banks; it would be more desirable if it that debt was in
the hands of conventional local banks. This holds for economies as diverse as,
for instance, Poland, Hungary, and Romania, where, respectively 35%, 40%
and 42% of this household debt is owned by major foreign banks.

Conclusion

This is not the first time the financial sector has used housing to develop instrument for investors. The first residential-mortgage-backed securities were produced
in the late 1970s. The concept, a good one in many ways, was to generate another source for funding mortgages besides the traditional one, which was basically
bank deposits in their many variants. In their benign early form, mortgage-backed
securities served to lower interest rates on mortgages and to stabilize the loan supply: that is, they allowed banks to continue lending even during downturns.

However, that earlier incarnation of subprime mortgages was a state
project. The one developed in the United States at the beginning of the
twenty-first century and now spreading internationally is built by and for the
financial sector. It is not about helping households to get housing but rather

is intended to build a financial instrument, an asset-backed security, for use in financial circuits. Two features make this innovation different. One is the extent to which these mortgages function purely as financial instruments, in that they can be bought and promptly sold. Ownership of the instrument may just last for a matter of hours. Thus, when an investor has sold the instrument, what happens to the house itself is irrelevant; indeed, the firms or bank divisions that suffered sharp losses were largely those specialized subprime lenders or divisions within banks that did retain ownership of the debt. Further, as already described, since these mortgages have been divided, spliced, and distributed across diverse investment packages, there is no single component in such a package that actually represents the whole house. In contrast, the owner loses the entire house and all the value she has in- vested in it if she is unable to meet the mortgage payments for a few months—no matter who owns the instrument and the slice of her house inside that instrument.

The second difference from traditional mortgages is that the source of profit for the investor is not the payment of the mortgage itself but the sale of the financial package that bundles hundreds or thousands of mortgage slices. This particular feature of the instrument enables lenders to make a profit from the vast potential market represented by modest-income households. The billions of these households across the world can become a major target when the source of profit is not the payment of the mortgage itself but the sale of the financial bundle. What counts for the lender is not the credit- worthiness of the borrower but the sheer number of mortgages sold to (often pushed onto) those households. This particular feature might be fine if the target for such mortgages is the world of wealthy speculators. But it becomes alarming when less well-off households are the targets.

The asymmetry between the world of investors (only some will be affect- ed) and the world of homeowners (once they default, they will lose the house no matter what investor happens to own the instrument at the time) creates a massive distortion in the housing market and the housing finance market. While homeowners unable to meet their mortgage obligations cannot escape the negative con- sequences of default, most investors can, because they buy these mortgages in order to sell them; there were many winners among investors and only a few losers in the years before the crisis broke in August 2007. Thus, investors could relate in a positive way to even the so-called subprime mortgages (poor-quality instruments), and this indifference in itself was bad for potential homeowners. We see here yet another sharp asymmetry in the position of the di- verse players enacting an innovation.

The current period makes legible a third asymmetry. At a time of massive concentration of financial resources in a limited number of super-firms, any that owned a large share of the subprime mortgages when the mortgage default crisis hit in 2007–2008 got stuck with massive losses. In an earlier period, ownership of mortgages was widely distributed among a huge number of banks and credit unions, and hence losses were more widely distributed as well. Ruthless practices, the capacity of firms to dominate markets, and the growing inter- connectedness of the markets have made these super-firms vulnerable to their own power, in a sort of network effect.[4]

Finally, as many of these instruments can be deployed globally, the risk mounts for a broader and broader range of modest households. Household debt in small and modest countries (mortgage debt, household general debt, etc.) can now be combined with high-grade debt and generate instruments to the high-level investment circuit. What we have seen in extreme form in the US is now spreading to more and more parts of the world. These are actors and firms that can generate impoverishment in growing sectors of a country's population by generating debt in ways that destroy the debtors but enable the financial sector to create whole new speculative instruments and sources of super-profits by mixing a little bit of asset (the modest house) with vast corporate and financial high-grade debt. The supply of modest-income households across the world is vast, and so is the capacity of the financial sector to use these households and discard them once used.

CHAPTER 5

Complex Inequalities in the Age of Financialisation: Piketty, Marx, and Class-Biased Power Resources

Eoin Flaherty

Introduction

Financialisation is widely acknowledged as a stressor of income equality as severe as those once considered staples of the political economy literature—globalization, welfare retrenchment, and skill-biased technological employment. Since the financial crisis, research has more pointedly fleshed out the institutional and regulatory characteristics of financialisation, allowing more specific causal channels linking the rise of finance to greater disparities in wealth and income to be established. Coupled with fears of continued stagnation across advanced capitalist democracies, Piketty's prognosis concerning the future distribution of income appears warranted. Accordingly, where slack national growth rates fall below those returns offered by rentier income streams; inequality, he claims, should rise as a consequence.

Whilst Piketty rightly links the rising ratio of capital-labor income to loosed bargaining constraints on top earners (through falling top marginal tax rates, especially since the 1970s), there is little sense of how wider institutional contexts may have played into this, nor how the institutional structure of capitalism has assumed various forms throughout time—financialisation merely the most recent. The temptation is thus to view the rise of the 'super rich' as a consequence of misguided fiscal policy, without interpreting this phenomenon as part of a wider package of neoliberal reforms aimed both at the labor movement, and the welfare state. By shifting focus toward a systemic understanding of how these measures are inherent to specific historical epochs of capitalist accumulation, we can better understand how a wider range of remedies is necessary, beyond narrow changes to specific aspects of fiscal policy alone.

Whilst much recent work has focused on different *discrete* aspects of the income distribution (for example, 'the 1% and the rest', or 'capital vs. labor'), there is a wider class politics underpinning the rise of inequality since the 1980's. The last twenty years have seen the consolidation of 'shareholder managerialism' approaches to human resource management, providing a direct link to the imperatives of corporate shareholders, and the lived experience of employment precarity. Coupled with a decline in the power of unions, real wage stagnation, and the rise of credit to shore up consumption, there now appears a clear institutionalization of class-biased power asymmetries. Whilst the 'very rich' may rely on investment and rent-generating income streams, 'the rest' now depend on debt, falling social transfers, and stagnant wages to subsist.

Finally, the tendency to focus on different aspects of the income distribution in isolation from each other has blinded us to the ways in which they are functionally inter-related. Inequality research has generally under-addressed the connection between the different aspects of income, such as the respective share of GDP accruing to capital and labor, the income shares of top fractiles such as the 1%, and the gap between rich and poor. There is strong reason to suspect that the era of financialisation has established even more profound links between these components of inequality however, due to the monopolization of rentier income streams by broad class groups. Thus we find that whilst the share of GDP accruing to labor has fallen as a result of deunionisation and globalization, this has facilitated a greater share of productivity being captured by an ever-shrinking pool of recipients. Similarly, the monopolization of financial instruments linked to securitization by resource-endowed individuals is implicated in the changing shape of the Gini income distribution, as those at the bottom assume the debt, which is subsequently leveraged by those at the top.

In the following discussion, I suggest that there is much we can learn by re-situating a class-based, relational analysis of inequality and its underlying power dynamics, drawing on the work of heterodox Marxian political economy in the social structures of accumulation tradition. Complementing this framework with discussion of a body of evidence showing the responsiveness of inequality to a range of institutional, economic, and regulatory variables, we come to see how class-biased power resources—in the form of control over terms of work, fiscal policy, and regulation—play a central role in the dynamics of modern inequality. In doing so, we also address a fundamental weakness in Piketty, by showing how inequality is necessarily embedded in wider systemic logics of accumulation, underpinned by distinct institutional and regulatory architectures.

Distributions of Income: The Personal, Functional, and Fractile, and Their Interrelations

It has been apparent for some time that long-term income distribution trends have not followed the typical Kuznets curve pattern, and that inequality has not fallen due to economic development and falling occupational dualization.

This 'classic' model depicted an initial disruptive phase of dualist growth during a country's putative stage of industrialization and urbanization, followed by a period of decline as economic development progressed. A transitional phase of initial high-income inequality was thus hypothesized by Kuznets, due to dual employment in both low-income agriculture, and non-agricultural work, followed by a period of declining inequality as growing non-agricultural employment raised per-capita incomes of the entire economy.[1] Despite ongoing faith in economic growth as the great leveler, toward the turn of the 21st century, it was apparent that this 'secular' promise of income equalization—in the absence of concerted political redistribution—had not come to pass. Instead, inequality has entered a 'great U-turn',[2] undoing decades of decline with a sustained upsurge since the 1980s, with globalization, de-unionisation, and retrenchment often cited as prime culprits.[3] The issue appears to have finally captured public imaginations, attracting critics from the Pope, to the U.S. president. NGOs now routinely point to rising global inequality as both consequence, and pretext to further economic and personal hardship, with the holdings of the bottom half of humanity equaling that of the wealthiest 62 individuals in 2015.[4] In light of these trends, the detachment of economic growth from any meaningful measure of human progress has never been clearer.

A number of issues are apparent here, and it is clear that despite the political importance of inequality entering public consciousness, clarity is needed on both working definitions of inequality, and the institutional factors that drive the distribution of income at various levels. The distinction is not merely academic and such clarity is essential for ordering the political project of redistribution. There are multiple means of measuring the distribution of income, as well as various definitions of income itself, along with 'stock' items such as capital. The issue of measurement is further complicated by rising debt in recent decades, with personal and household debt as a complement to stagnating real incomes, and heightened commercial trading in financial instruments. Furthermore, there are important distinctions to be made between, and inter-relations to be articulated amongst, the various aspects of inequality. The gap between rich and poor is but one component

---

1   Simon Kuznets, "Economic growth and income inequality," *The American Economic Review*, vol. 45 (1) 1955, p. 15.

2   Arthur S. Alderson and Francois Nielsen, "Globalization and the Great U-Turn: Income Inequality Trends in 16 OECD Countries," *American Journal of Sociology*, vol. 107 (5) 2002, pp. 1244–1299.

3   Britain and the U.S. are exemplars amongst Anglo-Saxons of this trend, see: http://piketty .pse.ens.fr/files/capital21c/en/pdf/F9.2.pdf Accessed February 22, 2017

4   Oxfam, *An Economy for the 1%: How Privilege and Power in the Economy Drive Extreme Inequality and how this can be Stopped* (London: Oxfam Briefing Paper, 2016). p. 210.

of the historical inequality narrative, with the rise of the 'super-rich', changing composition of capital and wealth, and a more generalized shift in the balance of power between 'capital and labor' playing complementary roles. The political importance of this becomes apparent once working definitions are dealt with.

Of the various possible measures of inequality, three have featured most in published work on the distribution of income: (1) the personal income distribution as captured by the Gini coefficient, which typically measures the overall spread of income amongst reporting earners or households in a given country, (2) the share of gross domestic product or national income accruing to wage and salary earners, also referred to as the functional income distribution or labor's share, and (3) the shares of total personal income accruing to the top 1% (the percentage income share of those residing above the 99th percentile/P99). The statistical properties and suitability of these measures is a matter of ongoing debate. Whilst the Gini coefficient is sensitive to variation about the mode, its intuitive interpretation as the ratio of observed inequality to perfect equality curves is appealing.[5] However, the survey-based sources on which such measures are often produced under-representation of top incomes, requiring the use of taxation records and interpolated control totals for population and income.[6]

The predominant trend amongst countries since the 1960s is that of rising inequality: falling factor shares, rising gaps between rich and poor, and rising top incomes. Figures 5.1 through 5.3 and Tables 5.1 and Table 5.2 illustrate these trends for a selection of countries with available data (note the use of restricted y-axes to emphasize trends). This secular trend is not uniform. The years of the 1980s are often noted as an important structural break for the Anglo-Saxon world, where labor's share of income began to decline, and top incomes began to rise under the combined pressures of neo-liberalization, state welfare retrenchment, and financialization. This characterization is especially applicable to the U.S. and U.K., often held as exemplars of the standard narrative of shifting power resources and rising inequality. There are strong correlations between the various components of the income distribution also, as noted in Table 5.2. Some caution is needed when interpreting these correlations, as the relationship between Gini inequality and the income shares of the top 1% is endogenous—however the partial effect is substantiated in multivariate panel work.[7] Table 5.2 adds basic dynamics by lagging the row variables

5   GINI, *Inequalities Impacts: State of the Art Review* (GINI Project, 2011), p. 14. http://www.gini-research.org/system/uploads/253/original/GINI_State-of-the-Art_review_1.pdf?1308916502. Accessed July 14, 2016.

6   Anthony B. Atkinson and Jes Sogaard, *The long-run history of income inequality in Denmark: Top incomes from 1870 to 2010* (EPRU Working Paper Series, 2013).

by one year, thus allowing us to better assess the relationship between income components, and the effect of institutional correlates on inequality. Overall, this basic inspection suggests not only a degree of commonality in the experiences of the tabulated countries (their long-term dynamics, as well as their susceptibility to common institutional protections and stressors), but also a relationship between the various income distribution components warranting further consideration. The top income share for example, closely tracks other measures of inequality such as the Gini/Atkinson coefficients and income percentile ratios. This observation suggests that factors often found to influence the bottom and mid-range of the income distribution may have similar effects at the top[8], albeit through qualitatively different mechanisms.

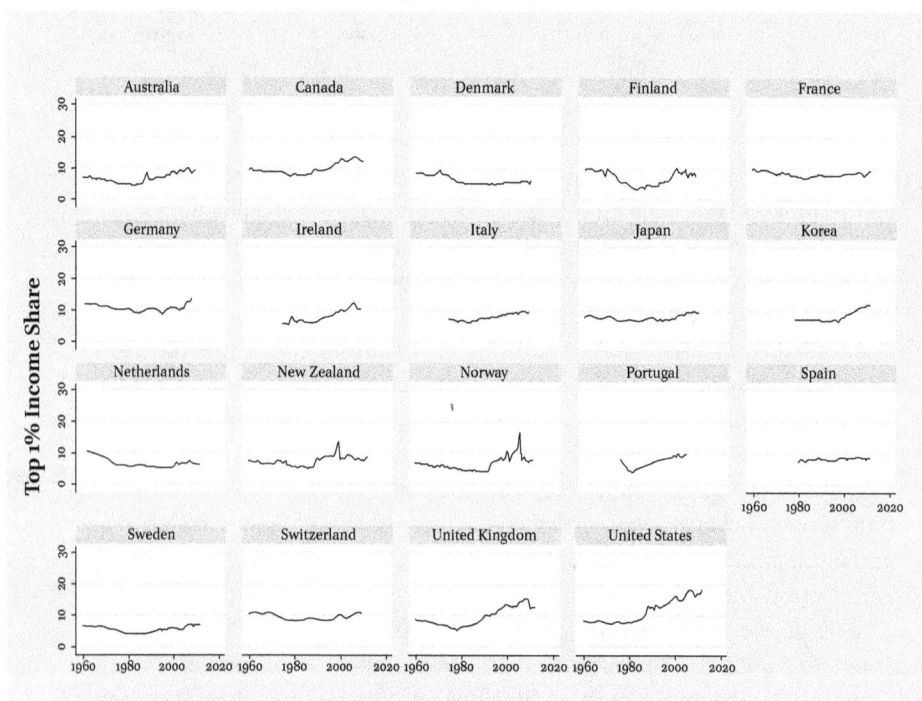

FIGURE 5.1   *Income share of the top 1% (1960–2012)*

7   Eoin Flaherty, "Top incomes under finance-driven capitalism, 1990–2010: power resources and regulatory orders," *Socio-Economic Review*, vol. 13(3) 2015, pp. 417–447. Emilie Daudey and Cecelia García-Penalosa, "The personal and factor distribution of income in a cross-section of countries," *The Journal of Development Studies*, vol. 43(5) 2007.

8   Andrew Leigh, "How closely do top income shares track other measures of inequality?" *The Economic Journal*, vol. 117 (524) 2007, pp. 619–633.

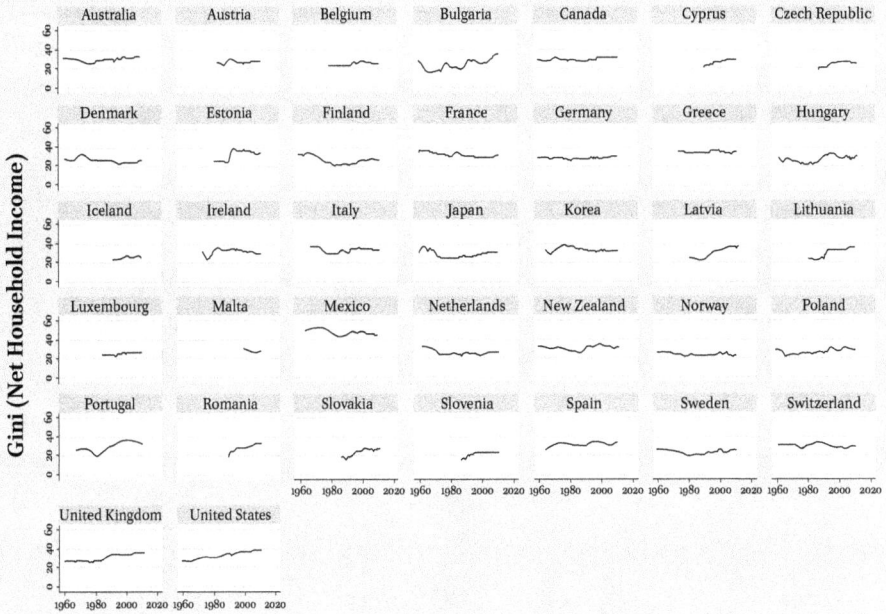

FIGURE 5.2 *Gini income inequality (1960–2012)*

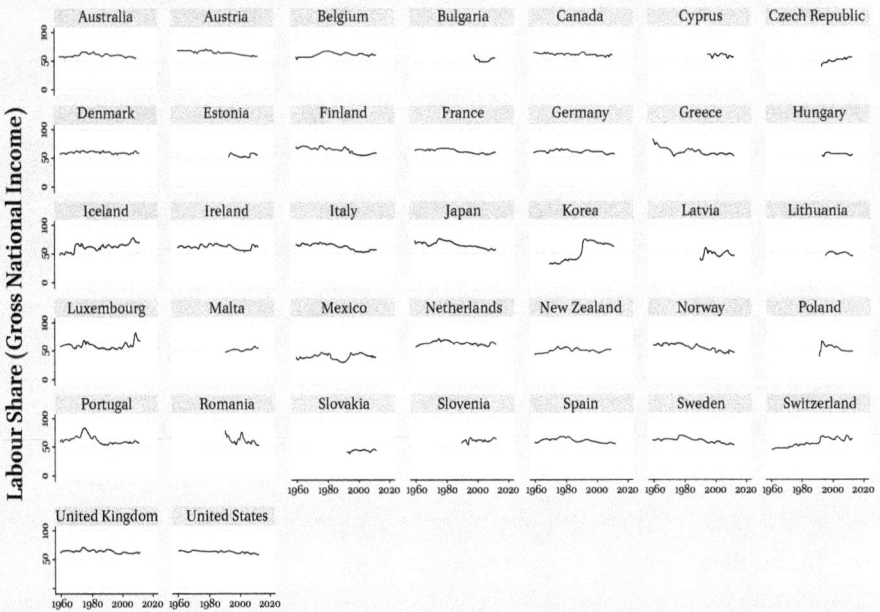

FIGURE 5.3 *Labour's share of national income (1960–2012)*

TABLE 5.1 *Inequality, linear trend regression slopes*[a]

	Top 1%[b]	Gini[c]	Labour share[d]
Australia	.066***	.061**	−.046
Austria	-	.057	−.206***
Belgium	-	.141***	.072*
Bulgaria	-	.279***	−.053
Canada	.089***	.059***	−.115***
Cyprus	-	.391***	−.160
Czech Republic	-	.260***	.652***
Denmark	−.062***	−.115***	−.032
Estonia	-	.404***	.044
Finland	−.029	−.124***	−.298***
France	−.015*	−.134***	−.192***
Germany	.012	.021*	−.074***
Greece	-	.004	−.285***
Hungary	-	.153***	−.031
Iceland	-	.198***	.351***
Ireland	.177***	.041	−.093**
Italy	.097***	.003	−.292***
Japan	.023**	−.057	−.257***
Korea	.146***	−.040	1.158***
Latvia	-	.555***	.082
Lithuania	-	.530***	−.154
Luxembourg	-	.171***	.047
Malta	-	−.214**	.198***
Mexico	-	−.116***	.060
Netherlands	−.056***	−.062*	−.059*
New Zealand	.051***	.040	.053
Norway	.077***	−.061***	−.336***
Poland	-	.115***	−.517**
Portugal	.164***	.382***	−.232***
Romania	-	.534***	−.593***
Slovakia	-	.426***	.141
Slovenia	-	.283***	.186*
Spain	.030***	.078**	−.143***
Sweden	.006	−.003	−.209***
Switzerland	−.007	−.043*	.425***
United Kingdom	.159***	.227***	−.080***
United States	.232***	.235***	−.109***

a   For a full discussion and sources of all variables cited in this chapter, see Flaherty, *Top incomes under finance-driven capitalism*.
b   Data taken from available countries as provided by: Facundo Alvaredo, Anthony B. Atkinson, Thomas Piketty and Emmanuel Saez, *The World Wealth and Income Database*, accessed on August 8, 2016 at http://www.wid.world/
c   Frederick Solt, "Standardizing the World Income Inequality Database," *Social Science Quarterly*, 90, 2009.
d   Constructed using data from: European Commission, *Annual Macro-Economic Database*, accessed on July 1, 2016 at http://ec.europa.eu/economy_finance/ameco/user/serie/SelectSerie.cfm

TABLE 5.2 *Lagged correlations, top income inequality and institutional drivers*

	Top 1%	Gini	Labour share	Union density	Govern- ment cons- umption	Economic globali- sation
Gini$_{(t-1)}$	.656***					
Labour Share$_{(t-1)}$	−.114**	−.389***				
Union Density$^a_{(t-1)}$	−.572***	−.579***	.164***			
Government Consump.$^b_{(t-1)}$	−.265***	−.141***	.035	.091*		
Economic Globalisation$^c_{(t-1)}$	.096*	−.051	−.078*	.107**	−.016	
Financial Liberalisation$^d_{(t-1)}$	.502***	.089**	−.120**	−.256***	−.052	.659***

a   Jelle Visser, *Database on Institutional Characteristics of Trade Unions, Wage Setting, State Intervention and Social Pacts in 34 countries between 1960 and 2012*, accessed on July 15, 2013 at http://www.uva-aias.net/207
b   Alan Heston, Robert Summers and Bettina Aten, *Penn World Table Version 7.1*, (University of Pennsylvania: Centre for International Comparisons of Production, Income and Prices, 2012).
c   Axel Dreher, Noel Gaston and Pim Martens, *Measuring Globalisation—Gauging its Consequences* (New York: Springer, 2008).
d   Abdul Abiad, Enrica Detragiache and Thierry Tressel, *A New Database of Financial Reforms*, (International Monetary Fund: IMF Working Paper WP/08/266, 2008). Note: Greater value = greater financial liberalisation.

The components of income itself are also not time-invariant. As such, the changing relevance of rentier items such as business and farm income, dividends, rents, and interest in the fortunes of top earners, demands that greater historical attention be paid to the factors driving accumulation amongst the rich.[9] The presence of human slaves as a substantial share in the pre-abolition composition of u.s. capital, and the declining significance of land in the composition of British capital, for example, can be tied to different narratives of social change, driven by both domestic and global factors.[10] Debate continues within research on labor's share of national income over the significance and estimation of self-employment income, a subject which has arguably not yet come to terms with the relevance of de-standardization, precarity, and informal employment as key issues in labor income. The tone of discussion is also very much divided between practitioners of a neoclassical tradition who view it as a self-equilibrating outcome of relative factor endowments, and those of political economists who view changes in the ratio of capital to labor income as the result of ongoing power struggles between opposing class groups.

These three measures sit within differing yet interrelated sociological narratives of inequality and class, with the income shares of the top 1% capturing the fortunes of the 'super-rich' as a social and class group distinct from that of the wider income distribution.[11] Research on the functional income distribution implicates analyses of key collective power resources, such as unionization, labor market regulation, and leftist political power.[12] Meanwhile, the personal income distribution is arguably of key concern to theorists of social class, as employment becomes ever more detached from previous occupation-based models of stratification.[13] And yet, despite the detailed body of empirical research available on these components of inequality, there is a sense of

---

9   Petra Duenhaupt, "Financialization and the rentier income share– evidence from the USA and Germany," *International Review of Applied Economics*, vol. 26 (4) 2012.

10   For the u.s., see: http://piketty.pse.ens.fr/files/capital21c/en/pdf/F4.10.pdf. Accessed July 14, 2016.
      For Britain, see: http://piketty.pse.ens.fr/files/capital21c/en/pdf/F3.1.pdf. Accessed July 14, 2016.

11   Jerry W. Kim, Bruce Kogut and Jae-Suk Yang, "Executive Compensation, Fat Cats, and Best Athletes," *American Sociological Review*, vol. 80 (2) 2015; Thomas W. Volscho and Nathan J. Kelly, "The Rise of the Super-Rich: Power Resources, Taxes, Financial Markets, and the Dynamics of the Top 1 Percent, 1949 to 2008," *American Sociological Review*, vol. 77 (5) 2012.

12   Tali Kristal, "Good Times, Bad Times: Postwar Labor's Share of National Income in Capitalist Democracies," *American Sociological Review*, vol. 75 (5) 2010.

13   Mike Savage, *Social Class in the 21st Century*, (London: Penguin, 2014).

conceptual disconnect. Whilst the statistical link between the personal and fractile income distribution is obvious, the linking of all three within an over-arching framework of inequality and its determinants is lacking. Therefore, whilst changes in the measured (Gini) spread of personal income are func-tionally related to changes in upper fractiles, a rising concentration of income at the top also brings concentrations of economic and political power, offering opportunities for further enrichment. Exploring this implication is thus not a singularly statistical task.

This conceptual disconnect is well illustrated by Atkinson's remarks on the capital-labor split as a central problem in political economy.[14] In his paper, At-kinson claims the study of this division offers sharper insight into the con-nection between macroeconomic outcomes, and the fortunes of individual incomes, as well as getting us closer to the normative question of fairness. The former was addressed by the International Labour Organisation,[15] which ques-tioned, in light of falling labor shares and rising economic productivity across the OECD, to whom the gains of high-performing economies had accrued—as rising profit rates outstripped those of wages. Furthermore, the report noted a worrying trend of falling shares of productivity amongst unskilled workers, and modest increases for the high-skilled. With this apparent violation of the self-correction and relative constancy of the capital-income ratio (a staple of neoclassical growth theory), the question turns to the mix of institutional and political factors which facilitate this rising income capture. Answering this question requires situating inequality in its uniquely modern context: a sit-uation where the fortunes of the wealthiest have grown almost unabated for decades, where 'capital' as a loosely defined social group have appropriated a greater share of the collective labor of workers, and where access to earned income is no longer a guarantor of economic security.

Financialization—A New Regime of Global Inequality?

For many analysts, the common timing of changes in the various distributions of income, as well as their correspondence with indicators of institutional and

---

14   Anthony B. Atkinson, "Factor shares: the principal problem of political economy?" *Oxford Review of Political Economy*, vol. 25 (1) 2009.

15   International Labour Organization, *Global Wage Report 2012/13: Wages and equitable growth* (Geneva: International Labour Office, 2013), accessed on July 14, 2016 at http://www.ilo.org/global/research/global-reports/global-wage-report/2012/WCMS_194843/lang--en/index.htm

economic change is evidence of a distinct historical regime of global inequality. Historical changes in the three central components of the distribution of income may be united in a common framework by adequately conceptualizing this new regime, identifying a set of common inequality drivers, and specifying the common channels through which they impact inequality. Such clarity is given by the concept of financialisation, which has been conceptualized in a number of different ways: the diversification of firms into financial activities away from core 'real economy' pursuits;[16] the growing use of securitization and tradable financial instruments as distributors of risk,[17] a realignment of corporate strategies in favor of profiteering and cost saving,[18] and the use of credit to shore up consumption under real wage stagnation.[19] The specific timing of financialisation is a matter of loose consensus, with many locating its origins in the post 1970s stagflation era, where the twin pressures of capital account openness and financial market deregulation combined to usher an era where finance assumed a greater role in the economic fortunes of both states and households. As a contributor to economic output, it surpassed manufacturing and services in many advanced economies during the 1990s, whilst stagnating real incomes fostered growing dependence on consumer credit to shore up earnings. In the U.S. alone, Tomaskovic-Devey and Lin estimate that up to

16   Greta Krippner, *Capitalizing on Crisis: The Political Origins of the Rise of Finance*, (Cambridge: Harvard University Press, 2011).

17   Fredrik Movitz and Michael Allvin, "What does Financial Derivatives really got to do with Jobs? Examining Causal Mechanisms between Aspects of Financialization, Work Intensification and Employment Insecurity," (London: Paper for ILPC 7–9th March 2014), accessed on July 11, 2016 at https://www.researchgate.net/publication/272495936 _What_Does_Financial_Derivatives_Really_got_to_do_with_Jobs_Examining_Causal _Mechanisms_between_Aspects_of_Financialization_Work_Intensification_and _Employment_Insecurity. Accessed July 17, 2016.

18   Paul Thompson, "Disconnected capitalism: or why employers can't keep their side of the bargain," *Work, Employment and Society*, vol. 17 (2) 2003, pp. 359–378; Paul Thompson, "Financialisation and the workplace: extending and applying the disconnected capitalism thesis," *Work, Employment and Society*, vol. 27 (1) 2013.

19   Robert Guttman, "A Primer on Finance-Led Capitalism and Its Crisis," *Revue de la regulation*, ¾, 2008, accessed on July 13, 2016 at http://regulation.revues.org/5843; Basak Kus, "Consumption and redistributive politics: The effect of credit and China," *International Journal of Comparative Sociology*, vol. 54 (3) 2013; International Labour Organization, *Global Wage Report 2012/13: Wages and equitable growth*; Engelbert Stockhammer, "Financialization, income distribution and the crisis," *Investigación Económica*, 71, 2012; Natascha van der Zwan, "Making sense of financialization," *Socio-Economic Review*, vol. 12 (1) 2014, pp. 99–129.

6.6 trillion dollars in profits and compensation was captured by the financial sector from 1980–2008, 65% of which went to the banking sector.[20]

The results of this finance-driven phase of economic and regulatory change were distinctly class-biased, with the emergence of what Foster and Holleman term a 'financial power elite',[21] deriving their wealth primarily from financial profits, real estate, and executive compensation. From 1979–2005, CEO pay increased from 38 times that of the average worker, to 262.[22] The comparative advantage of this group was sustained through a parallel increase in the structural powerlessness of labor relative to capital since the 1980's, linked to the weakening of the labor movement under the combined pressures of service sector growth, labor market deregulation, and the loosening of capital restraints as an engine of post-Fordist economic growth.[23] The result was an overall negative impact on non-financial sector output, where the resulting falloff in employment was borne by core labor, and where senior corporate officers netted gains from compensation packages linked to capital income such as stock options.[24] The institutionalization of this new regulatory order is thus strongly implicated in greater accumulation at the top of the income distribution, rendering the social, political, and policy underpinnings of the fortunes

20   Donald Tomaskovic-Devey and Ken-Hou Lin, "Income Dynamics, Economic Rents, and the Financialization of the U.S. Economy," *American Journal of Sociology*, vol. 76 (4) 2011, p. 553.

21   John Bellamy Foster and Hannah Holleman, "The Financial Power Elite," *Monthly Review*, vol. 62 (1) 2010, pp. 1–19.

22   Basak Kus, "Financialisation and Income Inequality in OECD Nations: 1995–2007." *The Economic and Social Review*, vol. 43 (4) 2012, pp. 477–495.

23   Olivier Blanchard and Francesco Giavazzi, "Macroeconomic effects of regulation and deregulation in goods and labor markets," *The Quarterly Journal of Economics*, vol. 118 (3) 2003, pp. 879–907; Arjun Jayadev, "Capital account openness and the labour share of income," *Cambridge Journal of Economics*, vol. 31 (3) 2007, pp. 424–443; Bob Jessop, "State theory, regulation, and autopoiesis: debates and controversies," *Capital and Class*, vol. 25 (3) 2001, pp. 83–92; Bob Jessop, "Revisiting the regulation approach: Critical reflections on the contradictions, dilemmas, fixes and crisis dynamics of growth regimes," *Capital and Class*, vol. 37 (1) 2013, pp. 89–110; William K. Tabb, "Financialization in the Contemporary Social Structure of Accumulation." *Contemporary Capitalism and Its Crises*, in Terrence McDonough, Michael Reich and David M. Kotz, (eds.) (Cambridge: Cambridge University Press, 2010).

24   Donald Tomaskovic-Devey, Ken-Hou Lin and Nathan Meyers, "Did financialization reduce economic growth?" *Socio-Economic Review*, vol. 13 (3) 2015, pp. 525–548.

of this group ever more visible.[25] The implications of rising inequality—particularly redistribution toward capital, and to the top of the personal income distribution—are that without political intervention to effect greater redistribution, inequality may undermine the very basis of democratic legitimacy.[26] This concern stands beside a basic interest in fairness in the distribution of productivity and economic rewards, which are inherently labor-driven.

Meanwhile, evidence of the damaging impact of financialisation on a range of aspects of economic and social life is mounting. Income is not allocated in a political vacuum, and evidence shows how apparently secular 'market equilibria' of income distribution are politically structured, and how income advantage above market rates is often secured through political manipulation of regulatory structures.[27] This observation chimes well with the role of falling top marginal tax rates as an incentive for top earners to bargain for greater incomes, without the threat of losing their gains through direct income tax—a prime culprit identified by Piketty for rising top income inequality since the 1970s. Evidence from panel studies of the three aspects of income inequality shows a consistent connection between financialisation and inequality.[28] Institutions linked to workers' organizational power show a consistent negative effect on inequality, with unionization working both

---

25 Ishac Diwan, *Debt as sweat: Labor, financial crises, and the globalization of capital* (World Bank: Working Papers, 2001), http://info.worldbank.org/etools/docs/voddocs/150/332/diwan.pdf accessed on July 14, 2016.
Anastasia Guscina, *Effects of Globalization on Labor's Share in National Income* (IMF Working Paper No. 06/294, 2006), accessed on July 13, 2016 at https://www.imf.org/external/pubs/cat/longres.aspx?sk=19244.0; Kristal, "Good Times, Bad Times: Postwar Labor's Share of National Income in Capitalist Democracies."

26 Thomas Piketty, *Capital in the Twenty-First Century*, (Cambridge: Harvard University Press, 2014).

27 Donad Tomaskovic-Devey and Ken-Hou Lin. "Income Dynamics, Economic Rents, and the Financialization of the U.S. Economy," *American Journal of Sociology*, vol. 76 (4) 2011, pp. 533–79.

28 Petra Dunhaput, *An empirical assessment of the contribution of corporate governance and financialisation to the rise in income inequality* (Working Paper, 2015) accessed on July 15, 2016 at http://recursos.march.es/web/ceacs/actividades/miembros/duenhaupt.pdf;_Flaherty, "Top incomes under finance-driven capitalism, 1990–2010: power resources and regulatory orders."; Olivier Godechot, "Financialization is Marketization! A Study of the Respective Impacts of Various Dimensions of Financialization on the Increase in Global Inequality," *Sociological Science*, Online First, 2016, https://www.sociologicalscience.com/articles-v3-22-495/ Accessed on July 11, 2016; Karsten Kohler, Alexander Guschanski and Engelbert Stockhammer, *How Does Financialization Affect Functional*

through collective bargaining capacity, and threats of strike action.[29] This works both through the functional income distribution by shifting the general balance of power in favor of labor, and the personal income distribution by promoting inter-sectorial wage equalization. Government consumption and leftist political representation typically record negative associations, both by promoting pro-labor social policies, and effecting direct redistribution through social transfers.[30]

The ways in which financialisation impacts inequality are diverse, and as evidence mounts, our understanding of the mechanisms producing these effects is sharpening. Indicators of stock market capitalization show evidence of the inequality-enhancing role of the 'shareholder value' model, with greater firm participation in finance—linked to the application of intensive equity-oriented HR practices, geared toward sustaining dividends.[31] The net effect of this regime is often a reduction in employment security to maintain tighter overheads and employee performance. Financial sector profitability is shown to enhance the incomes of top earners, linked to non-indexed performance bonuses, but also the generation of greater rents for staked investors. The result

Income Distribution? A Theoretical Clarification and Empirical Assessment (Kingston University: London Economics Discussion Papers, 2015), https://ideas.repec.org/p/ris/kngedp/2015_005.html Accessed on July 13, 2016; Basak Kus, "Financialisation and Income Inequality in OECD Nations: 1995–2007." _Division II Faculty Publications. Paper 173_ (2012). htp://wesscholar.wesleyan.edu/div2facpubs/173; Engelbert Stockhammer, "Determinants of the Wage Share: A Panel Analysis of Advanced and Developing Economies," _British Journal of Industrial Relations_, Online First, 2015, http://onlinelibrary.wiley.com/doi/10.1111/bjir.12165/abstract accessed on July 11, 2016; Thomas W. Volscho and Nathan J. Kelly, "The Rise of the Super-Rich: Power Resources, Taxes, Financial Markets, and the Dynamics of the Top 1 Percent, 1949 to 2008." _American Sociological Review_ vol. 55 (5) 2012, pp. 679–699.

29   Eoin Flaherty, "Top incomes under finance-driven capitalism, 1990–2010: power resources and regulatory orders." Basak Kus, "Financialisation and Income Inequality in OECD Nations: 1995–2007." SSRN Electronic Journal vol. 12 (4) 2015, pp. 20–32.

30   Eoin Flaherty and Seán Ó Riain, "The Variety of Polanyian Double Movements in Europe's Capitalisms." In _The Changing Worlds and Workplaces of Capitalism_, edited by Seán Ó Riain, Felix Behling, Rossella Ciccia and Eoin Flaherty, (London: Palgrave Macmillan, 2015), pp. 38–57.

31   Paul Thompson, "Disconnected capitalism: or why employers can't keep their side of the bargain," _Work, Employment and Society_, vol. 17 (2) 2003, pp. 359–378; Jean Cushen and Paul Thompson, "Financialization in the workplace: Hegemonic narratives, performative interventions and the angry knowledge worker," _Accounting, Organizations and Society_, vol. 38 (4) 2013, pp. 314–331.

has been a decoupling of surplus generation from production, enhancing executive compensation while excluding the wider workforce from wage-setting as resources were steadily reallocated away from core production.[32] Indicative of a wider class dynamic, financialisation also negatively impacts the functional income distribution (labor's share). Heightened financial market dependence loosens the dependence of firms on specific locations, enhancing their global mobility at the expense of relatively immobile workers, whilst emphasis on profitability within firms puts pressure both on wages and working conditions.[33] Of the four stressors examined, Stockhammer found financialization to exert a stronger downward pressure on labor's share than globalization, technological change, and welfare retrenchment.[34] A crucial error, however, would be to strategize for change merely on the basis of a collection of disparate effects. This observation brings us to the crux of the issue with suggested remedies for inequality based on tinkering with the tax system, enacting universal basic income, or implementing financial transaction charges—the systemic capitalist context in which financialisation operates.

Class Biased Power Resources: The Rich and the Rest under Finance-Driven Capitalism

The data on inequality point ever more to a sharp polarization of opportunity—whether through the monopolization of rentier income sources by top earners, or greater accrual of national product to capital. Many of the income-generating mechanisms of financialisation are also strongly class biased. In the U.K., the volume of domestic credit issued by the banking sector has risen from 118% of GDP in 1990 to 224% in 2010, with similar gains in the U.S.[35] This phenomenon is class biased to the extent that it reflects a parallel squeeze on the incomes of low-median earners, and an opportunity

32   Ken-Hou Lin and Donald Tomaskovic-Devey, "Financialization and U.S. Income Inequality, 1970–2008," *American Journal of Sociology*, vol. 118 (5) 2013, pp. 1284–1329.

33   Engelbert Stockhammer, "Determinants of the Wage Share: A Panel Analysis of Advanced and Developing Economies," *British Journal of Industrial Relations*, Online First, vol. 5 (1) 2015, pp. 3–33.

34   Engelbert Stockhammer, "Determinants of the Wage Share: A Panel Analysis of Advanced and Developing Economies."

35   World Bank, "Domestic Credit Provided By Financial Sector (% of GDP)," *World Bank Databank*, accessed on July 11, 2016 at www.data.worldbank.org

for those at the top. At the top, innovation in debt instruments underpinned by consumer credit (for example, the mortgage-backed securities which provided so disastrous a context to the financial crisis in the U.S.), allows greater appropriation of these financial rents by specialized actors, resulting in heightened inequality.[36] On the flipside of this process is the 'democratization' of consumer credit, with the proportion of low-income households owning credit cards rising from 2% in 1970, to 38% by 2001.[37] The pernicious political consequences of this are twofold; the bias of income redistribution from labor toward capital is facilitated by state and semi-state actors through, for example, bailout and recapitalization programmes,[38] whilst increased credit use skews individuals' assessments of their relative income position, and lowers support for redistribution.[39]

The capital-labor dynamic of the financialisation era marks a distinct break from that of other capitalist epochs—neoliberalism has had its role to play in this, by securing an institutional context for continued accumulation through deregulation. Regulation theory offers a useful framework for thinking through both the systemic underpinnings of inequality—particularly how the unique institutional and policy frameworks associated with the era of financialisation serve to skew bargaining power in favor of capital. This perspective emphasizes how states and trans-national polities facilitate accumulation in different ways, with the neoliberal model of lightly regulated, finance-driven capitalism merely the most recent.[40] The role of states in capital accumulation is viewed by social structures of accumulation practitioners (SSA) through their maintenance of institutions of law and private property, systems of financial

36 Olivier Godechot, "Financialization is Marketization! A Study of the Respective Impacts of Various Dimensions of Financialization on the Increase in Global Inequality," *Sociological Science*, June 29, 2016. https://www.sociologicalscience.com/articles-v3-22-495/ Accessed September 14, 2016.

37 Basak Kus and Wen Fan, "Income Inequality, Credit and Public Support for Redistribution," *Intereconomics*, vol. 50 (4) 2015, pp. 198–205.

38 Olivier Godechot, "Financialization is Marketization! A Study of the Respective Impacts of Various Dimensions of Financialization on the Increase in Global Inequality" *Sociological Science*, June 29, 2016. https://www.sociologicalscience.com/articles-v3-22-495/ Accessed September 14, 2016.

39 Basak Kus and Wen Fan, "Income Inequality, Credit, and Public Support for Redistribution." *Intereconomics* Vol. 50 (4), 2015, pp. 198–205.

40 Bob Jessop, "Revisiting the regulation approach: Critical reflections on the contradictions, dilemmas, fixes and crisis dynamics of growth regimes" *Capital & Class*, vol. 37(1), 2013.

exchange and governance, and labor markets.[41] Whilst the notion of a post-war capital-labor accord, or a 'Fordist' model of Atlantic capitalism featured prominently in the historical sociology of industry, regulation theorists treat theses epochs as sequential SSAS. As such, the successor to the Fordist model of accumulation is identified in the form of a finance-based regime of accu-mulation, predicated on a disembedding of capital from regulatory constraints and a commodification of the social wage through cheap credit.[42] The concept bears a clear affinity with heterodox/Marxist approaches to political econo-my, where class-biased accumulation is the core imperative of capitalism, and where the neoliberal state plays a facilitating role.[43]

The SSA, and broader Marxian approach is a crucial addition to the work of Piketty, insofar as it places institutions and power at the core of any understand-ing of inequality. It thus protects against the 'essentialising' tendencies of vari-able-based analysis, by theorizing financialisation not only as a specific regulatory order, but also as a logic of capitalism inherently disposed towards rising inequal-ity.[44] The policy context of this era is well-defined; as deregulation was instituted partly to address post oil-crisis stagflation, it instead ushered a shift from com-mercial to investment banking, and from loans to securities, disproportionately benefitting wealthy investors.[45] These shifts were underpinned by policy measures including the US Monetary Control Act of 1980, later Financial Services Mod-ernization Act of 1999[46] and the European Second Banking Directive of 1989.[47]

---

41   Terrence McDonough, Michael Reich, David M. Kotz (Eds.), *Contemporary Capitalism and its Crises: Social Structure of Accumulation Theory for the 21st Century.* (Cambridge: Cam-bridge University Press, 2010).

42   William. K. Tabb, "Financialization in the Contemporary Social Structure of Accumu-lation." In *Contemporary Capitalism and its Crises*, edited by Terrence McDonough, Michael Reich, and David M. Kotz, (Cambridge: Cambridge University Press, 2010), pp. 145–167.

43   Petra Duenhaupt, "Financialization and the Crises of Capitalism," *Institute for Internation-al Political Economy Berlin Working Paper 67*, 2016, accessed on July 13, 2016 at http://www.ipe-berlin.org/fileadmin/downloads/Papers_and_Presentations/IPE_WP_67.pdf

44   Natascha van der Zwan, "Making sense of financialization." *Socioeconomic Review* 12 (1) 2014, pp. 99–129.

45   Robert Guttman and Dominique Plihon, "Consumer Debt at the Center of Finance-Led Capitalism," *Texte d'une communication au colloque international organise á Paris par le CEPN at le SCEPA*, 2008, http://www.univ-paris13.fr/CEPN/IMG/pdf/wp2008_09.pdf. Ac-cessed on July 16, 2016

46   Ken-Hou Lin and Donald Tomaskovic-Devey, "Financialization and U.S. Income Inequal-ity, 1970–2008."

47   Rober Guttman, "A Primer on Finance-Led Capitalism and Its Crisis." *American Journal of Sociology* vol. 118 (5) 2013, pp. 1284–1329.

The regulatory process is ongoing; research is revealing how the enactment of the Dodd-Frank Act, which provided for federal oversight of consumer protection in the wake of the financial crisis, was rife with disagreement between financial actors over the characterization of root causes, and appropriate remedies.[48]

Meanwhile, understanding of the damaging consequences of finance-driven inequality, and indeed the role of inequality itself as a precursor to crisis, is growing. Stockhammer has already shown how financialisation has reduced accumulation rates (the capital stock growth rate within firms), by incentivizing managers to identify as rentiers, with a reduced stake in the wellbeing of firms, and more oriented toward raising dividend ratios.[49] This was achieved through the introduction of new financial instruments such as tender offers facilitating hostile takeovers, and the wider use of performance-indexed pay, which incentivized the allocation of corporate resources toward 'downsizing and distribution'.[50] The results for labor security and wellbeing are well documented,[51] and the raising of rentier returns is a crucial mechanism in the growth of top incomes, and widening gap between rich and poor.[52] The greater share of national income (GDP, GNP, or GNI) accruing to capital during the 1990s was also facilitated by greater capital account openness, which increased capital mobility relative to labor since the 1990s, disproportionately raising capital returns.[53] Central banks and government finance

---

48   Basak Kus, "Dodd-Frank: From Economic Crisis to Regulatory Reform," *Sheffield Political Economy Institute Research Institute, SPERI Paper No. 29*, 2016, See: http://speri.dept .shef.ac.uk/wp-content/uploads/2016/06/SPERI-Paper-29-Dodd-Frank-From-Economic -Crisis-to-Regulatory-Reform.pdf, Accessed on July 13, 2016.

49   Engelbert Stockhammer, "Financialization and the slowdown of accumulation," *Cambridge Journal of Economics*, vol. 28 (5) 2004, pp. 719–741.

50   Engelbert Stockhammer, "Financialization and the slowdown of accumulation," *Cambridge Journal of Economics*, vol. 28 (5) 2004, p. 721.

51   Jean Cushen and Paul Thompson, "Financialization in the workplace."(Workshop: University of Leicester, 2013) https://www2.le.ac.uk/colleges/ssah/research/cswef/conferences/ 2018financialization2019-2013-what-does-it-mean-for-work-and-employment/professor -paul-thompson-financialization-and-the-workplace-why-labour-and-the-labour -process-still-matters. Accessed on November 7, 2016.

52   Petra Duenhaupt, "Financialization and the rentier income share." https://www.econstor .eu/bitstream/10419/105926/1/imk-wp_2010-02.pdf. Accessed November 18, 2017. See also Eoin Flaherty, "Top incomes under finance-driven capitalism, 1990-2010." *Socio-Economic Review*. Vol. 13 (3) 2015, pp. 417–447. https://academic.oup.com/ser/ article-abstract/13/3/417/1668494/Top-incomes-under-finance-driven-capitalism -1990?redirectedFrom=fulltext Accessed October 12, 2016.

53   Gerald Epstein and Dorothy Power, "Rentier incomes and Financial Crises: An Empirical Examination of the Trends and Cycles in Some OECD Countries," Working paper

departments also played a role in fostering pre-crisis economic instability through anti-inflationary monetary policies which raised real interest rates leading to greater capital gains, growing profits in financial intermediation.[54]

Most distressing of all is the observation that financialisation is destructive of economic growth. Using an expanded concept of value added incorporating the claims of charities, government, and corporate debt holders due interest, Tomaskovic-Devey et al. show that greater financial investment by non-financial firms was destructive of non-financial sector economic growth. Their component-disaggregated effects show how financialisation depressed labor compensation and state tax receipts, whilst raising interest and dividend payments, to the benefit primarily of top earners.[55] This finding is deserving of immediate attention, as the necessary implication is that the shortfall in growth has been met primarily by labor, and by the state. States are doing little to redress this balance. While many countries have seen cuts or stagnation in their capital gains and top income taxation rates,[56] reliance on regressive redistribution measures such as indirect consumption tax often does little to alter the balance of income around the median.[57] Worryingly, the redistributive capacity of some welfare states (the percentage reduction in Gini from market to net income) is falling even amongst social democracies such as Denmark which dropped from 50% in 1995, to 46% in 2010.[58] As the opportunities to redress the balance of equality through the state shrink further,[59] the capacity of an unrestrained capitalism to meaningfully redistribute, must be questioned.

———————

    2003: http://scholarworks.umass.edu/peri_workingpapers/54/ Jayadev, "Capital account openness and the labour share of income" *Cambridge Journal of Economics* 2007. http://people.umass.edu/econ721/arjun_cje_cap_acct_open.pdf pp. 1–21.

54   Gerald Epstein and Dorothy Power, "Rentier incomes and Financial Crises: An Empirical Examination of the Trends and Cycles in Some OECD Countries," Working paper 2003: http://scholarworks.umass.edu/peri_workingpapers/54/ pp. 234–235.

55   Donald Tomaskovic-Devey, Ken-Hou Lin Nathan Meyers et al., "Did financialization reduce economic growth?" *Socio-Economic Review* vol. 13 (3) 2015, p. 538.

56   GINI, *Inequalities Impacts: State of the Art Review*, p. 93. http://www.gini-research.org/system/uploads/253/original/GINI_State-of-the-Art_review_1.pdf?1308916502

57   Pablo Bermandi and David Rueda, "Social Democracy Constrained: Indirect Taxation in Industrialized Democracies," *British Journal of Political Science*, vol. 37 (4) 2007, pp. 619–641.

58   Frederick Solt, "Standardizing the World Income Inequality Database" *Social Science Quarterly* vol. 90 (2) 2009, pp. 231–242.

59   Jason Beckfield, "European integration and income inequality." *American Sociological Review* vol. 71(6) 2006, pp. 964–985; Jason Beckfield, "Remapping inequality in Europe: The

What Can Piketty Learn from Marxism?

Whilst the foregoing paints a pessimistic picture, there is some cause for optimism. In a climate where economists can declare inequality a distraction from the study of growth,[60] where the distribution of value added between labor and capital can be assumed constant by fundamental macroeconomics texts,[61] and where concern with redistribution can be dismissed as '... envy raised to a theoretical and ethical proposition,'[62] Piketty's work, and indeed its antecedent projects such as the world top income studies,[63] lends useful empirical weight to normative criticism of the basic inequity of capitalism. Despite its largely rhetorical deployment by politicians and public figures, the greater positioning in public consciousness of inequality, and its role as cause and effect of economic and social insecurity, should be welcomed. Our chief criticism should be leveled at the limited degree to which Piketty's work treats the disparate institutions of capitalism as an interrelated whole, and the extent to which the mechanisms of income capture of the financialisation age represent a more thoroughgoing consequence of class-biased economic and political power. As with McCloskey,[64] it is possible to engage in such criticism whilst respecting the scientific effort of his work—and without writing off its potential sociological merit with epistemic caricatures aimed at this methodology.

David Harvey characterizes the tendency toward rising inequality as a central contradiction of capitalism, and in doing so, lays substantial criticism at Piketty for failing to grasp the role of 'capital' as a loosely coherent class, in sustaining high levels of inequality vis-à-vis the maintenance of high capital

---

Net Effect of Regional Integration on Total Income Inequality in the European Union," *International Journal of Comparative Sociology*, vol. 50 (1) 2009, pp. 1–24.

60   Donald Tomaskovic-Devey Ken-Hou Lin Nathan Meyers, "Did financialization reduce economic growth?" *Socio-Economic Review* vol. 13 (3) 2015, pp. 525–548.

61   Anthony B.Atkinson, "Factor shares: the principal problem of political economy?" *Oxford Review of Economic Policy* vol. 25 (1) 2009, pp. 3–16.

62   Deirdre N. McCloskey, "Measured, Unmeasured, Mismeasured, and Unjustified Pessimism: A Review Essay of Thomas Piketty's Capital in the Twenty-First Century," *Erasmus Journal for Philosophy and Economics*, vol. 7 (2) 2014.

63   Anthony B. Atkinson and Thomas Piketty, *Top Incomes Over the Twentieth Century: A Contrast Between Continental European and English-Speaking Countries*, (Oxford: Oxford University Press, 2007); Anthony B. Atkinson and Thomas Piketty, *Top Incomes: A Global Perspective* (Oxford: Oxford University Press, 2010).

64   Deirdre N. McCloskey, "Measured, Unmeasured, Mismeasured, and Unjustified Pessimism: A Review Essay of Thomas Piketty's Capital in the Twenty-First Century," *Erasmus Journal for Philosophy and Economics*, vol. 7 (2) 2014, 73–115.

returns.[65] According to Harvey, the politics of high capital returns are laid bare through a Marxist analysis of the ways in which neoliberalism has pursued an aggressive crusade against both organized labor, financial regulation, and top income and capital taxation—much of which is absent in Piketty's account. In more moderate formulations, post-Keynesians have suggested as much by emphasizing the alignment of firm mangers with the interests of rentiers under the 'shareholder managerialism' model, offering an empirical link between the general tendencies identified by Harvey, and the organization of modern work.[66] The overarching criticism seems to be a lack of institutional and political grounding in Piketty's expounding of 'r>g' (an excess of capital returns over economic growth rates) as the central inequality-producing tendency in capitalism.

Reviewers have tended toward similar criticisms, with Duménil and Lévy[67] suggesting that Piketty ignores the complexity of factors affecting wealth distribution, and Michel[68] drawing attention to the role played by financialisation in dis-incentivizing capitalist investment and saving, thus slowing the rate of growth. These factors, as we have observed, are not accidental. They are embedded in the very logic of the deregulation-driven SSA of financialisation, with all its attendant distributional consequences. More specifically, Foster and Yates[69] point to a central problem identified by Piketty—that in the absence of restraint, there is no inherent tendency in capitalism toward stability and equality. Yet many proposed remedies to inequality are silent on the lurking question of capitalism, and even when confronted in political economy,

65   David Harvey, "Afterthoughts on Piketty's Capital," May 17, 2014, http://davidharvey
      .org/2014/05/afterthoughts-pikettys-capital accessed on July 14, 2016. David Harvey, *Seventeen Contradictions and the End of Capitalism* (Oxford: Oxford University Press, 2014).

66   Jean Cushen and Paul Thompson, "Financialization in the workplace." *Accounting, Organizations and Society* Volume 38, Issue 4, May 2013, Pages 314–331, Olivier Godechot, "Financialization is marketization! A study on therespective impact of various dimensions of financialization on the increase in global inequality", MaxPo Discussion Paper, 2015. No. 15/3; http://hdl.handle.net/10419/125777 Accessed March 12, 2016; Engelbert Stockhammer, "Financialisation and the slowdown of accumulation." *Cambridge Journal of Economics*, vol. 28 (5) 2004, pp. 719–741.

67   Gérard Duménil and Dominique Lévy, "Thomas Piketty's Historical Macroeconomics: A Critical Analysis," *Review of Political Economy*, 28, 2016.

68   Thomas R. Michel, "Capitalists, Workers, and Thomas Piketty's Capital in the 21st Century," *Review of Political Economy*, 28, 2016.

69   John Bellamy Foster and Michael D. Yates, "Piketty and the Crisis of Neoclassical Economics," *Monthly Review*, 66, 2014, accessed on July 12, 2015 at http://monthlyreview.org/2014/11/01/piketty-and-the-crisis-of-neoclassical-economics/ Accessed March 22, 2016

the question often takes the form of the relative merits of 'varieties of capitalism' (whether coordinated or liberal), in a body of work which tends more toward questions of growth capacity and innovation, rather than distribution. The most politically credible remedies also largely remain within the confines of liberal capitalism—government savings schemes, universal basic income, and capital receipt/transaction taxes.[70]

In sum, the lessons for students of inequality within a sociological/political economy tradition are to acknowledge the complexities of the distribution of income—to recognize that inequality is multifaceted, and that there are common class dynamics at play across the various levels (between capital and labor over national product, and between 'the rich and the rest'), which are an inherent—rather than aberrant—consequence of a capitalist mode of production. The study of inequality should thus be productively married to the study of other fundamental institutions of capitalism which are the subject of renewed interest—the monetary system (of credit and debt), property (in terms of the 'enclosure' of new opportunities for profiteering such as intellectual property and privatization of public services), as well as the political processes which sustain domestic and transnational compacts geared toward deregulation (TTIP, and more recently the prospect of Brexit undermining fundamental workers' rights as enshrined in various pieces of European regulation). The SSA approach is but one element of the overall political economy toolbox which allows us to contextualize financialisation as but the most recent phase of inequality-prone capitalism. The task of the sociologist is to show how these questions are ones of class, and class-biased control over economic and political resources, rather than a mathematical inevitability.

---

70   Anthony B. Atkinson, "Can we reduce income inequality in OECD countries?" *Empirica*, Online First, 2015.

CHAPTER 6

Piketty and Patrimonialism: A Frankfurt School Critique of Piketty's Use of Marx, Weber, Political Economy, and Comparative Historical Sociology

J. I. (Hans) Bakker

"There is no royal road to science, and only those who do not dread the fatiguing climb of its steep paths have a chance of gaining its luminous summits."— Letter of March 18, 1872 from London by Karl Marx to Citizen Maurice La Châtre, cited in Louis Althusser's Reading Capital.[1]

Introduction

One of the best recent attempts to re-orient "economics" to more fundamental questions having to do with social class and income inequality is the widely-discussed book by "political economist" Thomas Piketty. Piketty is a "liberal" intellectual and not a "radical" of either the Left or the Right.[2] His work goes further than more journalistic accounts of recent trends.[3] But it does not go far enough in terms of political economy and "historical materialism."

---

1 Louis Althusser, Étienne Balibar, Roger Establet, Jacques Rancière and Pierre Macherey, *Reading Capital: The Complete Edition* (Trs. and Eds.) Ben Brewster and David Fernbach (London: Verso, 2015), p. 9. [This translation is the first Complete Translation in one volume based on the third French edition of 1996. The first edition dates back to 1965. The complex publishing history is detailed, 1–8.] Hereafter Althusser *Reading Capital*.

2 Thomas Piketty, *Capital in the Twenty-first Century* (Cambridge, MA: Belknap Press of Harvard University Press, 2014), pp. 447–451. Belknap Press is associated with Harvard University Press. Harvard spends approximately US$ 100 million a year to manage its endowment of $30 billion, the largest university endowment of any university in the world. See Thomas Piketty, *Capital in the Twenty-First Century*. Translated by Arthur Goldhammer. (Cambridge, MA: The Belknap Press of Harvard University, 2014), pp. 447–451.

3 Thomas Piketty, Emmanuel Saez and Gabriel Zucman. "Distributional National Accounts: Methods and Estimates for the United States since 1913." Presentation to the 2016 Allied Social Science Associations annual meeting, San Francisco, Calif., Jan. 3–5. {Accessed November 22, 2016 at http://piketty.pse.ens/fr/files/pikettysaezzucman2015dina.pdf} An example of a more journalistic account is Robert B. Reich, *Supercapitalism: The Transformation of*

He does not deal, for example, with the kinds of arguments put forward by Marxists in France.[4] In some ways, the fact that Piketty is very well versed in Neo-Classical Economics and yet does not see contemporary econometrics as the essence of wisdom is exactly what makes him so acceptable to so many. He has opened up "economics" and made the study of wealth rather than just "equilibrium" relevant again. He argues that the disparity between the top one percent and the bottom ninety-nine percent has grown considerably in most European countries and the United States. His data sets span more than one hundred years. His writing style is straightforward and comprehensible with no knowledge of mathematics required. All of the essays in this book are inspired by the fact that Piketty and his colleagues have opened up a window to discussions that were often ignored in the discipline of economics but that were not widely appreciated elsewhere either.

He touches on topics that many sociologists have discussed. But he himself does not make specifically sociological arguments except in so far as he touches on some sociological ideas found in Marx. Of course, he is not a sociologist. What he did in political economy is admirable. He utilizes the techniques of Neo-classical economic modeling but changes key assumptions. His contribution is significant. But precisely because it is so good we need to take the limitations seriously as well. Many key classical theorists in the social sciences have been influenced by political economy but have taken those ideas in different directions.

Piketty has been critiqued in many different ways, but the contribution this chapter seeks to make is to examine his overall assumptions about exploitation,

---

Business, Democracy, and Everyday Life. (New York: Alfred A. Knopf, 2002). Reich has a knack for taking complex arguments and stating them in ways that allow his books to reach a wide audience.

4   "Of course, we have all read, and all do read *Das Kapital.* ... But someday it is necessary to read *Das Kapital* to the letter" Althusser *Reading Capital,* op cit., 11. Althusser died at age seventy-two in 1990 after having been suddenly rejected almost universally because he (accidentally?) strangled his wife on November 16, 1980. For a long time, his work was taboo; but there is still great respect for his graduate students and many academics were influenced by his ideas, including fellow Algerian Jacques Derrida. Thomas Piketty would definitely have known about the details of the Althusserian oeuvre when he wrote his own book. Althusser is famous for postulating an epistemological break between the young Marx and the mature Marx of *Capital.* The so-called Paris School of Economics provides what could be called a Neo-Althusserian analysis of how the taken-for-granted logic of capitalism increases inequality in a way that is not simply evident to human beings who are embedded in capitalist relations of production, processing, exchange and distribution.

class relations and wealth in what can be described as a Neo-Marxian and Neo-Weberian Frankfurt School perspective. One aspect of Piketty's work that weakens the overall argument to some extent is his relative lack of attention to the early stages of capitalist imperialism and colonialism in what became the global modern capitalist economy as a whole. Another possible weakness is a lack of discussion of the transition from inequalities in traditional, pre-capitalist societies to inequalities within modern capitalist societies and then global "finance capitalism."

Is it possible that neo-patrimonial families of today are somewhat like the Patrimonial-feudal families of 14th century England? Would that imply they are closer to 14th century English than the very rich of the Patrimonial-prebendal Ancient Sinitic, Ancient Indic, or Ancient Roman Empires? Is Saudi Arabia today neo-patrimonial or truly Patrimonial-prebendal? Are today's "baronial" elites "quasi-feudal," albeit on an even larger (almost completely global) scale? Is the notion of a neo-patrimonial-feudal family or clan tied in any way to contemporary Feminist critiques of patriarchy and contemporary discussions of neo-patrimonialism? Piketty does not ask those questions and therefore we will not find answers to those questions in his otherwise remarkable, stimulating and heuristic work.

Overall the key criticism of Piketty made here is that he does not utilize an intellectual framework involving Comparative Historical Sociology (CHS). In particular, he does not develop the kind of political economy and economic theory associated with Karl Marx and Max Weber. He does not refer primarily to the extensive sociological literature on Marxist and Marxian "historical materialism".[5]

He remains within an intellectual framework that ultimately goes back to Scottish thinkers like Adam Smith and David Ricardo.[6] Nevertheless, many Marxists and Marxians appreciate Piketty's work because he has opened up debate on the question of wealth and has done an excellent job of utilizing the quantitative data available. For that he should be applauded. But if we start to think that is enough then we fall into a deep error. Social scientific generalizations about societies and wealth should be based not only on the last hundred years or so but should incorporate what we know about the last ten thousand years, or more. At the very least we have to pay attention to the

---

5   Anthony Barnes Atkinson and Thomas Piketty, (eds)., *Top Incomes Over the Twentieth Century*. (New York: NY: Oxford University Press, 2007).

6   John Chamberlain, 1965 [1959] *The Roots of Capitalism, Revised Edition* (Princeton, NJ: D. Van Nostrand, 1965 [1959]). It is remarkable that the classical political economists were Scottish and not English.

last four thousand years of recorded history, starting with Babylonia, Egypt and China in 2000 BCE.[7] A theory of historical social change that presumes to make cogent comments on wealth distribution and relational social class should follow Karl Marx's theory of Modes of Production. Marx's ideas concerning the dialectic are important. Social change involving the distribution of wealth goes back at least to the Slave Mode of Production and the so-called Asian Mode of Production. Moreover, those are just initial building blocks for a sociological theory based on research conducted since Marx's death. One way to think of this is to consider the possibility that Max Weber built on aspects of Marx's insights in somewhat the same way as Marx himself built on Hegel's dialectic.[8] Today's "supercapitalism" poses new questions that neither Marx nor Weber could have anticipated fully while they were alive. Thomas Piketty, for all his erudition, does not make use of Max Weber's ideas concerning traditional legitimate authority and "domination" (*Herrschaft, Macht*), especially the ideal type of patrimonialism. Does that matter? Yes, it definitely does. Weber was not "just" a sociological theorist. Weber held Professorships in Political Economy. Any discussion of modern capitalism that completely ignores Weber cannot be said to be a definitive treatment. Piketty has been critiqued in many different ways but the contribution this chapter seeks to make is to examine his overall assumptions about class relations and wealth in a Neo-Marxian and Neo-Weberian Frankfurt School perspective.

Piketty does mention Marx, but he does not really do justice to Marx's central insights concerning the dialectic involving Modes of Production. He does not cite Weber once. Yet, if we are going to apply Neo-Marxian and Neo-Weberian insights characteristic of the Frankfurt School ignoring Weber is a bit like ignoring Marx. Several commentators have pointed out that Piketty is not actually fair to Marx's theories, although he has provoked many thinkers into re-examining the idea of "capital." Piketty's book could be entitled: *Wealth in the Last Decade of the Twentieth Century and the First Decade of the Twenty-First Century*. But that more accurate title would be cumbersome and even just a title like *Wealth in the Global System* would not draw the same degree of attention from such a wide spectrum of political orientations and disciplines.

Much has been written about Thomas Piketty's ideas concerning income and wealth distribution. In order to avoid repeating what has been said in

---

7   Alf Henrickson. *Through the Ages: An Illustrated Chronicle of Events From 2000 BC to the Present* (London: Orbis Publishing, 1983 [1978]).

8   Theodore Adorno, *The Stars Down to Earth, and Other Essays on the Irrational in Culture*. Stephen Crook (Ed.). (London and New York, NY: Routledge/Taylor & Francis, 2015 [1994]), pp. 172–180.

dozens of first rate scholarly articles and hundreds of more popular venues, this chapter will focus on Piketty's use of the terms "patrimonialism" and "hyper-patrimonialism." In Canada today the Quebecois term *patrimonie* is translated in official government documents as "heritage." But Piketty both limits and then extends the term to mean inherited wealth. One's cultural heritage is not what he means, although no doubt the super-rich sometimes feel that they are the carriers of a rich heritage. He is concerned with *rentier* classes, a concern shared much earlier by Karl Marx. That rentier elite has some of the characteristics of a kind of neo-feudal baronial "aristocracy" even though the cultural beliefs of most u.s. citizens tend toward a notion of "egalitarianism." Few citizens seem concerned about the existence of so many billionaires and very few ordinary voters make any kind of association between a billionaire elite and exploitation of the so-called "middle class." Yet a family making $75,000 or $100,000 a year (after taxes) is hardly "rich" compared to billionaire families. The unemployed and underemployed are, of course, often left out of many discussions of the "working class," if the idea of proletarianized labor is even mentioned.[9]

The study of patrimonialism and neo-patrimonialism has had a small resurgence but in general the social science literature has not focused on the term.[10]Weber's original Ideal Type Model (ITM) involves one aspect of patriarchy and patrimonialism but the term can be extended to cover patrimonial ownership and wealth in contemporary modern capitalist societies as well, as

---

9   A peculiarity of u.s. mass media is the way in which the term "middle class" is used to cover anyone who would be considered "working class" (typically in industrial production or service jobs) in sociological theory and yet lower management is not regarded as being proletarianized labor. In other words, there is very little relational class analysis in popular media. The very notion of "middle class" obscures the very notion of class and class difference.

10 Max Weber, "Politics as a Vocation." *From Max Weber: Essays in Sociology*. (Tr. and Eds.) H. H. Gerth and C. Wright Mills. (New York, NY: 1958 [1919]), p. 79. Weber discusses "traditional domination" as a "pure type" and says it is "... exercised by the patriarch and the patrimonial prince of yore." Many sociologists seem to have skipped that line altogether. Weber spoke at Munich University in 1918 and the speech was first published in 1919. He contrasted "Politics" (*Politik*) with "Science" (*Wissenschaft*). A social scientific understanding of the sources of legitimate authority yields three pure types: traditional, charismatic and legal. The three pure types are not found in concrete reality but are purely analytical types. Less "pure" are the ideal types and a set of ideal types can constitute what I (and not Weber) call an Ideal Type Model (ITM). One ITM is Patrimonial-prebendalism. See Max Weber *Essays in Sociology*. (London: Routledge and Kegan Paul, 1946).

Piketty himself has done.[11] *Fortune* magazine carried a succinct article about the 185 billionaire "clans" in the United States.[12] The cover picture is of sixth generation Matthew Taylor Mellon II, the great, great, great grandson of Thomas Mellon. The nuclear family of the Mellons is worth about twelve billion dollars. Nicole and Matthew are the parents of Force (5) and Olympia (3), the seventh generation. They are a patrimonial family in the sense in which Piketty uses the phrase. Sometimes the idea is diluted to include a notion of neo-feudal family power and a "baronial" class. That is as misleading in terms of academic scholarship as phrases like "Mandarins" or "Brahmins" when journalists are discussing powerful politicians. The Mellons are a very rich or even super rich nuclear family. Does it add anything to think of them as a patrimonial family? Moreover, should the idea be extended to "mere" multi-millionaires and their nuclear families? Does it mean the same thing in the U.S. as it means in, say, France? How comparable were the 1990s to the 1890s? We could profitably discuss them as neo-patrimonial families.[13] The idea of "patrimonial capitalism" is now widely discussed in the social science literature but the link to Weber's Ideal Type Models is often ignored. An exception is academic work that has not received wide recognition.[14] Piketty's use of the idea, on the other

---

11   See the collection of essays in Julia Adams and Mounira May Charrad (eds.), *Patrimonial Power in the Modern World* (Thousand Oaks: Sage Publications, 2011) [This is Book 636 of the Annals of the American Academy of Political and Social Sciences.]. Hereafter Julia Adams and Mourina May Charrad *Patrimonial Power*. Also, see Mounira May Charrad and Julia Adams, *Patrimonial Capitalism and Empire* (Somerville: Emerald, 2015). Hereafter, referred to as Charrad and Adams *Patrimonial Capitalism*.

12   Abram Brown and Alex Morrell, *"Manor-born Entrepreneurs*: ["Meet the Mellons" and "America's Richest Families: From the Waltons to the Kennedys: The First Definitive Ranking of the Nation's 185 Billionaire Clans"]. *Forbes* 194 (1) [July 21]: pp. 62–88 (New York: Forbes Magazine, 20 [Editor-in-Chief Steve Forbes] 2014). The term "American" is used to mean U.S. citizens and not inhabitants of the Americas and not even North America, of course.

13   The term "one percent" covers far more families than the term "neo-patrimonial" families. There is actually tremendous variation among the fifty states as to what it means to be among the one percent in a specific state, from the less affluent states to the most affluent states. Also Washington, D.C. has among the highest incomes of the one percent in that district, due in part no doubt to the salaries of lobbyists. See Richard Lachmann, "American Patrimonialism: The Return of the Repressed" in Julia Adams and Mounira May Charrad *Patrimonial Power in the Modern World*, (Thousand Oaks: Sage Publications, 2011).

14   Julia Adams and Mounira May Charrad (Eds.) *Patrimonial Power* in *the Modern World*, (Thousand Oaks: Sage Publications, 2011). My own work on the use of Max Weber's Ideal Type Model of Patrimonial-prebendalism and Patrimonial-feudalism has been largely ignored, perhaps in part because the empirical case study material has concerned

hand, has been very influential. One of the reasons for his influence is his excellent use of quantitative data. But another factor is his willingness to connect
with literature. He makes the term "patrimonial capitalism" come alive by utilizing references that many people in the humanities and the arts who are not
keen on data analyses can nevertheless associate with directly.

Piketty's use of the ideas found in the novels of Henri de Balzac and Jane
Austen make his book in "political economics" and "economics" more palat-
able. It may even come as a shock to some readers of literary novels to realize that they have been reading about rich, very rich and super rich families
of earlier eras. But his is not a work of literary criticism. The real thrust of
the book is the analysis of national wealth. He utilizes modern technological improvements to pull together data sets for many of the modern capitalist nation-states. But he does not put that analysis into a broader literary
framework along the lines of "sociology and literature." Great novels like
James Joyce's *Finnegans Wake* and David Foster Wallace's (2016) *Infinite Jest*
are ignored.[15] In a way it would be a better book if he had also referred to
historical novels that deal with Medieval Europe and pre-modern empires.
He ignores the fictional literature on those themes and does not refer to the
extensive work on imperialism that comes from the Marxist and Marxian
traditions.[16]

For the political economist and comparative historical sociologist Max
Weber the term *Patrimonialismus* had a broader meaning. In the sections on
Patriarchy, Patrimonialism and Feudalism in the work commonly known in

---

traditional authority in Java and Bali prior to imperialist incursion by Europeans. See
for example: J. I. (Hans) Bakker, "Patrimonialism, Involution, and the Agrarian Question
in Java: a Weberian Analysis of Class Relations and Servile Labour." in John Gledhill, B.
Bender and M. T Larsen (Eds.) *State and Society the Emergence and development of Social
Hierarchy and Political Centralization* (London: Routledge, 1995), pp. 279–301. Hereafter
Bakker *Patrimonialism Java*.

15   Wallace's one finished novel, first published in 1996, is considered by many literary thinkers in the U.S. to be "the novel of its generation." Arguably, it is to the American literature
of the turn of the twenty-first century what Joyce's work was to the turn of the twentieth
century. However, Wallace and Joyce do not deal with the super-rich or neo-patrimonial
capitalist class the way Balzac and Auden sometimes do.

16   Richard B. Day and Daniel Gaido, (Trs. and Eds.) *Discovering Imperialism: Social Democracy to World War I* (Chicago: Haymarket Books, 2012). [Originally published by Koninklijke
Brill NV in Leiden, the Netherlands, in 2011.] The authors cited span 1897 to 1916 and
include Max Beer, Karl Kautsky, Rudolf Hilferding, Rosa Luxemburg, Karl Radek, Otto
Bauer and Anton Pannekoek as well as others who are not as well known. Hereafter Day
and Gaido *Imperialism*.

English as *Economy and Society*[17] (Weber 1968) he provides a set of ideal types
concerning "traditional authority." What he means by traditional authority is
pre-modern legitimate authority and the pre-modern exercise of raw force. To
distinguish the pre-modern from the modern requires accepting Weber's notion that traditional capitalism was greatly transformed in the sixteenth and
seventeenth centuries by modern capitalism and modern bureaucracy. The
traditional bureaucratic structures of various kinds of Patrimonial and Feudal
societies were not modern. Often when Weber's theory of bureaucracy is discussed authors lose track of the fact that Weber did not just discuss modern
bureaucracies. A key ideal type characteristic of pre-modern bureaucracies
was the existence of officials who received tribute. In some passages Weber
calls those tributary officials "prebendal officials." A careful reading of Weber's
texts reveals that a key aspect of his general argument about traditional legitimate authority is the ways in which there were often oscillations between a
strictly prebendal form of traditional bureaucracy and a form of traditional
bureaucracy that also included the existence of a "baronial" or "feudal" class.
The aristocratic owners of demesnes were not the Patrimonial rulers *per se*,
but they did rule within a system that can be designated as Weber's implicit
"Patrimonial-feudal" Ideal Type Model (ITM). It was only in some regions of
the world where the Patrimonial-feudal ITM tends to apply fairly well. In most
parts of the world the incipient Patrimonial-feudal principle of legitimate authority and traditional bureaucracy was nipped in the bud. Thus, for example,
Weber argues that in what we call "China" (i.e. technically Sinitic Civilization)
the principle of legitimacy of one Patrimonial ruler was reinforced many
times. The Chinese prebendal officials (the *Hou*) were not autonomous.[18] Does
that mean that the "baronial" nuclear families, extended families and clans of
the contemporary global "modern capitalist" system are in some ways like the
extended families and clans of the Sinitic or Indic or "Europic" (i.e. not yet "European" but "Roman") pre-modern capitalist, traditional civilizations and cultures? Is it possible that patrimonial families of today are like the patrimonial
families of Ancient Sinitic, Ancient Indic, or Ancient Roman Empires, albeit
on an even large (almost completely global) scale? In some ways, the answer is
that they are obviously very different. The wealth that has been accumulated
in the United States is far greater than total wealth in any pre-capitalist society before circa 1500 or any modern nation-state that participates in one way

---

17   Max Weber, *Economy and Society* (Berkley: University of California Press, 1978 [first
      English translation, 1968]).
18   See Max Weber, *The Religion of China: Confucianism and Taoism.* (New York: MacMillan,
      1951 [1915]).

or another in the global finance capitalist system today. But the key fact that Piketty makes abundantly clear is that income inequality has increased significantly from the late 1970s to today. "For the United States overall, the top 1 percent captured 85.1 percent of total income growth between 2009 and 2013. In 2013 the top 1 percent of families nationally made 25.3 times as much as the bottom 99 percent."[19]

Piketty misleads his readers by using the English version of a French term. We cannot blame that on bad translation. He is very precise in his use of North American English. He has chosen to use the terms patrimonialism and hyper-patrimonialism, terms not widely associated with Marx or Marxism. Yet, as stated, there is no use made of Max Weber's social theories or his explicitly "political economic sociological" theories. Yet Weber's views are heuristic for understanding many aspects of traditional authority and "Patrimonial prebendalism" in neo-patrimonial societies today.[20]

Cogent discussions are found in law reviews.[21] That may be in part because as Heilbron makes it clear, the structure of the French discipline of "*economie*" is different from the u.s. discipline of economics.[22] In France there has been a split among three approaches of 1) the *École libre des sciences politiques* in

---

19   Estelle Sommeiller, Mark Price and Ellis Wazeter,"Income inequality in the u.s. by state, metropolitan area, and county," Economic Policy Institute Report (Washington: Economic Policy Institute, 2016). www.epi.org/107100. Accessed on November 22, 2016.

      This forty-seven page report is an analysis of wealth inequality state by state. In twenty-four states the top one percent captured between half and all income growth. The top one percent earn far less on average in states like New Mexico, Arkansas, West Virginia and Mississippi than in states like Connecticut, New Jersey, Massachusetts and New York. They also present data for the top .01%. Somewhat surprisingly Wyoming has a small, very rich, elite that represents an enormous top to bottom ratio for that state.

20   J. I. (Hans) "Weber's oscillation thesis: Patrimonial prebendalism and [patrimonial] feudalism." *Perspectives*,34 (1) (2012) and J. I. (Hans), "Why is Weber's prebendalism ignored? Considering a post-ISIS caliphate." *Perspectives* vol. 37 (1), 2015, pp. 22–25. See Max Weber, *Essays in Sociology.* (London: Routledge and Kegan Paul, 1946) See especially "India: The Brahman and the castes" pp. 306–444, 460–467 and "The Chinese Literati" in, and ff. is especially 400, 402, 405, 411–412, 413, 419, 420, 424, 432. The Hans Gerth and Charles Wright Mills volume *From Max Weber*, (New York: Oxford University Press, 1946) is frequently cited. The term "prebends" is used frequently by Weber yet very few sociological theorists are familiar with the term. I submit that he has in mind traditional authority and therefore Patrimonial-prebendalism and in the case of the Warring States period in China, an incipient Patrimonial-feudalism nipped in the bud.

21   David Singh Grewal, "Book Review [of Piketty 2014]: The laws of capitalism." *Harvard Law Review* vol. 128 book review 626, 2014, pp. 626–667.

22   Johan Heilbron, *French Sociology* (Ithaca: Cornell University Press, 2015), pp. 32–37.

1871, 2) the *sciences humaines* (which included *ethnologie, sociologie* and psychologie but also *philosophie*) in the Faculty of Letters, and 3) the Faculty of Law. Political economics (*economie politique*) became a compulsory subject for law students in 1877.

In 2004 Emmanuel Saez at the University of California, Berkeley, prepared a paper for the Berkeley Symposium on Poverty, the Distribution of Income and Public Policy. He thanks Thomas Piketty for helpful discussions and cites several of Piketty's French-language publications. Ten years later Piketty[23] writes that an explanatory model that he developed with Saez and Stefanie Stantcheva to explain skyrocketing executive pay involves "political, social, and cultural as well as economic factors" and that part of the "beauty" of the social sciences is that complex and comprehensive questions cannot be answered in absolutely definitive ways. That is true, of course. But it is also true that sometimes it is possible to hide behind the numbers and avoid key theoretical questions. The problems with the poll data in the 2016 election made it clear that the numbers do not always speak for themselves. Analysis is necessary in any political economic approach, especially the somewhat modified Frankfurt School framework advocated here.

It is not generally recognized that both Karl Marx and Max Weber were both political economists.[24] They engaged in what can be called *Sozialökonomie*. They approached the study of political, economic and social issues from a framework that does not fit easily into three separate disciplines. We could say, of course, that they were political scientists, economists and sociologists. But focusing on the fact that they themselves thought in terms of a critique of certain aspects of the Classical Political Economy of Adam Smith and David Ricardo helps to put their insights into a new light. Marx the economist

---

23   Thomas Piketty and Emmanuel Saez, 2004. "Income Inequality in the United States, 1913–2002." In *Top Incomes over the Twentieth Century,* edited by Anthony Barnes Atkinson and Thomas Piketty. (New York, NY: Oxford University Press, 2014) supplemented by Thomas Piketty and Emmanuel Saez with 2014 data updates. http://eml.berkeley.edu/~saez/tabfog2014prel.xls{Downloadable Excel files} Accessed November 22, 2016.

24   I myself did not fully appreciate until fairly recently the important way in which Max Weber was primarily a political economist. I had been educated to view him as primarily a sociologist and historian. It was reading Richard Swedberg, *Max Weber and the Idea of Economic Sociology* (Princeton: Princeton University Press, 1998) that made Weber's intellectual affinities with political economy much clearer. See my discussion of this issue in J. I. Hans Bakker (ed.), "Introduction" and "Conclusion" in his *The Methodology of Political Economy: Studying the Global Rural-Urban Matrix* (Lanham: Lexington Books/Roman and Littlefield, 2015), pp. 1–29 and 211–255. Also, see: Richard Swedberg, *Essays in Economic Sociology/Max Weber* (Princeton: Princeton University Press, 1999).

was a political economist. Weber the sociologist was a Professor of Political Economy during the relatively few years he actually taught. What we call his *verstehede Soziologie* is not at all comparable to what is generally called sociology today. In so far as both Marx and Weber contributed to sociology it was mainly to Comparative Historical Sociology (CHS). Their CHS continues to be an important framework. Because the majority of academic economists today practice some form of neo-classical economics the main focus on Marx and Weber's contributions has been in the discipline of sociology. They are both considered "sociological theorists." Economists are familiar with Marx but often dismiss his ideas. Hardly any economists bother to read Weber. One argument frequently accepted is that Marx's work is irrelevant to academic economics because (it is alleged) the labor theory of value is either misleading or completely incorrect.[25] Economists rarely mention Weber at all. But, if we examine the distribution of wealth from a Marx-Weber "New Political Economy Perspective" (NPEP) a number of issues are clarified. The key idea is that we have to consider the political, the economic and the social as one set of interlocked problems. It can be useful to simply focus on one of the three for certain kinds of mathematically-sophisticated or statistically intriguing arguments, but thinking about problems in the real world requires something more than mathematical or statistical gymnastics. That point is made by Thomas Piketty. He provides a wealth of qualitative information and quantitative data but he makes it clear that he is fundamentally making the kinds of arguments that a political economist makes about the distribution of wealth in advanced, modern capitalist societies in the global capitalist system and global food regimes.

An alternative view of capital, familiar to Classical Political Economy, is that capital is fundamentally a social relation. In other words, what we call capital is not a "thing" but a set of relationships. That idea was revived to counter the assumption in Neo-Classical Economics that capital is an abstraction that can be aggregated into what has come to be known as the "production function." This

---

25   David L. Prychitko, "Marxism." *The Concise Encyclopedia of Economics* (Indianapolis: Liberty Fund, Inc., 2007). *http://www.econlib.org/library/Enc/Marxism.html*, The second edition of this book came out in December 2007. It is available both in print through Liberty Fund, Inc. and online at Econlib. (The 1st edition continues to be available online at Econlib.) A key text for an overview of what is meant by "Marxism" is Leszek Kolakowski, *Main Currents of Marxism*, 3 volumes (New York: Oxford University Press, 1985). See also Ed. W. W. Bartley III The Liberty Fund generally presents a critique of Marxism and Marxist theory based in part on the work of Friedrich Hayek, *The Fatal Conceit: The Errors of Socialism* (Chicago: University of Chicago Press, 1988). There have been many different critiques of the labor theory of value.

is not the place to enter into that complex debate.[26] It would involve also going back to work by Eugen Böhm von Bawerk, Rudolf Hilferding, Rosa Luxemburg, Ernest Mandel, Paul Sweezy and many others. Suffice it to say here that Piketty's work has made those debates relevant again just as Joan Robinson's work in the period after WWII brought Marx back into academic discussion.

Instead, the focus here is on a somewhat different aspect of the problem, one that can be associated with the Frankfurt School attempt to meld ideas from Marx with CHS put forward by Weber. It has been argued that Frankfurt School of Critical Theory needs to be "resurrected,"[27] in order to better understand the nature of the 21st century with the domination of Global Modern Finance Capitalism (GMFC). The intellectual context of the 1920s, immediately after World War I, was both quite different and, at the same time, quite similar to the intellectual context of the 2010s. By the 2020's the situation will be somewhat different again, depending in part on U.S. federal politics. The recent election of Donald Trump makes it clear that the issue of neo-patrimonialism is not going to go away in the U.S. context. Trump himself is a kind of neo-patrimonial figure and there seem to be elements of prebendalism in his selection of members of his inner circle.[28] One very important question is whether the 1920s

---

26 Joan Robinson, "The Production Function and the Theory of Capital," *Review of Economic Studies*, vol. 21 (2), 1953–1954, pp. 81–106. Reprinted in part with comment in Joan Robinson, Collected Economic Papers, vol. II (Oxford: Basil Blackwell). See the essays in Bill Gibson (ed.), Joan Robinson's *Economics: A Centennial Celebration*. (Cheltenham, and Northampton: Edward Elgar, 2003), especially Claudio Saroni, "Robinson on Marx," pp. 43–56. The book has an excellent bibliography of on work relevant to Robinson and of Joan Robinson's published work, pp. 351–386, especially pp. 375–379. Hereafter: Gibson *Robinson*.

27 Lauren Langman, "Bringing the critical Back In: Toward the resurrection of the Frankfurt School," in Dahms, Harry (ed.), *Mediations of Social Life in the 21st Century: Current Perspectives in Social Theory*, Vol. 32. (Bingley: Emerald, 2014), pp. 195–227.

28 The notion of "nepotism" did not exist in traditional systems of legitimate authority where the general framework conformed to a great extent to Max Weber's Ideal Type Model (ITM) of Patrimonial prebendalism. There were no rules against involving family members in governance. Quite the reverse. The general ITM of Patrimonialism is divided into three aspects: Original Patriarchy, Prebendalist kinds of Patrimonialism and more clearly feudal kinds of Patrimonialism. Many academics are not familiar with the term "prebendalism." Hardly any journalists use the term. However, it is still used by the Anglican Church to represent the "prebends" given to church officials. A Patrimonial prebendal ruler in traditional societies often depended on immediate family members in order to insure a degree of reliability, a strategy that did not always work. To have a 21st century President of the United States rely heavily on his children and his son-in-law is clearly an echo of traditional prebendalist and feudal versions of Patrimonialism. Hence, it can be thought of in terms of the ITM of Neo-patrimonialism, a kind of patriarchal rulership adapted to modern global capitalism.

and 1930s will be repeated in significant ways in the 2020s and 2030s. There is no question about the existence of Neo-Fascist political currents in Europe today, but there is a question whether they will become even more dominant as the threat of Wahabi-influenced Islamic terrorist activities continues. There has never been an end to major wars. World War II was not the end of war but only the beginning of a new stage of more localized kinds of wars. But can war be more or less contained to specific nation-states like Korea, Vietnam, Iraq and Afghanistan? Or will wars start to involve larger and larger regions of the world, like most of the Middle East or much of East Asia?

Piketty and Patrimonial Families: Is His Analysis Linked to Comparative Historical Sociology?

Piketty's excellent analysis has much to offer. It has also been critiqued in many ways and for many reasons. Some of the critiques are ideologically motivated. Right wing thinkers do not like the way he offers suggestions that do not conform to their stereotypes of *laissez faire*. Left wing thinkers do not like the way he slights Karl Marx and the Marxism of the Second International as well as aspects of some 20th and 21st century "Marxian" approaches. This discussion concerns one very specific conceptual problem in Piketty, a problem due in part to translation from French to English. That is the use of the word "patrimonial."

It may seem to some that the question of Piketty's use of the word "patrimonialism" is a trivial concern. But our use of words has an impact. The neglect of the word patrimonialism in modern academic scholarship reflects a significant failure to fully grasp a very important aspect of the political economy of social formations. The use of the word patrimonial must be examined in terms of its relevance to class analysis. If there is such a thing as an elite of patrimonial families in the U.S. (and the Global North generally) then we need to pay attention to social class and we need to put the analysis of social class and exploitation into a wider Neo-Marxian and Neo-Weberian framework.

One would think that the link between Marx and Weber would be widely recognized in sociological theory, but there are still many thinkers within the discipline who tend to see the two as being opposed.[29] Also noteworthy

---

29   Marcuse's critique of Weber does not really tackle the questions discussed here. If Marcuse had made a clear distinction between value-rational and goal-rational social action, then many of his criticisms would have to be significantly modified. Instead, he plays with the idea of "Reason" in an ahistorical sense.

is the fact that even well-known Weber experts have not paid a lot of attention to the arguments about patrimonialism. Some tend to write about a contrast between "patrimonialism" and "bureaucracy" but that is very misleading. There were traditional bureaucracies in patrimonial society and thus we really should specify whether we mean a traditional bureaucracy or a "modern bureaucracy" of the type that did not come into existence before the advent of modern capitalism. For example, in Medieval Europe the Roman Catholic Church provided most of the traditional bureaucracy that supported the administration of the Medieval Holy Roman "Germanic-Italic" Empire. It was not a modern bureaucracy, but it was efficient. Monks, priests and nuns were the officials who served as traditional bureaucrats. They were not paid a salary. But they did receive tribute in the form of arrangements involving "prebends." The highest officials of the Roman Catholic Church had control over vast resources but they were not in and of themselves politically independent. At least in theory they could be removed by the Patrimonial prebendal ruler: the Pope. The struggle between Holy Roman Emperors and Popes concerned the ultimate source of legitimate authority. Because of that struggle, it was eventually possible for those who held domains to declare themselves somewhat independent of Patrimonial prebendal control. That is, they were somewhat independent of the Roman Catholic Church. That also led to imperial cities which became somewhat independent of both the Pope and the Emperor. Weber presents arguments about all of that and much more. But instead of continuing to discuss pre-modern societies and Weber's ideas concerning Patrimonialism it is useful to turn to contemporary societies and social class. After the Protestant Reformation and the emergence of modern capitalism we eventually get the establishment of the nation-state principle, an idea fully recognized in the seventeenth century. Most of our analyses of social class today are based on ideas about social class in modern nation-states that participate in the global finance capitalist system that got consolidated after WWII and became especially significant after technological changes in transportation and communications led to greater international connectedness. With globalization, however, there has also been a rise in income inequality.

Wright and Relational Social Class: *Ambiguous* Use of Class in Piketty

Wright discusses Piketty's work on social class in terms of the recent rediscovery of the topic of "inequality." The popularity of Piketty's book is due in part, he argues, to the "salience of inequality as an issue of broad public concern."[30] One reason Marxian thinkers may be drawn to the book is that Piketty does not hesitate to argue in favor of political intervention. He makes it clear that spontaneous processes are not going to do the trick. Wright briefly summarizes the arguments and conclusions found in Piketty's book, but then discusses the way that Piketty analyzes his own specialization: the study of social class. The summary is excellent[31] and does not have to be repeated here, except to point out that income inequality and wealth inequality are closely related. Let us focus on the very large inequalities of both sky high incomes and inherited wealth in terms of the concept of contemporary "patrimonial families." Wright states that Piketty's use of the term "class" is somewhat ambiguous. That is primarily because Wright feels that an analysis within the "Marxist" tradition of academic scholarship requires a "relational analysis" emphasizing the exploitation of "labor" by the "owners" of capital. The owners of capital are also often among the top ten percent of all those who receive various forms of remuneration for high level management activities. The process whereby the top class and status groups reproduce themselves is well understood. Even the ownership of real estate in terms of residential owner-occupied real estate can have an important impact on social class, whether or not we should classify a super-rich family's estate as one aspect of their "capital" (in the Marxian sense) or not. Inequalities that result from the ownership of "capitalist capital" (as opposed to capitalist personal property) are the core of the problem in Marx's analysis of capital. Class relations in contemporary modern capitalist societies still generate economic inequality, as they have done since the earliest stages of modern capitalism in the 16th century. But in recent decades those inequalities have escalated. A "relational understanding of class" today also requires the kind of analysis of huge salaries of CEOs and other top executives that were not necessarily characteristic of earlier stages of modern capitalism. The owners of capital (many of whom have inherited at least a part of their wealth) appropriate a share of the wealth that is produced by the labor power of those of live in humble (if not always wretched) conditions. However, both Piketty and Wright tend to neglect the CHS dimension of the problem. Piketty does a marvelous job of utilizing the available data for the last hundred years or so and Wright is analytically precise when discussing U.S. social class since World War II. But the 15th through 18th centuries are largely ignored. Why is that important? The earliest stages

30   Erik Olin Wright, *Understanding Class*. (London and New York: Verso, 2015). See also
       Chapter 1 above.
31   Erik Olin Wright, *Understanding Class*. (London and New York: Verso, 2015), pp. 129–
       134.

of modern capitalism are central to Weber's theory of "rationalization." In the last four or five hundred years there has been a huge increase in the importance of goal-rational, instrumental social action and a consequent decline in traditional, effectual ("emotional") and value-rational social action. Similarly, there has been a gradual expansion of modern bureaucracy and a gradual decline of traditional, pre-modern capitalist, bureaucracy. But when Piketty and Wright discuss these issues their generalizations are mostly only relevant to the last hundred years. That is due in part to the lack of available and relevant quantitative data. Wright[32] discusses Weber's theory of life chances but tends to neglect Weber's broader CHS, with the exception of comments on slavery. Relational social class can refer to either: 1) social inequalities and relations throughout human recorded history (with some archeological and anthropological speculation about non-written history) or 2) strictly just the kind of social class and status relations found in "modern capitalism." Then everything hinges on how we define "modern capitalism" (as opposed to generic capitalism) and we think is more important about social class in modern capitalist relations of production: life chances or "exploitation." But what is exploitation? Does possession of extreme wealth automatically indicate exploitation of the poor? Would the 99% be any better off if the 1% were to lose almost all of their wealth?[33]

But, as mentioned, Piketty, despite some discussion of Marx, does not utilize any insights found in Weber. Wright does cite Weber, drawing heavily on the

---

32   Erik Olin Wright, *Understanding Class.* (London and New York: Verso, 2015), pp. 21–56.

33   In traditional, pre-modern capitalist societies there was very little money wealth and therefore very little "capital" in the form of money. It could be argued that under Patrimonial-prebendal and Patrimonial-feudal systems of rulership the exploitation of the ninety-nine percent (or even 99.8%) was so pervasive that very few people even asked the question whether the nine-nine percent would be better off if the Patrimonial rulers lost much of their wealth. Indeed, anything more than windfall, sporadic accumulation of any kind in the kind of generic or "pariah" capitalism that existed very widely before 1500 was minimal. It is only with "modern capitalism" (starting in the 16th century, long before industrialization) that we see the beginnings of real capital accumulation over time. There were some incipient forms of capital accumulation in the last stages of Patrimonial feudalism when free cities in the Italian peninsula made a significant break from *direct* control by the Holy Roman Empire and the Roman Catholic Church. Simplistic critiques of Weber's Protestant Ethic thesis fail to take note of the fact he fully understood such incipient kinds of early versions of modern capitalism prior to the Protestant Reformation-especially in the Italian City-States. His doctoral dissertation on early trade explicitly discusses such early pockets of a qualitative transformation that became far more widespread after the Reformation and Counter-Reformation.

now highly disputed work we know in English as *Economy and Society*.[34] Contemporary Weber scholars draw attention to the fact that much of *Wirtschaft und Gesellschaft* (even in its fifth German-language edition) is still misleading (so, of course, is the English-language version).

The Original Frankfurt School

The first generation of the Frankfurt School strongly influenced by Gyorgy (Georg, George) Lukàcs, Karl Korsch and Wilhelm Reich, included Max Horkheimer, Herbert Marcuse, and Walter Benjamin. Theodor W. Adorno joined somewhat later. Fromm and Reich in particular used Sigmund Freud's more sociological ideas as well as his psychoanalytic insights. But all first generation Frankfurt School theorists seem to have been at least somewhat familiar with the work of Max Weber (1865–1920).[35] Weber is considered an important contributor to "sociology" and his *verstehende Soziologie* definitely has had a significant impact on many thinkers. But what is often forgotten is that Weber was first and foremost an academic political economist. His official positions were in *Sozialökonomie*.[36] That German word is a translation of the French *economie sociale*, which is a French translation of the Scottish-English phrase "political economy." The fact that Weber was also a historian, comparative historian, lawyer, jurist, methodologist, and many other things should not obscure the fundamental importance of the political economy approach for most of his work. Weber was never an academic philosopher, but he definitely had a deep knowledge of the German Idealist philosophical tradition of Kant, Fichte, Schelling, Hegel, Nietzsche and others. (It is not clear if he read Kierkegaard deeply.) He also read the Classical Political Economists (CPE) and the critique of CPE by Karl Marx. Most of his criticisms of "Marxism" were of certain aspects of the Second International and not necessarily of Karl Marx himself. Marx's Critique of Political Economy, as contained in the *Grundrisse*

---

34   Max Weber, *Economy and Society* (Oakland: University of California Press, 1978).

35   Weber's writings on rationality, bureaucracy and modernity, influenced his close friend, Lukacs, whose analysis of reification joined Reason, bureaucratic logic, with Marx's critic of commodity fetishism and ideological domination.

36   For a brief time at the very end of his of his life Weber was a Professor of Political Economy *and Sociology* at the University of Munich. Nevertheless, his career was mostly that of a Political Economist. *Economy and Society* is not "just" a sociological magnum opus. It is a largely unfinished work, which attempts to combine political economy with social psychology and Comparative Historical Sociology.

and the parts of Capital published in his own lifetime, were definitely also a kind of Political Economy. But Marx's own works should not be confused with what is commonly called "Marxist Economics." Marx the political economist influenced Weber the political economist at least as much as Marx the social psychologist and sociologist influenced Weber the social psychologist and sociologist.[37]

What is most relevant here is the precise way in which Weber used his ideal types of traditional authority. There has been much misinterpretation of Weber's theory of patrimonialism. Sometimes, for example, a short-hand version contrasts "patrimonialism" with "bureaucracy." But that is completely incorrect. For Weber there was traditional bureaucracy in patrimonial empires. Moreover, such traditional patrimonial bureaucracies still exist in many parts of the world despite the emergence of a global, modern capitalist system. Sometimes, as in the literature on Africa, they are called "neo-patrimonial" bureaucracies and states. Modern, goal-rational, formal legal bureaucracies are often discussed with the one word bureaucracy without any further clarification. But the context should make it clear that only goal-rational bureaucracy is really being discussed. When Weber's original German-language drafts are read very carefully and statements are taken in context it is sometimes the case that we need to be very discerning to make it clear what he means. Hence, there is all the more reason to read with a classical hermeneutic framework and not jump to unwarranted conclusions. There is no opportunity here to enter into precise quotations of the German-language versions of Weber's subtle ideas, but the texts are widely available now in the *Gesamtausgabe*.[38]

---

37   Some Frankfurt School theorists attacked Weber's views. See Herbert Marcuse, "Industrialization and Capitalism" *New Left Review* vol. I. (30) 1965, pp. 3–17. Some of Marcuse's criticisms hinge on his failure to distinguish between traditional authority and modern capitalist authority. At times, he also does praise Weber.

38   Max Weber, *Wirtschaft und Gesellschaft: Die Wirtschaft und die gesellschaftlichen Ordnungen und Mächte*. [Economy and Society: The Economy and the Societal [Social] Orders {Organizations, Institutions} and Powers {*Herrschaften*, Rulerships, Dominations}.] *Nachlaß. Teilband 4: Herrschaft. Herausgegeben von* [edited by] Edith Hanke *in Zusammenarbeit mit* [in collaboration with] Thomas Kroll. *Max Weber Gesamtausgabe* [Collected Works of Max Weber]. *Abteilung I: Schriften und Reden, Band 22–4*. [*MWG I/22–4*] (Tübingen, Deutschland: J. C. B. Mohr [Paul Siebeck], 2005), Max Weber, *Abriß* [*Abriss*] *der universalen Sozial- und Wirschaftgeschifte: Mit- und Nachschriften 1919/1920*. [Universal Social and Economic History, 2011] *Max Weber Gesamtausgabe* [Collected Works of Max Weber] *Abteilung III: Vorlesungen und Vorlesungsnachriften/ Band 6*. [*MWG III/6*]. *Herausgegeben von* Wolfgang Schluchter *in Zusammenarbeit mit* Joachim Schröder (Tübingen: J. C. B. Mohr [Paul Siebeck], 2011).

It is sufficient to state here that one possible interpretation is that Weber moves beyond the notion of a specifically "Asian" Mode of Production to a theory of the universal *oscillation* (at various times in history and various locations) between the Ideal Type Model (ITM) of Patrimonial-prebendalism and the ITM of Patrimonial-feudalism. In other words, it is not a transition from one Mode of Production (e.g. Slave) to a Feudal Mode of Production. It is not a transition along some more or less deterministic evolutionary path or even some kind of Hegelian or Neo-Hegelian dialectical path. Weber did not accept an evolutionary theory (in the usual sense of a social scientific "progressive" evolutionary dialectic). The symbol of the more progressive aspect of Patrimonial-feudalism is the very gradual, very reluctant acceptance of the legitimate authority of a baronial landed elite. We do not tend to think of the landed elite as progressive in any sense, but in Weber's political economy the gradual encroachment on absolute authority of a Patrimonial-prebendal leader is a significant breakthrough toward a very long term possibility of some level of what we today call democratization. One example of a Patrimonial-prebendal state in the world today is North Korea. At times in Sinitic history the Emperors were Patrimonial-prebendal rulers over much of the geographic territory now claimed as part of the so-called People's Republic of China. But in so-called "warring states" periods Sinitic civilizations did not encompass all of the contemporary land mass. Similarly, the European Holy Roman "Germanic-Italic" Empire was an effective Patrimonial-prebendal system throughout much of Europe for at least hundreds of years between 800 and 1806. Both Napoleon and Hitler sought to create a new empire ultimately based on Patrimonial-prebendalism. Space precludes a full discussion of those ideas here. But we need to mention the concept in order to make the critique of Piketty clear. He has an implicit critique of the ways in which extreme concentrations of wealth tend to result in a kind of "baronial elite" in the Global North. That would seem to be a regression to "feudalism."

Moreover, Piketty does attempt to discuss three hundred years of capitalism. He does not entirely lack a historical and comparative dimension in his work. Rather than simply discuss capitalism in a kind of "ethnographic present" he makes it clear that the modern finance capitalism of the 21st century has both similarities and differences with the 18th, 19th and 20th century forms of capitalism. However, he does not really tackle the question of 16th and 17th early modern capitalism. Nor does he examine Modes of Production in the period before the first emergence of modern capitalism. Thus, he does not discuss the Mode of Production in the "twilight stage" or "Autumn" of the Feudal Mode of Production. He also does not examine the continued existence of slave and serf relations of production in the late Feudal and early Modern period of the 15th century or slavery and serfdom in later stages of gradually more industrialized modern capitalism.

The word "patrimonialism" is not used in English a great deal in the 21st century, but it does get used by some scholars, primarily those familiar with Max Weber. But even there the original meaning that Weber had in mind tends to be lost. The ideal type model (ITM) of "Patrimonialism" found in Weber's posthumous (1922) *Wirtschaft und Gesellschaft*[39] (Weber 2005) is often misunderstood, even by academics. The definitive sections on the Ideal Type Models (ITMs) of "Patrimonialism" and "Feudalism" have not been translated into English, although it must be said that the Guenther Roth and Claus Wittich translations of those sections are more than adequate for our purposes here. The discussion of patrimonially organized "communities" by Julia Adams is directly relevant here.[40] But it would take us too far afield to start to discuss the best way to pull together Weber's work on the earlier draft and the later draft of what is now commonly known as *Economy and Society*.[41] Instead, we can return to some comments on history.

U.S. Imperialism and Social Darwinism

One aspect of Piketty's work that weakens the overall argument to some extent is his relative lack of attention to the early stages of imperialism and colonialism in what became the global modern capitalist economy as a whole. To fully comprehend the United States as a nation-state first formed during the late

---

39   Max Weber, *Economy and Society*, (Berkeley: University of California Press, [1922] 2013).

40   Charles Camic, Philip S. Gorski and David M. Trubek (eds.), *Max Weber's Economy and Society: A Critical Companion* (Palo Alto: Stanford University Press, 2005). This excellent collection contains penetrating analyses by Richard Swedberg, Eric Olin Wright, Guenther Roth, Wolfgang J. Mommsen, Mustafa Emirbayer, Donald N. Levine, Duncan Kennedy, Harvey Goldman, Julia Adams, Hans Joas, Hans G. Kippenberg, Randall Collins, and Regina F. Titunik, as well as the editors. See the book review by Thomas M. Kemple, "Max Weber's Economy and Society: A Critical Companion," 2005, in the *Canadian Journal of Sociology*, Available online at http://www.cjsonline.ca/reviews/mweconsoc.html Kemple takes issue with the interpretations put forward by Donald N. Levine and Mustafa Emirbayer. Also, see Julia Adams and Mary Charrad (Eds.) *Patrimonial Power* (Thousand Oaks: Sage Publications, 2011).

41   See Horst Baier, M. Rainer Lepsius, Wolfgang J. Mommsen and Wolfgang Schluchter, "Overview of the Text of *Economy and Society* by the Editors of the Max Weber *Gesamtausgabe*," translated by Austin Harrington, Max *Weber Studies* 1 (1) [2000], pp. 104–115. Available at Stable URL: http://www.jstor.orgn/stable/i24574210

eighteenth century (c. 1775–1789) we must retain an awareness of the extent to which the ideology of Social Darwinism concerning race allowed for colonialism within the "continental" u.s. and further imperialism and colonialism outside of the continent. The u.s. "American" expansion in the Pacific is worth noting.[42] One important step was the military take-over of the Kingdom of Hawai'i. Although now Hawaii is one of the fifty states, it has always been a bit different than the forty-eight states on the mainland. (Alaska is also different, but in distinct ways.) The invasion of Mexico, the Spanish-American War, the Cuban-American War and the invasion of the Philippines are all part of the story. u.s. military actions in the Philippines were ruthless and resemble the situation in the Belgian Congo.[43] We are all familiar with My Lai in Vietnam, but few u.s. citizens know there were many My Lai type incidents in the Philippines. The u.s. would not be the powerful nation-state that it became after the Great War, and that reached its highest point of "greatness" after WWII as one of the two super powers, if the Westward expansion had not taken place.[44] Yet the u.s. frontier is hardly ever discussed as an imperialist expansion of the sort that European nation-states like Great Britain and France practiced outside of Europe. Particularly interesting in Bradley's account is the way in which Theodore Roosevelt considered the Japanese "honorary Aryans" but made fun of the Chinese[45] Everything that u.s. elite liked about Japan relative to Korea and China at the turn of the century (1890s to 1905) later became qualities that were critiqued after Pearl Harbor. Japan invaded and maintained Korea and Manchuria as colonies in large part due to the u.s. go ahead. But Japanese military action against the u.s. was completely in line with earlier Japanese surprise attacks against Russia in 1905. Surprisingly, Theodore Roosevelt set the stage for the "day of infamy" that Franklin Delano Roosevelt may have had

---

42   James Bradley, *The Imperial Cruise: A Secret History of Empire and War.* (New York: Little, Brown and Co., 2009).

43   Adam Hochschild, *King Leopold's Ghost: A Story of Greed, Terror, and Heroism in Colonial Africa* (Boston: Mifflin Book and Houghton Mifflin Company, 1999 [1998]).

44   The 2016 presidential election sidestepped this obvious fact and there was no mention of u.s. imperialism by any candidate. However, to "Make America Great Again" in the same sense in which the u.s. has been deemed by many citizens to have been great in the twentieth century would require imperialism rather than globalization. Globalization required international free trade agreements that affect corporations due to extreme differences in the cost of labor. Just as it is not possible for the United Kingdom to go back to the kind of imperialism that once characterized the British Empire it is not feasible for the u.s. to continue the kind of expansion that involved imperialism on the continent of North America and imperialism abroad, particularly in the Pacific.

45   Op. cit., Bradley, 167–200.

a significant role in creating.[46] Conservative Social Darwinist racist beliefs were central to U.S. expansion against indigenous "Indian" nations and later expansion abroad. Somewhat surprisingly, even Robert Park, known in part for his work with Book T. Washington at Tuskegee, was a Social Darwinist of sorts.[47] The neo-patrimonial families which are super rich today are often families that benefited either directly or indirectly from U.S. imperial expansion and colonialism in the North and South Americas as well as the Pacific. It is likely that in 1776 or 1789 few of the so-called Founding Fathers (or Founding Mothers) would have anticipated the way in which thirteen small states eventually became part of a nation-state with fifty states and many overseas territories. The U.S. Empire replaced the British Empire to a large extent after WWII. The existence of huge income inequalities in the U.S. are not just due to free market capitalist forces but are also closely associated with the expansion of U.S. territory from thirteen states on the Eastern Seaboard to large swaths of territory on the continent and around the world. The German nation-state lost its overseas colonies after the Treaty of Paris of 1919 and the British and French lost their overseas empires after World War II. Coming decades will likely see a gradual weakening of U.S. neo-colonial power and a situation where income inequality will start to have the kinds of effects that Marx predicted long ago. One of his main theoretical mistakes concerning the declining rate of profit was to think primarily in terms of decades rather than centuries. But the economic forces at work were understood in an essential way by Marx. Piketty has given added weight to those aspects of Marx's theory of capital that can now be studied empirically in a highly-sophisticated manner.

Conclusion

The focus has been on the way in which Piketty's use of the term patrimonialism is both heuristic and misleading.[48] It is fruitful because it draws attention to the ways in which billionaire clans in the U.S. and elsewhere have a kind of "baronial" influence comparable in a metaphorical sense to the

---

46   A very controversial argument has been put forward by Robert A. Theobald, *The Final Secret of Pearl Harbor*. (Old Greenwich: The Devin-Adair Company, 1954).

47   Aldon Morris *W. E. B. DuBois and the Birth of Modern Sociology* (Berkeley: University of California Press, 2015), pp. 100–148.

48   Space limitations preclude extending this discussion further even though there are many other topics that could be considered, including the question of whether or not there is one relatively unified power elite in the U.S. Are there several different competing power

power of aristocratic classes like the British and French landed elites. Neo-patrimonialism is a reasonable way to think about the top one percent and especially the top one tenth of one percent or top one hundredth of one per-cent. The Prussian *Junkers* could also be discussed in this context, but Piketty does not draw attention to Bismarck and the founding of the new nation-state of *Deutschland* and its overseas imperial aspirations. If we use terms strict-ly and in the spirit of *Wissenchaft* ("science") and historical materialism as a trans-historical theory then it is misleading to write about the one hundred and eighty-five billionaire clans of the U.S. as a baronial or neo-patrimonial elite. The strength of the "civil sphere" and the importance of "Anglo-Saxon" traditions of "civility" make a return to a Patrimonial-feudal, much less a Patrimonial-prebendal, system largely inconceivable in the U.S., France or Germany, although not necessarily in Russia or China. On the other hand, the recent presidential election makes the idea less inconceivable than it might have been a year ago. Neo-Patrimonialism is characteristic of Saudi Arabia and continues to be important in many parts of the Middle East, despite the Arab Spring. Today North Korea comes very close to a contemporary version of Weber's Ideal Type Model of Patrimonial-prebendalism and not just neo-patrimonialism. If we step outside of Weber's initial discussion then the pre-cise boundary line between traditional and modern is very difficult to draw.

If we are going to "bring the Critical back in" and resurrect Frankfurt School insights, then simply reading Piketty is only one small step in the right direction.[49] We need to pay attention to Wright's critique of the ambigu-ities in Piketty's analysis of class. But to go the whole route we need to move beyond "rhetorical hypostatizations" of market equilibrium as a bedrock phenomenon and look at complex background assumptions that go back hundreds of years—if not longer. Bringing the interdisciplinary approach of the Frankfurt School back into the discussion is important and Piketty could easily have utilized some of the key insights of both Karl Marx and

---

elites? Do the "higher circles" not only represent "wealth" but also power independent of wealth? My feeling is that C. Wright Mills who was not himself part of any power elite, tended to over-emphasize unity within *one* power elite, although he did emphasize the somewhat independent roles of the economic, political and military *institutions*. That, however, can then also lead to a Structural-Functionalist sociological theory of a dozen or more "institutions" in "society" and a neglect of political economic questions central to the sociology of exploitation, wealth and relational social class.

49   Lauren Langman, "Bringing the critical Back In: Toward the resurrection of the Frankfurt School," in Dahms, Harry (ed.), *Mediations of Social Life in the 21st Century: Current Per-spectives in Social Theory*, Vol. 32. (Bingley: Emerald, 2014), pp. 195–227.

Max Weber. It is also important to go back to Theodor Adorno.[50] Without that broader set of theoretical ideas his approach—despite its sophistication— remains somewhat like "Cargo Cult" science described by Feynman.[51] Key aspects of the problem are ignored. In addition to cogent criticisms of the notion of general laws of economics already found in the literature[52] the full range of views in "economic sociology" should also be considered. But even more than that, the dialectical downside of the French Enlightenment belief in rational progress should also be considered in terms of the fragility of democracy, especially now.[53]

In this analysis the main goal has been to utilize insights of Marx and Weber that Frankfurt School theorists brought together. Of course, many of the ideas presented here could be further developed, discussed and debated. It has not been my intention to state any of this in a dogmatic fashion. Rather, this has been an exploration of one aspect of Piketty's work that seems to require further consideration. That is his relative neglect of the Comparative Historical Sociological (CHS) big picture. It is certainly understandable that he has limited his generalizations mostly to those trends for which it was possible to collect adequate data. What he has done is a major accomplishment. But precisely because Piketty has opened up topics relatively neglected outside of relatively small intellectual networks it is now useful to broaden the questions even beyond the already macro level inquiry he has undertaken and succeeded in getting recognized by both academics and non-academic intellectuals. Some of those questions go back to Max Weber's Ideal Type Models (ITMs) of traditional legitimate authority, especially Patrimonialism. Since Piketty himself uses the term patrimonialism it is fair to ask if we cannot expand that topic and look into it more theoretically. Weber used that term, which is not widely

---

50   Stephen Crook, "Introduction." in Adorno, Theodore, *The Stars Down to Earth, and Other Essays on the Irrational in Culture.* (Ed.) Stephen Crook. (London and New York: Routledge/Taylor & Francis, 2015 [1994]), pp. 1–45.

51   Richard P. Feynman, *The Pleasure of Finding Things Out* (Cambridge: Helix Books, Perseus Publishing, 1999).

52   Daron Acemoglu and James A. Robinson. "The Rise and Decline of General Laws of Capitalism." *NBER Working Paper* 20766, (December, 2014).

53   Leo Damrosch, *Tocqueville's Discovery of America.* (New York: Farrar, Straus and Giroux, 2010). Tocqueville speculated on the future. He presents possible dangers that attend democracy, including the possibility of a tyrannical form of government. He had insights into the ways in which democratization could be linked to totalitarianism. He was among the first to think about the problem of relative deprivation, also called the Tocqueville Effect. Today a family income of US$45,000 a year is very high on a world scale but not regarded as sufficient by many U.S. citizens. Extreme inequality can lead to dis-satisfaction.

used in American English or even British English today. It may be because of
his French background that Piketty felt comfortable using the term, although
here the idea of "*neo*-patrimoniaism" has been emphasized when discussing the one hundredth (0.01%) and the one, one hundredth of one percent
(0.001%) as the true "baronial" global capitalist elite.

The situation in the U.S. and in the world generally has been radically
altered as a result of the U.S. presidential election. The Electoral College
system created a situation where the majority of votes cast for president gave
way to a system of electors. That system was designed long ago to ensure that
full-fledged democratization would not get out of hand. The eighteenth and
early nineteenth century electors were always wealthy white men with very
high status who could be relied upon to select a President from the capitalist
elite. But in recent decades the Electoral College system has worked in a
different way. Now the smaller populations in relatively less urban areas with
more scattered populations have a greater overall influence on the outcome
than the densely packed metropolitan and big city parts of the country. Since
each state, large or small, has two Senators the electoral system reflects the
original compromise that small states like Rhode Island and Connecticut
insisted on against larger states like New York, Pennsylvania, Massachusetts
and Virginia. After the Civil War the Republican Party was able to largely shape
many aspects of the political geography, for example creating two states, North
Dakota and South Dakota, where conceivably there could have been only one
state, perhaps simply called Dakota. Today the so-called fly-over states have an
influence on the outcome of a nation election that is not entirely proportional
to their size or economic importance. But in every state there is an elite group,
a neo-patrimonial social class that to a certain degree controls many aspects of
the situation when it comes to the precise way in which political decisions are
made. It is not just a matter of an elite in Washington, D.C. or New York City.
There are many billionaire families who not only have economic wealth but also
significant political influence. The study of the political economy of the U.S.
continues to be of vital concern. Utilizing insights from Marx, Weber, Adorno,
Horkheimer, and many other thinkers we could consider to be contributors to
what might loosely be called the Frankfurt School will be beneficial for better
theoretical understanding and praxis. However, what many Marxists, Neo-
Marxists Marxians, Neo-Marxians and even Weberians have tended to neglect
is Weber's extremely valuable theories concerning Patriarchy, Patrimonial
prebendalism and Patrimonial feudalism. That is an area of inquiry that will
be relevant for the study of the U.S. and all countries around the world where
neo-patrimonial structures still exist. Weber's Ideal Type Model is also directly
relevant to the study of terrorist organizations like ISIS/ISIL and nation-states

like North Korea, Iran and Saudi Arabia that still aspire to what could be called an essentially Patrimonial prebendal form of governance.[54]

What this discussion has not done is to apply aspects of this analysis more broadly to a whole range of issues that need to be developed. However, perhaps the book as a whole will resolve many of the problems that need to be considered. What is needed today is greater recognition of the heuristic value of the Ideal Type Models of Patrimonial prebendalism and Patrimonial feudalism. While Piketty himself was not directly concerned with those models he nevertheless opened a window on the concept of patrimonialism in general. His ideas about patrimonial capitalism bring out the element of elitism in contemporary global finance capitalism, especially as that plays itself out in modern nation-states. To full comprehend what neo-patrimonialism means in corporations and governments requires also including at least some awareness of neo-patrimonialism in the Global South. Piketty analyzed data from what is essentially a core part of the Global North. But in other parts of the world there are also neo-patrimonial social and cultural aspects of political economy. The world of the twenty-first century can only be fully comprehended in a thorough manner if we take a long view of historical social change and also go all the way back to the earliest aspects of patrimonial rulership and traditional societies. Inequality did not start with modern capitalism in the sixteenth century. In the twentieth century fascism was neo-patrimonial. In the twenty-first century, there are still many echoes of pre-modern, traditional patrimonialism, both quasi-feudal ("baronial") and even quasi-prebendal ("Mandarin-like"). Moving to less inequality will involve keeping the whole sweep of world history in mind. That can only be done if we move beyond economics and even political economics to the kind of Comparative Historical Sociology characteristic of much of the best work of both Karl Marx and Max Weber.

---

54   See J. I. (Hans) Bakker "Weber's oscillation thesis: Patrimonial prebendalism and [patri-
      monial] feudalism." *Perspectives*, vol. 34 (1) 2012, and J. I. (Hans), Bakker, "Why is Weber's
      prebendalism ignored? Considering a post-ISIS caliphate." *Perspectives*, vol. 37 (1) 2015.

CHAPTER 7

The Missing Element in Piketty's Work

Roslyn Wallach Bologh

Introduction

Drawing on the classic works of Marx and Weber and the contemporary work of economist Michael Hudson, I identify the key missing element in Piketty's work on capital and the significance of that omission, particularly with respect to social and economic development. In his classic work on social stratification, "Class, Status and Party," Max Weber identifies the defining feature of inequality as that of power. For Weber, classes, status groups and parties must be understood as "phenomena of the distribution of power within a community."[1] For Karl Marx, capital entails power over a society's productive powers, the power over society's development, the development of social life and social relations. Marx identifies the defining feature of any society as its "relations of production." For Marx, social stratification and social class must be understood in terms of production.[2]

Much social science research on social stratification, often explicitly drawing on Weber's discussion of status along with class, tends to use the concept of 'socio-economic status:' a combination of status group stratification (related to social honor and life style due to education and occupation) and class stratification (based on income due to position in the market). Social science researchers may acknowledge power as an incidental consequence of socio-economic status, as in the power of the "upper class" to influence state politics and policies, or in the power to consume more and different goods and services. However, for these researchers neither relations of power nor relations of production are inherent in their conception of classes or inequality.

Essentially, the conceptualization of class for these researchers is one of *gradations* not *relations*. Unlike Marx and Weber who elaborate on the qualitative differences between classes—related to power and production—these social science researchers, including for the most part, Piketty, treat stratification

---

1   Max Weber, *From Max Weber.* Hans Gerth and C. Wright Mills (eds). (New York: Oxford University Press, 1946).

2   See Marx, *Grundrisse,* transl. Martin Nicolaus (New York: Random House 1973) where he addresses the connection between distribution, production and power.

in terms of quantitative differences: greater or lesser income, wealth or status. For these researchers, where one draws the line between socioeconomic groupings and how many groupings or strata into which one may divide a population derives from the researcher's interest: upper, middle, lower; top 1% or top 10%, or top 20%; etc., not something inherent in the relations of production.

Among such researchers, Piketty's work stands out because he uses historical data to show that the extreme form of inequality into which we are heading looks just like the extreme form of inequality that characterized the *patrimonial society* of the past—and that such inequality seems to be the rule rather than the exception (unlike what had been believed). In other words, he warns that the existing quantitative difference between classes is transforming the classes and the relations between them into a new (or return to an old) form of stratified society: *"patrimonial capitalism."* As Marx and Engels point out quantitative differences do become qualitative differences. Moreover, Piketty is aware of one qualitative difference between the classes—the difference between those wealthy enough to live off "unearned income" (a category recognized by the IRS) and those who live off "earned income." Unfortunately, he does not go far enough in his analysis of "unearned income."

The use of the term "patrimony" indicates the kind of difference that Piketty points to: the importance of inheritance. Through the inheritance of wealth (in this case capital instead of land ownership) a group is able to maintain its status (including especially its lifestyle) and its position—including its political power, the power that comes from money. Piketty identifies today a tendency that Weber had described as the tendency of stratification by economic class to become, under certain historical conditions, increasingly like stratification by status group. Piketty does not distinguish between status group and class nor does he elaborate on the significance of such a "patrimonial capitalism," but he does call it "terrifying."

Weber on Status Groups and Legal Privilege

Weber spells out the difference between economic classes and status groups. Economic classes are based primarily on location in a market—with ownership and non-ownership of property being decisive. Weber defines class as people having in common a specific causal component of their life chances (such as chances for a "good life" related to consumption, personal experiences, opportunities, living conditions, health and longevity) as far as these life chances are determined by their power in the market. "'Property' and 'lack of property' are, therefore, the basic categories of all class situations."[3] Because slaves could not sell their labor on the market, they did not constitute a class according to Weber.

Weber defines a status group in terms of a shared life style; a privileged status group requires education or social immersion as well as ownership of property or wealth, but mere wealth is not sufficient, and in some instances, members may not even own property or wealth. But because style of life is dependent on property or wealth, over the long run it becomes difficult to maintain membership without property (hence the term, déclassé). Essential to status group stratification are restrictions on 'social intercourse,' including confining marriage to the same status group—that is, social exclusion. In addition to life style (and the property to ensure it) and social exclusion, stratification by status also involves legally privileged monopolization of economic opportunities. Weber talks about 'pariah groups' as well as privileged and 'disprivileged' status groups. Weber distinguishes status groups from classes also in terms of the communal nature of the former. That is, status groups maintain a shared social identity that enables them to take social action (act cohesively or collectively) on their own behalf. Taking issue with Marxists, Weber claims that this is not the case with economic classes, except under certain conditions.

Where stratification by status group was replaced by economic class stratification, the consequences were revolutionary. The idea of "natural superiors" and "natural inferiors" grounded in sacred tradition, the idea of a "higher" or noble class of people ruling over the "lower orders," based on the traditional "noble" life style of the former gave way to new ideas of social and political equality. However, and this is important, Weber suggests that even in societies based on economic "class"—a market economy—and formally organized on the basis of political democracy and social "equality," status groups tend to emerge.

Critical to the continued existence of status groups is "legal privilege." Jim Crow laws after the Civil War would be a feature of status group stratification that continued within a society based on class stratification—position and power in the market. Weber asserts that "the road ... to legal privilege, positive or negative, is easily travelled as soon as a certain stratification of the social order has in fact been 'lived in' and has achieved a stability by virtue of the stabilization in the distribution of economic power."[4] For

---

3   Max Weber, *From Max Weber,* Hans Gerth and C. Wright Mills (eds.) (New York: Oxford University Press, 1946), p. 182.

4   Max Weber, *From Max Weber,* (eds.) Hans Gerth and C. Wright Mills (eds.). (New York: Oxford University Press, 1946), pp. 1, 188.

Weber, stabilization in the distribution of economic power is critical to status group stratification. New technological developments create a dynamic economy that tends to destabilize the distribution of economic power.[5] Technological developments destabilize economic power and status group stratification.

Piketty's concept of patrimonial capitalism presupposes legal privilege—the privilege to inherit great wealth which he discovers is accumulating at a faster rate than the rate of economic growth leaving less and less for those not born into the privileged class/status group and increasing the gap between them. That is why Piketty argues for the importance of changing the laws to create a global tax on wealth.

Piketty, Weber, and Marx on Growth and Development

Piketty declares that there are only two ways to prevent the severe inequality that leads to patrimonial capitalism: either through economic growth or through a global tax on wealth—redistribution. Piketty and Weber both see economic growth as the essential factor making possible social mobility and preventing the ossification of status group stratification. Instead of talking about growth in general, Weber, like Marx, specifies the critical factor as technological development. Marx's writings on capital emphasize the importance of ongoing technological development.

Marx, in the Communist Manifesto, notes that capitalism has produced wonders far exceeding all the great wonders of the ancient world—showing what social labor is capable of accomplishing. Marx stresses the need to keep developing our productive powers, the forces of production, not only or primarily to reduce economic inequality but to enable free socially self-conscious individual and social development.

Both Weber and Piketty warn that without ongoing technological development and rapid economic growth status group stratification will re-emerge. Because Picketty sees significant technological development and economic growth as unlikely, he recommends a global tax. Without such a tax, he warns, a type of status group stratification based on inherited wealth will inevitably re-emerge.

---

5   Max Weber, *From Max Weber*, Hans Gerth and C. Wright Mills (eds.). (New York: Oxford University Press, 1946), p. 194.

Wealth as Fortune, Wealth as Capital: Types of Economic Power

Piketty does not directly address the power of capitalists, other than as power to sway politicians. In other words, Piketty does not focus on *how* capitalists invest their capital, *how* it is that capital can increase faster than the rate of economic growth, nor *that* capitalists own big capital and hence have the power to determine how economic growth and development occur or do not occur. This is the missing dimension in Piketty's work. He does not examine the dynamics within capitalism—the relations of production and exchange. Instead, Piketty focuses on class in terms of distribution of the power to consume more (and more highly valued) goods and gain more wealth. He does not focus on class in terms of distribution of the *power to control production*—including growth and the technological development of forces of production.

Weber goes further in his analysis of class differences; he explains that owning and disposing of property "gives to the propertied a monopoly on the possibility of transferring property from the sphere of use as a "fortune" [enabling appropriation and consumption of goods and services] to the sphere of "capital goods"; that is, it gives to them the entrepreneurial function and all chances to share directly or indirectly in returns on capital."[6] Piketty tends to treat capital as a source of income, particularly of income that exceeds the amount spent on consumption (necessary and luxury goods and services). This excess income then increases the owner's capital; by investing a larger sum, the income from the increased capital also increases, creating an ever-growing amount of capital. The owner of capital keeps increasing his or her capital—becoming wealthier and wealthier. However, Piketty does not address the process by which new value is produced, creating economic growth. He does not explain the process by which wealth as fortune accumulates faster than the production of wealth in the form of tangible values—real economic growth. In Marx's terms, Piketty is describing an increase in exchange value (money) that is much greater than the increase in use values. Marx refers to the potential for this type of capital to become "fictitious capital." Piketty tends not to focus on different types of capital.

In discussing social stratification, Weber does distinguish among types of property ownership and types of capital. He writes, "'Property' and 'lack of property' are ... the basic categories of all class situations ... However, within these categories, class situations are further differentiated, on the one hand,

---

6 Max Weber, From Max Weber, Hans Gerth and C. Wright Mills (eds.) (New York: Oxford University Press, 1946), p. 182.

according to the kind of property that is usable for returns [*the kind of capital*] and, on the other hand, according to the *kind of services* that can be offered in the market" [italics added].[7] We are all well aware of the significance of the differences among kinds of services that are offered in the labor market (persons offering their services as hedge fund managers and persons offering their services as hairdressers, etc.) However, we are less aware of the significance of the differences among "the kinds of property that is usable for returns." "Ownership of domestic buildings; productive establishments; warehouses; stores; agriculturally usable land, large and small; ownership of mines; cattle; men (slaves); disposition over mobile instruments of production, or capital goods of all sorts, especially money or objects that can be exchanged for money easily and at any time ... all these distinctions differentiate the class situations of the propertied ... Accordingly, the propertied, for instance, may belong to the class of *rentiers* or to the class of entrepreneurs."[8]

For Weber, it is the rise of a class of entrepreneurs (for which the Protestant Ethic was hugely important according to Weber) particularly the ones he identifies as "captains of industry" that makes all the difference. Although Weber acknowledged his own economic situation as that of *rentier* (living off income from invested, inherited wealth), he also acknowledged that the landowning *rentiers* of Germany, the Junkers, were a political force responsible for holding back the potential of Germany, a political force whose interests were antithetical to the further development of Germany as a great power in the world.

Rentiers, Industrial Capitalists, and Conjunctural Crisis

The distinction between *rentiers* and entrepreneurs is critical to understanding what may be called the "conjunctural crisis" of our time. Piketty does not explore the profound significance for our lives today of this distinction. Because Piketty focuses exclusively on the distribution of wealth and income, he divides the world into strata based on having more or less wealth or income—a quantitative difference. For Piketty what makes the class of *rentiers* so important is that the "unearned income" (defined as such by our tax system) of *rentiers* accumulates more quickly than the growth of our economy,

---

7   Max Weber, *From Max Weber*, Hans Gerth and C. Wright Mills (eds.) (New York: Oxford University Press, 1946), p. 1.
8   Max Weber, *From Max Weber*, Hans Gerth and C. Wright Mills (eds.) (New York: Oxford University Press, 1946), p. 1.

meaning that they are receiving a bigger and bigger share of the economy's production or wealth.

However, the qualitative differences among owners based on different kinds of properties are not reducible to a quantitative difference in income. Marx and Marxists have focused on the qualitative difference between *owners and non-owners*, capitalists and wage workers, in terms of the power of the former and the disempowerment of the latter. However, the qualitative differences among owners of different kinds of property—different kinds of capital(ists)—and the significance of those qualitative differences in terms of power has not been made so abundantly clear. Marx does distinguish between types of capital. He identifies finance or bankers' or lenders' capital—a very old type of capital in human history—which he called "usury capital," money used to make more money by lending at high interest rates. The usurious lender appropriates anything and everything belonging to the debtor who cannot pay back the loan with interest—in the past that included not just the land and the cattle but the children and wives—debt slavery—as well as the labor power—debt peonage—belonging to the debtor. In Volume 3 of Capital, Marx discusses the rapaciousness of usury capital and also the creation of fictitious capital (associated today with Wall Street) under modern capitalism. The critical economist, Michael Hudson,[9] however, reminds us that for the most part Marx expected finance capital to finance and hence *serve* industrial production.

Just as the change that Piketty notices in wealth and income inequality suggests a return to a patrimonial type of society, the change that Michael Hudson analyzes with respect to the rise of *rentier* (or finance) capital suggests a conjunctural crisis that can return us to a new dark age and the kind of class struggle over credit and debt that Weber tells us predominated in earlier times. Weber recounts the history of class struggles, describing the different types that have existed at different times and places, and claims that with modern industrial capitalism, "it is not the *rentier*, the share-holder, and the banker who suffer the ill will of the worker, but almost exclusively the manufacturer and business executive who are direct opponents of workers in wage conflicts." He continues, "This is so in spite of the fact that it is precisely the cash boxes of the *rentiers*, the share holder, and the banker into which the more or less unearned gains flow, rather than into the pockets of the manufacturers or of the business executives" (Gerth and Mills, 186) Weber goes on to say that this state of affairs plays out in political parties, such as in the varieties of "patriarchal

---

9   Michael Hudson, *The Bubble and Beyond* (Dresden: ISLET, 2012).

socialism," possibly a reference to parties that focus on industrial capitalists or "big business" without focusing on financial capitalists: *rentiers*, share holders and bankers.

The fact that the *rentier*, the shareholder, and the banker tend not to suffer the ill will of the worker is a fact that engages us today. The occupiers of Occupy Wall Street did direct their ill will toward the *rentier* class. Political candidates and parties (such as Bernie Sanders and his Democratic Party campaign staff) were drawing from and directing such ill will towards Wall Street. However, it has been relatively unusual for socialists or organized labor to focus primarily on Wall Street—the *rentier* class of capitalists—rather than Corporate Main Street—the industrial capitalists, employers of wage labor.[10]

Consciousness and Conjunctural Crisis

The connection between the life chances of the working class and the actions of *rentiers* is particularly opaque. Weber explains that communal action on the part of an economic class requires "intellectual conditions," that is, "transparency of the connections between the causes and the consequences of the 'class situation.' ... It is only then that people may react against the class structure, not only through acts of an intermittent and irrational protest but in the form of rational associations." Without such transparency or intellectual conditions, "the contrast of life chances can be felt as an absolutely given fact to be accepted."[11]

The unexpected surge of support for Trump and Sanders in 2016 suggests that a large percentage of people in the U.S. do not feel that their life chances are an 'absolutely given fact to be accepted.' However, in terms of 'intellectual conditions' mainstream economists today are claiming that these life chances depend on economic growth that cannot be much increased—and hence those (diminished) life chances must be accepted as an absolutely given fact! Moreover, they argue that there is a need to reduce even further the life chances of the non-owning classes—specifically targeting "the elderly" who are being 'supported' by a relatively smaller population of younger workers. Others

---

10   See Hudson's in "Introduction" to *Killing the Host* (Petrolia: Counterpunch Books, 2015) where he talks about his own experience teaching at the New School, where the relationship between industrial capitalists and workers was the only important relationship from a critical perspective. In Michael Hudson, *Killing the Host,* (Dresden: ISLET, 2015).

11   Max Weber, *From Max Weber,* Hans Gerth and C. Wright Mills (eds.) (New York: Oxford University Press, 1946), p. 184.

may target other groups (immigrants, the unemployed, the homeless, the undereducated, or ethnic and racialized groups, impoverished single mothers, or the government) as reducing the economic pie available for a struggling 'middle class' or of a dominant status group such as white, Christian, native born workers. Such 'intellectual' analyses incite intra-class conflict—the kind of Malthusian politics that can lead to war, genocide and fascist outcomes. Whether from the conservative right or from the liberal left (with the latter focusing on taxing the wealthy), the intellectual analysis offered tends to frame the issue as a matter of dividing up a *limited and shrinking* economic pie—a matter of distribution.

We seem to have reached a historical period where relative economic 'stagnation' is not a temporary event—a result of crisis—but inherent in the nature of today's monopoly capitalism.[12] Economists are once again talking about the need for fiscal policies—government spending, especially on infrastructure—to improve the economy.[13] Such investment is essential. However, after considering the various possibilities, how much improvement do such economists expect? "Mr. Summers says better policies could add from a half to a full percentage point to growth. And he holds out hope that substantial investments in advanced technologies that have not yet shown large productivity benefits will eventually do so."[14] But even with the best of intentions, cautions Douglas

---

12   Eduardo Porter, "The Mirage of a Return to Manufacturing Greatness," NY Times: April 26, 2016.   http://www.nytimes.com/2016/04/27/business/economy/the-mirage-of-a-return -to-manufacturing-greatness.html?_r=0. Accessed December 18, 2016. Baran and Sweezy originally called attention to this phenomenon in their book, *Monopoly Capital* (New York: Monthly Review Press, 1968). Lawrence Summers is now also claiming that the historically low economic recovery from the 2008 financial crisis is not simply a matter of a slow recovery but a long term condition of stagnation that began before the crisis and was not obvious because of the previous economic bubble that made the economy appear to be growing—until the bubble burst—a situation that mainstream economists often claim can only be recognized after the fact or in hindsight.

13   Eduardo Porter, "Government Must Play a Role Again in Job Creation," NY Times: May 10, 2016.   http://www.nytimes.com/2016/05/11/business/economy/as-jobs-vanish-forgetting -what-government-is-for.html?rref=collection%2Fcolumn%2Feconomic-scene&action =click&contentCollection=business&region=stream&module=stream_unit&version=latest &contentPlacement=3&pgtype=collection. Accessed January 22, 2017.

14   Eduardo Porter, "A Growth Rate Weighed Down by Inaction," NY Times, May 17, 2016. http://www.nytimes.com/2016/05/18/business/economy/a-growth-rate-weighed-down -by-inaction.html?rref=collection%2Fcolumn%2Feconomic-scene&action=click &contentCollection=business&region=stream&module=stream_unit&version=latest &contentPlacement=2&pgtype=collection. Accessed January 22, 2017.

W. Elmendorf, a former Congressional Budget Office chief who is now dean of the Kennedy School of Government at Harvard, 'we are not going to get back to 3 percent with anything we know how to do now.'"[15] That is a frightening assessment. It also misses, as does Lawrence Summer in the quotation above, that corporations and the government have reduced investment in research and development to practically nothing compared to what it had been. Yet it is science and technology that has made possible the revolutionizing of production that Marx described. Investment in science and technology, research and development along with infrastructure development made possible the ongoing radical transformation of production and increase in productivity that had characterized capitalism. As Marx noted in his analysis of relative surplus value, competitive capitalism had an incentive to keep revolutionizing the means of production. However, monopoly capitalism does not have that incentive: monopolies confer *rentier* privilege on owners who have little or no incentive to revolutionize or invest in research and development—especially when there is more money to be made (and less risk) through finance.

Economists now predict economic stagnation (historically slow economic growth) for the 'foreseeable future.' This is a terrifying prospect. If our stagnating economy must, for the most part, simply be accepted and lived with as an absolute fact, as economists suggest, then we may expect more intra-class conflict—a kind of Hobbesian world of the working class—a war of each against all as everybody seeks "their share" at the expense of others. If, instead, class-consciousness or intellectual conditions of transparency of a critical type do develop then we may see more inter-class struggle. Hence, the conditions we confront are those of a conjunctural crisis, a confrontation with major repercussions. Moreover, this does not even include the global elements of the crisis—including potential global political-economic-conflagration.

Relations of Distribution, Relations of Production

The Great Recession of 2008 and the Big Bailout together with almost half a century of working class loss of (middle class) status, jobs and disposable income and rising debt and foreclosures (without any big bailout for

---

15   Eduardo Porter, "A Growth Rate Weighed Down by Inaction," NY Times, May 17, 2016. http://www.nytimes.com/2016/05/18/business/economy/a-growth-rate-weighed-down -by-inaction.html?rref=collection%2Fcolumn%2Feconomic-scene&action=click &contentCollection=business&region=stream&module=stream_unit&version=latest &contentPlacement=2&pgtype=collection. Accessed January 22, 2017.

homeowners) may be responsible for a more or less 'naked and transparent class situation' (and diminished life chances). In today's class situation, the relations between *rentier* or financial capitalists and the working class may be as significant as the relationship between industrial capitalists and the working class. Moreover, industrial capitalists are using corporate capital as finance capital at the expense of long-term investment that can produce economic and social growth and development.

Piketty treats class inequality as a world in which a few own great fortunes; those fortunes are getting larger, growing faster than the gross domestic product; and the gap between them and everybody else keeps widening. However, Piketty stays away from explaining the actions that are producing this phenomenon. He does not consider the qualitative differences within the capitalist class and the role of financial capitalists and the financialization of industrial capital. For Piketty the problem is one of distribution of wealth. For Hudson the problem is the power of financial capital and how it operates—its impact on production and on the working class, which I interpret broadly as the bottom 90% who work for a living. Marx addresses the question in *Grundrisse*[16] of whether the determining feature or starting point of analysis should be production or distribution. After an intensive and extensive examination of this question, he concludes that the starting point must be production.[17] This is very different from the perspective of social scientists who study social stratification in terms of distribution of income and wealth.

Marx spells out the dynamics of industrial capitalism, the role of wage labor in the production of value and surplus value, the ways that capitalists find for increasing profit and also increasing productive power and real use values in the world: increasing and revolutionizing the means/forces of production, developing the productive power of society through investing in science and technology, reducing turn over time (use of middlemen or wholesalers), requiring shift work, globalizing production, using and issuing credit. He also shows the inevitable crises that accompany capitalist production. Marx uses the term, 'periodic crises,' whereas economists use the term, 'business cycle'— naturalizing it and erasing the pain it causes and the people who suffer the pain. Crisis becomes important for Marx, for he feels that crisis makes transparent the connection that Weber described above and impels workers to take social action rather than just accepting their pain as an absolute given, reacting only as individuals trying to deal with their personal 'life fate.'

---

16   Karl Marx, *Grundrisse,* translated by Martin Nicolaus (New York: Random House, 1973).
17   See, Roslyn Wallach Bologh, *Dialectical Phenomenology, Marx's Method* (London: Routledge, 2010) for an extended analysis of Marx's *Grundrisse.*

Finance Capital: Fettering vs. Fostering Economic
Growth and Social Development

The commitment that drove Marx's analysis and critique of political economy
was not only the alleviation of working class immiseration. His commitment
was to revolutionizing society in the sense of moving society and social life
forward—a commitment to the further development of social life and human
beings. Marx asked how the mode of production under feudalism became rev-
olutionized so that a new mode of production—new relations of production,
a new form of social life: new political, economic and cultural forms—came
about. He answered the question by noting that under feudalism the forces of
production that had been developed were being fettered—held back by the
feudal order. The fetters had to be "burst asunder" in order to free the forces of
production to be utilized and further developed, and in so doing revolutionize
society.

The crises of capitalism represent a 'fettering' of today's forces of production. With crisis, productive powers of society do not get utilized and some
even get destroyed at the same time that increasing numbers of people are
unable to find work. They experience privation or deprivation with respect
to their life conditions (recognizing also that 'need' is always historical and
cultural as well as biological) creating desperation and mental and physical
deterioration, including a rise in suicide rates as Durkheim was one of the first
to note. This contradiction between the appearance and experience of scarcity in the context of real power to produce plenitude will give impetus, Marx
anticipated, to the revolutionizing of society so as to realize that potential and
to usher in new social relations, new relations of production—bursting the
fetters that hold back the productive powers of social labor. Marx asserts that
historically class conflict ends either with the revolutionizing of society (revolutionizing the relations of production) or the common ruin of both classes
and the rise of a new dark age.

Hudson's work describes the nature of the new Dark Age to which today's
relations of production are leading. He explains that today's crisis may be understood not only in relation to already developed forces of production that
are being fettered (as per the loads of cash that corporations are hoarding).
Hudson argues that the crisis must also be understood in relation to the uses
to which financial capital are being put: non-productive debt-leveraged speculation and the kind of credit creation—which is also debt creation—which
results in asset price inflation or speculative bubbles followed by bursting of
the bubble and financial crisis. This kind of crisis results in debt deflation—a
downward spiraling of the economy—as paying down debt and interest diverts

money from consumption on the part of individuals and from expanding production on the part of corporations. With reduced consumer, demand (due to loss of discretionary income and increased debt) comes reduced production (stagnation), which means fewer business and job opportunities, rise in unemployment, and increased competition for jobs resulting in lower wages. With reduced production and reduced income on the part of taxpayers, not just individuals but nation states and cities end up unable to pay their interest laden debts resulting in demands by creditors for austerity and selling of public goods to private companies—raising the value of the companies and hence the price of their stocks and providing new sources of profit in the form of "rent" from charging high fees for "public goods"—both of which enrich the *rentier* class while further impoverishing nation states, cities and working class consumers.

The creation of a new social and economic order for Marx was premised on revolutionizing the relations of production. This meant a new society in which the social, economic, political and legal orders all served the same end. For Marx revolutionizing the relations of production would mean socially organizing production towards the end of ongoing economic, social and individual growth and development. This would require organizing society around a social commitment to the ongoing development of the forces of production, ongoing development of technology (with corresponding changes in social life) and the ongoing development of human beings—human beings who are free to engage in free conscious development. For Marx, the end is always human freedom to develop which requires a socially self-conscious mode of production grounded in a commitment to ongoing development—both social and individual.

Inequality, Finance Capital (*Rentiers*) and Relations of Production

Piketty treats inequality as a problem of distribution and not as a problem of production. He does not focus on production and how relations of production and exchange (including banks and credit, or debt-creation) are fettering rather than expanding and developing the productive forces. He focuses on the increase in economic inequality and foresees a 'terrifying' world in which status group stratification becomes prominent—as the legal order upholds the inheritance of 'unearned' wealth. Because that wealth increases faster than the society's rate of economic growth, workers will fall farther behind and remain in a particular status group whose life chances are diminished. They will be excluded by birth from a status group with its own life style, that engages in endogamous marriage and that monopolizes certain legal privileges—the privilege of inheriting wealth and 'investing' it for private gain, the privilege of being able to provide their children with the resources to excel in academics and attend elite universities which in turn allow them access to (and monopolization of) those economic opportunities with the greatest income potential—a situation that belies the foundational myth of the United States that it is a society based on social and political equality with ample social mobility and a growing middle class whose income and hence wealth keeps increasing while economic inequality decreases. Michael Hudson claims that "neither Piketty nor the Fed make an attempt to explain the dynamics causing the [extreme] polarization. They merely measure its broad parameters."[18]

For Hudson, the key analysis that is missing from Piketty's work is an analysis of the actions of finance capitalists—*rentiers*—and their *power* over the economy (the *relations of production*). Since the 1970s, and intensified by the 1990's repeal of the Glass Steagal Act, the role of finance capital has become apocalyptic in its increasing impact on society in general and on nation states and individuals in particular. I am referring to the economic relations between *rentiers* and the productive economy, a relationship that Hudson compares to a relationship between parasites and their host, a metaphor that comes from Marx in Volume 3 of Capital—in this case a relationship in which the parasites are "Killing the Host," the title of Hudson's recent book.

Rentiers are owners who live off unearned income from payments they can extract merely by the fact of their ownership. They may own land and extract ground rent; they may own monopolies and extract exorbitant prices; they may own public goods and extract high fees, and they may own "debt" or "collaterized debt obligations" and collect on that debt by extracting more labor and causing more impoverishment. They may enjoy unearned income (capital gains) from asset appreciation or asset price bubbles in stocks (where the stock market value of the company rises due to increased amount of money buying up shares rather than due to real value in terms of tangible assets and actual production) or in bonds or in real estate (or even in art). They may collect dividends from stock ownership; they may collect "interest" from debt ownership (credit cards, mortgages, student loans).

Banks' unearned income comes from debt—the more capital it has, the more it must lend and the more debt it must produce, that is, the more borrowing it must induce. When financial capitalists (banks) make credit

---

18   Michael Hudson, "Piketty vs. the Classical Economic Reformers," *Real-World Economics Review,* vol. 69, Oct. 2014, p. 122.

available—creating debt—for financing and thereby increasing (leveraging) investments in financial assets (rather than productive assets, infrastructure, research and development), it drives up the prices of those assets and causes speculative bubbles—asset price inflation. When the bubbles burst, we get a crisis of debt deflation or debt crisis: the deflation that occurs as money gets tied up paying back debt, rather than being used for the production and consumption of goods, leading to a downward spiral and what is currently being called economic stagnation.[19] This problem becomes magnified when, through the repeal of Glass Steagall, banks (including those that are federally insured by taxpayers—FDIC) are allowed to finance (create credit which is also debt) and leverage their own speculative, non-productive gambling and trading. With the bursting of speculative bubbles, huge financial institutions that the government deems 'too big to fail' are bailed out because it is believed that such failure would undermine the whole economy that is based on financial transactions involving those institutions and because of the intimate relationship between the financial capitalists and the government. With the bursting of speculative bubbles, huge financial institutions that the government deems 'too big to fail' are bailed out because it is believed that such failure would undermine the whole economy that is based on financial transactions involving those institutions. Where does the money come from that governments use to bail out banks?

As indicated earlier, rentier (ir) rationality now pervades not just Wall Street but the industrial/entrepreneurial/corporate sector. The invasion of this socially irrational but privately 'rational' action—(alienated rationality—action that increases the monetary wealth of individual financiers but diminishes the social and productive wealth of society)—has taken the form of leveraged buyouts from outside, and from inside it takes the form of buybacks of company shares (or investing in hedge funds or in 'financing' consumer purchases by charging high rates of interest) rather than investing corporate funds for long term growth and development that has tangible social benefits. As rentier (ir) rationality pervades economic relations, income (interest and fees) from debt (or credit creation)—not production—becomes the most decisive feature of the economy—debt that strangles the economy and produces austerity and stagnation rather than growth and development. Debt that cannot be paid back either must be re-structured or "forgiven" or result at the individual level in debt peonage (debt from student loans, debt from credit cards, debt from

---

19   See Michael Hudson, "The Bubble Economy: From Asset-Price Inflation to Debt Defla-
        tion," in *Killing the Host, How Financial Parasites and Debt Destroy the Global Economy*
        (Dresden: ISLET, 2015), pp. 157–171.

bank mortgages, debt from payday lenders) resulting in changed life chances and a changed "life style:" adults living with their parents, not marrying, not having children or becoming single parents, taking drugs, selling drugs, dying earlier[20] and committing suicide at rising rates. On the nation-state level debt that cannot be paid back leads to austerity and privatization (private, "for profit" ownership of public goods and provision of public services including running prisons for profit and even ambulance services)[21] with reduced services, increased fees—and more debt peonage.

Just as the intra-national political consequences of the fettering of production are compelling—witness the rise of Donald Trump and Bernie Sanders—the political consequences in terms of international relations are compelling as well: economic stagnation and creditor imposed austerity leading to unimaginable rates of *youth unemployment and migration* as well as increasing desperation of nation states leading to conflicts over *access to resources* needed for production and subsistence as well as resources such as waterways needed for transportation or distribution of goods (resources that become commodities to be bought and sold in the market or appropriated militarily). Economic stagnation and debt crises also lead to demands for privatized takeovers of a nation's public goods and resources often by foreign creditors, demands that are upheld by legal institutions that are external to the particular nation state. All of these consequences spell trouble for international relations.

Conclusion

To conclude, Piketty's book calls attention to the extreme inequality that is developing within the advanced industrialized nations today. He calls attention to the nature of this extreme inequality by identifying it as patrimonial capitalism—the increasing concentration of capital in the hands of *rentiers*

---

20   Recent studies have shown increases in the mortality rate within the white working class in the U.S. Within the U.S. the level of economic inequality within a state had a significant effect on women's life spans ("New Clues in the Mystery of Lagging Life Expectancy for American Women," NY Times, August 23, 2016). The rise in mortality rates mostly affects working class whites http://www.nytimes.com/2016/06/01/health/american-death-rate-rises-for-first-time-in-a-decade.html?

21   See Danielle Ivory, Ben Protess, and Kitty Bennet, "When You Dial 911 and Wall Street Answers," NY Times, June 25, 2016. http://www.nytimes.com/2016/06/26/business/dealbook/when-you-dial-911-and-wall-street-answers.html?

who inherit their wealth and live off the unearned income from that wealth. He sees this as a problem of distribution and recognizes that relations of distribution are upheld by the legal order, and hence laws must be enacted—a global tax on wealth—that protect against extreme, fixed inequality in the distribution of wealth through inheritance—patrimonial capitalism. But Piketty does not explore the specific dynamics of what Marx calls relations of *production and exchange* (finance). Piketty treats capital as a self-expanding 'thing' that is owned and inherited or distributed, and not as a set of *social relations entailed in production and exchange*, a set of social relations and actions that are restraining production, restraining social and human development, and threatening the world with a new dark age of debt deflation—with its dire and dangerous social and political implications.

With socially self-conscious investment, we would invest a part of our total social "capital" or surplus in research and development. We would do this based on self-consciousness of ourselves as essentially social beings, shaped by a social world that we (re)produce. Instead of the condition of being alienated from ourselves as social producers of our world, a world that determines our life chances, we would self-consciously shape the social world that shapes our being, our life fate, our life chances. This would mean organizing our production self-consciously—self-consciously organizing the economy that determines our life chances. The aim would be to continually revolutionize our socially developed and produced forces of production to contribute to our ongoing social and human development. For Marx, self-consciously developing and shaping the forces that shape our lives means freedom—the freedom to realize our potential as creative social beings—that is, self-realization and self-potency—the freedom to realize our potential as social beings endowed with the capacity for social self-conscious activity, the capacity to reflect on and shape the social world that we (re)produce.

Instead of socially self-conscious relations of production aimed at social and individual development (unalienated life activity, self-realization through self-consciously contributing to the ongoing development of our social world including especially the forces of production), we have a world in which social and human development is being 'fettered' along with the forces of production. This 'fettering' takes the form of economic slowdown or *stagnation* (with attendant unemployment, underemployment, non-employment, and low wages); *austerity* (governments cutting spending for public services and public goods including infrastructure); *privatization* (governments selling off public goods so that creditors can now gain income from charging high fees for those public goods) and *crises:* financial crises, 'business cycle' crises, and the crisis of stagnation itself. The fettering of the economy and deterioration of economic opportunities along with alienated labor leads to personal deterioration (where one's life seems to lack value, purpose and meaning) and deterioration of social relations (self-destructive competition between individuals; ambition and greed that leads to the dehumanization of others and self-protective attitudes and behaviors that result in indifference and hostility to others)—as well as political deterioration including the rise of politically reactionary social groups and terrorism.

As Weber informs us, an intellectual analysis, such as Hudson's analysis of finance capital today, makes possible transparency that can lead to 'rational associations' rather than 'intermittent and irrational protests' or acceptance 'as an absolutely given fact' of the worsening 'contrast in life chances,' about which both Marxists and Piketty have been sounding the alarm.

CHAPTER 8

Critical Theory, Radical Reform, and Planetary Sociology: Between Impossibility and Inevitability

Harry F. Dahms

Introduction

The early twenty-first century is a time when many assumptions that used to inform the outlook of individuals, members of social groups, citizens, activists, scholars and researchers, and decision-makers at all levels of organizations and institutions, are requiring rather rapid and even radical reassessments and adjustments, in an equally rapidly changing societal context. Politics, culture, society, and especially the economy, are changing at a speed and according to patterns that are difficult to follow and discern, as are changes in constellations between these dimensions of life in global civilization.[1] For many people, in societies that began to undergo modernization processes more than two centuries ago, and in societies in which those processes set in or were imposed much later, it is difficult to grasp just how much the world under the aegis of globalization is in flux, and how many and how much prevailing assumptions are being invalidated and revalidated in different forms ever more quickly.[2] Moreover, changes are observable both as a direct consequence of globalization, in terms of globalization, as well as in reaction to globalization, especially the strengthening of right-wing movements and politics, in modern western societies and elsewhere, that many had assumed were a phenomenon of the past. For a growing segment of populations in modern societies that have been especially stable for decades, if not longer—such as the United States, the United Kingdom, France, Germany, Austria—the pace and extent of change appears to be reaching a critical mass that exceeds tolerable levels and the capacity and willingness to cope with experiences of cognitive dissonance, especially on the issue of migration and immigration, and the conspicuous

---

1 Hartmut Rosa and William E, Scheuerman (eds.), *High-Speed Society: Social Acceleration, Power, and Modernity* (University Park: Pennsylvania State University Press, 2009).

2 To be sure, this pattern does not prevail everywhere equally, nor is it consistent or readily discernible. See Tony Smith, *Globalisation: A Systematic Marxist Account* (Chicago: Haymarket, 2009).

inability of governments to meet proliferating challenges. Peculiarly, in societies that used to be at the forefront of social, political, cultural and economic progress, with regard to social justice, civil and political liberties, equality of opportunity, and similar markers of rights, entitlements, recognition, and success, more and more people are willing to react strongly, if not violently to what they see as forms of disenfranchisement in favor of "others", especially immigrants, or those who traditionally were in structurally inferior positions or who had to conceal their identities and life choices, such as women, members of minorities, or individuals who do not adhere to traditional conceptions of gender and sex differences.

This also appears to be a time when the kind of perspectives that would provide a basis for confronting mounting challenges, particularly in the area of public policy and in ways that are constructive and consistent with stated standards and objectives, are increasingly difficult to sustain and advocate. It is becoming apparent that there is an absence of positions and practices which would translate into confronting effectively those challenges in ways that are consonant with their nature, respectively. With each crisis and set-back, it would appear, the inability or refusal on the part of different, often conflicting types of actors and decision-makers to anticipate unintended and unexpected consequences resulting from the established constellations of business, labor and government, as well as from efforts to better the latter, is becoming more glaringly apparent, with the resolve to face facts more directly, weakening further.[3]

In this context, the kind of perspectives that have been advocated and developed in the tradition of critical theory since the 1930s, along with a notion of radical reform that would foster the conception of practical alternatives to the well-established and counterproductive opposition between systems-stabilizing reforms and radical revolutions, and an understanding of planetary sociology as a discipline charged with illuminating global rather than national society, are urgently needed. Yet, during the post-war era, and especially since the 1980s, critical theory has become more concerned with efforts to reconcile with mainstream and liberal traditions of philosophy, social and sociological theory, than with scrutinizing the inner workings of modern society.[4] Furthermore, whereas the concept of radical reform has been suggested more

3   See Harry F. Dahms, *The Vitality of Critical Theory* (Bingley: Emerald, 2011), pp. 157–222

4   See Michael J. Thompson, *The Domestication of Critical Theory* (Lanham: Rowman & Little-field, 2016); Harry F. Dahms, "Modernity," in G. Honor Fagan and Ronaldo Munck (eds.), *Globalization and Security. An Encyclopaedia*, vol. 2 (Santa Barbara: Praeger Security International, 2009), pp. 303–20.

or less implicitly as early as the 1920s—e.g., by the "reform economists" at the New School, including especially sociologist Eduard Heimann[5]—and formulated explicitly decades later—e.g., by André Gorz[6]—social and political theorists and practitioners concerned with the slow pace of social progress and rapidly rising economic inequality in recent decades tend to continue to adhere to "reform vs. revolution" to too great an extent, or have abandoned the distinction entirely, along with the willingness to concede that radical reform may be a more promising option. Finally, as it is becoming ever more apparent that human civilization on Earth resembles a closed—and, for instance, as far as natural resources and food stuffs are concerned, probably a shrinking—system, rather than the open and expanding system suggested by positive conceptions of globalization, sociology as the social science of modern society is called upon even more strongly, to include in its analyses the level of planetary society—as the penultimate reference frame envisioned implicitly in the classical frameworks developed by Marx, Durkheim and Weber.[7]

Ironically, however, the current age appears to be less and less conducive to maintaining a rigorous concept of critical theory that is concerned above all with the problematic nature of modern society;[8] to conceiving public policies and strategies for qualitative social transformations in terms of radical reform; and to actualizing the promise of sociology by developing theories and methods that comprise the planetary level of societal integration. In this sense, the early twenty-first century appears to be a time when it is exceedingly difficult, if not impossible, to inform our understanding of the circumstances and forces that shape our societies, political practices, and economic processes and forms of organization, and individual and social lives, through rigorous conceptualizations of critical theory, radical reform, and planetary sociology. On the other hand,

---

5   Claus-Dieter Krohn, *Intellectuals in Exile. Refugee Scholars and the New School for Social Research*, trans. R. And R. Kimber (Amherst: University of Massachusetts Press, 1993); Eduard Heimann, *Soziale Theorie des Kapitalismus. Theorie der Sozialpolitik* [1929] (Frankfurt: Suhrkamp, 1980).

6   André Gorz, Strategy for Labor. A Radical Proposal (Boston: Beacon Press, 1967).

7   See Harry F. Dahms, *Modern Society as Artifice: Critical Theory and the Logic of Capital* (London/New York: Routledge, forthcoming).

8   See Harry F. Dahms, *The Vitality of Critical Theory* (Bingley: Emerald, 2011), pp. 249–303; "Critical Theory in the Twenty-First Century: The Logic of Capital between Classical Social Theory, the Early Frankfurt School Critique of Political Economy, and the Prospect of Artifice", in Daniel Krier and Mark Worrell (eds.), *The Social Ontology of Capitalism* (New York: Palgrave, forthcoming) and "Critical Theory as Radical Comparative-Historical Research," *The Palgrave Handbook of Critical Theory*, ed. by Michael J. Thompson (New York: Palgrave, forthcoming).

in the interest of the survival of modern society and the indubitable achievements it brought about and represents at the global scale—keeping in mind the multifarious costs they entailed and continue to involve—advancement of and reliance on those concepts and the practices they imply, should be nothing less than inevitable.

As modern society maintains itself in a manner that is intrinsically entwined with and inconceivable independently of the continuous process of capital accumulation within a system of structural social, political, legal and economic inequalities, any attempt to identify and assess the circumstances and forces that shape our lives and societies demands that we consider the importance of and diverse implications resulting from this process. Thomas Piketty's well-known work, *Capital in the Twenty-First Century*, is the most noticed effort to provide much-needed historical and empirical knowledge and information about this process in recent years.[9] In what follows, however, I will focus not on the intricacies of Piketty's analysis of "capital"—especially the link he identifies between the rate of return of capital (r) and the rate of economic growth (g), with economic inequality increasing wherever and whenever the former is greater than the latter ($r > g$)—but on reactions in society to perceptions of the intensifying shaping power of globalization, e.g., in the form of China's increasing weight and influence, and on prospects for practical strategies to diminish the increase in inequality, or at least its rate of growth, especially in the form of a global tax on profits. How did Piketty frame the link, under conditions of globalization, between reactions to growing economic inequality on the part of more and more people around the world, and the heightening need to tackle inequality by means of public policies, in ways that would be consistent with the principles of democratic politics and society?

Piketty on Fantastic Fears, Partial Irrationality, and Utopian Ideals

In the third part of *Capital in the Twenty-First Century*, on "The Structure of Inequality," in the chapter on "Global Inequality of Wealth in the Twenty-First century," in the section on "International Divergence, Oligarchic Divergence,"

---

9   Thomas Piketty, *Capital in the Twenty-First Century*, trans. Arthur Goldhammer (Cambridge: The Belknap Press of Harvard University Press, 2014). For my earlier treatments of Piketty's work, see "Toward a Critical Theory of Capital in the 21st Century: Thomas Piketty between Adam Smith and the Prospect of Apocalypse," *Critical Sociology* 41 (2) 2015: 359–74, and "Which Capital, Which Marx? Basic Income between Mainstream Economics, Critical Theory, and the Logic of Capital," *Basic Income Studies* 10 (1) 2015: 115–140.

Thomas Piketty addresses one source of proliferating concerns about globalization and how it purportedly divests control, in myriad ways, from democratic citizens presumably having been accustomed to being in charge of their own affairs and countries. In this particular instance, Piketty contends that fears of the perceived "threat of international divergence owing to a gradual acquisition of the rich countries by China" are more likely to be the result of oligarchic divergence, i.e., "a process in which the rich countries would come to be owned by their own billionaires or, more generally, in which all countries, including China and the petroleum exporters, would come to be owned more and more by the planet's billionaires and multimillionaires"[10]—a process that has been underway for some time. With global growth slowing and competition for capital heating up at the international level, it is highly likely that the rate of return on capital (r) from here on out will far exceed the rate of economic growth (g). With the size of initial endowments expanding, r will increase as well, especially with global financial markets becoming more and more complex, so that the preconditions are fulfilled for the gulf between the top 1% and 0.1% of the global distribution of wealth, and the rest, to widen further and further. Still, it is impossible to predict the speed of this oligarchic divergence, though it seems to be clear that the related risk is much greater "than the risk of international divergence",[11] so much so that

> the currently prevalent fears of growing Chinese ownership are a pure fantasy. The wealthy countries are in fact much wealthier than they sometimes think. The total real estate and financial assets net of debt owned by European households today amount to some 70 trillion euros. By comparison, the total assets of the various Chinese sovereign wealth funds plus the reserves of the Bank of China, represent around 3 trillion euros, or less than one-twentieth the former amount. The rich countries are not about to be taken over by the poor countries, which would have to get much richer to do anything of the kind, and that will take many more decades.[12]

Piketty goes on to ask, "[w]hat, then, is the source of this fear, this feeling of dispossession, which is partly irrational?"[13] He first identifies the "universal

---

10   Thomas Piketty, *Capital in the Twenty-First Century*, trans. Arthur Goldhammer (Cambridge: The Belknap Press of Harvard University Press, 2014), p. 463.

11   Thomas Piketty, *Capital in the Twenty-First Century*, trans. Arthur Goldhammer (Cambridge: The Belknap Press of Harvard University Press, 2014)

12   Thomas Piketty, *Capital in the Twenty-First Century*, trans. Arthur Goldhammer (Cambridge: The Belknap Press of Harvard University Press, 2014)

13   Thomas Piketty, *Capital in the Twenty-First Century*, trans. Arthur Goldhammer (Cambridge: The Belknap Press of Harvard University Press, 2014), p. 464.

tendency to look elsewhere for the source of domestic difficulties" as partial source of the feeling of dispossession, whose primary cause is "the fact that wealth is very highly concentrated in the rich countries (so that for much of the population, capital is an abstraction) and the processes of the political secession of the largest fortunes is already well underway."[14] The notion alluded to earlier, that China owns only one-twentieth of European households is difficult to imagine for people in wealthy countries, especially since the wealth of European households is privately held and impossible to mobilize for public purposes by governments. Piketty observes that this wealth nevertheless is real and could be tapped if the EU governments were to decide to do so:

> But the fact is that it is very difficult for any single government to regulate or tax capital and the income it generates. The main reason for the feeling of dispossession that grips the rich countries today is this loss of democratic sovereignty. This is especially true in Europe, whose territory is carved up into small states in competition with each other for capital, which aggravates the whole process. The very substantial increase in gross foreign asset positions (...) is also part of this process, and contributes to the sense of helplessness.[15]

To begin to tackle this situation and the corresponding feelings of dispossession and helplessness, Piketty suggests the establishment of a global tax on capital as a means to overcome related "contradictions."[16] Yet, he cautions that oligarchic divergence is both more likely than international divergence and a far greater challenge to prevent or alleviate, as doing so would require much more international coordination between and across countries that usually are in the habit of competing with each other: "the secession of wealth tends ... to obscure the very idea of nationality, since the wealthiest individuals can to some extent take their money and change their nationality, cutting all ties to their original community. Only a coordinated response at a relatively broad regional level can overcome this difficulty."[17]

---

14   Thomas Piketty, *Capital in the Twenty-First Century*, trans. Arthur Goldhammer (Cambridge: The Belknap Press of Harvard University Press, 2014)

15   Thomas Piketty, *Capital in the Twenty-First Century*, trans. Arthur Goldhammer (Cambridge: The Belknap Press of Harvard University Press, 2014)

16   Should a global tax be impossible, Piketty identifies a European tax as a good start. In the next part of the book, he discusses 21st century versions of a social state, progressive income tax, and a global tax in detail.

17   Thomas Piketty, *Capital in the Twenty-First Century*, trans. Arthur Goldhammer (Cambridge: The Belknap Press of Harvard University Press, 2014), pp. 464–65.

In the fourth part of his book, "Regulating Capital in the Twenty-First Century," Piketty turns to possible remedies for the problem of increasing inequality. In the chapter on "A Social State for the Twenty-First Century," he sets out "to draw lessons for the future."[18] To begin with, World War I and II had destroyed the past and structurally transformed inequality, but in the current decade, levels of wealth inequality are beginning to exceed the highest levels that had been reached previously:

> The new global economy has brought with it both immense hopes (such as the eradication of poverty) and equally immense inequities (some individuals are now as wealthy as entire countries). Can we imagine a twenty-first century in which capitalism will be transcended in a more peaceful and more lasting way, or must we simply await the next crisis or the next war (this time truly global?). ... [C]an we imagine political institutions that might regulate today's global patrimonial capitalism justly as well as efficiently?[19]

As far as Piketty is concerned, "the ideal policy for avoiding an endless inegalitarian spiral and regaining control over the dynamics of accumulation would be a progressive global tax on capital ... [which] would expose wealth to democratic scrutiny."[20] Without such scrutiny, it would be impossible to effectively regulate banks and flows of international capital. Unlike strategies to retreat into national identities or the like, such a tax would favor the general interest rather than private interests, and preserve economic openness and competition. "But a truly global tax on capital is no doubt a utopian ideal."[21] Thus, we are left with the question of what role government should play in the process of producing and distributing wealth in the current century, and what shape the social state should take.[22]

Though Piketty evidently is reluctant to be optimistic, he contends that Keynesian fiscal instruments should continue to provide the reference frame

---

18   Thomas Piketty, *Capital in the Twenty-First Century*, trans. Arthur Goldhammer (Cambridge: The Belknap Press of Harvard University Press, 2014), p. 471.

19   Thomas Piketty, *Capital in the Twenty-First Century*, trans. Arthur Goldhammer (Cambridge: The Belknap Press of Harvard University Press, 2014)

20   Thomas Piketty, *Capital in the Twenty-First Century*, trans. Arthur Goldhammer (Cambridge: The Belknap Press of Harvard University Press, 2014)

21   Thomas Piketty, *Capital in the Twenty-First Century*, trans. Arthur Goldhammer (Cambridge: The Belknap Press of Harvard University Press, 2014).

22   Thomas Piketty, *Capital in the Twenty-First Century*, trans. Arthur Goldhammer (Cambridge: The Belknap Press of Harvard University Press, 2014), p. 471–72.

for identifying means to remedy the problem of expanding economic inequality, assuming that it will be possible to apply the political will—an objective that will not be easy to attain. However, as a professional economist with the evident ability to phase into and out of sociological concerns and questions, Piketty does not address explicitly, and may not be in a position to consider fully, the degree to and manner in which the conditions that were conducive to Keynesianism during the decades following World War II may, or in fact do, no longer prevail. As the demise of what I will refer to as the "seventy-year peace"—the period of time since 1945 that saw first the expansion and then the contraction of social welfare states, the qualitative and then merely quantitative solidification of democracy, and the absence of open military conflicts either between European countries, or between European countries and other democratic countries or their World War II antagonists (the US, UK, USSR, and Canada)—seems to be increasingly imminent, many of the precepts that appeared to provide a reliable basis for public policies and international relations, until the end of the twentieth century, are in danger of becoming outdated and superseded by new developments, more or less rapidly, generating an increasingly aggravated condition of uncertainty in the process.[23] In part, the latter is the result, at any and all levels of social, political, and economic structure, institutions, and processes, of decades of neoliberal policies, ideology, and neglect, and their compounded consequences—of the logic of capital transposed to different forms and levels of social life.[24] From processes of individual identity formation to globalization, and mediated by myriad forms of consumerism, intensifying resource extraction, competition for scarce resources, and a persistent breakdown in social ties, forms of solidarity, and the capacity to engage in, adhere to, and maintain shared norms and values, beyond temporary states of excitement and anger, modern society as well as human civilization is undergoing a process of transformation that amounts to an entirely novel and unexpected reconfiguration between and across constellations of

---

23   Evidently, this is not to suggest that there have been no armed conflicts within Europe or between European nations, as in the former Yugoslavia, Northern Ireland, the Bask Country in Spain, the Falkland War between the UK and Argentina, and so forth. However, none of these conflicts pitted European nation-states against each other—an unprecedented historical achievement of tremendous proportions. However, the fact that this peace held for seventy years in no way is evidence for the prevailing pattern being reliable from here on out. See Harry F. Dahms, "Democracy," in G. Honor Fagan and Ronaldo Munck (eds.), *Globalization and Security. An Encyclopedia*, vol. 1 (Santa Barbara: Praeger Security International, 2009), pp, 42–60.

24   See Fred Block and Margaret R. Somers, *The Power of Market Fundamentalism* (Cambridge: Harvard University Press, 2014).

business, labor, government, political parties and ideologies, the populations that identify with and support and promote them, in ways that we are poorly positioned to grasp and track.

The Constitutional Logic of Modern Society between the Logic of Capital and the Persistence of Inequality

It would be a tall order to fully explain the economic and financial logic at work in modern capitalist societies with available conceptual tools in the mainstream social sciences, and even more so in everyday life, especially as far as growing economic inequality and the proliferation of fears and irrationalities relating to the forces that have been shaping social and individuals lives are concerned, and even more, to contain or channel the logic with existing political tools. Those fears and corresponding irrationalities, which have been amplifying at least since the beginning of globalization, may appear to be exaggerated in light of circumstances that are open to empirical examination, but they also may be expressive of sentiments that are more worrisome, as their roots and potential implications neither may be conceivable, nor accessible, within the established framework of modern capitalist societies. Indeed, discerning these sentiments might require a type of critical reflexivity with regard to the constitutional logic of modern society that the latter is prone to discouraging, and they could be an expression of the discrepancy between categories that purportedly enable us to make sense of the world today but which, in the face of ever more unsettling trends and developments, foster ever greater cognitive dissonance and consternation, as those categories describe how modern society supposedly is maintaining order and functioning, rather than how it actually does maintain order and function. Without digging far enough below the realm of surface appearances, it is not likely to be possible to reach the level at which causal explanations would have to be anchored, so as to translate into tangible insights capable of illuminating the contradictory de facto operations that sustain the different instances of modern societies, at the general level, and in their distinctive specificity, respectively. As concrete societal systems of order, processes and structures, modern societies tend to wrap symptoms that are indicative of the urgency of present conditions and trends, in a cocoon of rationalizations that ought to account for why things are the way they are, and why we should accept that they cannot be any other way.

Indeed, there are strong indications that feelings of disenfranchisement, experiences of fragmented rationality, and the futility of pursuing policies that should be perfectly viable strategies to tackle concrete problems rather than utopian ideals, may point towards features of modern societies that cannot be grasped adequately with categories and conceptual tools that are manifestations of the counterintuitive constitutional logic of modern society, of the pervasiveness of the logic of capital at all levels of social integration, and the shackles of structural inequalities, rather than means to critically scrutinize these features. Critical theorists have been rejecting the notion that it is sufficient to try to "explain" surface manifestations of social life with reference to other surface manifestations, e.g., frustration with immigration as directly the consequence of increased numbers of immigrants. Advocates of radical reform have been contesting the claim that the binary of reform vs. revolution provides a productive reference frame for developing strategies to tackle inequalities effectively, since both reformist and revolutionary approaches tend to disregard how individuals are constructed through and within systems of inequality. Reforms usually protect both the existing social structure and the range of identities constructed via and in the former. By contrast, revolutions endeavor to destroy, dismantle, disrupt or improve existing systems of inequalities, without acknowledging or addressing the fact that identities that formed in contexts fraught with inequalities are prone to function through some kind of system of inequalities, and thwart the construction of new social structures which would be more consonant with the validity claims about individual opportunity and freedom, and collective responsibility, in modern societies. A program of planetary sociology, finally, starts out from the acknowledgment that challenges such as global inequality rising, climate change accelerating, and resources being depleted, among others, must be confronted globally, on the basis of knowledge and theoretical frames which correspond with how modern societies actually work, as opposed to how we would prefer to suppose that they work.

Despite Piketty's willingness to break with prevailing conventions in economics as a social-science discipline, he evidently continues to work with assumptions that, presumably, facilitated political stability and economic growth during the postwar era, especially during and after the era of Keynesianism. Evidently, during the early decades of the "seventy-year peace", the exceedingly unusual circumstances of the Cold War era facilitated the expansion of social-welfare states in western Europe, North America, and elsewhere, and the adoption of different kinds of social legislation and public policies designed to stabilize post-World War II democratic societies and to protect them from the Soviet threat that would have been highly unlikely or outright impossible in any other context, with the present increasingly resembling the latter rather than the former. On the other hand, if the Great Depression would not have derailed intellectual, theoretical, political and policy developments that had emerged during the 1920s, World War II may not have happened, and instead, during the 1930s and 1940s, an entirely novel public policy paradigm might have taken hold to contain or channel the logic of capital in ways more consistent with social goals and standards, and which would have made the "achievements" of the 1950 and 1960s pale, by comparison. In any case, as a mainstream economist, the kind of concerns that drive Piketty's research do not pertain to the fact that in modern societies, the fabric of social life changes on an ongoing basis, reflecting at least in part macro-changes in political economy, in ways that are more likely to be inversely related to the perceptions of societal change on the part of individuals, social scientists, and decision-makers. Especially with regard to the ways in which societal change manifests itself in constellations of business, labor and government, of politics, culture, society and the economy, and in modes of interaction between individuals, organizations, institutions, and society, the categories employed to identify and "process" patterns of social change frequently have been developed in circumstances in which those patterns no longer applied, as they literally belonged to a by-gone era. To whatever extent the categories employed may have facilitated a measure of correspondence between perceptions of patterns that presumably were responsible for the nature and direction of changes, and the patterns that in fact were responsible for those changes, they inevitably are fraught with prevailing ideologies and the notions members of society need to subscribe to in order for society to maintain order and function, regardless of whether those notions are conducive to illuminating the nature and direction of social change or not.

Critical Theory and the Logic of Capital

In capitalist societies, it would be unrealistic to assume the absence of a close link between the dominant mode of economizing and social, political, and cultural forms and practices. Whereas economics as a discipline neither is concerned with related issues, nor in the position to analyze corresponding phenomena due to the absence of tools that would be required to do so, sociology as the social science of modern capitalist societies does have the tools, but as a discipline, lacks the mind-set to put to use those tools in a manner that would illuminate rigorously the links between the forces that shape social life and those that shape economic life. Moreover, as an established and professional discipline concerned with scientific standards and legitimacy within academia, beyond the social sciences, sociology lacks the special tools, the motivation, and the critical impetus to scrutinize the inner workings of the capitalist process, even in economic sociology. As disciplines, neither economics nor sociology are interested in illuminating the underlying forces that are constitutive to a large degree, both qualitatively and quantitatively, of social, political, cultural, institutional and organizational forms in modern society: the logic of capital.

Given this dilemma, which has burdened efforts to analyze and theorize modern society from its earliest beginnings, critical theory during the 1930s developed with the purpose of confronting the challenge of how to study modern society in ways that do not replicate the social, political, cultural and economic patterns prevalent in modern society and which the latter relies upon, but to dedicate the requisite energy and time to illuminating precisely those patterns. As I have put it elsewhere, especially in the works of Max Horkheimer, Critical Theory began as the project of illuminating the gravity concrete socio-historical circumstances exert on the process of illuminating this circumstances.[25] This gravity is a problem especially in modern society, as it relies on the willingness of researchers, and individuals generally, to subscribe to the spurious notion that under the sign of enlightenment, modern society is much more conducive to critical reflectivity with regard to its governing principles, than any other form of social organization.[26] In modern capitalist societies, moreover, such reflexivity is particularly important for illuminating the influence and shaping power the process of capital accumulation, and the corollary logic of capital, have been exerting on concrete forms of modern social, political and cultural life and the direction of their development.

While the critical theorists of the early Frankfurt School did not develop a 20th-century version of Marx's critique of political economy, their concern with the ongoing permutations of capitalism was sufficiently rigorous to track and examine the increasingly problematic cultural consequences of capitalism becoming ever more ingrained in society, and in this sense, their work was compatible with interest in the logic of capital. Yet, critical theory did not have a discernible impact in philosophy or the social sciences until, later in the century, leading representatives, such as Habermas and Honneth, abandoned any interest in the machinations of the logic of capital, and instead endeavored to make critical theory more compatible with traditional and mainstream approaches in the social sciences and humanities. Outside of this "mainstream" of critical theory, especially in Germany, however, social theorists and philosophers inspired by the early Frankfurt School began to try to reconfigure and

25   Harry F. Dahms, "Critical Theory as Radical Comparative-Historical Research," in Michael J. Thompson (ed.), *The Palgrave Handbook of Critical Theory* (New York: Palgrave, forthcoming).

26   John Ralston Saul, *The Unconscious Civilization* (New York: The Free Press, 1995).

apply Marx's critique of political economy for the purpose of illuminating the changed conditions in advanced capitalist societies, at a rather high level of theoretical sophistication.[27]

Radical Reform and the Persistence of Inequality

During the 1920s, before the social scientists and social theorists who later became known as associates of early Frankfurt School critical theory had to emigrate from Germany, they were convinced that intellectual, theoretical and research efforts had to be oriented toward the prospect and realization of the proletarian revolution. During the 1930s, the members of the Institute for Social Research, after its relocation to New York—especially Max Horkheimer, Herbert Marcuse, and Theodor W. Adorno—began to realize, more or less painfully, that the likelihood of a successful socialist revolution, with the proletariat as the "subject of history", was in precipitous decline.[28] Yet, rather than turning to reformism as the strategy of choice to promote or bring about qualitative social transformation in the name of social justice, equality, and real freedom, the critical theorists Horkheimer, Marcuse, Adorno and Leo Lowenthal abandoned the focus on practical political strategies to confront the threat to modernity, turning instead to the effort to deepen the theoretical understanding of the contradictions at the core of modern societies in such a manner that the conclusions reached would not be in danger of being a function of existing conditions, but transcend the latter in rigorous fashion.[29]

---

27   Moishe Postone, *Time, Labor, and Social Domination: A Reinterpretation of Marx's Critical Theory* (Cambridge: Cambridge University Press, 1993); Hans-Georg Backhaus, *Dialektik der Wertform: Untersuchingen zur marschen Ökonomiekritik*, 2nd ed. (Freiburg: Çaira, 2011); Helmut Reichelt, *Neue Marx-Lektüre: Zur Kritik sozialwissenschaftlicher Logik* (Freiburg: Ça ira, 2008); Robert Kurz, *Geld ohne Wert: Grundrisse zu einer Transformation der Kritik der politischen Ökonomie* (Berlin: Horlemann, 2012); Neil Larsen et al. (eds.), *Marxism and the Critique of Value* (Chicago: McM' Publishing, 2014); Anselm Jappe, "Kurz, a Journey into Capitalism's Heart of Darkness," *Historical Materialism* vol. 22, 3–4, pp. 395–407.

28   Helmut Dubiel, *Theory and Politics: Studies in the Development of Critical Theory* (Cambridge: MIT Press, 1985).

29   Max Horkheimer "Traditional and Critical Theory" [1937], in *Critical Theory: Selected Writings* (New York: The Seabury Press, 1972); Max Horkheimer and Theodor W. Adorno, *Dialectic of Enlightenment: Philosophical Fragments* (Stanford: Stanford University Press, 2002).

It appears that the circumstances in which we find ourselves today, as far as reconciling theory and praxis is concerned, are comparable to those Horkheimer, Marcuse, and Adorno confronted in the 1930s. The present does not appear to be a time when qualitative change is likely, or even possible, however much it may be needed. Rather, even consolidating gains made in recent decades along an array of economic, legal, and social-justice indicators looks rather difficult, beyond the politics of intersectionality and identity. Indeed, the well-established distinction between reform and revolution seems practically useless, in the sense that even reforms are too much of a challenge if they would permeate structures of inequality generally, and especially economic inequalities, and capitalist processes and forms of organization. Such reforms certainly are conceivable theoretically, but efforts to engender qualitative changes, or even to establish preconditions for the latter, do not appear to be promising, or even viable. The probability of revolutionary action in terms of stated goals, as opposed to myriad unintended consequences that would pervert related efforts, may be beyond linguistic expression, considering that Piketty describes a global tax on profits as "a utopian ideal."

Before it will be possible to conceive of and apply successfully strategies to slow or buffer continuing growth in economic inequality, it is necessary to first develop a concept of radical reform for the twenty-first century which reflects that economic policies must be interlinked with other types of public policies, at the planetary level. In order to develop such a concept, reconnecting with debates during the inter-war years in the German-speaking world, especially in Germany and Austria, and corresponding debates in countries with similar levels of political, economic and industrial development, before the rise of National Socialism and fascism, when the foundations of critical theory were laid and—in the aftermath of the revolutions in Russia, Germany, and Austria—new perspectives on mediating between capitalism were being formulated, especially on how to bridge or overcome the divide between capitalism and socialism, in the writings of such social scientists and theorists like Adolph Lowe, Eduard Heimann, Emil Lederer and others. It is imperative that we remember that and how the thread of thinking beyond "reform vs. revolution" was dropped during the age of totalitarianism, and that there have been few noteworthy efforts to pick it up again.[30]

---

30   Claus-Dieter Krohn, *Refugee Scholars and the New School for Social Research*, (Amherst: University of Massachusetts Press, 1993); *Eduard Heimann, Soziale Theorie des Kapitalismus. Theorie der Sozialpolitik* [1929] (Frankfurt: Suhrkamp, 1980) and André Gorz, *Strategy for Labor. A Radical Proposal.* (Boston: Beacon Press, 1967) regarding the concept. See

Planetary Sociology and the Constitutional
Logic of Modern Society

In the final analysis, the penultimate level of analysis sociology must include and tackle is planetary in nature. The kinds of political, economic, organizational and social challenges that have been proliferating under conditions of globalization for the most part are of a scale and scope that cannot be tackled at the national level. It is impossible to conceive of necessary strategies at levels that do not require coordination at lower levels of complexity across nations, as far as individual and group culpability, participation and responsibility are concerned, e. g., with regard to practices in terms of energy and resource use and depletion, and production of pollutants and waste that all have been intensifying rapidly and which are detrimental to all forms of life, including the biosphere as a whole. Moreover, globalization is a process fraught with ideology, both positively and negatively. For now, it is not possible to discern clearly how the globalization process will shape future developments on Earth at the societal level, and whether—in terms of a rigorous cost-benefit analysis— globalization increases or undercuts, possibly once and for all, the likelihood of qualitative progress according to clearly identifiable standards. The concept of "globalization" continues to be, above all, a framing devise for the purpose of formulating questions that can and must be addressed, but for which it is not possible to find definite answers. Indeed, it is equally conceivable that globalization will advance or thwart the ability of human beings, societies, and human civilization to engender modes of interaction, to construct institutions and forms of organization, and to establish constellations between business, labor, and government that are conducive to the attainment of collective objectives in terms of stated goals. Whether globalization will be a positive

---

also Philippe van Parijs (ed.) *Arguing for Basic Income: Ethical Foundations for a Radical Reform* (LMax Horkheimer "Traditional and Critical Theory" [1937], in *Critical Theory: Selected Writings* (New York: The Seabury Press, 1972); Max Horkheimer and Theodor W. Adorno, *Dialectic of Enlightenment: Philosophical Fragments* (Stanford: Stanford University Press, 2002).

31   Claus-Dieter Krohn, *Refugee Scholars and the New School for Social Research,* (Amherst: University of Massachusetts Press, 1993); Eduard Heimann, *Soziale Theorie des Kapitalismus. Theorie der Sozialpolitik* [1929] (Frankfurt.: Suhrkamp, 1980). André Gorz, *Strategy for Labor. A Radical Proposal* (Boston: Beacon Press, 1967); regarding the concept, see also Philippe van Parijs (ed.) *Arguing for Basic Income: Ethical Foundations for a Radical Reform* (London: Verso, 1992); Tariq Ramadan, *Radical Reform: Islamic Ethics and Liberation* (Oxford: Oxford University Press, 2008).

and constructive or a negative and destructive force indeed will depend on how stated goals relate to shared norms and values in societies and human civilization. Who defines the goals, how are they being defined, and is their attainment contingent on the application and maintenance of force, or realizable in a manner that is consistent with and conducive to the application and strengthening of democratic principles, without the latter aggravating further the gulf between the purported *modi operandi* of modern society and the ways in which modern society maintains order by further violating the standards according to which it is supposed to function?

Even though globalization is not an analytical category, it is an excellent means to anchor and focus analyses and diagnoses in the interest of illuminating current trends, dilemmas, tensions and contradictions. Moreover, sociology is the only discipline with the tools to track globalization and to discern, more or less systematically, the different types of changes that come with it. However, as a discipline, sociology does not work with the kind of reference frame, nor does it have the methodological, theoretical or substantive cohesiveness, that would be required to confront the vicissitudes of globalization in terms of the dichotomy between progress and regression, and costs and benefits, that would promote pointed determinations about whether and how and to what extent and in what ways globalization overall is a process that is beneficial to modern societies, or humanity, or the planet Earth with all of its inhabitants, or whether it is more destructive than productive, and conducive or not to sustainability.

Radical Transformation in the Vortex of Impossibility and Inevitability

It is a trope in papers of this kind to call for a different kind of mind-set, for a shift in thinking, a new type of perspective and intellectual discipline with regard to an established set of practices and problems. In light of the above, it ought to be apparent that the precepts regarding the links between critical theory, social science (especially economics and sociology), and praxis have been problematic for decades, and we still continue to work with assumptions about how to identify desirable objectives, how to confront a proliferating array of challenges, and how to attain stated goals. Meanwhile, the transformations and re-configurations at the macro-level of social, political, cultural and economic life continue to play out in ways that are not in discernible ways related to what we expect, would prefer to see happening, or are in the position to grasp on their terms, rather than ours. In fact, we appear to be engaged in language games that redefine the underlying logic of macro-processes so as to be consistent with our individual or collective self-understanding, as if these processes were a function of our goals, aspirations, intentions and notions. Yet, the modes of interpreting macro-processes that shape our existence are a strange combination of categories of our "desire" on the one hand—what we want, are supposed to want, think we are supposed to want, expect, are supposed to expect, think what we are supposed to expect—and on the other, a function of the processes themselves, expressing of a logic that is beyond rigorous scrutiny.

Piketty suggests that we should struggle for a global tax on profits, and for a social state in the twenty-first century, to contain capital's proclivity to generate ever-greater inequality. However, the virtual reality that we have all existed in for decades—with public policies a function of the imperative to maintain social order, in the face of accelerating socio-economic change, rather than the nature and direction of socio-economic change being a function of democratically arrived at public policies—has eroded the capacity of most individuals, organizations, and institutions to consider the possibility that problems merely have been managed, rather than acknowledged or tackled in terms that would be consistent with the nature of those problems, and the scope of related challenges. Inequality is not a problem that is ancillary to modern societies; rather, inequalities constitute part of the core of modern societies, even though—in the interest of protecting stability in modern societies—elected and unelected officials and decision-makers must insist that inequality is incongruous with the values, norms and principles according to which modern societies function and maintain order. However, as the classical social theorists knew, and as most sociologists, if pressed, would admit, when we refer to modern society, we are inferring the system of inequalities without which it could not exist.

Ergo, there is a profound gap between perceptions of modern society, and its actuality, between what is impossible and inevitable, in the sense that inequality is supposed to be incompatible with modern western capitalist democratic societies, even though—evidently—modern society would be inconceivable without the motivational infrastructure it is contingent on. This motivational infrastructure relies to a large degree on the fact of inequalities: they provide the scaffolding within which individual identities emerge and on which their integrity relies, both positively and negatively; and inequalities provide organizations and institutions with the hierarchical mode of organization in politics, culture, and society that facilitate selection processes designed to fill positions in the ever more important bureaucratic and managerial hierarchies in economy and government.

PART 2

Inequality

∴

CHAPTER 9

Beyond Piketty's Economism: History, Culture, and the Critique of Inequality[1]

Daniel Krier and Kevin S. Amidon

Introduction

Thomas Piketty's *Capital in the Twenty-First Century* (2014) was that rare social science book that reignited heated discussions of inequality within academia and, for a time, in popular media. The attention and praise received by *Capital in the Twenty-First Century* was well deserved. Piketty built on the work of dozens of sophisticated economists, and his book contains a wealth of empirical time-series data on comparative income distribution. This makes it an impressive resource for future scholarship and analysis. Nonetheless, the book remains impaired by its excessively narrow disciplinary focus within contemporary academic economics and its economism that emphasizes one-sided strictly economic causation while discounting complex historical, cultural and political forces. Piketty's work clearly strains to remain entirely economic while avoiding any whiff of the political. Most notably, the book shies from an engagement with Marx and Marxist interpretive traditions that have long sought a differentiated analysis of the institutional mechanisms and historical dynamics of capital. It therefore fails to connect with important strands of current critical theory that we highlight below.

Piketty appears—doubtless for good reason within academic economics— to be so committed to first-order empiricism within the economic realm that his book seems uninterested in, even dismissive of, interpretive political conclusions that incorporate history and culture. This is understandable across the European and American spheres, where central banks, technocratic policy institutions, think tanks, and academic work hew compulsively to a rhetoric of apolitical economic science. Unfortunately, *Capital in the Twenty-First*

1   The authors wish to thank David Fasenfest for permission to reproduce text previously published in *Critical Sociology* and Lauren Langman for the opportunity to rethink and update our views of Piketty's book. We also wish to thank Robert J. Antonio (University of Kansas, USA), Tony Smith (Iowa State University), and Mark P. Worrell for comments that significantly enriched this chapter.

Century thus becomes at once too much and too little: it sets up expectations in left-progressive readers familiar with Marx that it might in fact contribute to critical social theory by putting its data at the service of a causal-functional analysis of capital. Unfortunately it does not, for it does not interrogate capital per se. Rather, the book is a description of the historical relations between national income and the return on capital. It therefore provides less a causal explanation of the return on capital as it does an accounting of the income that accretes to the owners of capital. This distracts from the complex, layered, and dynamic nature of capital by flattening it into income, and income into wealth. Thus for all its strengths, Piketty's work constrains critical approaches to political economy, and serves further to evacuate the political from the sphere of the economic. Critical theorists have much work to do to turn Piketty's near-compulsive empiricism into work that can go beyond the narrow disciplinary confines of academic economics and reveal and develop understanding of the historical dynamics and political core of all economic policy.

Piketty's "Laws"

Reading Piketty's *Capital* carefully requires commitment. The work is a substantial, well-argued depiction of systemic wealth and income inequality in modern capitalism. Though the book is voluminous, at its heart is a large series of straightforward line graphs depicting long term patterns within an impressive array of data: centuries-long time series of national income and wealth statistics across several continents. The simplicity of the graphs is in keeping with the spare, even austere, mathematically reduced theses that are presented as *laws of capitalism*. In a world awash in complex, contingent and relativistic theories, Piketty's rather old-fashioned claim to the discovery of unvarying laws is unusual. It further helps to account for the public fascination with the book, especially among those who—despite Piketty's own studiously apolitical stance—represent left-progressive policy positions.

What are the "fundamental laws of capitalism" that Piketty claims to have discovered? Expressed in properly scientific Greek letters, the formula of the first such law is $\alpha = \tau \times \beta$: the share of national wealth that accrues to capital (α) is equal to the rate of return on capital (τ) times the ratio of capital to income (β). This law is a "pure accounting identity ... tautological ..." but Piketty argues that it is important since it places the "three most important concepts for analyzing the capitalist system" in relation to each other.[2] The second law is expressed $\beta = s / g$: the ratio of capital to income of a country (β) is equal to the savings rate (s) divided by the economic growth rate (g).[3] Though not expressed as a fundamental law (which serves to distance him from Marx), the formula from the book that expresses Piketty's central argument about inequality in capitalism most directly is $r > g$: the rate of return on capital (r) is greater than the economic growth rate (g). In short, capital accumulates. Piketty distills long-range figures for "the inequality r > g" (of 4–5 percent return on capital and about 1 percent long term growth) but the variation in time and place is considerable, so that r > g "should be analyzed as a historical reality dependent on a variety of mechanisms and not as an absolute logical necessity."[4] Though mathematically expressed, Piketty avoids complex statistical analysis to pictorially represent variations among income, wealth, growth, and rates of return in a variety of places and times. There is nothing complex about the math: Piketty's conclusions result from inferences not inferential statistics.

To us, the great strength of the book is Piketty's rigorous aggregation of national statistics from very diverse sources that make possible such powerful, large-scale time-series. This was an immense undertaking, and Piketty and his collaborators deserve the accolades they have received for making this laboriously constructed data set available on his website. Such strenuous aggregation of data into such straightforward representative schemas without shilly-shallying is unusual in the contemporary academy. Indeed, it is reminiscent of the 19th and early 20th century economic scholarship that Piketty frequently cites and openly admires, such as Willford King's (1915) *The Wealth and Income of the People of the United States.*[5]

At the same time, however, Piketty scrupulously avoids interpretive claims that might pigeonhole him as "left" or "radical"—or even as "French." His work has impressive scale, but its scope is narrow, even pinched, such that no accusation that his academic work might be tainted with political motivation be allowed to stick. Even where Piketty admits that political factors play a major role in the historical processes he elucidates, he buries his claims deep

2 Thomas Piketty, *Capital in the Twenty-First Century.* (Cambridge: Harvard University Press, 2014), p. 52.

3 Thomas Piketty, *Capital in the Twenty-First Century.* (Cambridge: Harvard University Press, 2014), p. 166.

4 Thomas Piketty, *Capital in the Twenty-First Century.* (Cambridge: Harvard University Press, 2014), p. 361.

5 Willford King, *The Wealth and Income of the People of the United States.* (New York: Macmillan, 1915).

in the text and shies away from interpretive conclusions. For example he states flatly that "the price of capital is … always in part a social and political construct…." This significant admission is, however hedged rhetorically between two phrases that give it a throwaway character: "Last but not least" and "This is obvious …"[6] It thus remains for other scholars to use Piketty's material, restrictively couched in economism, to found critical and interpretive arguments that do not accede to an evacuation of the political.

Piketty is thoughtful, careful and transparent about the sources of this data, and is cautious to specify what he feels are appropriate interpretive limitations. Standing back from the book, its most impressive accomplishment is the revelation of the magnitude and near universality of income and wealth inequality. Reviewing the graphs, clear law-like structural relationships between Piketty's concepts come into view: despite massive historical and political changes, the ratio of capital to income varies within a surprisingly narrow range across nations and centuries. In Piketty's graphs, patterns of wealth and income inequality appear surprisingly similar across national borders that demarcate distinctive political economies. Yet, American critical theorists and left-progressives attuned to history and culture will find it affirming to see that our time (post-1970s) and our place (Anglo-American liberal market economies) are indeed especially unequal relative to the recent past and to other nations.

In an interesting and revealing move, in the service of his arguments about patrimonial capitalism in the nineteenth century and earlier, Piketty even seems to privilege the *literary* above the political-economic as an interpretive scheme. The income and wealth dynamics distilled into formulas and graphically depicted by Piketty are frequently illustrated with literature, particularly Honoré de Balzac and Jane Austen. The most compelling of these illustrations is drawn from Balzac's *Pere Goriot* and turns upon a young man's calculations as he ponders the relative returns to the pursuit of a professional career versus marriage to a wealthy woman.[7] Austen's characters engage in the same ethical calculus, though in a different context and with different results. The dilemmas faced by impecunious, literary dowry-hunters who acquire patrimony through matrimony captures Piketty's own moral stance toward inherited wealth in capital: given the long-run tendency for r > g, returns to wealth frequently exceed returns to work. This turns out to be one of Piketty's most vigorously emphasized themes: as economic growth slows, capitalism reinforces inherited wealth while reducing rewards for work.

---

6   Thomas Piketty, *Capital in the Twenty-First Century*. (Cambridge: Harvard University Press, 2014), p. 188.

7   Thomas Piketty, *Capital in the Twenty-First Century*. (Cambridge: Harvard University Press, 2014), pp. 238–40.

Piketty's *Capital* and Marx's *Capital*

Clearly, Piketty's failure to engage Marx impairs *Capital's* utility for critical theorists. Piketty does make reference to Marx at several points in his work, which contains within its rhetorical framing—though obliquely—a response to and criticism of Marx's analysis of capital. Unfortunately, it also seems that Piketty's commitment to the maintenance of his credibility within transatlantic academic economics leads him to be unduly dismissive of Marx, and to appear unwilling to raise serious Marxist questions about the nature and functioning of capital. Throughout the book we see a range of rhetorical moves that serve to mask the political moments always present within economic activity.

Piketty has even represented himself as unfamiliar with, if not uninterested in, the basic arguments of Marx's *Capital*. In an interview with Isaac Chotiner published in *The New Republic* in May 2014, Piketty was asked to "talk a little bit about the effect of Marx on your thinking and how you came to start reading him?" Piketty's responded: "Marx? ... I never managed really to read it. I mean I don't know if you've tried to read it. Have you tried? ... *The Communist Manifesto* of 1848 is a short and strong piece. *Das Kapital*, I think, is very difficult to read and for me it was not very influential." Chotiner prompted Piketty by noting that "... your book, obviously with the title, it seemed like you were tipping your hat to him (Marx) in some ways." To which Piketty responded, "No not at all, not at all! The big difference is that my book is a book about the history of capital. In the books of Marx there's no data."[8]

Chotiner's questioning of Piketty about his engagement with Marx is reasonable given that the first reference to Karl Marx occurs in the third sentence of the first page of Piketty's *Capital*: "Do the dynamics of private capital accumulation inevitably lead to the concentration of wealth in ever fewer hands, as Karl Marx believed in the nineteenth century?"[9] On pages seven through eleven, Piketty criticizes Marx's *Capital*, boiling it down to several theses that he perceives as flawed, including the principles of "infinite accumulation" and "perpetual divergence." Piketty reads Marx's analysis as symptomatic of economists' "no doubt overly developed taste for apocalyptic predictions."[10] Piketty

---

8   Isaac Chotiner, "Thomas Piketty: I Don't Care for Marx: An Interview with the Left's Rock Star Economist." *New Republic* (5 May 2014) at: http://www.newrepublic.com/ article/117655/thomas-piketty-interview-economist-discusses-his-distaste-marx. Accessed November 21, 2014.

9   Thomas Piketty, *Capital in the Twenty-First Century*. (Cambridge: Harvard University Press, 2014), p. 1.

10 Thomas Piketty, *Capital in the Twenty-First Century*. (Cambridge: Harvard University Press, 2014), p. 11.

often pairs Marx's name with the idea of apocalypse: "My conclusions are less apocalyptic than those implied by Marx's principle of infinite accumulation and perpetual divergence."[11]

Piketty reads Marx as wrongly theorizing an "inexorable tendency for capital to accumulate and become concentrated in ever fewer hands, with no natural limit," signaling an "apocalyptic end to capitalism."[12] Marx's "dark prophecy" was in error because of Marx's ignorance of productivity improvements, because he "totally neglected the possibility of durable technological progress and steadily increasing productivity," which Piketty views as "a counterweight to the process of accumulation and concentration of private capital."[13] This is perhaps the most glaring misunderstanding of Marx in the book: Piketty's repeated claim that Marx "implicitly relies on a strict assumption of zero productivity growth over the long run."[14]

Marx is further criticized for methodological errors, because he "no doubt lacked the statistical data needed to refine his predictions" and intellectual dishonesty because he "decided on his conclusions in 1848, before embarking on the research needed to justify them."[15] In a footnote to the text, Piketty adds that Marx "occasionally sought to make use of the best available statistics of the day but … in a rather impressionistic way and without always establishing a clear connection to his theoretical argument."[16] Piketty diminishes Marx as one of a number of proto-economists who "had been talking about inequalities for decades without citing any sources whatsoever or any methods for comparing one era with another or deciding between competing hypotheses."[17] Even when Marx did use statistics, he "usually adopted a fairly anecdotal and unsystematic approach to the available statistics."[18] At moments, Piketty views

---

11   Thomas Piketty, *Capital in the Twenty-First Century*. (Cambridge: Harvard University Press, 2014), p. 27.

12   Thomas Piketty, *Capital in the Twenty-First Century*. (Cambridge: Harvard University Press, 2014), p. 9.

13   Thomas Piketty, *Capital in the Twenty-First Century*. (Cambridge: Harvard University Press, 2014), p. 10.

14   Thomas Piketty, *Capital in the Twenty-First Century*. (Cambridge: Harvard University Press, 2014), p. 27.

15   Thomas Piketty, *Capital in the Twenty-First Century*. (Cambridge: Harvard University Press, 2014), p. 10.

16   Thomas Piketty, *Capital in the Twenty-First Century*. (Cambridge: Harvard University Press, 2014), p. 580.

17   Thomas Piketty, *Capital in the Twenty-First Century*. (Cambridge: Harvard University Press, 2014), p. 13.

18   Thomas Piketty, *Capital in the Twenty-First Century*. (Cambridge: Harvard University Press, 2014), p. 229.

Marx as a vigorous stylist who "evidently wrote in great political fervor" making "hasty pronouncements from which it was difficult to escape,"[19] and adds that "Marx's literary talent partially accounts for his immense influence."[20] At other moments, Piketty criticizes Marx at once for lack of rigor and for unclear writing style: "Marx did not use mathematical models, and his prose was not always limpid, so it is difficult to be sure what he had in mind."[21]

We will not narrate full correctives to Piketty's statements regarding Marx. Even a cursory reading of Marx's *Capital*, the *Grundrisse*, or the essay, "Value, Price, Profit" will demonstrate Marx's emphasis upon productivity growth as a consequence of the pursuit of relative surplus value. Marx strove to address the statistical evidence that was reliably available in his time, and dialectically reconsidered his positions throughout his life. The degree to which Piketty is unschooled in Marx is not a significant issue for us. Rather, the disciplinary boundaries of the economics necessarily privileged by Piketty foreclose Marx and Marxian analytics.

The most important consequence of Piketty's foreclosure of Marx is that capital remains fundamentally fetishized as an undifferentiated object that radiates power. Marx's value theory defetishizes commodities, money, and capital, revealing value as generalized labor embedded during the labor process and socially validated in exchange. Piketty does not analyze value, leading him to conflate capital with wealth, using these terms "interchangeably, as if they were perfectly synonymous."[22] To Piketty, capital is "the sum total of nonhuman assets that can be owned and exchanged," a long list that includes real estate (even private homes) and "financial and professional capital (plants, infrastructure, machinery, patents, and so on) used by firms and government agencies."[23] To Marx, capital as such refers to wealth invested in the process of commodity production where it mixes with living labor to produce an excess known as profit. Even King's (1915) analysis distinguished between active wealth (invested and circulating) and inert or passive wealth. Piketty makes

19   Thomas Piketty, *Capital in the Twenty-First Century*. (Cambridge: Harvard University Press, 2014), p. 10.

20   Thomas Piketty, *Capital in the Twenty-First Century*. (Cambridge: Harvard University Press, 2014), p. 580.

21   Thomas Piketty, *Capital in the Twenty-First Century*. (Cambridge: Harvard University Press, 2014), p. 228.

22   Thomas Piketty, *Capital in the Twenty-First Century*. (Cambridge: Harvard University Press, 2014), p. 47.

23   Thomas Piketty, *Capital in the Twenty-First Century*. (Cambridge: Harvard University Press, 2014), p. 46.

no such distinction, and thus ventures no analysis of the constitutive nature of capital (value, the labor process, the working day, the extraction of surplus). For him, such work ventures beyond the legitimate discursive boundaries of the discipline of economics.

Marx's *Capital, Volume 1* focuses upon the analysis of production: by defetishizing the capital process (seeing commodities as value, as crystalized labor power, by analyzing the working day), Marx kept in view the social relationships and political systems that constitute an economy. Remaining within the confines of economic disciplinarity, Piketty was unable to defetishize capital and to analyze it in terms of a historically determined, culturally contingent labor process. For example, Piketty's discussion of the contradictory status of slaves as capitalized labor focused upon the money-value of slaves and the fact that they constituted a large percentage of capital in the antebellum American South. Remaining within economic-calculation rather than historical and cultural interpretation, Piketty does not describe how slavery contributed to Northern capital or how slavery operated as a variegated mode of deeply exploitative production, as recently revealed in Baptist's (2014) *The Half has Never Been Told*.[24] The social ontology and historical determinants of workplace inequality, even slavery, remain unanalyzed. To Piketty, domination and exploitation is economic rather than political, as though the primary problem with slavery was reducible to the low incomes and meager possessions of the slaves, whereas to Marx, exploitative labor processes—whether involving chattel slaves, servile peasants, or industrial workers—are alienating in historically and culturally determined ways. Piketty's book does not venture into these historical workplaces nor examine work process, locations central to Marx's politically potent work.

Convergence and Divergence, Commons, and Enclosures

Piketty analyzes national inequalities of income and wealth as shaped by contradictory forces pushing toward "convergence" (reduced inequality) and "divergence" (increased inequality). The failure to defetishize capital by analyzing the labor process is especially limiting when Piketty explains the two forces of "convergence," both emanating out of colleges and universities: diffusion of knowledge and acquisition of skills and training. Piketty views increased acquisition of skills and knowledge as the foundation of a "patrimonial middle

---

24   Edward Baptist, *The Half Has Never Been Told: Slavery and the Making of American Capitalism.* (New York: Basic Books, 2014).

class" that reduces inequality within nations. The same forces—increased education and acquisition of know-how—also lead to reduction of inequality between nations. Poor countries of the world take note: "by adopting the modes of production of the rich countries and acquiring skills comparable to those found elsewhere, the less developed countries have leapt forward in productivity and increased their national incomes...." The mechanism is "fundamentally a process of the diffusion and sharing of knowledge—the public good par excellence—rather than a market mechanism."[25]

Here Piketty gestures toward but fails to articulate with the political-economic arguments of "alter-modernity" theorists like Michael Hardt and Antonio Negri, who see the "commons" or "commonwealth" as byproducts created and enriched through capitalism.[26] Forms of association, know-how, information, and knowledge generated within capitalism flow into the "cultural commons." Political struggles in our time are less focused upon labor and working class activism than struggles against appropriation, privatization, and enclosure of the commons in order to foster a de-commodification of social life. Piketty's uncomplicated assurance that knowledge-diffusion and skill-acquisition spread readily to the lower orders underestimates capital's power to enclose. Hardt and Negri see political struggle as necessary to overcome capital's surveillance and control systems, including the army of property lawyers that enforces the trademark, copyright and patent machinery securing intellectual property.

While Piketty incorporates "immaterial capital" (patents, intellectual property, brands, goodwill, trademarks) into his definition of capital, he provides no separate analysis of them. Similarly, his disciplinary constraints do not allow him to recognize the "fictitious" nature of immaterial capital (as understood by theorists including Marx, Rudolf Hilferding, and David Harvey). Piketty therefore cannot follow Hardt and Negri into a political analysis of the growing importance of immaterial production and the important role intellectual property law plays in the privatization of culture.[27] The book's constricted economic disciplinarity excludes most culture from view, including capitalized culture that is legally enclosed from the public domain as intellectual

25   Thomas Piketty, *Capital in the Twenty-First Century*. (Cambridge: Harvard University Press, 2014), p. 21.

26   Michael Hardt and Antonio Negri, *Commonwealth*. (Cambridge: Harvard University Press, 2011).

27   On intellectual property law, see James Boyle, "The Second Enclosure Movement and the Construction of the Public Domain." *Duke Law School Public Law and Legal Theory Research Paper Series* (2003).

property. Analysts who study the unpaid labor of consumers point to a condition of double-exploitation that consumers rarely understand with clarity and that lies beyond Piketty's disciplinary horizon.[28]

Disciplinary conventions further seem to limit Piketty's understanding of the primary force behind divergence to the outsized earnings of "super-managers": "this spectacular increase in inequality largely reflects an unprecedented explosion of very elevated incomes from labor, a veritable separation of the top managers of large firms from the rest of the population."[29] Piketty attributes this rise to the selfish interests and exceptional bargaining power of top managers in corporations, who "have the power to set their own remuneration, in some cases without limit and in many cases without any clear relation to their individual productivity."[30]

Such framing of excessive executive compensation as a classic principal/agent hazard, though consistent with academic economic discourse, discounts the politicized financial deregulation of recent decades and how it dramatically increased the power of large, speculative stockholders to control corporate affairs. Beginning in the 1980s, stockholders of U.S. corporations grew more organized and active, electing boards of directors who awarded immense stock options to the executives they appointed. Stock options (and bonuses tied to stock price) ensured that U.S. executives were focused "liked a laser" upon increasing the short-term value of corporate stock by giving them a "piece of the action."[31] Contrary to Piketty's narrow interpretation, executive stock options were not "incomes from labor" that were economically justified by "clear relation to their individual productivity" but rather payments akin to bribes.[32] Piketty makes a category mistake when he views executive compensation and stock options as labor income: they are, in fact, a redistribution of the return to capital meant to incentivize management to increase returns. The large growth in income inequality that Piketty graphs was not due to pay for efficient work, but was a means to forge an unusually powerful corporate control structure.

---

28   Bernard Cova and Danielle Dalli, "Working Consumers: the Next Step in Marketing Theory?" *Marketing Theory* vol. 9, 2009, pp. 315–339.

29   Thomas Piketty, *Capital in the Twenty-First Century*. (Cambridge: Harvard University Press, 2014), p. 24.

30   Thomas Piketty, *Capital in the Twenty-First Century*. (Cambridge: Harvard University Press, 2014), p. 24.

31   Dan Krier, *Speculative Management: Stock Market Power and Corporate Change* (Albany: State University of New York Press, 2005).

32   Thomas Piketty, *Capital in the Twenty-First Century*. (Cambridge: Harvard University Press, 2014), p. 24.

The Varieties of Capital and the Social State

Piketty documents significant divergences in national patterns of inequality and depicts them graphically in his book, but shies away from historical or cultural causal analysis of them. Often, his discussion introduces but then minimizes national variations while drawing attention to overarching similarities in pursuit of his unitary, strictly economic theory of wealth and income inequality. Piketty misses an important opportunity to dwell upon the historical, political and cultural foundations of divergent national capitalist systems. In the late 20th century, research into enduring, deeply-structured "varieties of capitalism" gave rise to an extensive interdisciplinary literature in the hinterlands between academic economics, sociology, and business studies.[33] Interpreting the historical, cultural and political embeddedness of capitalist institutions with a variety of ideal types, this literature differentiated between "liberal market economies" (primarily Anglo-American) and "coordinated market economies" (Northern European Social Democracies). Some approaches identified additional varieties of capitalism clustered in the Catholic countries of southern Europe.[34] We have recoded the data files that Piketty has (meritoriously) provided to scholars on his website, sorting the nations in his database into three groups that loosely correspond to these "varieties of capitalism": Northern European social democracies (whose economic ethics align closely with Weber's Pietists), Anglo-American liberal market economies (whose economic ethics align closely with Weber's Calvinists) and Catholic economies (whose economic ethics align closely with Weber's traditionalism).

---

33 Gøsta Esping-Andersen, *The Three Worlds of Welfare Capitalism*. (Princeton: Princeton University Press, 1990); M. Albert, *Capitalism vs. Capitalism*. (New York: Four Walls Eight Windows, 1993); P.A.Hall and D. Soskice (eds), *Varieties of Capitalism: the Institutional Foundations of Comparative Advantage*. (Oxford: Oxford University Press, 2001); L.A. Scruggs and J.P. Allan, "Social stratification and welfare regimes for the Twenty-First Century: Revisiting the Three Worlds of Welfare Capitalism." *World Politics* Vol. 60, 2008, pp. 642–664; Wolfgang Streeck, *"E Pluribus Unum?* Varieties and Commonalities of Capitalism." *SSRN Working Paper Series.* (2010); Dan Krier, "Critical Institutionalism and Financial Globalization: a Comparative Analysis of American and Continental finance." *New York Journal of Sociology* Vol. 1 (1), 2008, pp. 130–186. For an important antecedent to this literature, see Max Weber, "Capitalism and Rural Society in Germany." *From Max Weber: Essays in Sociology*. (London: Routledge and Kegan Paul, 1946), pp. 363–85.

34 Gøsta Esping-Andersen, *The Three Worlds of Welfare Capitalism*. (Princeton: Princeton University Press, 1990). See also Max Weber, "Capitalism and Rural Society in Germany." *From Max Weber: Essays in Sociology*. (London, Routledge and Kegan Paul, 1946), pp. 363–85.

Differences between these three varieties of capitalism became apparent, suggesting that deep historical, cultural and political structuring are particularly important to explain large variations in the capitalist "social state." The correlation of risk-pooled social insurance with political subjectivity[35] predicted by the varieties of capitalism literature, indicates that significant differences in politics and culture continue to separate coordinated from liberal capitalist economies (See Appendix). Piketty's focus upon national economic statistics misses these important cross-national clusters.

Specifically, national statistics further limit Piketty's view of diverse, historically contingent, regional and sectional patterns of inequality within a given nation-state. For example, *Capital's* dataset does not parse economic statistics into counties, states or regions, but remains aggregated at the national level. The remarkable diversity of regional cultures and regional identities within France, the subject of much academic study,[36] was masked by Piketty's reliance upon national data. This is unfortunate, since the historical structuring, remarkable endurance and uneven decay of these regional cultures in the face of capitalist modernization were central to classic large-scale studies of capital.[37]

Regional and sectional analyses of u.s. inequality make scant appearance in Piketty's book. Piketty notes that u.s. Northern states, during the 19th century at least, had extraordinarily low levels of inequality while southern states had very high levels of inequality that rivaled or exceeded aristocratic Europe, and he further notes the significance of slaveholding in this dynamic especially in the late 18th and early 19th centuries. However, he ventures no deeper reflection upon how these historical politics of expropriation might continue to affect capital formation.[38] This is unfortunate, because county-level u.s. census

35   Kevin S. Amidon and Z.G. Sanderson, "On Subjectivity and the Risk Pool; or, Žižek's Lacuna." *Telos* (160), pp. 121–138.

36   Emile Durkheim, *Suicide: A Study in Sociology*. (Glencoe: Free Press, 1951); Marc Bloch, *Feudal Society*. (London: Routledge, 1964); Eugen Weber, *Peasants into Frenchmen: the Modernization of Rural France, 1870–1914*. (Redwood City: Stanford University Press, 1976).

37   Fernand Braudel, *Civilization and Capitalism, 15–18th Century, Volume 1: The Structures of Everyday Life*. (Fortuna: University of California Press, 1981); Fernand Braudel, *Civilization and Capitalism, 15–18th Century, Volume 2: The Wheels of Commerce*. (Fortuna: University of California Press, 1982); Immanuel Wallerstein, *The Modern World-System 1: Capitalist Agriculture and the Origins of the European World-Economy in the Sixteenth Century*. (New York: Academic Press, 1974).

38   Thomas Piketty, *Capital in the Twenty-First Century*. (Cambridge: Harvard University Press, 2014), pp. 158–163.

data on income inequality reveal enormous cultural differences across U.S. regions.[39] Northern tier states and the Midwest consistently exhibit low levels of inequality (on par with contemporary European social democracies) while the southern states exhibit exceptionally high levels of inequality (on par with Aristocratic Europe at its most unequal peak). Such patterns of regional distinctiveness are consistent with Fischer's (1989) *Albion's seed* and with other social histories mapping distinctive subcultures laid down by British and European laws and customs.[40] While these European folkways were modified in the American setting, the translation of old world cultures to the colonies often resulted in concentration and clarification: the New World setting enabled certain contradictions and tonal disharmonies to be worked out, creating cultures with great logical self-consistency, durability and self-clarity.

The Evacuation of the Political and Its Retrieval

For critical theorists accustomed to historical and cultural analysis and interested in the possibilities of politics, what can be learned from Piketty's constrained disciplinarity? In his writing and in interviews, Piketty does not simply set himself apart from politically engaged scholarship, but projects the entire category of the political into the utopian and its dialectically opposed double, apocalyptic prophecy.[41] Such distancing is necessary for Piketty to maintain credibility within the branches of disciplinary economics committed to positivist, non-Marxist, and economic reductionist positions. Critical theorists can only find it perverse, however, that Piketty, in the name of retaining disciplinary credibility and legitimacy within technocratic, bureaucratic policymaking, eliminates practical political engagement. In order to preserve possibilities to technically influence administrative policy, Piketty blunts his book's potential for politics. Piketty not only distances himself from Marx, but discounts his own proposal for a global tax on wealth as "utopian."[42] The most

---

39   U.S. Census Bureau, *Household Income Inequality within US counties: 2006–2010.* (Available (consulted 25 August 2014) at: http://www.census.gov/prod/2012pubs/acsbr10-18 .pdf).

40   David Hackett Fischer, *Albion's Seed: Four British Folkways in America.* (New York: Oxford University Press, 1989).

41   Thomas Piketty, *Capital in the Twenty-First Century.* (Cambridge: Harvard University Press, 2014), pp. 6–12.

42   Thomas Piketty, *Capital in the Twenty-First Century.* (Cambridge: Harvard University Press, 2014), p. 471, pp. 515–34.

dispiriting aspect of Piketty's *Capital* then is not the dark projections of future inequality, but the work's almost total resignation to disciplinary conformity, such that the scholarly precondition for serious consideration by those who determine policy is an abandonment of politics as purely utopian. What is even more disheartening is the remarkable modesty, even banality, of Piketty's "utopian" dreams: he calls for a mere 5% tax upon wealth. His proposed solution is as narrowly economic as the rest of the book.

Piketty's *Capital* is the product of disciplinary conventions that define anything other than descriptive empiricism as utopian. Within the boundaries of economics, Piketty's single-minded focus upon national income statistics need not be disturbed by any serious, culturally-sophisticated challenge to the nation-state as a meaningful economic unit. Such economism allowed his analysis to remain free of Foucauldian interrogation of the motives underlying the historical development of state surveillance and control that make possible the collection of the data he analyzed.

Conclusion

We have argued that while Piketty's *Capital in the Twenty-First Century* sparked renewed *academic* discussion of inequality, the *political* impact of the book was limited. We traced this political inefficacy to Piketty's location within the disciplinary boundaries of academic economics. Piketty's *economism* overemphasized economic forces while underemphasizing complex social causation. We found that economism was especially evident in Piketty's faint engagement with Marx and his dismissive treatment of Marx's ideas. Economism was also evident in his drive to generate global and transhistorical data on national income distribution that reduced capitalism's institutional complexity to numerical causal laws. Finally, economism was bound up with his preference for technically calculated policy over socially engaged politics. We argued that politically potent critical theories of inequality must reach beyond economism to comprehend the historical development and cultural determinations of capital. We highlighted historical and cultural approaches that transcended economic reductionism: labor process studies, research on speculative capitalism, and research on distinctive varieties of capitalism at the regional and cross-national levels (Figure 9.1). While Piketty's book may punch his admission ticket into the corridors of policy, the messier realities of history, culture and politics remain for critical theorists to analyze.

Comparison of Economic Ethics

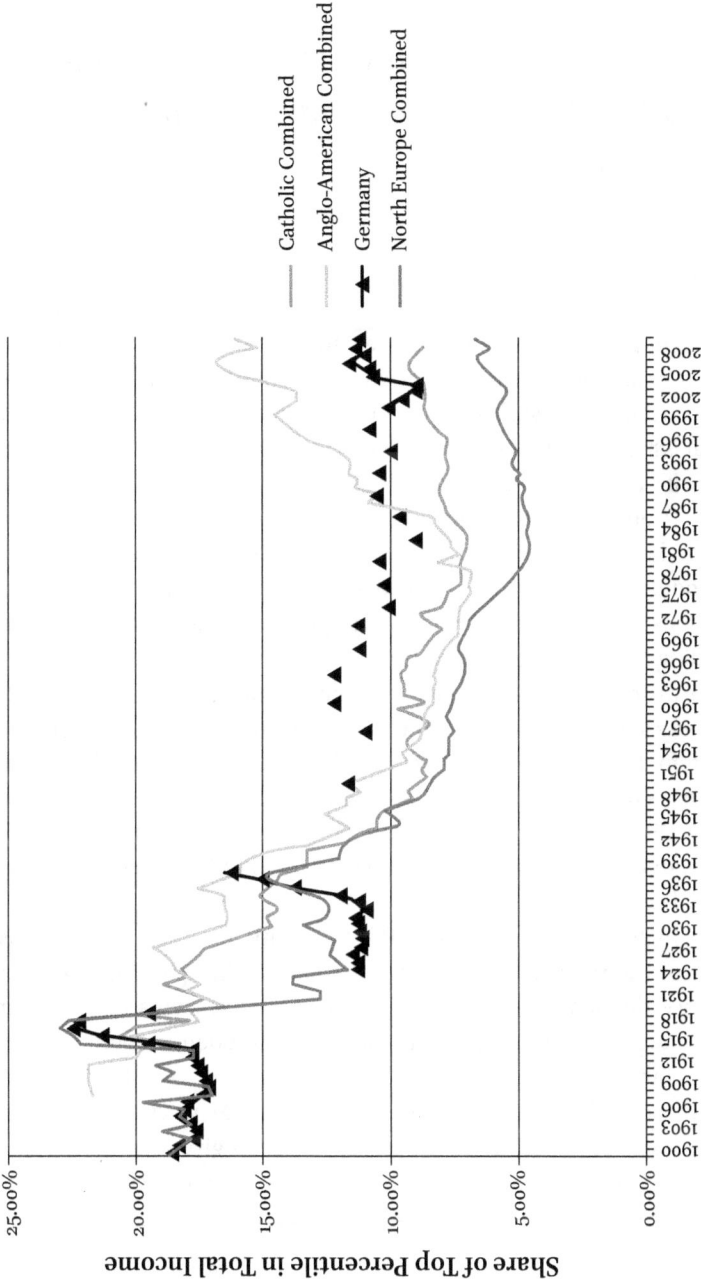

FIGURE 9.1 *Income inequality and varieties of capitalism*

CHAPTER 10

Accounting for Inequality: Questioning Piketty on National Income Accounts and the Capital-Labor Split

Charles Reitz

Thanks in part to Occupy Wall Street, and in part to the media attention bestowed upon Thomas Piketty's new book, *Capital in the Twenty-First Century*, the "distribution of wealth is one of today's most widely discussed and controversial issues" [1].[1] A big problem with this important discussion, says Piketty, is that it's a "debate without data" [2]. The introduction and analysis of large data sets on inequality would seem to be his forte. Furthermore, he wants to look at data diachronically as its patterns evolve over time. These are clearly methodological strengths that encourage confidence in his work. Theoretical questions, however, also inevitably arise in the debates and controversies surrounding the meaning of the data.

The distribution of wealth has been given short shrift in most conventional economics textbooks, yet it is arguably the most basic element in our economic system. The topics such as where wealth comes from, how it is accumulated, what is its relationship to income flows and income inequality are usually absent in discussions among conventional economists. Piketty rightly counters this tendency, and advocates "putting the distributional question back at the heart of economic analysis" [15].

The high profile emergence of Piketty's work raises our hopes and is to be welcomed. Furthermore, his heart seems to be in the right place: "There is little evidence that labor's share in national income has increased significantly in a very long time" [22]. Also from 1980 to about 2000, he points out, the top 10% of income earners in the U.S. increased its share such that it is now about 50% percent of the national income [23]. These are weighty matters in terms of the wide-spread fairness and justice concerns given the pattern of intensifying inequality here and labor's nearly total dependency on market-based

---

1   Page numbers in brackets refer to Thomas Piketty, *Capital in the Twenty-First Century*. (Cambridge: Harvard University Press, 2014). This essay has been strengthened through critical comments from Victor D. Lippit, David Barkin, Christopher Gunn, Stephen Spartan, Mehdi Shariati, and Morteza Ardebili. Weaknesses that remain are my own.

access to necessities of life. Some interpretations of globalization have questioned whether intensifying inequalities are self-evidently tied to fairness and justice issues. It is suggested that globalization together with technological change might mean that income that would otherwise go the U.S. middle class might instead accrue to emerging middle classes and the poor in developing countries, and that it is not necessarily unjust that they catch up while middle-class incomes in the U.S. stagnate. Scott Sernau[2] has argued to the contrary, and Piketty would seem to agree,[3] that globalization has led paradoxically to "worlds apart," both within and between nations. Austerity policies, centering on forms of structural adjustment, have reduced social-needs-oriented government spending while subsidizing banking and investment institutions. Increasing exploitation is occurring today through the "race to the bottom" as global capitalism scours the world for the lowest wage labor markets and presses domestic labor for steep cuts. Policies of the World Bank, the International Monetary Fund, and NAFTA (North American Free Trade Agreement) have led to structural adjustments that exemplify policies of domination that hurt the poor and middle classes.

Most U.S. adults typically have little awareness of the nature of *wealth* or the pattern of its distribution in society. This generally also means lack insight into the connection of *income flows* to relations of capitalist property (i.e. *wealth*) *ownership* and the commodification of labor and life. The distinction between an income flow *from wealth*, and how the economic assets owned by a person or family (rent, interest, dividends, and profit) differ from the income flow *from labor* (i.e. salary and wages) is key to critical understanding and its impacts will soon be elaborated below. An examination of these kinds of social dynamics is a vital part of a critical or radical pedagogy. A widely-used sociology text, *Social Problems,* by Macionis[4] stands out in this regard, pointing out that inequalities of wealth are linked to inequalities of *life chances.* "Life chances" is a technical term used to indicate the relative access a household has to the society's economic resources: decent housing, health care, education, employment, etc. The greater the wealth in one's household, the greater one's life chances. Life chances (including access to jobs and income) are today being transferred

2   See Scott Sernau, *Worlds Apart: Social Inequalities in a Global Economy* (Thousand Oaks: Pine Forge Press, 2006), p. 44.

3   Piketty writes of the "Inequality of Total Income: Two Worlds" [263] and his chapter 8 is entitled "Two Worlds" [271–303], yet close examination shall reveal below significant areas of divergence from both Sernau's analysis and my own. Thomas Piketty, *Capital in the Twenty-First Century.* (Cambridge: Harvard University Press, 2014)

4   See John J. Macionis, *Social Problems* (Boston: Prentice Hall, 2012), p. 31.

away from the vast majority of households and redistributed to the advantage of the wealthiest.

A pattern of polarization has transpired with regard to incomes, over time, such that today "income inequality has soared to the highest levels since the Great Depression."[5] "The increase in incomes of the top 1 percent from 2003 to 2005 exceeded total income of the poorest 20 percent of Americans ..."[6] In February 2013 Emmanuel Saez, of the University of California, Berkeley, reported that during the current recovery the incomes of the top 1 percent rose 11.2 percent, while the incomes of the remaining 99 percent fell by 0.4 percent.[7] Saez also reported that in the U.S. "Excluding earnings from investment gains, the top 10 percent of earners took 46.5 percent of all income in 2011, the highest proportion since 1917."[8]

Investigating the origins of inequality and its intensification in the U.S. my colleague, Stephen Spartan, and I have sought to understand the generative structures undergirding today's increasingly unequal and irrational patterns of wealth and income distribution.[9] In the U.S. even the current recovery is a further indicator of a distorted political economy in which taxpayer/government subsidies to finance capital have permitted a redistribution of wealth to the advantage of the largest banks and high income individuals—reducing the global payroll. Governments can alter these patterns of inequality through macroeconomic interventions involving policies of taxation, central banks, and education. In the U.S. over the last several decades a rising tide of growth certainly did not lift all boats. The primary gains of globalization have accrued to the wealthiest; the wealth gap is the widest in decades.[10]

---

5   Annie Lowrey, "Costs Seen in Income Inequality," *The New York Times,* October 17, 2012, p. B-1.

6   U.S. Congressional Budget Office in Douglas Dowd, *Inequality and the Global Economic Crisis* (New York: Pluto Press, 2009), p. 122.

7   Annie Lowrey, "Incomes Flat in Recovery, but not for the 1%," *The New York Times,* February 16, 2013, p. B-1.

8   Piketty and Saez in Lowery, Ibid. p. B-4.

9   Charles Reitz and Stephen Spartan, "The Political Economy of Predation and Counterrevolution," in Charles Reitz (ed.) *Crisis and Commonwealth: Marcuse, Marx, McLaren* (Lanham: Lexington Books, 2013), pp. 19–41. Elements of the present essay, its political economic foundations, though not the critique Piketty, are drawn from this earlier work.

10   See Patricia Cohen, "Fueled by Recession, U.S. Wealth Gap Is Widest In Decades, Study Finds," *The New York Times,* December 18, 2014, p. B-3. Cohen reports that the scale of global inequality is staggering and intensifying. Nearly 1 percent of the world's population owns 50 percent of the world's wealth. See also Patricia Cohen, "Study Finds Global Wealth Is Flowing to the Richest," *The New York Times,* January 19, 2015, B-6. Joseph

Thomas Piketty's study of capital and inequality begins with a standard ten-et of national income accounting, that "All production must be distributed as income in one form or another, to either labor or capital ... National income = capital income + labor income" [45]. Further, "income can always be expressed as income from labor and income from capital" [242].

In other words, a key criterion in understanding inequality is *the capital-labor split* with regard to their respective shares of the national income.[11] Spartan and I develop a model (see Figure 10.1) that derives precisely from our shared understanding with Piketty as just described above: $Ni = Ci + Li$, where Ni is national income, Ci is capital income, and Li is labor income.

The first half of Piketty's extensive analysis is taken up by his meticulous search for the historical development of global patterns of Ci as a percentage of Ni. Should this be increasing, as is indicated in the work of others highlighted above, this would have clear implications for the justice and fairness issues connected in our view to the reality of intensifying inequalities.

Clearly, if Ni (national income) and Li (labor income) are known quantities, then Ci (capital income) is easily determined. Our efforts were much more modest than those of Piketty; still, we proceeded in a straightforward manner to ascertain capital income by expressing the relationship Piketty acknowledged above ($Ni = Ci + Li$) in an equivalent form, namely as $Ci = Ni - Li$. Hence, we were able to determine Ci when Ni and Li were known in the economy's manufacturing sector.

Piketty might have done this also, but in his work, the analysis shifts almost immediately away from the $Ni = Ci + Li$ relationship, to an examination of what he calls the "First Fundamental Law of Capitalism" [52]. Piketty assigns α to represent capital income (which we have designated as Ci, above). The fundamental law of capitalism as he sees it is that α (or Ci) equals the product of r times $ß$, where r is the rate of return on capital and $ß$ is the capital/income ratio [50]. Here we enter vast new data territory and a new assertion of variables standing in formal equilibrium with α or Ci. This method's logic appears to achieve his objective, the determination of α (capital income, Ci),

---

Stiglitz points out that inequalities of income and wealth are larger in the U.S. in comparison to other advanced industrial countries, and they are increasing unusually fast. He adds that those with power tend to use that power to enhance their positions. See Joseph E. Stiglitz, *The Price of Inequality: How Today's Divided Society Endangers our Future* (New York: W.W. Norton, 2012), pp. 28–39.

11   As the essay proceeds, distinctions will be drawn between certain of Piketty's views on labor income and my own, notably his inclusion of the total supersalaries of executives as remuneration for labor.

START	VALUE ADDED	END
Value of Production Inputs	in	Value of Production Outputs
	PRODUCTION	
Total costs of supplies, fuel, raw materials, electricity, tools, etc.	PROCESS ▶--------------------------------------▶	

Total New Value
Produced in 2008
in manufacturing:
$2,274,367 million.
This total was distributed as income to Labor and
to Capital

Nim

(100%)

↓	↓
Lim	**Cim**
(26%)	(74%)
Income returned to Labor = Payroll	Income returned to Capital =
Wages and Salaries $607,447 mil.	Rent, Interest, Dividends, Profit $1,666,920 mil.

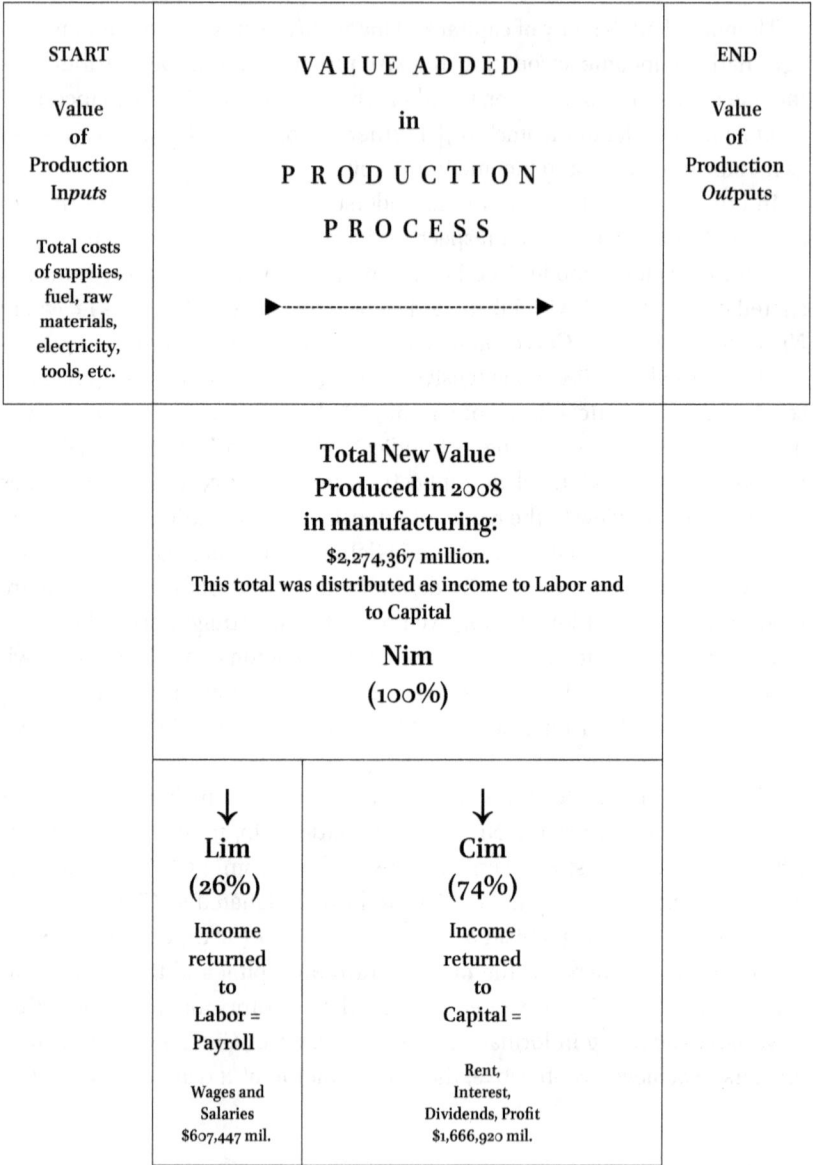

FIGURE 10.1 *The capital-labor split in U.S. manufacturing*

but for Piketty the research road to α and Ci takes a convoluted turn involving three new variables. This may take us where we want to go, or it may well lead him (and us) to inaccuracies and erroneous conclusions. His procedure to find Ci or α presumes that the total value of the capital stock of any economy may be confidently and immediately determined as well as the *rate* of return on capital overall (**r**).

Piketty acknowledges that a nation's capital is comprised of a variety of assets: "residential capital, professional capital used by firms and government" [51] farmland, housing stock, etc. [119]. Piketty [48–49] is not bothered that the dot.com bubble and the real estate bubble have made it clear distortions can inflate (and deflate) prices beyond real value. These factors would seem to pose insurmountable difficulties in accurately ascertaining the total value of capital stock. Such distortions would likewise introduce fluctuations in the rate of return or growth in sectors and subsectors of the economy, and damage our ability to assess **r** for the economy overall. Thus seeing "α = **r** X ß" as the fundamental law of capitalism [50–52] seems methodologically questionable. Because of the difficulty in gaining access to such data as well as uncertainties in assessing it, our methodology makes use instead of the basic formula that Piketty agrees to at the outset: **Ni − Li = Ci**. Thus the potential pitfalls of Piketty's circuitous research route can be avoided. Let us explain our approach.

The standard methodology utilized to calculate the gross domestic product and national income looks at the amount of *new wealth created, i.e. value added* through production in each firm and each industry. In each sector of U.S. manufactures, for example, this is calculated by deducting the dollar costs of the *inputs* (supplies, raw materials, tools, fuel, electricity, etc.) from the dollar value of the *outputs* for each firm. Very importantly, these national income accounts—unlike conventional business accounts—do *not* include the "cost" of labor among the *input* costs in the conception of the production process they utilize. Instead, they treat workforce remuneration and capital remuneration as do Locke, Smith, and Marx—as income flows stemming from the *value production process* itself.[12]

When looking at data on the gross domestic product and national income with regard to the U.S., it makes sense to look *first* at that portion of the national income generated in manufacturing. This is because data in that sector

---

12 Another customary approach to the measurement of national income calculates it as the aggregate expenditure of private and government consumption as well as business purchasing (Y=C+K+G): factors expressing demand—and this may undergird a Keynesian *demand*-push policy towards growth. The *value-added* approach, which I prefer, takes *supply* seriously. It emphasizes the importance of production as the key factor in the generation of real growth in national wealth and in the assessment of national income in terms of real, value-added outputs. This approach is extremely fruitful, and has more critical potential than is generally recognized—something radical political economists might well take up further.

are clearly reported to the U.S. Department of Commerce with regard to labor income from manufacturing and national income from manufacturing. This latter figure we can call **Nim**, and analogously consider it to be composed of **Cim** (capital income from manufacturing) and **Lim** (labor income from manufacturing). Thus: **Nim** = **Cim** + **Lim**. National income from manufacturing (**Nim**) minus labor income from manufacturing (**Lim**) = capital income from manufacturing (**Cim**), which may be restated as: **Nim** – **Lim** = **Cim**.

The *Statistical Abstract of the United States 2011* (*SAUS*, sadly the U.S. Census Bureau terminated the collection of data for the Statistical Compendia program effective October 1, 2011, and since then the *SAUS* has no longer been published) includes the data we need in this regard from the U.S. Department of Commerce. In terms of the nomenclature of this Table: "Value added by manufactures" is what we call **Nim**. The "total payroll" is what we call **Lim**, and **Cim** is found by subtracting **Lim** from **Nim**. From that we get:

Value Added by Manufactures (Nim) – Total Payroll (Lim) = Income Returned to Capital (Cim)

The *Statistical Abstract of the United States 2011* reported the new wealth created (value added) in manufacturing in 2008 (the most recent available figure). This is contained in Figure 10.2 (its Table 1006, http://www.census.gov/prod/2011pubs/11statab/manufact.pdf retrieved June 11, 2011).

That portion of the U.S. national income derived from manufacturing is given as $2,274,367 million. This is listed under the heading "Value Added by Manufactures." Every dollar of the value added in U.S. manufacturing—for example this $2,274,367 million[13]—was distributed into one of the two basic income categories: 1) as **Lim**, income to the workforce—given as the *payroll* (wages and salaries)—$607,447 million; and 2) as **Cim**, income to owners and investors—as *profit (including dividends), rent, and interest*—which we can calculate (**Nim** – **Lim** = **Cim**) as the remainder: $1,666,920 million. Something very like this disproportionate division of the added value between capital income in manufacturing (**Cim** = **74 percent**) and labor income in manufacturing (**Lim** = **26 percent**)—the capital-labor split—is structured by unequal property relations into other sectors of the economy and into the division of the gross domestic product and national income overall. Spartan and I emphasize that incomes returned to capital and labor are *structurally determined*, i.e. conditioned primarily by societal, rather than individual, factors.

Looking further at some of the disaggregated data from Table 1006, our Appendix B below, we see, for example, that in category 3152, *cut and sew*

---

13   This and other figures from: Table 1006. Manufactures—Summary by Selected Industry, 2008. *Statistical Abstract of the United States: 2011*, p. 634. See this as **Appendix A** below.

[12,781.2 represents 12,781,200. Based on the Annual Survey of Manufactures; see Appendix III]

Industry based on shipments	2002 NAICS code[1]	All employees			Production workers[2] (1,000)	Value added by manufactures[3] (mil. dol.)	Value of shipments[4] (mil. dol.)
		Number[2] (1,000)	Payroll				
			Total (mil. dol.)	Per employee (dol.)			
Manufacturing, total	**31–33**	**12,781.2**	**607,447**	**47,527**	**8,872.9**	**2,274,367**	**5,486,266**
Food[5]	311	1,437.8	51,818	36,039	1,113.7	246,222	649,056
Grain and oil seed milling	3112	53.2	2,817	52,953	39.5	28,988	94,000
Sugar and confectionery products...........	3113	61.9	2,625	42,431	47.3	13,184	26,648
Fruit and vegetable preserving and specialty food	3114	167.7	6,232	37,161	138.5	28,045	63,187
Dairy products...........................	3115	132.3	5,899	44,592	95.6	27,072	98,118
Animal slaughtering and processing	3116	505.7	15,217	30,094	438.9	50,823	169,925
Bakeries and tortilla.......................	3118	271.6	9,442	34,760	172.8	34,108	58,701
Beverage and tobacco products	312	152.8	7,322	47,905	87.0	76,292	125,520
Beverage.................................	3121	134.7	6,223	46,196	73.5	44,833	88,085
Textile mills	313	135.6	4,661	34,383	113.1	12,471	31,845
Textile product mills.......................	314	136.3	4,151	30,455	104.9	11,540	26,630
Apparel	315	148.9	3,887	26,112	116.2	9,237	19,596
Cut and sew apparel....................	3152	118.5	3,075	25,951	92.2	7,385	15,608
Leather and allied products.................	316	31.7	994	31,361	23.9	2,619	5,411
Wood products[5]	321	461.6	15,619	33,834	365.5	34,577	88,004
Sawmills and wood preservation............	3211	91.7	3,394	37,024	76.9	7,278	24,272
Paper....................................	322	403.2	20,546	50,957	311.6	79,175	178,749
Pulp, paper, and paperboard mills...........	3221	117.8	7,794	66,142	93.6	40,476	82,923
Converted paper products..................	3222	285.4	12,752	44,687	218.0	38,700	95,826
Printing and related support activities........	323	605.9	25,138	41,491	422.4	60,003	99,167
Petroleum and coal products................	324	105.9	8,415	79,444	68.2	91,559	769,886
Chemical[5]..............................	325	780.1	50,766	65,074	448.8	355,481	751,030
Basic chemical...........................	3251	151.8	10,880	71,656	92.2	83,629	244,174
Pharmaceutical and medicine..............	3254	249.1	18,771	75,347	117.8	142,773	194,478
Soap, cleaning compound, and toilet preparation	3256	104.4	5,667	54,259	62.7	46,661	97,431
Plastics and rubber products................	326	796.5	31,580	39,651	613.2	91,431	204,679
Plastics products	3261	651.8	25,299	38,815	499.7	76,503	167,423
Rubber product	3262	144.7	6,281	43,415	113.5	14,929	37,256
Nonmetallic mineral products	327	443.4	19,372	43,694	338.0	61,994	115,920
Glass and glass product	3272	93.9	4,227	45,042	74.0	12,562	23,197
Cement and concrete products.............	3273	213.6	9,106	42,637	161.8	29,774	57,779
Primary metal[5]	331	418.3	22,693	54,245	328.7	93,564	282,141
Iron and steel mills and ferroalloy	3311	109.3	7,668	70,150	87.4	43,036	126,332
Foundries................................	3315	144.0	6,435	44,689	116.3	15,492	31,842
Fabricated metal products[5]................	332	1,572.7	69,231	44,021	1,153.4	188,072	358,363
Forging and stamping	3321	123.5	5,763	46,663	92.0	15,834	34,899
Architectural and structural metals	3323	408.5	17,253	42,239	293.1	44,878	94,980
Machine shops, turned product and screw, nut, and bolt.............................	3327	398.5	17,748	44,537	298.5	39,941	64,064
Coating, engraving, heat treating, and allied activities...............................	3328	136.0	5,360	39,403	104.0	16,432	27,740
Machinery[5]	333	1,127.4	57,212	50,749	726.1	168,153	356,954
Agriculture, construction, and mining machinery	3331	209.2	10,279	49,147	143.0	39,037	94,334
Industrial machinery	3332	127.6	7,648	59,919	67.6	18,703	35,612
Ventilation, heating, air conditioning, and commercial refrigeration equipment	3334	145.8	6,019	41,297	104.7	19,092	40,702
Metalworking machinery	3335	161.3	8,305	51,502	112.1	17,325	29,277
Computer and electronic products[5]	334	1,034.1	66,345	64,156	493.8	234,390	391,082
Computer and peripheral equipment.........	3341	92.6	5,908	63,792	34.7	38,727	68,110
Communications equipment	3342	132.8	8,961	67,481	53.9	30,504	53,865
Semiconductor and other electronic component...........................	3344	371.6	20,486	55,123	227.9	71,258	116,809
Navigational, measuring, medical, and control instruments	3345	395.1	29,033	73,475	151.3	88,473	139,775
Electrical equipment, appliance, and component.............................	335	411.9	19,038	46,226	285.3	61,975	131,759
Electrical equipment	3353	144.4	6,890	47,705	96.1	21,840	44,301
Transportation equipment[5]	336	1,474.4	82,532	55,976	1,018.6	252,187	666,807
Motor vehicle............................	3361	163.0	11,318	69,424	139.5	52,337	210,978
Motor vehicle body and trailer	3362	123.5	4,789	38,790	95.0	10,208	29,764
Motor vehicle parts	3363	523.7	24,771	47,297	391.6	62,812	174,646
Aerospace product and parts	3364	439.8	30,892	70,240	235.2	93,036	178,709
Ship and boat building	3366	149.0	6,857	46,016	103.1	16,665	30,430
Furniture and related products[5]	337	459.8	16,344	35,544	343.3	43,965	80,466
Miscellaneous[5]	339	642.9	29,782	46,322	397.1	99,460	153,200
Medical equipment and supplies............	3391	313.7	16,151	51,491	188.3	60,424	84,029

[1] North American Industrial Classification System, 2002; see text, Section 15. [2] Includes employment and payroll at administrative offices and auxiliary units. All employees represents the average of production workers plus all other employees for the payroll period ended nearest the 12th of March. Production workers represent the average of the employment for the payroll periods ended nearest the 12th of March, May, August, and November. [3] Adjusted value added; takes into account (a) value added by merchandising operations (that is, difference between the sales value and cost of merchandise sold without further manufacture, processing, or assembly), plus (b) net change in finished goods and work-in- process inventories between beginning and end of year. [4] Includes extensive and unmeasurable duplication from shipments between establishments in the same industry classification. [5] Includes industries not shown separately.

Source: U.S. Census Bureau, Annual Survey of Manufactures, "Statistics for Industry Groups and Industries: 2008," June 2010, <http://www.census.gov/manufacturing/asm/index.html>.

634 Manufactures

FIGURE 10.2 *Table 1006. manufacturers—summary by selected industries 2008*

apparel, **total** value added (in millions) was *$7,385*. The payroll (in millions) was *$3,075*. Therefore the amount returned to capital (in millions) was *$4,310*. This latter figure is an amount equal to 100 percent of what was paid to the workforce *plus* an extra 40 percent. What is true in this sector of the economy holds true in several other branches, often more dramatically.[14] In category 3118, *bakeries and tortilla,* total value added (in millions) was *$34,108*, the payroll was *$9,442*; hence *$24,666* was returned to capital, more than double the amount returned to labor. The *pattern of returns to capital and labor* is clear in every sector and sub-sector of manufacturing.

At the start of his book Piketty asks: "But what do we really know about ... [the evolution of the capital-labor split] over the long term?" [242]. Here he raises a good question, one that he only gets to however, in the second half of this major work. In the first half, among other things, Piketty takes pains to make clear his own theoretical perspective, and explains that (growing up at the time he did) he: "was vaccinated for life against the conventional but lazy rhetoric of anticapitalism." "If capital plays a useful role in the process of production, it is natural that it should be paid" [423]. He declares he has "no interest in denouncing inequality or capitalism per se—especially since social inequalities are not themselves a problem as long as they are justified ..." [31].

In terms of the justification for labor's share, it is conventionally held that the increasing use of labor-saving technology reduces labor's role in production; hence reductions in the share of the value added that will be distributed as remuneration to labor are legitimate. Herbert Marcuse noted in *One-Dimensional Man* (1964) that manufacturing would utilize ever-increasing automation technologies such that labor's role would be increasingly diminished and ultimately eliminated. He did not conclude however that this should mean that the bulk of the compensation from manufacturing *should* go to capitalist owners. Instead he saw this tendency as lowering the real per-unit costs of production almost to nothing and making abundance an historical possibility.[15] We should also understand that the technologies are often developed through a web of scientific support activities at public research institutions, not by manufacturers themselves. They build upon productive forces that are part of a social fabric, such that the gains of technological advance should properly accrue to the public as commonwealth. Under capitalism however the powers

---

14   It is true that the return to capital is composed of rent and interest as well as profit (including interest); the margins in the apparel industry are notoriously thin and can actually be less than returns to labor.

15   See Herbert Marcuse, *One-Dimensional Man* (Boston: Beacon, 1964), pp. 24–25, 35–36.

of technology are used to intensify reductions in labor compensation through de-skilling and outsourcing/offshoring.

A key theme in Piketty's work and ours is thus the notion of a capital-labor split in the distribution of the national income. Piketty asks: what is the "right" split between capital and labor? [41, 263]. We on the other hand (as apparently indolent anticapitalists) offer Marx's radical admonition to the rising labor force: "Instead of the *conservative* motto '*A fair day's wage for a fair day's work!*' they should inscribe on their banner the revolutionary watchword 'Abolition of the wages system.'"[16]

Piketty tells us that the split of the national income between labor and capital is traditionally calculated to be "[r]oughly *65–70 percent for wages and other income from labor and 30–35 percent for profits, rent, and other income from capital*" [41, 583]. He notes at the outset however that the reality is more complicated than that. The complications take up the first two hundred pages of his book (more on this below). *Our calculation* of the split between labor and capital (looking specifically at the capital-labor shares in the manufacturing sector of the u.s. and using u.s. Census Bureau data, as we have seen above), *has these proportions just the other way round, with the lion's share (almost three quarters) going to capital!*[17] In the light of this official government information, the thought that businesses can reduce inequality by "creating jobs" would seem to be politically deceptive and pathetic for labor, given that each quantity q of income flow from such a job is generally accompanied (in the private manufacturing sector) by an income flow of $3q$ to capital.

Our analysis, outlined above, utilizes a straightforward model of income flows. Piketty side-steps this in what to us seems to be a curious circumvention. Thus he begins his analysis of the changing features of inequality in the world by asserting: "The most fruitful way to understand these changes is to analyze the evolution of the capital/income ratio (that is, the ratio of the total stock of capital to the annual flow of income) rather than focus exclusively on the capital-labor split (that is, the share of income going to capital and labor, respectively)" [42]. With this, his study is off in a new direction, yet a few pages later the analysis swerves and takes a back flip: "The capital/income ratio for the country as a whole tells us nothing about inequalities within the country. But β does measure the overall importance of capital in a society, so analyzing this

---

16   Marx in Reitz and Spartan, op. cit., p. 35–36.

17   Piketty deals with data from France and more than a dozen other countries including the United States. While Spartan and I share certain methodological presuppositions, our focus is exclusively on the u.s. This precludes any unmediated comparisons of our findings to Piketty's, yet a careful comparison of conclusions will be presented below.

ratio is a necessary first step in the study of inequality."[18] Then we are in for 1) an assertion that seems designed to reduce *what he will consider* as income from capital (Ci): "a portion of what is called 'the income of capital' may be remuneration for entrepreneurial labor, and this should no doubt be treated as we treat other forms of labor," [41] and 2) a big surprise: "... this spectacular increase in inequality largely reflects an unprecedented explosion of very elevated incomes from labor, a veritable separation of the top managers of large firms from the rest of the population" [24]. Piketty may have deftly set the stage to underestimate income to capital to a very significant degree, helpful also to his *reinterpretation of the meaning* of rising inequality overall.

Piketty tells us that, in France and the U.S. especially, executive supersalaries [276, 298] are the factor most responsible for the intensifying inequalities. Piketty's method also overestimates the labor share of the national income because he defines executive pay as remuneration for *labor*. He finds that of the top 10% of income earners in the U.S., only the top 1% receive most of their income from capital [277, 280]. The bottom 9% of these get their remuneration primarily from their executive labor [279], though he admits that this remuneration cannot be adequately demonstrated as deserved in terms of the executives' own marginal productivity [308, 330]. Rather the *norms* of the corporate boards' compensation committees have become permissive [333]!

The failure of the theory of marginal productivity to explain CEO compensation and its disjunction from the practices of corporate compensation committees seems a blatant contradiction. It raises two immediate questions: if the top executives themselves do not produce a major share of the substance of their own remuneration, who does? And if much of this compensation is given as stock or stock options, then must not this portion be considered *apart* from Li (Labor income) as a redistribution or transfer of a property claim on assets composed of already extant wealth/capital? Compensation through rights to stock ownership, if this is to be considered a flow from the value added through the production process, must be seen *by definition* in national income accounting as Ci (Capital income). Compensation packages of top executives used to recruit and retain skilled managerial and technical labor are composed of several components, reflecting a *multiple class positioning*. Salary due to their marginal product might with some warrant be seen as labor compensation. Compensation beyond their marginal product, which Piketty acknowledges as routine, i.e. bonuses, stock options, etc., may be due to their

---

18   Piketty, op. cit., p. 51. Piketty says understanding why the capital/income ratio varies from
       country to country is a goal of Part Two of his study. Thomas Piketty, *Capital in the Twenty-
       First Century*. (Cambridge: Harvard University Press, 2014)

relative monopolization of a key decision-making position and the seeking of rent-like possibilities, rather than to the scarcity of their talents within a managerial labor pool.

Piketty's *Capital in the Twenty-First Century* is significantly burdened by obfuscation. This becomes abundantly clear when Piketty diminishes the question of income from inherited wealth as a social justice issue: "To be sure income from labor is not always equitably distributed, and it would be unfair to reduce the question of social justice to the importance of income from labor versus income from inherited wealth" [241]. Starting with a consideration of "Inequalities with Respect to Labor and Capital" [242] any ostensible concern Piketty might have had with the injustice of the given patterns of the capital-labor split is recast here as a discourse on "Two Worlds"—which becomes a 100-plus page excursion into a description of inequalities *internal to* the flow of income to labor that are considered in disjunction from inequalities *internal to* the flow of income to capital! We are treated to Table 7.1 on "Inequality of labor income across time and space" [247]. Table 7.2 presents "Inequality of capital ownership across time and space" [248]. Table 7.3 gives us "Inequality of total income (labor and capital) across time and space," [249] and hypotheses are proffered concerning the meaning of inequality in the u.s. So, we read, for example, how "inequality with respect to capital is always greater than inequality with respect to labor" [244]. Further, "If inequalities are seen as justified, say because they seem to be a consequence of a choice by the rich to work harder or more efficiently than the poor ... then it is perfectly possible for the concentration of income to set new historical records. That is why I indicate in Table 7.3 that the United States may set a new record around 2030 if inequality of income from labor—and to a lesser extent inequality of ownership of capital—continue to increase as they have done in recent decades. ... " [This would be] "a very inegalitarian society, but one in which the peak of the income hierarchy is dominated by very high incomes from labor rather than inherited wealth" [264–265]. "[W]hat primarily characterizes the Unites States at the moment is a record level of inequality of income from labor ... together with a level of inequality of wealth less extreme than the levels observed in traditional societies or in Europe in the period 1900–1910" [265].

If top incomes have grown far in excess of the economy's overall rate of growth, something had to give. These grew at the expense of what? Piketty tells us the top incomes grew at the expense of many in the labor force, but this shift is not to be explained by heightened returns to capital—rather by heightened returns to supersalaried executives, in his estimation, labor's elite.

Thus some of the key causes and consequences of capitalist inequality in its historical and political context are diminished: it's not that following decades of labor speedup,[19] the recovery continues to facilitate enormous amounts of capital accumulation[20] and the intensification of poverty.[21] Piketty does *not* see inequality as primarily a matter of the structural relationships in the economic arena between propertied and non-propertied segments of populations. Capitalism generates some extreme inequalities, but apparently not primarily through a system of appropriation is embedded within the relationship of wage labor to capital in the distribution process. In his view U.S. capitalism a less a society dominated by a parasitic rentier class than by (non-parasitic?) supermanagers. Stiglitz and Greider are renowned for macroeconomic analyses demonstrating just the opposite.[22]

Entrenched CEOs can gain so much structural power that they are virtually independent of boards of directors and corporate compensation committees, directing the strategic mission and the organizational culture, and acquiring unearned advantages (rents). At the same time their decisions may be exploitative and detrimental to the labor force overall. Critical Marxists like Erik Olin Wright have demonstrated in contrast to Piketty that certain class locations can exhibit overlap and structural social complexity.[23] Supersalaried executives should *not* be seen as *labor's* elite, but rather as occupying *interpenetrating class locations*. This shows why such

---

19   See Monika Bauerlein and Clara Jeffery, "Speedup. All Work and No Pay," the cover story in *Mother Jones* July and August 2011, pp. 18–25. Also Ben Agger, *Speeding Up Fast Capitalism* (Boulder: Paradigm Publishers 2004).

20   In December 2014, the Pew Research Center using data from the Federal Reserve reported that income inequality in the U.S. had reached to its widest point in the last three decades, intensifying the wealth gap. At the median of top wealth quintile in 2013 owners held twice as much as they did in 1980. See Patricia Cohen, "Fueled by Recession, U.S. Wealth Gap Is Widest In Decades, Study Finds," *The New York Times,* December 18, 2014, p. B-3. 2014 was also the third consecutive year of a "bull run" in which Standard & Poor's stock index rose more than 10 percent, according to Peter Eavis, "Markets Hit Highs in '14 As Bull Run Endured," *The New York Times,* January 1, 2015. See also "Companies Spend on Equipment, Not Workers," *The New York Times,* June 10, 2011, p. A-1.

21   Sabrina Tavernise, "Poverty Reaches 52-Year Peak, Government Says," *The New York Times,* September 14, 2011, p. A-1.

22   See Stiglitz, op. cit., chapter 2, "Rent Seeking and the Making of an Unequal Society," pp. 28–51. Also "The Rentiers' Regime" in William Greider, *One World Ready or Not: The Manic Logic of Global Capitalism* (New York: Simon & Shuster, 1997), pp. 285–315.

23   The issues of the boundary dispute were treated in and Erik Olin Wright's *Class Structure and Income Determination* (New York: Academic Press, 1979).

supersalaries should *not* be counted as remuneration to labor. Wright's dialectical conception of class and multiple class positioning sets my analysis apart from Piketty's, and leads to different conclusions. Here we see that the real debate revolves *not around data*, but rather around the *interpretation of the data, theory.*

Seldom discussed among students (or among faculty) is the question of where wealth comes from or the nature of the relationship of wealth to labor. These issues were first formulated, and for many economists settled without controversy, in the classical economic theory of John Locke and Adam Smith. As is well known, they held that a person's labor is the real source of all wealth and property that one might have the right to call one's own. Locke emphasized the natural equality of human beings and that nature was given to humanity in common. My perspective builds upon Locke and Smith, but stresses with Marx that labor is a *social* process; that the value created through labor is most genuinely measured by socially necessary labor time and its product rightfully *belongs* to the labor force as a *body*, not to individuals as such, i.e. grounding a theory of common ownership and social justice. Where Locke and Smith saw individual labor as the source of private property, in an atomistic (Robinsonian) manner, Marx recognized that all humans are born into a social context. Humanity's earliest *customs*, i.e. communal production, shared ownership, and solidarity assured that the needs of all were met, i.e. including those not directly involved in production like children, the disabled, and the elderly. This right of the commonwealth to govern itself, and humanity's earliest ethic of holding property in common, derive only secondarily from factual individual contributions to production; they are rooted primarily in our essentially shared species nature as humans, as empathic social beings. Communal labor sustained human life and human development. When commodified as it is today, labor's wealth-creating activity is no longer a good in itself. The overall "value" of the activity of the workforce, governed by capitalist property relations, is reduced to its aggregate payroll. The workforce is never fully remunerated for its contribution to the production process precisely because its contribution, when commodified through the labor market, *tends to be reduced to the equivalent of the bare cost of labor force reproduction,* and the "surplus" is appropriated as property by powerful non-producers.

This essay has questioned critical aspects of Piketty's methodology, use, and interpretation of data, as well as his conventional assumptions on the meaning of inequality, the origins of income and wealth, and the nature of economic justice. It urges that we need to get beyond Piketty to understand both capital and inequality; likewise it advocates for a radical political economy that stresses the transformation of commodified labor into decommodified *public* work, work for the public good, common*work* for a common*wealth.* "The very achievements of capitalism have brought about its obsolescence *and* the possibility of *the alternative.*"[24]

---

24   Herbert Marcuse, "Why Talk on Socialism?" in Charles Reitz (ed.) *Crisis and Commonwealth: Marcuse, Marx, McLaren* (Lanham: Lexington Books, 2013), p. 309.

CHAPTER 11

The Political Dimensions of Economic Division: Republicanism, Social Justice, and the Evaluation of Economic Inequality

Michael J. Thompson

Introduction: The Problem

Economic inequality is one of the most salient and concrete expressions of social power. It entails inequality of control—over resources, over people, over the purposes and goals of the community itself. The idea that economic inequality is a matter of power, however, continues to elude the dominant mainstream discussions of it as a social problem and social reality in the social sciences and in political philosophy as well. The empirical investigation into the dynamics and contours of economic inequality has ballooned in recent years. These studies have benefitted from contemporary statistical models, large datasets, and computer analyses to give us a generally consistent picture of economic divisions. The results have been nothing short of staggering. Indeed, what Alderson and Nielsen have termed the "great economic U-turn," can now be seen to have come full circle.[1] Whereas gains by labor unions and the progressive democratic pressures of the public during the 1960s and 1970s had led to a significant reduction in inequalities of wealth and income, the 1980s and onward have witnessed a return to the bloated inequalities of the pre-Depression period. What we now call "neo-liberalism" is therefore a new phase of economic inequality where economic elites have unbridled capacity to control the economic resources and the ends toward which they are employed for society as a whole. Despite this, analyses of economic inequality remain stuck in the liberal values that have consistently accompanied capitalist society. It is therefore crucial, in my view, that we seek to construct an alternative set of values and evaluative categories that can help in sustaining a critical account of economic inequality and the kinds of capitalist dynamics that impel them.

---

1   See Arthur. S. Alderson and Francois Nielsen, "Globalization and the Great U-Turn: Income Inequality: Trends in 16 OECD Countries." *American Journal of Sociology* vol. 107 (5) 2002, pp. 1244–1299.

In what follows, I would like to propose an understanding of economic inequality that is distinct from the more economistic thinking that so deeply marks our policy and ethical debates. According to this "thin" understanding, economic equality is an issue mainly of distributive justice alone; it concerns the extent to which the gap between incomes and wealth can be narrowed so that individuals may have equal access to other personal and social goods—such as political participation, levels of consumption, educational and employment opportunities, and so on. What I propose is a different understanding of economic equality and inequality, one rooted in a republican understanding of politics that relies on a "thicker" understanding of the descriptive account of economic divisions. A republican conception of politics, briefly stated, holds that the purpose or end of social institutions should be to enhance and pursue the common interest of the society as a whole. According to this view, inequality in the economy can be seen as the extent to which certain members of the community are able to control the common resources of the society as well as redefine the purposes and ends of that society as a whole. As a result, economic inequality leads ineluctably to a degradation of the common interest and the re-orientation of public, common goods toward elite, particular interests.

Liberal-distributive theories of justice generally fail to penetrate into this level of the structure of social life. In another sense, liberalism can be seen to reinforce and even justify economic inequality based on market principles.[2] John Rawls, for instance, argues that the two basic principles of justice—the equality of basic liberties and the "difference principle"—are principles of distributing rights and duties throughout the basic structure of social institutions.[3] But in an attempt to achieve "justice as fairness," there is no sense that we can conceive of a basic set of purposes or ends toward which these institutions ought to be oriented. We are left unable to judge the purposes and projects of individuals, even when they come to steer the purposes of the rest of society as a whole. As I see it, a deeper understanding of the importance of economic inequality can be addressed by understanding how the activities and purposes of economic actors come to affect the common interest of the community: whether or not they violate the two conditions of public maintenance and equal power relations. Beyond the *deontological* concerns with equality of access and opportunity, there is the more substantive issue of the *consequences* of the interests of private power and its ability

---

2   Michael J. Thompson, *The Politics of Inequality: A Political History of the Idea of Economic Inequality in America.* (New York: Columbia University Press, 2007).

3   John Rawls, *A Theory of Justice.* (Cambridge: Harvard University Press, 1971).

to affect and shape social and public life more broadly. Economic inequality is therefore an expression of power, it concerns the issue of living according to the interests of a shared public life, or according to the interests and power of private groups.

The Limits of the Contemporary Analysis of Economic Inequality

Thomas Piketty's much-discussed recent study of economic inequality has provoked many to look anew at the problem. Although Piketty is able to chart the empirical contours of inequality, what is lacking from his empiricism is a critical account of what makes inequality a normative problem. Indeed, the mainstream approaches of modern economics basically confine themselves to the utilitarian and welfarist problems of inequality. According to this account, inequality may be unfair in the sense that some individuals are unable to attain a basic standard of welfare or that the overall sum of utility has not been maximized. But these are very thin and minimal accounts of the problem of inequality. The prime limitation seems to me to be that these positions are defined by merely distributional concerns of personal forms of welfare and utility. They are unable to grasp a deeper and more important concern: that economic relations need to be seen as political relations, as relations of social power. What I would like to suggest is that inequality be evaluated not according to the individualist account of welfare and utility or, as the liberal approach to political philosophy would have it, an equality of opportunities or basic primary goods, and instead conceive of inequality as a pathology of the common good itself. According to this account, we should measure inequality according to the extent to which it is able to reduce the overall good to which members of the community as a whole have access. This common or public good is the condition to be maximized, something I call the *public maintenance maxim* which holds that all resources should be put toward common, public goods and purposes before they can be utilized for merely private ends. In this sense, inequality should be seen as the advancement of private ends over public ones. It violates what I will basically refer here to as a republican conception of social justice.

At the root of the liberalism is a set of ideas that, as I see it, stand in opposition to a kind of egalitarianism that would be just in an optimal sense. Most importantly there is the notion that individuals are free to the extent that they can *secure freedom from the interference from the state in their own chosen courses of life and in their affairs*. It seeks a society that is structured, as William Galston has put it, "to create and sustain circumstances within which individuals may pursue—and to the greatest possible extent achieve—their good."[4] In particular, this doctrine holds that socio-economic affairs require immunity from state interference. From this basic principle derives two logics that, in addition to defining the general field of American political culture, come into contradiction with the other. On the one hand, it allows for the development of an equality of rights between all individuals, assigning them an equal weight in terms of the law and in terms of their basic access to protection of the law. It seeks to promote the freedom of the individual. But the second logic that stems from liberalism is that one can dispose of their property without the interference of the state since property is attached to the individual, who is, according to the essence of this principle, to be free as an individual from state interference.

Central to the liberal view on economic inequality, however is its ability to constrain the opportunities and life chances of the poor. One manifestation of this idea is found in the "difference principle" of Rawls which states that an equal distribution of goods should be preferred unless an alternative scheme can be shown to help the least disadvantaged. For Rawls, the key principle behind equality is the notion that each will have the adequate "primary goods" to be able to pursue their own conceptions of the good. This becomes a core structural element of liberal theories of equality: that behind it is a principle of fairness that allows all to be able to follow their own interests and conceptions of the good life. Hence, Brian Barry argues that any conception of social justice must subsume liberal justice which holds that all must be treated equally. For Barry, social justice consists of "the claim that the distribution of opportunities and resources within a society ... makes for a society's being just or unjust."[5] Similarly, Amartya Sen argues that we should see inequality as affecting the chances that poorer individuals possess to realize their capabilities and functionings.[6] Poverty therefore reduces the capacity of the poor to be able to convert their functionings into capabilities. Equality must therefore be concerned with taking into consideration the different needs that different individuals may possess.[7]

These philosophical positions, despite the differences between them, all possess a basic a priori assumption: that inequality reduces the ability of individuals to act on the choices and opportunities they have to live their lives.

---

4   William Galston, *Liberal Purposes: Goods, Virtues and Diversity in the Liberal State*. (New York: Cambridge University Press, 1991), p. 183.

5   Brian Barry, *Why Social Justice Matters*. (Cambridge: Polity, 2005), p. 22.

6   Amartya Sen, *On Economic Inequality*. (New York: Oxford University Press, 1997).

7   See Amartya Sen, *Choice, Welfare and Measurement*. (Cambridge: MIT Press, 1998).

These approaches basically focus on distribution as a means to allow individuals to live an abstract conception of the good. But we can instead choose to see economic inequality as a thicker phenomenon: one which shapes the relations of power among individuals, but also the shape and content of the social product or social wealth as a whole. The key to evaluating an unequal society is to keep in view the extent to which inequalities are not simply concerned with depriving individuals of primary goods, opportunities, functionings, or whatever, but more importantly, how it affects the social whole and the ends to which economic activities and resources are employed. One can easily imagine a society that fulfills an equality condition in liberal terms—according to those of utility, welfare, primary goods, or whatever—without considering the extent to which the society that these individuals have access to, toward which they work, and how the human and natural resources are employed and utilized, all can still be for ends that are not beneficial in a social, public sense. As I see it, economic inequality should be judged precisely on this basis, and a more compelling, more robust theory of social justice can be derived from understanding the ways that economic divisions reshape and reorient the utilization of collective resources and efforts away from collective, public goods and ends.

The Mechanism of Inequality

Before proceeding to the specific ways that economic inequality creates the conditions for injustice and the introduction of alternative evaluative categories that should be employed to judge economic inequality more generally, I would like to outline what I see to be the basic mechanism of economic inequality and the different forms it can take in market societies. This descriptive aspect of my argument will be important in formulating the critical categories I will use to open up a more compelling conception of social justice. As I see it, basic to the generation of inequality in market societies is the phenomenon of unequal exchange (see Figure 11.1). An unequal exchange occurs for a multiplicity of reasons, but in its essence, it is defined as a surplus benefit gained from extracting some resource from another. Hence, anytime person A exchanges some good with person B, their exchange will result in $A > B$ if A is able to extract some benefit from B. We do not need to understand unequal exchange in strict, zero-sum terms. According to this logic, the benefit gained by A is exactly the amount lost by B. But this is an unrealistic and overly demanding criterion. For one thing, the benefit needs to be a surplus benefit for A, but need not be a total loss for B. Unequal exchange simply means that B is not as well as off after his exchange with A. Hence, in any capitalist relation between a worker and an owner, the owner will pay a wage for the labor time worked by the worker. The owner benefits by selling the product of the laborer for more than what the laborer put into it in terms of wages.

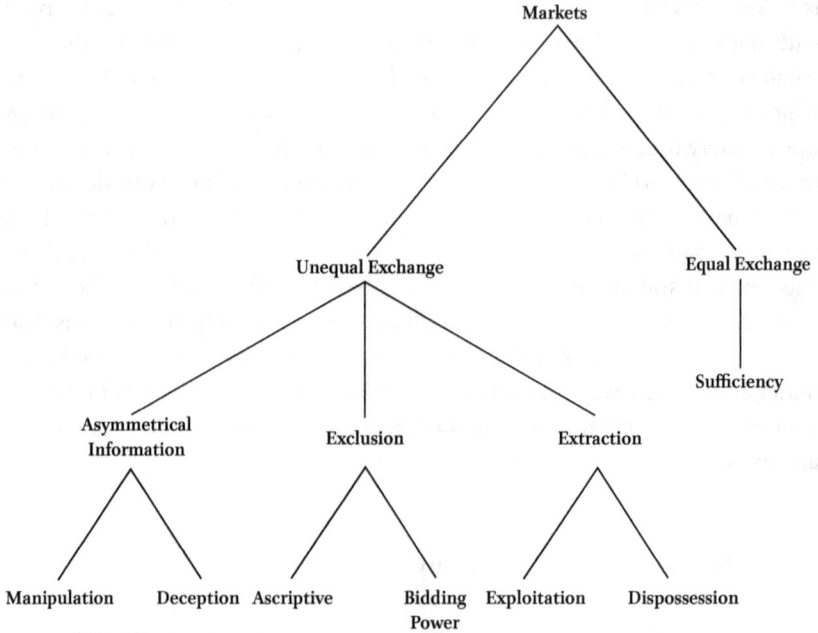

FIGURE 11.1 *Breakdown of market forms in terms of type of exchange and their features*

But the worker still received wages at the end of the day. In other words, the total benefit received by the owner is not equal to the total loss from the laborer. Therefore, there can be unequal exchange without person A receiving all of the benefit that person B has lost within an exchange. In this case, A and B can still be unequal within a dynamic model of overall growth. If we denote the benefit received, k, at different time periods, t, for each agent, the simple expression of unequal exchange given above, $A > B$, would be rewritten as: $(A^{t_1}_{k_A} > B^{t_1}_{k_B}) \rightarrow (A^{t_2}_{k_A} > B^{t_2}_{k_B})$ where growth of the overall condition gives us $(k^{t_1}_A + k^{t_1}_B) < (k^{t_2}_A + k^{t_2}_B)$ but the structural relation of unequal exchange continues in any subsequent exchange $(k^{t_1}_A < k^{t_2}_A)$ and $(k^{t_1}_B < k^{t_2}_B)$. This means that unequal exchange can, and indeed does, persist beyond any kind of zero-sum logic. B can be better off than he was before his interaction with A, but this does not mean that B has not been extracted from and that surplus benefit has not been absorbed by A. In this case, we can see that unequal exchange can coexist with an increasing benefit to both parties and that a rejection of the argument of unequal exchange is not countered based on a rejection of the simplistic zero-sum logic.

An equal exchange exists when each person in the exchange relation are able to receive roughly equal benefit from one another without surplus gain being received by either party. Hence, in any equal exchange, the outcome between persons A and B must result in $A \cong B$. The outcome of any equal exchange relation is therefore *sufficiency*; it is the condition that emerges from any relation of equality.[8] The essential mechanism of economic inequality is therefore unequal exchange. But this entails unpacking the kinds of unequal exchange that can manifest itself in socio-economic relations. Inequalities of income and wealth are not sufficient in themselves to account for the contours of inequality that exist. At the core of the mechanism of unequal exchange is the capacity of privately controlled surplus to exercise other forms of power over others. In this sense, the reality of economic inequality cannot be simply understood through the micro-social relation of interpersonal exchange since patterns of individual micro-interactions migrate into larger social processes, institutions, practices, and so on—quantity turns into quality.[9] Rather, it is the product of certain logics of social action that are patterned, legitimated and often times necessitated by social-structural form and the norms and constraints it imposes on social actors.

Unequal exchange can occur in three different scenarios that we find frequently in modern capitalist-market societies. These are *extraction, asymmetrical information* and *exclusion*. These are not exhaustive, and they can overlap, but they are analytically distinct categories. According to the first, I can extract benefit from you when I exploit you or when I dispossess you from something. In an exploitive relation, I gain benefit from you by extracting surplus from your labor or from some capacity that you possess. But in dispossession, I am able to accumulate surplus by taking away things you already possess or things which were previously public and are now absorbed into private control. This can be done by changing laws, cutting entitlements and

---

8   It should not be deduced from this that any condition of equal or sufficient exchange need result in economic stagnation. Economic growth does not necessitate the kind of unequal exchange characteristic of extractive/capitalist forms of market structure.

9   This view is against those who see inequality as emerging from micro-market interactions. For this argument, see James Child "Profit: The Concept and its Moral Features." In Ellen Frankel Paul, Fred D. Miller and Jeffrey Paul (eds.) *Problems of Market Liberalism*, (New York: Cambridge University Press, 1998).

so on so as to transform property rights and to disenfranchise a group from accessing and utilizing that good.[10] But I can also *exclude* you from certain goods, opportunities, services, social networks, relations, and so on. Social networks, circumscribed by class relations, can act as exclusionary boundaries to access certain jobs and the like. Municipalities can erect tax barriers that keep out certain racial (what we can call "ascriptive exclusion") or class groups, thereby restricting access to certain kinds of public goods (education, sanitation, and so on).

Unequal incomes and wealth can also lead to inequalities in *bidding power* where groups and individuals are excluded because of their inability to access certain kinds of goods and services. This inequality of bidding power leads to a differentiated market for many kinds of goods and services creating a multi-tiered society: quality of education, public goods and social networks are structured according to the bidding power of individuals. Similarly, phenomena such as gentrification and the transformation of public space succumb to the interests of those that can afford to invest in property and controlling shares in them. Lastly, *asymmetrical information* is an unequal exchange that can occur because of the incapacity of certain individuals and groups to be able to understand the nature of the exchange or the value of the objects being exchanged. I can get you to purchase an item that you may not need; I may persuade you to purchase something for a price that far exceeds its worth; or I may be able to manipulate you in other ways to get you to sell something, to enter into a contractual relation, or whatever, that is not in your best interest and from which I stand to gain at your expense. This is the situation of *manipulation* where *A* possesses more information about a transaction or good than *B* and uses that in some sense to cheat or otherwise benefit from that inequality of information.[11]

---

10   For a fuller account of what he terms "accumulation by dispossession," which includes "the commodification and privatization of land … conversion of various forms of property rights to the commons; commodification of labor power and the suppression of alternative forms of production and consumption," see David Harvey, *A Brief History of Neoliberalism* (New York: Oxford University Press, 2005), 159 and *passim*. It should be noted that this can also include transforming previously public entitlements into the private realm, such as the privatization of public education, the move from pension funds to retirement accounts, the elimination of health and other kinds of public insurance, and so on. All of these are done for the purpose of extraction, but they are, in essence, distinctive forms of unequal exchange.

11   See George Akerlof and Robert Shiller, *Phishing for Phools: The Economics of Manipulation and Deception*. (Princeton: Princeton University Press, 2015).

But it can also lead to more fundamental problems of *deception*, which is the capacity to manipulate demand and tastes based on the intentional manipulation of facts (such as health or environmental impact of particular goods or products, and so on).

From this brief discussion of the different dimensions of unequal exchange, we can see that markets are not simply relations of exchange, but also mechanisms of social power. They are structural relations between individuals and groups that allow for the exercise of different kinds of inequality and control. Of course, not all market relations are this way. If I purchase a house from you for a fair price, or any other purchase where you do not gain at my expense, then sufficiency is the result. But the dominant mode of economic life governed by accumulation and capital mitigates against these kinds of exchange. Ideological defenders of the market therefore seek to confuse by casting all market relations in terms of the equal exchange model, obfuscating from view the more prevalent forms of unequal exchange that predominate economic life. The reality of unequal exchange is more than simply a plausible outcome of economic relations, it is the express purpose of capitalist forms of economic life. Unequal exchange also undermines the basic thesis that pro-market writers hold: that markets enable choice and allow the expression of individual agency. As my theoretical analysis demonstrates, the opposite will more likely be the case: that unequal exchanges will form patterns of inequality, of power and of the constriction of choice (Singer 1978), instead leading to the institutionalization of unequal power relations.[12] But even more, theorists who hold that markets are in some basic sense expressions of "spontaneous order" are holding to an ideal understanding of markets at best and a theoretically deficient understanding of them at worst.[13] In the end, these three broad forms of unequal exchange, extraction, exclusion and asymmetrical information, lead to denser structures of inequality. These structures of inequality, as we should see them, may have unequal exchange as their basic starting point and generative mechanism, but they themselves come to take on their own dynamics. It is for this reason that we must turn to look at the ways that these structures of inequality violate the republican conception of social justice that I am outlining here.

---

12   Peter Singer, "Rights and the Market." In John Arthur and William H. Shaw (eds.) *Justice and Economic Distribution*. (Englewood Cliffs: Prentice-Hall, 1978), pp. 198–211.

13   For an example of this view and an attempt to fuse it to a theory of justice, see John Tomasi "Political Legitimacy and Economic Liberty." *Social Philosophy and Policy*, vol. 29 (1) 2012, pp. 50–80.

Economic Inequality and the Contours Social Injustice

Since unequal exchange cannot simply be conceptualized as a logic between isolated actors nor in terms of a micro-relation between individuals, we should instead see that unequal exchange is embedded in the institutional structures of society. Once this becomes the case, inequality can no longer be seen as a purely economic phenomenon but is now a distinctly *political* one. This means that unequal exchanges are not simply about the inequality of benefits, opportunities, or anything of that sort, but rather *inequalities of power*—power over the resources, people and purposes of the community as a whole. In this sense, economic inequality violates the principle of social justice by allowing for the unequal power of certain segments of the community over what could otherwise be utilized by the community as a whole according to the common or public interest. This criterion needs to be elaborated since it is the first major step beyond the liberal understanding of social justice. As I see it, goods within any society can be broadly categorized as those that essentially benefit all, or the public as a whole on the one hand and those that benefit a particular individual or group at the expense of another, a group or the community as a whole. I will call the first kind of good a *common* or *public* good and the second a *pleonexic* good.[14]

The important point here is that any pleonexic good can only be produced through the logic of unequal exchange or by in some sense exploiting or extracting some benefit from another. It is a structural relation between agents that places emphasis on the capacity of one agent to control in some sense the actions or capacities of another agent for the former's surplus benefit. In this sense, pleonexic goods entail *pleonexic social relations*; they necessitate that unequal exchange grant certain parties more power in society than others by which is meant more control over the decisions of what to produce and how; capacities to consume and utilize resources (natural and human) that according to their particular needs and ends; and the capacity to shape the aims and goals of the society as a whole.[15] Pleonexic goods and relations therefore, when they go unchecked and begin to proliferate throughout the economy, polity

---

14   I derive the term "pleonexic" from the Greek πλεονέξια which means "to want more than what one needs."

15   Marx therefore maintains that under the private control of economic resources and modes of production is a perversion of the true nature of modern social production, which is truly collective and socialized. However, the benefits of this process of socialized production flow to those who own and control capital. Hence, capital is, for Marx, "not a personal, it is a social power," Karl Marx, *The Communist Manifesto* (New York: Vintage, 1959), p. 21. The political moment therefore is the conversion of the private control of

and society, lead to a condition of *oligarchic wealth* which refers to the way that surplus is used to serve the ends of particular segments of the community (i.e., the wealthy) as opposed to the interests of the community as a whole. Since any society produces some degree of surplus, we can judge the extent of social justice within any community by evaluating how it manages and utilizes this surplus. Whenever surplus is controlled by the few for the interests of the few, we have a condition of oligarchic wealth. Oligarchic wealth is not only a kind of social wealth, it also entails a particular kind of socio-economic and political structure to sustain it: there are certain institutions, certain norms, practices, laws, and so on, that will be required to sustain and to enhance oligarchic wealth. The first and most important among these is the need to defend that wealth and the income gained from it.[16]

Comparing pleonexic and common goods means understanding the ways that unequal versus equal exchanges are privileged. In Figure 11.2, I compare the ways that two different benefit schemes can be shown to differ based on the kinds of goods that are pursued. Both curves α and β represent the frontier of benefits that different kinds of exchange/production relations can offer to two different agents, A and B. Pleonexic goods result in an unequal benefit for A and B. Hence, for α we can see that line y_1 delineates benefit for person A over person B, and y_3 delineates benefit for person B over person A. However, line y_2 represents an equal benefit for both A and B. Even under conditions of economic expansion and growth, giving us the curve β we can see that z_1 and z_3 both delineate pleonexic relations or goods and z_2 again a common good. Figure 11.2 therefore is meant to show how, in a simplistic sense, common versus pleonexic goods can be understood as bestowing not simply unequal benefit, but benefits that are tied to others. It is not simply a matter of person A getting a different amount of benefit from person B; what is essential in this concept is that the production of these goods, the purpose of their production and the kinds of relations that spring from them determine the distribution of benefit.

Of course, it would be absurd to argue that all benefit schemes must be wholly equal. One person may have more need for healthcare than another, therefore receiving more benefit from the healthcare system than another.

---

capital to social control, "into the property of all members of society, personal property is thereby not transformed into social property. It is only the social character of the property that is changed. It loses its class character," Marx, *Communist Manifesto*, 22. Marx is here outlining a republican conception of social justice insofar as he is stating the need for the accountability of the social product to society as a whole.

16   See the important discussion by Jeffrey Winters, *Oligarchy*. (New York: Cambridge University Press, 2011).

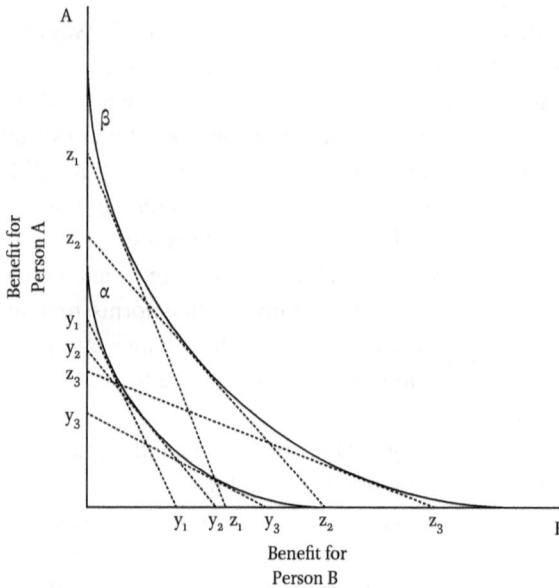

FIGURE 11.2 *Pleonexic and common good benefit schemes*

But healthcare satisfies a republican conception of justice only once we can show that the highest quality of healthcare is potentially available for all equally as any other.[17] The key issue here is that benefits are not being extracted from one individual or group in order to be converted or in some way transferred to another individual or group. It is essential that the resources, labor and capacities of society ought to be used for social ends and not extracted by private persons for their particular ends and projects. What is essentially common about the common interest or common goods is therefore that they promote the development of each individual within the community as an individual, but an individual who is mutually related to others, an individual who is part of a structure of interdependent relations and that these interdependent relations ought to promote the good of all

---

17   This is why Marx's concept of justice must be seen as moving beyond any liberal, "bourgeois," form of right: "one worker is married, another not; one has more children than another, and so on and so forth. Thus, with an equal performance of labor, and hence and equal share in the social consumption fund, one will in fact receive more than another, one will be richer than another, and so on. To avoid all of these defects, right instead of being equal would have to be unequal." Karl Marx, "Critique of the Gotha Programme," in *Karl Marx and Friederich Engels on Philosophy and Politics*, (New York: Vintage, 1959), p. 119.

and not be the basis for the particular ends and gain of particular interests and projects.[18]

But in circumstances of economic inequality, this is precisely what takes place: unequal benefit is the essence of unequal economic relations. We can contrast this with *democratic wealth* which is the condition that holds when the economic efforts of the community are oriented toward public or common needs rather than particular needs. In this sense, the term democratic entails the object for which social and economic institutions seek to provide, not simply a means of decision making. Hence, although any valid thesis concerning social justice must, I think, take into account the democratization of the workplace, the meaning behind democratic wealth is not a decision-making one, but refers to the character of the goods produced and the means by which they are produced.[19] A society characterized by democratic wealth is therefore one where the production of wealth is done according to democratic means (i.e., without exploitation, without other forms of unequal exchange) and the purpose is to fulfill democratic, i.e., common goods and purposes of need by the community. Democratic wealth also does not allow there to be barriers to entry based on income.

Indeed, common goods are common because *all members of the community have equal access to them*. A society that places emphasis on democratic wealth over the production and consumption of pleonexic goods therefore is closer to

---

18   In her interesting reconstruction of T.H. Green's conception of the common good, Avital Simhony argues that "the common good ethic forges a non-dichotomous moral framework which aims to occupy a moral terrain of human connectedness where one's good and the good of others are intertwined, where one's fundamental interest in one's own development is not pitted against one's interest in the development of others." Avital Simhony, "T.H. Green's Complex Common Good: Between Liberalism and Communitarianism." In A. Simhony and D. Weinstein (eds.) *The New Liberalism: Reconciling Liberty and Community*. (New York: Cambridge University Press, 2001), p. 73.

19   In this sense, Daniel Bell's comment that "If there is any meaning to the idea of workers' control, it is control—*in the shop*—over the things which directly affect his workaday life: the rhythms, pace, and demands of work; a voice in the setting of equitable standards of pay; a check on the demands of the hierarchy over him. These are perhaps 'small' solutions to large problems, what Karl Popper has called 'piecemeal technology,' but look where the eschatological visions have led!" Daniel Bell "Work, Alienation and Social Control." In Irving Howe (ed.) *The Radical Papers*. (New York: Anchor Books, 1966), pp. 89–98, p. 93). Bell's fear of Soviet models of collectivism should not confuse the issue at hand here: namely that it is not simply control over the workplace, but having the entire economic system accountable to public needs and goods that should be central to any substantive theory of social justice.

realizing what I am calling here the *public maintenance maxim*: or that criterion of social justice where common goods are given priority over other kinds
of goods.[20] A society therefore wastes its resources (natural as well as human)
whenever it invests or expends them on pleonexic goods in place of those
goods and purposes which satisfy common or public ends, or those goods that
would be beneficial to all.[21]

Now we can see that unequal exchange, which I pointed to as the primary
mechanisms of economic inequality, produces pleonexic goods and relations at
the expense of common or public goods. I have also shown that the former lead
to the condition of oligarchic wealth and the unequal control over the resources,
surplus and collective decisions of the goals and aims of the society. Now, since
this condition necessarily leads to hierarchical structures of social relations,
we should consider how this social-structural context affects other dimensions
of social life. Economic inequality also leads to other kinds of anti-democratic
pathologies within society. The main variable here is unequal control over economic and therefore social resources. The more unequal a society becomes in
terms of income and wealth, the more that the control over other, non-economic
institutions and resources becomes imperative to maintain wealth-defense.
Material power, conferred by unequal control of resources and the income that
it generates, therefore is capable of shaping political power over the legal and
coercive powers of the state. As a result, economic divisions not only confer
unequal political power on those that benefit from economic resources, it also
grants them unequal influence to the political system itself.

Oligarchic forms of inequality therefore lead to the erosion of democratic
practices, institutions and attitudes within the community. Economic inequality therefore undermines the very forces and resources that have the ability to
combat it. Since economic inequality can only be undone by redistributional
measures (of income, legal rights over property, power over the capacities of
production of the economy, and so on), it is crucial that de-mobilization of
democratic practices be successful. The more unequal a society becomes, the
less active non-wealthy (especially poor) citizens become politically. They are
less inclined to vote, less inclined to discuss politics and be aware of political
concerns, and less likely to participate in political groups and parties.[22] At the

---

20   Elsewhere I have explored this idea, see my paper, "The Limits of Liberalism: A Republi-
      can Theory of Social Justice." *International Journal of Ethics* vol. 7(3) 2011, pp. 1–18.

21   See my paper, "On the Ethical Dimensions of Waste." *Archiv für Rechts- und Sozialphiloso-
      phie* vol. 101(2) 2015, pp. 252–269.

22   See Frederick Solt, "Economic Inequality and Democratic Political Engagement." *Ameri-
      can Journal of Political Science* vol. 52(1) 2008, pp. 48–60.

same time, parties become less responsive to the poor and middle class and increasingly beholden to the wealthy.[23] Policies are therefore shaped by economic elites and their distended influence over elected officials and the kinds of policies that they enact and support.[24] Oligarchy now morphs from control over economic resources to control—either direct or indirect—of others sectors of society. Now, social policy, educational imperatives, regulation, cultural production, and so on, all become shaped and influenced by economic elites.[25]

But in addition to the erosion of political activity among non-elites, especially among the poor, inequality has an effect on the political culture more generally and the social psychology of individuals. As hierarchical relations become more predominant, individuals become more predisposed to hierarchical attitudes and world-views. They begin to internalize the legitimacy of social divisions and hierarchical power relations, seeing them as natural and their place within that hierarchical scheme as justified.[26] In place of critical attitudes toward elites, the ego becomes domesticated by consistent exposure to authority leading to penchant for accepting and respecting authority.[27] In addition, authoritarian attitudes toward racial groups become heightened as economic inequality feeds social and psychological feelings of anxiety.[28] What all of this leads to is a general *de-democratization of society*.[29] Civil society fragments, the attitudes of individuals becomes less critical, more affirmative of

---

23   See Larry Bartels, *Unequal Democracy: The Political Economy of the New Gilded Age*. (Princeton: Princeton University Press, 2008).

24   See E. E. Schattschneider, *The Semi-Sovereign People: A Realist's View of Democracy in America*. (New York: Holt, Rinehart and Winston, 1960) as well as Claus Offe, "Participatory Inequality in the Austerity State: A Supply-Side Approach." In Armin Schäfer and Wolfgang Streeck (eds.) *Politics in the Age of Austerity*. (Cambridge: Polity, 2013), pp. 196–218.

25   See Henry Kariel, *The Decline of American Pluralism*. (Stanford: Stanford University Press, 1961).

26   See Robert Lane, "The Fear of Equality." *American Political Science Review* vol. 53(1) 1959. pp. 35–51 as well as Jim Sidanius and Felicia Pratto, *Social Dominance: An Intergroup Theory of Social Hierarchy and Oppression*. (New York: Cambridge University Press, 1999).

27   See Frederick Solt, "The Social Origins of Authoritarianism." *Political Research Quarterly* 65(4) 2012: 703–713.

28   See Jim Sidanius and Felicia Pratto, "Racism and Support of Free-Market Capitalism: A Cross-Cultural Analysis." *Political Psychology* vol. 14 (3) 1993, pp. 381–401 as well as Edward J. Rickert, "Authoritarianism and Economic Threat: Implications for Political Behavior." *Political Psychology*, vol. 19 (4) 1998, pp. 707–720.

29   See Armin Schäfer, "Liberalization, Inequality and Democracy's Discontent." In Armin Schäfer and Wolfgang Streeck (eds.) *Politics in the Age of Austerity*. (Cambridge: Polity, 2013) pp. 169–195.

the hierarchical structure of the community, and the legal, political and cultural superstructure of society increasingly reflects the interests of elites and less the common needs of the community itself. This is the terminus, in many ways, of the original mechanism of basic unequal exchange that I outlined above. Economic inequality is therefore more than merely an issue of maximizing the benefits to the least well off; more than about distributional justice in terms of income and opportunity. It forces us into a deeper set of questions and concerns over its effects and goods that social life ought to provide. In the remainder of this paper, I will therefore focus on an alternative scheme for understanding social justice in republican, rather than liberal, terms.

Republicanism: An Alternative Scheme to Evaluate Economic Inequality

Now that I have explored the mechanisms of inequality as well as the pathologies that stem from it, I would like to outline what I see to be a more compelling set of concepts, both normative and descriptive, that can offer us a more critical engagement with economic inequality. To go back to my opening discussion, I think it is important for anyone critical of economic inequality not only to understand its true nature and mechanisms, but also to see that liberalism has so dominated the political philosophy we use to gauge and evaluate it that we require a new set of concepts to oppose it. According to the alternative conceptual scheme I am laying out here, any condition of social justice must be one where common or public goods are promoted over pleonexic goods. This is because, as I have sought to demonstrate, pleonexic goods and the kinds of relations that produce them entail the social and political pathologies of oligarchic wealth and the unequal, anti-democratic control over the purposes and goals of the society as a whole. It follows that a society characterized by social justice would need the thicker kinds of goods that common goods support. I will point to three of these principles here and argue that they are essential features of a republican theory of social justice. These three principles are (i) the *distributive principle* that deals with equality of *access to the social product*; (ii) the *qualitative principle* which deals with the *quality of the goods and services* to which these individuals have access; and finally (iii) the *directionality principle* which deals with the public orientation of economic activities and the extent to which they fulfill public or common ends and needs as opposed to private or particular ends, interests and needs. In the end, these three principles can be used to give us a richer and more robust account of the extent of social justice within any society.

The centrality of the state in securing freedom and broader social ends of a modern community was at the heart of the Progressive philosophy and social theory during the late nineteenth and early-twentieth centuries ultimately culminating in the New Deal and its reorganization of the relation between polity and economy.[30] Basic to this reformation was the argument that the state had a responsibility to the *public*, seen as an ontologically distinct from individuals and their various individual relations with one another. The idea of a public, or common interest or of a public good means that there is some set of goods and interests that can be beneficial to all outside of their various arbitrary preferences and which ought to be protected, even at the expense of violating some of the liberties of individual or corporate bodies. Isolating a *res publica*, a common interest, means that we seek to understand and to determine that set of goods that are beneficial to all in either an *immediate, developmental,* or *potential* sense. A good is beneficial in an *immediate* sense when it has a direct, positive effect in the life of any individual. An immediate good is the access to resources needed for life (food, shelter, free time, protection from harm, and so on). A good is *developmental* when it serves to cultivate the capacities and abilities of individual agents. Education, cultural institutions, civic groups, libraries, and so on, all provide developmental goods that serve the growth of individual capacities, skills, and so on. Lastly, there are *potential* goods by which I mean those goods that are of potential benefit for any individual. In this sense, healthcare, unemployment insurance, disaster relief, environmental protections, and so on, can all be seen as potential goods that an individual would be able to access, but is neither developmental nor immediately needed by everyone at any given moment but could potentially be needed by any individual or group.

These kinds of goods can be present in different forms and different degrees in many different economic models. But the republican approach to social justice that I am advocating here argues that these goods are essential features of common or public goods and that any society that seeks to maximize social justice must also maximize access to and the quality of these kinds of goods. The central concern here is that economic inequality and the pleonexic goods and relations that it produces detract from the ability for the community to provide for itself these kinds of goods in their fullest capacity. Any pleonexic good or relation detracts from a common good because the unequal exchange

---

30   For a discussion, see the excellent study by Brian Stipelman *That Broader Definition of Liberty: The Theory and Practice of the New Deal.* (Lanham: Lexington Books, 2012), pp. 263–307.

that lies at its base is subtracted from the common fund of access of the community as a whole and is captured by the particular interest of the owner of that surplus. Economic inequality is therefore not simply a matter of distributive justice, a matter of violating the condition of "fairness." Rather, it is a deeper pathology in that it reorganizes the efforts and aims of the community as a whole.

What I mean by "resources" are human capacities, skills, and so on as well as natural and social resources. Most centrally, we can begin to understand the common interest and make it something tangible and concrete once we are able to see that the resources that are employed, the ends and purposes to which our institutions are oriented, and the kinds of social relations that are structured for people do not violate the unequal power relations condition—i.e., that no single or corporate individual or agent is able to utilize the resources of individuals or society for their own arbitrary preferences. Hence, a republican conception of social justice requires that the state take, to some significant degree, a non-neutral position with respect to the ends or purposes to which public forms of resource utilization take place. Indeed, it necessitates that the ethical neutrality of the state be re-programmed to protect, promote, and to enhance common goods and to diminish pleonexic goods.

On this view, the public maintenance condition and the power relations condition come together to provide us with a principle that helps to determine the common interest of a modern public. Since traditional understandings of the common interest or common good derive from their origins in pre-modern political communities, we often mistake it for a conservative doctrine. Similarly, the more modern formulation of this concept made by utilitarianism is also mistaken in that it sees the common good as that which meets the preferences of the good of the maximum amount of individuals. But the idea of the public and common interest that I see as attractive is one that demarcates a set of those goods that are, in some way, shared by all who live within social life. The public cannot be reduced to the sum total of individual preferences, nor can it be understood as a social contract between rational individuals. Rather, the public and its interest is, following Aristotle, *ontologically prior* to individuals and their arbitrary interests. It is necessary therefore to articulate the kinds of common goods and the kinds of social structures that are most adequate to a shared reciprocally formed life among others. The public, in this sense, is not simply made of "other people," it is, in its essence, a particular logic of social relations, of social structure itself.

Economic inequality must therefore be recast in a thicker sense that distributive understandings of justice allow. In this sense, I follow Plato rather than

Aristotle: in place of questions of distributive justice, I believe the structural idea of justice organized around the common needs and ends of the society as a whole, as the non-metaphysical layer of Plato's text lays it out, is in fact the thesis that underpins a theory of justice that can be used to explode the sterile categories of liberalism.[31] Because the structure of liberal theory must allow for the individual (personal or corporate) to be free from the interference of the state and the community as whole, it simultaneously allows for the power of private interest to co-opt the power of the state and the common interest as well.

Inequality in the sphere of economic life therefore constitutes a violation of both the public maintenance condition as well as the equal social power condition by (i) depriving an individual of a right to any set of immediate, developmental, or potential goods; and (ii) by leaving him prey to the extractive power of other individuals. The basis of economic inequality in a deeper sense is therefore more than an issue of the distribution of "basic goods" made possible by liberal theories of social justice.[32] Economic inequality is not a matter of *desert*; it is more importantly a matter of whether individuals participate in an economy that promotes the maximum possible in the way of public goods to which they have access. At the same time, it means creating and defending forms of economic life that reduce the ability of private persons and groups to obtain extractive power over other individuals.[33] Inequality is therefore the ability for private individuals and groups to steer the efforts of society and its human and natural resources toward the arbitrary preferences of elites rather than toward public, common ends. In this sense, the common interest is diminished in two senses: first, by allowing for a society where an individual does not have access to the complete set of social goods that any community

---

31   This is also the principle of social justice that underwrites any valid theory of socialism. As Henry Pachter points out, reverberating with Plato's theory of justice in the *Republic*: "In the socialist economy, capital goods, once created, enter into the consumption funds of the society, to be drawn upon as the need occurs." Henry Pachter, "Three Economic Models: Capitalism, the Welfare State, and Socialism." In Irving Howe (ed.) *The Radical Papers*. (New York: Anchor Books, 1966), p. 53.

32   See the more extensive defense of this liberal theory of social justice by Barry, *Why Inequality Matters*.

33   I take the distinction between "extractive" and "developmental" power from C.B. MacPherson, *Democratic Theory: Essays in Retrieval*. (Oxford: Oxford University Press, 1973) as well as the more developed discussion of this idea in my paper, "The Two Faces of Domination in Republican Political Theory." *European Journal of Political Theory* (in press).

can provide; and second, by forcing individuals into forms of work and life that is directed by private concerns.

Conclusion: Economic Inequality and the Republican Theory of Social Justice

From the argument I have been exploring here, I think we can begin to distill the sketch of an argument that can serve as a means to move beyond the contradiction in liberal theory I have pointed to and toward a more compelling theory of justice, one along broadly republican lines.[34] Since economic inequality is a central mechanism of social power, it represents a basic and pervasive impediment to a richer reality of justice. A republican approach to economic equality must, I think, therefore be embedded within a different paradigm of social justice for it to break out of the sterile liberal categories that continue to define current debates. Economic inequality therefore becomes more about the ability of private persons to obtain and protect their power to utilize and employ the resources of the community toward their own projects and ends. The ways they are able to adapt other institutions—the state, education, culture, and so on—erodes the capacity of those non-economic institutions to provide a countervailing force within the economic sphere by blunting active citizenship and streamlining educational institutions toward instrumentalized ends fashioned by the business community.

The infiltration of these interests into the other spheres of social life also infects the state and its ability to defend those common purposes.[35] It also, however, affects the logics of social movements which become increasingly

---

34   I mean to define an understanding of republican political theory that in contrast to thinkers such as Philip Pettit, *Republicanism: A Theory of Freedom and Government*. (New York: Oxford University Press, 1997); John Maynor, *Republicanism and Modern Political Theory*. (Cambridge: Polity, 2003); Richard Dagger "Neo-Republicanism and the Civic Economy." *Politics, Philosophy, and Economics* vol. 5 (3) 2006, pp. 151–173; Frank Lovett, "Domination and Distributive Justice." *Journal of Politics* vol. 71(3) 2009, pp. 817–830; and Frank Lovett and Philip Pettit, "Neorepublicanism: A Normative and Institutional Research Program." *Annual Review of Political Science* vol. 12 (2009), pp. 11–29.

35   In this sense, the very legitimacy of the state, in a progressive sense, can be seen to rest on its ability to promote a social structure that is just in the deeper sense in which I am advocating here. See the discussion by Milton Fisk, *The State and Justice: An Essay in Political Theory*. (Cambridge: Cambridge University Press, 1989), pp. 65–138.

unable to formulate concrete forms of resistance to the imperatives of private power. By directing their attention toward the state as the object of dissent, many social movements and their theorists fail to understand the progressive potential of the state, rendering their power more diffuse than economic elites and, in the process, ineffective in more concrete terms.[36] Perhaps a republican understanding of the nature of economic life and inequality can help to reconstruct a more radical, more substantive form of resistance as well as a normative understanding of the kinds of public life that should be defended from the assault by private interest.

---

36 In a curious way, it is the need for a concentration of political power that can effectively countervail the powers of concentrated economic power. See Grant McConnell, *Private Power and American Democracy*. (New York: Vintage, 1966) as well as Kariel, *The Decline of American Pluralism.*

PART 3

Global Inequality

CHAPTER 12

Piketty on the World Market and Inequality within Nations

Tony Smith

Piketty's criticisms of neoclassical economics in *Capital in the Twenty-First Century* are devastating. At key points, however, his critical faculties abandon him. Two will be discussed here, his discussion of inequality in the world market, and his explanation of the strong tendency to inequality within national economies.

Inequality in the World Market

In over 650 pages exactly three are devoted to inequality in the world market. He begins with some critical comments on marginal productivity theory. It holds that returns to capital tend to be relatively high in regions where capital is relatively scarce. If we assume a reasonably free flow of capital across borders, then, capital investment should tend to flow from (capital abundant) wealthy regions to (capital scarce) poorer regions, leading to convergence in the world market over time.

Piketty points out a rhetorical slight of hand in this line of thought. It is natural to take "convergence" to mean that per capita *income* in poorer regions catches up to that of wealthier countries. In this context, however, it refers to a convergence in per capita *output,* which can be expected to lead to *increased* divergence of income in the world market as investors from wealthy regions come to own more and more of the productive resources of developing regions (69–70).[1]

A second problem Piketty mentions is that capital inflows from developed nations lead to alliances between foreign capitals and local elites, provoking a domestic reaction against governments supporting foreign investors to the detriment of their own businesses and workforce. This sets the stage for intractable political conflicts, discouraging further foreign investment—and thereby undermining the supposed path of convergence.

---

1 Thomas Piketty, *Capital in the Twenty-First Century* (Cambridge: Belknap Press, 2014).

Piketty's most damning criticism, however, is the simple fact that "(I)f we look at the historical record, it does not appear that capital mobility has been the primary factor promoting convergence of rich and poor nations" (70). Just the opposite; countries that are successful examples of convergence have *restricted* the free flow of capital across borders:

> China, for example, still imposes controls on capital: foreigners cannot invest in the country freely, but that has not hindered capital accumulation, for which domestic saving largely suffice. Japan, South Korea, and Taiwan all financed investment out of [domestic] savings.[2]

If successful development in the world market has not been due to the free flow of capital across borders, what has been the key? In Piketty's view,

> (T)he principle mechanism for convergence at the international ... level is the diffusion of knowledge. In other words, the poor catch up with the rich to the extent that they achieve the same level of technological know-how, skill, and education, not by becoming the property of the wealthy.[3]

This leaves one last piece of the puzzle: how can poor regions catch up in scientific-technological knowledge and know-how? International openness and trade are part of the story. But the central factor is the right sort of institutions:

> (K)nowledge diffusion depends on a country's ability to mobilize financing as well as institutions that encourage large-scale investment in education and training of the population while guaranteeing a stable legal framework that various economic actors can reliably count on. It is therefore closely associated with the achievement of legitimate and efficient government.[4]

Piketty concludes, "Concisely stated, these are the main lessons that history has to teach about global growth and international inequalities" (71). All that is required now is the political will in poor regions to learn and implement these lessons.

Needless to say, the causes of severe inequality and poverty in global capitalism are complex and controversial. I shall restrict myself here to the dimension

---

2   Thomas Piketty, *Capital in the Twenty-First Century* (Cambridge: Belknap Press, 2014), p. 71.

3   Thomas Piketty, *Capital in the Twenty-First Century* (Cambridge: Belknap Press, 2014), p. 71.

4   Thomas Piketty, *Capital in the Twenty-First Century* (Cambridge: Belknap Press, 2014), p. 71.

Piketty emphasizes, the diffusion of scientific-technological knowledge and know-how. A first point is compatible with Piketty's position, but not explicitly mentioned by him: in global capitalism the "default setting," so to speak, is for knowledge and technological know-how to serve as means enabling wealthy regions to reproduce and extend their relative advantages over time.

State of the art research and development tends to be extremely costly, and so in any given period research at the scientific-technological frontier is most likely to take place in wealthy regions of the global economy. Scientific-technological innovation is a major weapon in inter-capital competition, and so units of capital based in wealthy regions, with privileged access to advanced research and development relative to units based in other regions, have a tremendous advantage in the world market. Not every unit of capital based in wealthy regions is guaranteed to maintain a leading position in the world market over time. But taking wealthy regions as a whole, they are in a position to establish a virtuous circle in which advanced R&D provides the basis for successful innovations, successful innovations generate high returns, high returns (with their large positive multiplier effects) provide the revenues to fund the next generation of research at the scientific-technological frontier, setting the stage for further innovations, further competitive success, and further high returns.

In contrast, there is a strong tendency to vicious circles in poorer regions. An initial inability to fund R&D at the scientific-technological envelope makes it unlikely firms in those regions will be able to introduce significant innovations. This condemns them (as a group, if not in every individual case) to low returns.[5] Low returns, and the correspondingly small positive multiplier effects in the domestic economy, restrict the ability to fund advanced R&D in the succeeding period, limiting future profit opportunities from commercializable innovations.

The tendency for severe global inequality and poverty to persist is an essential determination of global capitalism, as essential as the technological dynamism so lauded by its defenders. The former is a dimension of the latter.[6]

---

5   Oil producing regions have a different dynamic. I shall not consider them here.

6   At the turn of the century more than 95% of all research and development was undertaken in the wealthy regions of the global economy. See Elhanan Helpman, *The Mystery of Economic Growth* (Cambridge: The Belknap Press of Harvard University 2004), pp. 64. Since then a higher proportion of global R&D has been subcontracted by multinationals to labs in poorer regions of the world economy, where scientific-technical labor is cheaper. This has reinforced, rather than limited, the advantages of multinationals from wealthy regions.

Piketty could grant this and still assert that this tendency for divergence can be put out of play if the right institutions and public policies are established, along the lines of the successful "developmental states" he mentions. In these cases:

* State expenditures and policies are consistently directed over time to creating an effective national innovation system, including measures such as direct state funding of R&D, support for the education and training of a scientific-technical workforce, government procurement policies offering secure markets to innovating companies, tax breaks for R&D, accelerated depreciation of investment in equipment embodying advanced technologies, and so on.

* State officials instruct agents in the financial system to provide innovating firms with abundant access to cheap credit, with effective mechanisms in place to ensure this directive is carried out. If the banking system is nationalized guidance can be conducted through formal channels. Informal guidance without nationalization can in principle be equally effective. Foreign capital inflows into the financial sector are restricted in order to maintain state capacities (foreign investors are much less likely to acquiesce to state guidance). Restrictions on capital outflows from the domestic financial sector are also required to prevent domestic banks from pursuing foreign investments promising higher profits than the extension of credit to domestic firms.

* Firms at a considerable technological disadvantage in global competition are protected from competition while they are in the process of catching up to the scientific-technical frontier. Significant tariff and non-tariff barriers against competing imports are imposed, combined with state support for imports of necessary inputs into production that the domestic economy cannot produce itself.

* Measurable benchmarks are established by the state to ensure that the firms benefitting from protection and from access to cheap credit are in fact successfully catching up to the technological level of leading competitors in the world market. Sanctions are imposed on those who are not.

The success of these policies in Japan, South Korea, Taiwan, and other countries in East Asia in recent decades, shows that poor regions in the global economy are not condemned to remain poor.[7] Or so Piketty supposes.

---

7   China is a special case. For all its astounding growth, China has not yet in fact "caught up." An estimated 90 percent of China's trade surplus is in processing trade (trade in goods assembled

There are two difficulties to consider. First of all, Piketty himself notes that catching up requires "large-scale investment." Establishing a capable national innovation system requires wealth, but a poor region must have an effective national innovation system to become wealthy. This chicken and egg problem could at least partially be solved by technology transfer from developed countries. But if technology is a major weapon in inter-capital competition, why would units of capital or states in wealthy regions support a policy of free technology transfer? Copying technologies provides a second option. But firms from wealthy regions can be expected to protect their intellectual property and trade secrets vigorously. Also, it can take considerable scientific-technological sophistication to copy sophisticated knowledge goods, another chicken and egg problem. And firms associated with the most effective national innovation systems will generally have moved to a new generation of knowledge goods by the time the previous generation has been successfully copied. Purchasing required technologies is a third option. But undertaking such purchases on the required scale generally requires a significant store of world money, and that is precisely what regions without an effective national innovation system already in place lack. Borrowing from global capital markets appears to offer a solution, and it has been highly touted as a development strategy by neoliberal theorists. But loans only spur development if the rate of return on investments significantly exceeds the rate of loan repayments. Corruption, nepotism, and vanity projects, the allocation of funds to sectors where there are limited opportunities to grow in the world market, undermine this goal. And even when they were not in play, the very high start-up costs required to participate in many leading global markets, purchases of soon to be obsolete technologies, and so on, has made the history of countries borrowing for development a history of countries falling into the "debt trap."[8]

A second difficulty is no less serious. For the developmental state project to succeed, there must be a wealthy region willing to accept imports from a developing region, despite the restrictions imposed by the latter on the former's exports and capital investments. Capitalist states are generally disposed

---

in China from imported parts and materials) generated by multinational corporations and foreign joint ventures (National Research Council, *Rising to the Challenge: U.S. Innovation Policy for the Global Economy* (Washington: The National Academies Press, 2012), p. 219).

8 In other words, new loans are required to pay off the interest on old loans, which were taken out to pay back the interest of yet earlier loans, and so on, back to the initial loan. Since the 1980s the "third world" has transferred funds to wealthy creditors in the 'first world' equivalent to almost 50 Marshall Plans (EricToussaint, *Your Money or Your Life! The Tyranny of Global Finance* (London: Pluto, 1999), pp. 123, 151; Richard Westra, *The Evil Axis of Finance* (Atlanta: Clarity Press, 2012), p. 100).

to further the interests of units of capital within their jurisdiction, and these restrictions harm "their" capitals. Why would a strong state agree to this arrangement?

After World War II Japan, South Korea, and Taiwan grew at historically unprecedented rates. Their firms caught up to the frontiers of scientific-technological knowledge in numerous leading sectors. How were the above difficulties overcome? Astoundingly, this question is all but ignored in left liberal contributions to the global justice debate. The answer is not hard to find: these nations were on the front lines of cold war, and the United States had an exceptional geopolitical interest in the prosperity and stability of key allies. U.S. political elites proved by their actions they fully understood that "free trade" does not bring prosperity and stability. While acquiescing to its allies' high tariff barriers, the U.S.'s own tariffs were lowered, allowing them to export as much to the U.S. domestic market as they could sell. No political pressure was put on these states to allow capitals from the U.S. to take over promising firms or banks, or to open their financial sector and let Asian firms and banks invest in the U.S. Tremendous amounts of money were funneled into these nations through military expenditures, regardless of human rights violations. Important technologies were simply given away.[9]

---

9 "Japan rapidly became the US frontline base for its operation in Korea ... with US spending on supplies from Japan totaling $3 billion. And this was on top of approximately $1.7 billion in aid the US channeled to Japan during the occupation years ending in 1952 ... As was the case with the Marshall Plan for West Germany and the nascent EU, Japan too overcame the abiding development 'catch-22' of having to export in order to pay for imports but being unable to produce for export without first importing material and machinery. ... Tens of thousands of patents for multifarious technologies were freely transferred to Japan. These factored into both the rise of key industries such as automobiles and machine tools as well as electronics and synthetic fibers, and resurrected industries like steel and shipbuilding/repair" (Westra, *The Evil Axis of Finance*, 54). "[B]etween 1953 and 1967 Taiwan received $1.3 billion in economic assistance largely as grants which, added to military assistance, amounted to $365 per capita at a point when in 1960 Taiwan's annual per capita income was a mere $110. From 1946 to 1976 South Korea received $12.6 billion in economic and military assistance from the US which, when topped up by funds from international institutions and Japan, amounted to approximately $600 per capita, equal to the total aid received by all of Africa or half that received by all Latin America during the same period, Between 1953 and 1962 such flows financed close to 70 percent of South Korean imports and constituted 75 percent of fixed capital formation. This fact surely vitiates the mainstream economic mantra of simple EGO [Export Oriented Growth] as, absent the anticommunist partnerships the region entered into with the US, it is not clear from where in a free trading 'free world' the capital underpinning globally competitive exports would have been generated" Richard Westra, *The Evil Axis of Finance* (Atlanta: Clarity Press, 2012), p. 60.

This was a contingent state of affairs, and it did not last. As the Cold War concluded the U.S. government withdrew its support for the developmental state model.[10] From now on access to the U.S. domestic market would be conditional on a reciprocal opening of their economies to U.S. exports and investments. And from now on technology transfer to poor regions would occur mostly within export processing zones, where transnational corporations could limit and control transfers to local subcontractors, suppliers, and distributors.

The systematic tendency to severe global inequality and poverty is an essential determination of the capitalist world market. While this tendency may be put out of play in exceptional circumstances, it cannot be dismantled as long as the property and production relations of capitalism remain in place. The roots of the problem do not lie in contingencies of public policies, as Piketty supposes. They lie in the role of technological innovation as a major weapon of inter-capital competition.[11] No account of "capital in the twenty-first century" should ignore this feature of the global capitalism.

Inequality within National Economies

Piketty's central claim is that the extreme levels of inequality within contemporary capitalist societies can be checked only by extraordinary catastrophes (world wars and their aftershocks), or extraordinary political measures, like the global wealth tax Piketty (unrealistically) advocates. Piketty discusses this tendency with the aid of the formula 'r>g'. Since the rate of return on capital (r) tends to exceed the rate of growth (g), those who own capital investments tend to see their wealth and income increase at a faster rate than those whose wealth and income are more closely tied to the lower average rate of growth (including the vast majority of those

---

10   The developmental state also cannot be maintained after local industrial firms and banks grow to the point where they can effectively resist state directives to focus on less profitable domestic opportunities when more promising ones are available elsewhere. The demise of the developmental state model in Asia was overdetermined, brought about by internal as well as external factors.

11   In the words of a leading mainstream growth theorist: "(I)nvestment in innovation widens the gap between rich and poor countries. The output gains of the industrial countries exceed the output gains of the less-developed countries. We therefore conclude that investment in innovation in the industrial countries leads to divergence of income between the North and the South" See Elhan Helpman, *The Mystery of Economic Growth*, (Cambridge: The Belknap Press of Harvard University 2004), p. 85.

working for a wage). It is crucially important for Piketty's position that he explain *why* r>g.

Here too Piketty notes that the marginal productivity theory of capital is in adequate. It implies that the rate of return on capital investment tends to decline relative to the return from hiring labor as relatively more amounts of capital are accumulated, with the result that investments in labor tend to be substituted for further investments in capital. Greater demand for labor tends to lift wages, so the division of income between capital and labor should supposedly shift in favor of the latter as capital becomes relatively more abundant. The fact that the return to capital has remained above the general rate of growth (and the growth of real wages in particular) as capital has become relatively more "abundant" shows that marginal productivity of capital theory once again does not explain what needs to be explained.

I believe the key factor in Piketty's answer to the question why the rate of return on capital exceeds the rate of growth—and therefore the key to his theory of capital—is presented in the following passage:

> (T)he observed historical evolutions suggest that is it is always possible—up to a certain point, at least—to find new and useful things to do with capital: for example, new ways of building and equipping houses (think of solar panels on rooftops or digital lighting controls), ever more sophisticated robots and other electronic devices, and medical technologies requiring larger and larger capital investments. One need not imagine a fully robotized economy in which capital would reproduce itself (corresponding to an infinite elasticity of substitution [of capital for labor, t.s.]) to appreciate the many uses of capital in a diversified advanced economy.[12]

At any level of accumulation, then, capital remains relatively "scarce" as long as there are new uses to which it can be put, putting out of play any tendency for returns to capital investment to diminish as additional increments of capital are accumulated.

It should take just a moment's reflection to realize that the fact that new things can have new uses utterly fails to explain what Piketty needs to explain. Many years ago creatures with DNA like ours discovered how to control fire, use stone tools, forge copper, bronze, and iron, and attach wheels to carts. Fire, stone, copper, bronze, iron, and wheels have all had countless uses ever since.

---

12   Thomas Piketty, *Capital in the Twenty-First Century* (Cambridge: Belknap Press, 2014), p. 221.

And yet for all but an exceedingly small fraction of the time our species has been on this planet the accumulation of capital has not been the dominant organizing principle of society as it is today.

We cannot hope to explain why r > g without comprehending Marx's point that capital is not a thing. It is a process aiming at valorization (the difference between the initial money invested and the money appropriated as a result of that investment), with each moment in the process a moment in the systematic reproduction of capital/wage labor relation.[13]

The key to this relationship is straightforward enough: in capitalist market societies most individuals are cut off from the material preconditions of human life. The goods and services needed to survive take the social form of commodities owned by others, as do the means of producing subsistence goods. In principle, at least, the "free" individuals of capitalism are not subjected to the personal compulsion imposed on slaves, serfs, and peasants throughout recorded history. They are, however, subject to relentless impersonal coercion, *forced* to obtain money to obtain the goods and services they and their dependents require to live even minimally acceptable lives. As a result, they are forced to sell their labor power to some unit of capital or other, and to create an amount of value exceeding the value of their wages, since their labor power will be purchased only so long as they do so. At the conclusion of a given cycle of production they will have spent their income on the goods and services required to reproduce themselves and their families, with perhaps a small amount set aside for savings. The owners and controllers of capital, in contrast, as a group (if not in every individual case) will have obtained a monetary return enabling them to reinvest at a higher level in the next cycle, even after (often considerable) funds have been deducted for their own personal consumption. Wage laborers must once again sell their labor power to holders of capital, and once again subordinate their living labor to the augmentation of value.

If we wish to understand why r > g in modern capitalism, we cannot do so in abstraction from these property and production relations. (If we wish to understand why there was inequality in slave, feudal, or tribute-extracting societies, the quite different social relations found in those quite different contexts would have to be examined.) And if we wish to understand why the divergence between r and g decreases or increases at a particular time and particular place, we must also investigate the relevant social relations, and not the property of things to be useful.

---

13   Marx is, of course, fully aware that there are other important social relationships. He insists, however, that considering them at later, more concrete, theoretical levels supplements, rather than contradicts, the account presented here.

Piketty explains the decline in inequality in most regions of the world market in the twentieth century as due to the losses inflicted on capital owners by catastrophic world wars, and the space this created for public policies keeping inequality in check. These factors are certainly an important part of the story. But they provide a very incomplete account.

In the decades after the devastation of World War II capitals could expand and grow rapidly as demand expanded. In this context public policies supporting the consumption of at least certain categories of worker households were not in fundamental tension with capital accumulation. Also, decades of labor struggles had successfully built labor organizations in the U.S. and elsewhere capable of maintaining pressure for increased real wages. Ideological competition with so-called "really existing socialism" encouraged capitalist countries to lift workers' conditions during the Cold War as well.

In 1945 the Japanese economy was roughly a century behind the U.S., while Germany lagged a half century or so.[14] By the 1970s both regions had more than caught up. In many of the most technologically sophisticated and economically crucial sectors of the world market—consumer electronics, autos, motorcycles, chemicals, business machines, steel—Japanese and European capitals were more efficient producers of higher quality products than established U.S. firms. The latter, however, did not withdraw from these sectors at a corresponding rate, and so productive capacity in the global economy increased faster than the growth of markets to absorb it. The result was *an overaccumulation crisis*, manifested in excess productive capacity and a corresponding decline in the rate of investment, profits, and growth.[15] The post-WWII "long boom" had also been characterized by relatively low levels of unemployment and relatively high levels of labor organization in the U.S. and other regions of the "center." The resulting ability of workers to win wage increases and partial control of the labor process squeezed profits. There was even a brief moment in which real wages increased at a faster rate than productivity growth, eroding surplus value production. The rate of investment necessarily tends to decline when surplus value is threatened. Piketty and other left liberals see the rise in inequality in recent decades as a failure of political will to tax, redistribute, and regulate sufficiently. But this ignores how capital responded to the significant fall in the rate of profit in the world market set off by the global crisis of the 1970s.

---

14   David McNally, *Global Slump* (Oakland: PM Press, 2010), p. 27.

15   Robert Brenner, *The Economics of Global Turbulence* (New York: Verso, 2006); Chris Harmon, *Zombie Capitalism* (Chicago: Haymarket Press, 2010).

The standard response by capital to overaccumulation is the destruction and devaluation of excess capacity of through a major downturn. Ruling strata across the globe had every reason to avoid this. Members of the ruling circles in the u.s. had an additional reason to avoid a severe global recession or depression in the 1970s: destroying or devaluing previous capital investments on the scale required would have inflicted massive harm on u.s. capitals in particular, due to their weaker competitive positions in key sectors of the world economy. The material foundation for the geopolitical hegemony of the u.s. would have been profoundly threatened. Another way forward for capital was desperately sought.[16] "Neoliberalism" is the general term for the path that was taken. Its major features include:

1) An unprecedented explosion of credit money; $50 trillion has been created in the u.s. alone since the conclusion of World War II.[17] This has enabled productive capacity to be valorized that would otherwise have been destroyed or devalued;

2) An attack on labor in every stage of the capital process: increased coercion in the labor market due to levels of unemployment that were previously considered politically unacceptable; speed-ups in the labor process, extensions of the work day, disciplining through household debt, and so on.

3) Globalization, which increased pressures on labor through, for example, to capital flight to regions where wages were 20% of u.s. levels (Mexico) or even just 5% (China), and enabled a partial and temporary "spatial fix" for overaccumulation difficulties by providing new outlets for investment;

4) Financialization; with overcapacity problems continuing to plague most non-financial sectors of the world market, credit money tended to flow to the financial sector, leading to serial bubbles in various categories of financial assets.[18]

---

16   In the industrial heartland of the u.s. there was brutal deindustrialization in the 1970s and early 80s, and the situation in the United Kingdom was even worse. But it was not sufficient to remove excess productive capacity in most major sectors of the world economy; there was no "'slaughter of capital values" on a scale sufficient to end [overcapacity and overproduction]' (Radhika Desai, *Geopolitical Economy, After US Hegemony, Globalization and Empire* (London: Pluto, 2013), pp. 24–5; see Harmon, *Zombie Capitalism*, pp. 231–33, 282.)

17   Richard Duncan, *The New Depression* (Hoboken: Wiley, 2012), p. 34.

18   Dan Krier, Speculative Finance Capital, Corporate Earnings and Profit Fetishism. *Critical Sociology* vol. 35 (5) 2009, pp. 657–75.

5) Global imbalances, with global growth generated by surplus regions exporting to regions with ever-growing deficits.

Neoliberalism was a tremendous success from the standpoint of capital. Profit levels significantly recovered after the slowdown of the 1970s. While levels of growth in the global economy may not have reached those of the post-WWII 'golden age,' they did not diverge significantly from what had been attained in previous periods of capitalist expansion.[19] The value of financial assets in general, and the U.S. stock market in particular, trended steeply upwards for an unprecedented period of time. A case could be made that the technological dynamism of this period was unsurpassed; at least it is doubtful whether there has ever been a technology trajectory with the steepness of the information technology revolution, or one that has spawned new firms and industries at a faster rate. The explosion of trade and foreign direct investment facilitated historically unprecedented rates of growth in East and South Asia. In poor regions of the global economy, by official measures, at least, more people were lifted out of poverty than in any previous period of human history. Most of all, *a destruction and devaluation of capital on anything approaching the scale the previous history of capitalism suggested was required to address the overaccumulation crisis of the 1970s did not occur.* Capital accumulation revived. But it did so at immense social costs, including the sharp increase in inequality Piketty laments.

Immense indebtedness, higher rates of exploitation, a declining share of wages in national income across the globe, recurrent financial bubbles, extreme global imbalances, and a sharp rise in inequality were not accidental occurrences that could have been avoided if only political elites had fulfilled their normative responsibilities.[20] *Measured by the standards of capitalist rationality, neoliberalism was a 'rational' response to the overaccumulation crisis of the 1970s.* In the present moment, when overcapacity continues to afflict the major sectors of the world economy, a renewal of neoliberalism remains capital's best hope even now, after its madness has been revealed for all who wish to see.

There is tremendous descriptive power in the simple r > g relation at the heart of Piketty's masterwork. But if we wish to explain this relation, Marxian

---

19   David McNally, *Global Slump*; Gérard Duménil and Dominique Lévy, *The Crisis of Neoliberalism* (Cambridge: Harvard University, 2011).

20   The risk of environment catastrophe must be added to this list as well. Richard Smith, Capitalism and the Destruction of Life on Earth: Six Theses on Saving the Humans. *Real-World Economics Review* 64, 2013, pp. 125–50.

theory remains far more useful than nostrums to the multiplicity of new things with new uses. Our critique must go beyond Piketty's assessment of a particularly irrational variant of capitalism to a critique of capitalist 'rationality' in general.[21]

21   Tony Smith, *Beyond Liberal Egalitarianism: Marxism and Normative Social Theory for the Twenty-First Century* (Leiden: Brill, forthcoming).

CHAPTER 13

Capital*ism* in the Twenty-First Century: Global Inequality, Piketty, and the Transnational Capitalist Class

William I. Robinson

Introduction

Why has Thomas Piketty's tome, *Capital in the Twenty-First Century*, sparked such a firestorm of debate on global inequalities in the world media, academic and policy circles? These inequalities are indeed truly savage. In 2015, the year after Piketty's book was released in English,[1] the development NGO Oxfam reported that the richest one percent of humanity would own more than the rest of the world in 2016.[2] This is up from the one percent owning 44 percent of the world's wealth in 2010 and 48 percent in 2014. If current trends continue, the one percent would own 54 percent by 2020. Even more shocking, the top 80 billionaires were worth $1.9 trillion in 2014, an amount equality to the bottom 50 percent of humanity and these 80 saw a 50 percent rise in their wealth in just four years. At the same time, the poorest 50 percent saw a drop in their wealth during this same four-year period from 2010 to 2014. In other words, there has been a huge transfer of wealth in a very short period of time from the poorest half of humanity to the richest 80 individuals on the planet.

I do not think however, that outrage over these inequalities explains the attention that Piketty's study has received. After all, Piketty is far from the first to draw attention to such expanding inequalities in recent years and he does not even show just how pronounced they are in the same way that Oxfam and other studies have done so. His exposition exhibits theoretical and analytical limitations, political blind spots and historical flaws, as I will discuss below. His proposed remedies—a global tax on capital and redistribution through progressive tax reform—are welcome yet hardly novel.

---

1 Thomas Piketty, *Capitalism in the Twenty-First Century* (Cambridge: Harvard University Press, 2014 [2013]).

2 Oxfam. *Wealth: Having It All and Wanting More* (London: Oxfam, 2015), https://www.oxfam .org/en/research/wealth-having-it-all-and-wanting-more. Accessed on November 3, 2015.

But that is precisely the rub. *Capital in the Twenty-First Century* has been so well received by the academic, media, and political establishment precisely because it converges with the reformist agenda of a rising number of transnational elites and intelligentsia. These elites have become increasingly concerned that the social conflicts and political turmoil sparked by such egregious inequalities may destabilize global capitalism and threaten their control. They seek to save capitalism from itself and from more radical projects from below. Like Piketty, they call for mildly redistributive measures such as increased taxes on corporations and the rich, a more progressive income tax, the reintroduction of social welfare programs, and a "green capitalism." They are also alarmed that extreme levels of inequality will undermine the prospects for growth and profit making. The Organization of economic Cooperation and Development (OECD), the club of the 34 richest countries, for instance, warned in a 2015 report that the "global inequality gap" has "reached a turning point." The report did not have much to say about the social injustice that such inequality represents, nor about the mass suffering it brings about. It did, however, highlight that "high inequality drags down growth" and recommend raising taxes on the rich.[3]

What accounts for escalating worldwide inequalities that have so alarmed transnational elites? As Marx analyzed in *Capital*, there is something going on in the capitalist system itself beyond sets of government policies that generates inequalities. Simply put, capitalists own the means of producing wealth and therefore appropriate as profits as much wealth as possible that society collectively produces. Capitalism produces social inequalities as a consequence of its own internal workings. But such inequalities end up undermining the stability of the system since the mass of working people cannot purchase the wealth that pours out of the capitalist economy to the extent that capitalists and the well-off retain more and more of total income relative to that which goes to labor. If capitalists cannot actually sell (or "unload") the products of their plantations, factories, and offices then they cannot make profit. This is what in critical political economy constitutes the underlying internal contradiction of capitalism, or the *overaccumulation* problem. Left unchecked, expanding social polarization results in crisis—in recessions and depressions, such as the

---

3   Organization for Economic Cooperation and Development, *In It Together: Why Less Inequality Benefits All* (OECD Publishing, 2015), http://www.keepeek.com/Digital-Asset-Management/ oecd/employment/in-it-together-why-less-inequality-benefits-all_9789264235120-en#page1. Accessed on November 3, 2015.

Notably, the report also called for greater gender inequality, not as a matter of justice but because gender equality is shown to decrease income inequality.

1930s Great Depression or the 2008 Great Recession. Worse still, it engenders great social upheavals, political conflicts, wars and even revolutions— precisely the kinds of conflicts and chaos we are witnessing in the world today. As Chris Harman showed so clearly in his eminently readable account, *A People's History of the World*, the struggle between the haves and the have-nots has driven civilization and its interminable crises for millennia.[4]

In the view of the reformers as well as that of Piketty, however, it is not the capitalist system itself but its particular institutional organization that is to blame for inequalities. They believe it can be offset by policies such as those Piketty proposes. Radical political economists refer to state redistributive policies or worker struggles for higher wages that offset the tendency towards social polarization, wars that may destroy existing capital stock and have a leveling effect, and so on, as countervailing tendencies. However, seen in light of the *systemic* contradictions of capitalism, inequality is not the result of "bad policies." Prevailing policies and institutions are not a "public choice" as insinuated by the *choice theoretic paradigm*[5] employed by Piketty, among others. This approach views state policies and their outcomes as the product of "choices" made by publics, as if publics and states are rational, unitary and coherent actors. Rather, policies are the outcome of ongoing and often unpredictable crises and social struggles among competing classes and groups.

The Class Warfare of the Transnational Capitalist Class

Capitalist globalization from the 1970s and on undermined the countervailing tendencies that in the mid-20th century attenuated some of the sharpest social polarization. The high rates of inequality registered in the wake of the industrial revolution reached a peak in the late 19th and early 20th centuries and then diminished somewhat—*in the heartlands of world capitalism*—in the wake of two world wars and the Great Depression. Colonialism and imperialism transferred surplus wealth from the periphery to the metropolitan centers of world capitalism and made possible the rise of a labor aristocracy in these centers, as both Vladimir Lenin and Cecil Rhodes noted early in the 20th century. Those sectors are now experiencing under capitalist globalization downward mobility, heightened insecurity and "precariatization" that threaten to undo the hegemonic blocs forged in the 20th century in the core countries through

---

4   Chris Harman, *A People's History of the World* (London: Bookmarks, 1999).

5   Alex Callinicos, *Social Theory: A Historical Introduction* (New York: New York University Press, 1999).

the incorporation of these (often white racially privileged) sectors. When reform-oriented transnational elites bemoan the "loss of the middle class" they are referring to the destabilization of these formerly privileged sectors among the working class and to the erosion of the earlier hegemonic blocs.

The "Fordist-Keynesian" social order that took shape in the 30 years following World War II involved high growth rates, a rise in living standards for substantial sectors of the working class, and a decrease in inequalities in the developed core of world capitalism. Why "Fordist-Keynesian?" It was Henry Ford who first recognized that the new system of mass, standardized production ("Fordism") could not be sustained without introducing as well mass, standardized consumption. This meant establishing a stable employment arrangement—or capital-labor relation—for a significant portion of the working classes and wages high enough for the working class to actually consume the goods and services that their labor produced—in exchange for workers' obedience to capital. In turn, John Keynes analyzed that the Great Depression owed to insufficient demand as a result of the concentration of wealth. The state needed in Keynes' view to intervene in the economy in order to regulate the market (especially financial markets) and to boost demand through state spending on public projects such as infrastructure and social serves as well as through the establishment of minimum wages, unemployment insurance, pensions, and so forth.[6]

The period of post-World War II prosperity in the core countries owed a great deal to this combination of Fordist production and regulated capital-labor relations and Keynesian monetary, budgetary and regulatory policies. Mainstream academics and policymakers shifted from the earlier classical economic theories of David Ricardo, Adam Smith, and Jean Baptiste Say to Keynesian economic theory. State intervention in the capitalist market and a component of redistribution came to define economic policy in the mid-20th century in the then-First World, as well as in the then-Third World in the wake of decolonization. Causal to this evolution of capitalism was the struggles between competing social and class forces around the world. The Fordist-Keynesian arrangement came about because of the mass struggles of working and

---

6 There is a great deal of good literature on Fordism and Keynesianism. Harvey, although somewhat outdated, remains for me an important statement on the subject. David Harvey, *The Condition of Postmodernity*, (Cambridge, MA: Blackwell, 1990). See also: Ash Amin, *Post-Fordism: A Reader*, (Cambridge: Blackwell, 1994); Robert W. Cox, *Production, Power, and World Order: Social Forces in the Making of History* (New York: Colombia University Press 1987); William I. Robinson, *Global Capitalism and the Crisis of Humanity*, (New York: Cambridge University Press, 2014).

popular classes from the late 1800s into the 1930s, including worker, populist, and socialist movements, the Bolshevik revolution, and the anti-colonial and national liberations struggles in the Third World. While these struggles cannot be discussed here, the epistemological point important to the critique of Piketty and our understanding of global inequalities in the twenty-first century is that social forces in struggle are what shape the nature and direction of social change. Class and social struggle is almost entirely absent from Piketty's account of capital and inequality in the twenty-first century. I will have more to say on this below.

Redistributive nation-state capitalism evolved, therefore, from capital's accommodation to mass upheavals from below in the wake of the to the crisis of the two world wars and the Great Depression. In the wake of the next great crisis, that of the 1970s, capital went global as a strategy of an emergent transnational capitalist class, or TCC, to reconstitute its social power by breaking free of nation-state constraints to accumulation. The post-WWII "class compromise" served capital well for several decades. Corporate profits rose sharply from 1945 to 1968, and then declined until the early 1980s, when it again rose very rapidly, this time as a result of globalization.[7]

Let us elaborate: the particular Fordist-Keynesian institutional arrangement came apart in the wake of the 1970s crisis of world capitalism. The corporate class and its agents identified the mass struggles and demands of popular and working classes and state regulation as fetters to its freedom to make profit and accumulate wealth as the rate of profit declined in the 1970s. Emergent transnational capital went global. As the TCC congealed it forged what became know as the "Washington consensus," or agreement around sweeping worldwide economic restructuring to put in place a new transnational corporate order and go on the offensive in its class warfare against working and popular classes.

Transnationally oriented elites and capitalists captured governments around the world and used states to undertake sweeping restructuring and integration into a new globalized production and financial system. The "neoliberal counterrevolution" opened up vast new opportunities for accumulation. Free trade agreements and financial liberalization lifted state restrictions on cross-border trade and capital flows. Privatization turned over everything from public industries, to educational and health systems, mail service, highways and ports to transnational corporations and provided an investment

---

7 Piketty demonstrates as much; see figure 6.8, p. 227. In Thomas Piketty, *Capital in the Twenty-First Century* (Cambridge: Belknap Press, 2014)

bonanza to the TCC as it concentrated wealth as never before. Labor market reform led to the erosion of regulated labor markets. As workers become "flexible" they joined the ranks of a new global "precariat" of proletarians who labor under part-time, temporary, informalized, non-unionized, contract, and other forms of precarious work.

All of this, it should be clear, has enhanced the structural power of transnational capital over states and popular classes worldwide and has had the effect of exacerbating inequalities. Popular and working classes have been less effective in defending wages in the face of capital's newfound global mobility. And states have seen the erosion of their ability to capture and redistribute surpluses given the privatization of public assets, ever more regressive tax systems and prospects for corporate tax evasion, mounting debt to transnational finance capital, inter-state competition to attract transnational capital, and the ability of the TCC to transfer money instantaneously around the world through new digital financial circuits (this is the notorious "loss of state sovereignty" about which so much has been written).

Emergent transnational capital experienced a major expansion in the 1980s and 1990s through globalization. The TCC undertook *hyper-accumulation* by applying new technologies such as computer and informatics, through neo-liberal policies, and through new modalities of mobilizing and exploiting a global labor force. The TCC conquered new markets in hothouse fashion in the former Soviet Union, Eastern Europe, and the Third World. Several hundred million new middle class consumers in China, India and elsewhere in the so-called "emerging countries" provided new global market segments that fueled growth. But at the same time hundreds of millions, perhaps billions of people, were displaced from the countryside in the Global South through new rounds of primitive accumulation brought about by neo-liberal policies as well as social cleansing, and organized violence such a the "war on drugs" and the "war on terror," both of which have served as instruments of primitive accumulation and for the violent restructuring and integration of countries and regions into the new global economy.[8] Banks and institutional investors began vast new land grabs around the world in the second decade of the 21th century in what amounts to a new round of global enclosures. All this has generated a vast army of internal and transnational immigrants who have swelled the ranks of the unemployed and the structurally marginalized—the new "surplus humanity"—placing downward pressure on wages everywhere.[9]

---

8 On this point, see Dawn Paley, *Drug War Capitalism* (Oakland: AK Press, 2014).

9 See William Robinson, *Global Capitalism and the Crisis of Humanity*, (Cambridge: Cambridge University Press, 2014).

The Cycle of Crisis and the Reformers

By the late 1990s stagnation once again set in and the system faced renewed crisis as privatizations dried up, the conquered regions were brought into the system, global markets became saturated, and new technologies reached the limits of fixed capital expansion. Escalating global social polarization and inequality fueled the chronic problem of over-accumulation. The global market has not been able to absorb the output of the global economy. Global inequalities and the impoverishment of broad majorities mean that transnational capital cannot find productive outlets for unloading surplus. By the turn of the century it was clear we were headed towards a new structural crisis. First came then Asian financial meltdown of 1997–98, which quickly spread, to Russia, Turkey and Brazil. Then came to dot-com bust and worldwide recession in 2000–01. In 2008–9 the financial system collapsed as stock market, mortgage market, and other bubbles burst.

The TCC turned to several mechanisms to sustain accumulation in the face of stagnation. One is militarized accumulation. Wars and conflicts unleashed cycles of destruction and reconstruction that fuel accumulation. We are now living in a global war economy. The global arms trade, prison-industrial complexes, homeland security systems, mass surveillance, militarized policing and border control, the deployment of armies of private security guards—all this keeps accumulation going in the face of stagnation yet it also further aggravates social inequalities and ultimately destabilizes the system. A second is the sacking and pillaging of public finances, reflecting a more general transformation of public finance. Predatory transnational finance capital extracts evergreater amounts of surplus value from labor via public finances recycled as bailouts, subsidies and the issuance of bonds. According to the International Bank of Settlements, the global trade in government bonds now exceeds $100 trillion. Public finance has become a mechanism for capital to make claim to the future income of workers. A third mechanism is frenetic financial speculation in the global financial casino. Fictitious capital now so exceeds the real output of goods and services that a new collapse of devastating proportions would appear all but assured. Although they helped keep the global economy sputtering forward, all three of these mechanisms have further aggravated inequalities, over-accumulation, social conflicts and political crises.

Tellingly, some of the very economists and policymakers who designed the neo-liberal program and pushed it on the world through such transnational state institutions as the World Bank, the International Monetary Fund and the U.S. and other powerful states are now leading critics of "market fundamentalism," a phrase first coined by George Soros. An Hungarian born billionaire financier and speculator, Soros achieved notoriety in 1992 when he threw the British economy into a tailspin by unloading some $10 billion worth of pounds onto international currency markets, making him a profit of $1 billion overnight. Previously, Soros established himself as a crusader for the overthrow of the former Soviet Union and the imposition of neo-liberal structural adjustment on Eastern Europe. The Wall Street tycoon first coined the phrase "market fundamentalism" in his best-selling 1998 book, *The Crisis of Global Capitalism*, which argued that blind faith in market forces was leading to widening inequalities and ongoing crises that threatened the stability of the system.

Joseph Stiglitz, who as Senior Vice President and Chief Economist of the World Bank from 1997 and 2000, helped imposed neo-liberalism around the world, also became a leading voice among the reformers in the wake of the 1997–98 Asian financial crisis. More recently, Lawrence Summers joined the ranks of the reformists. Previously he displayed impeccable neo-liberal logic in 1991 by claiming, as Chief Economist at the World Bank, that dumping toxic waste in Third World countries would bring economic benefits. "I have always thought that the under-populated countries in Africa are vastly UNDER-polluted," said Summers, "their air quality is probably vastly inefficiently low compared to Los Angeles or Mexico City." From the World Bank, Summers went on to design free trade and other neo-liberal policies for the Clinton and then later the Obama administration.[10] Fast forward to 2012; Summers argued that

---

10   The memo (Internal World Bank Memo dated 12 December 1991) was widely published in the press at the time and is reproduced in hundreds of web sites, among them Wikipedia at https://en.wikipedia.org/wiki/Summers_memo. Particularly useful is Foster's 1993 discussion of the memo. Following his work as Treasury Secretary in the second Clinton government Summers went on to become President of Harvard University, a post from which he resigned in disgrace for declaring that women are biologically less capable of learning math than men. It is worth recalling more of his infamous 1991 memo:

   "The measurements of the costs of health impairing pollution depends on the foregone earnings from increased morbidity and mortality. From this point of view a given amount of health impairing pollution should be done in the country with the lowest cost, which will be the country with the lowest wages. I think the economic logic behind dumping a load of toxic waste in the lowest wage country is impeccable and we should face up to that.... The demand for a clean environment for aesthetic and health reasons is likely to have very high income elasticity. The concern over an agent that causes a one in a million change in the odds of prostrate cancer is obviously going to be much higher in a country where people survive to get prostrate cancer than in a country where under 5 mortality is 200 per thousand. Also, much of the concern over industrial atmosphere discharge is about visibility impairing particulates. These discharges may have very little

escalating inequality should be tempered because it is fueling a growing disillusionment with capitalism.[11]

Jeffrey Sachs is perhaps most emblematic of the neo-liberal-cum-reformers. As a consultant for international financial institutions and governments Sacks designed and imposed the very first neo-liberal structural adjustment program, on Bolivia, in 1985. The program decimated Bolivia's poor: purchasing power dropped by 70 percent nearly overnight, unemployment shot up to 25 percent as thousands were fired and strikes made illegal, and throwing millions into untold hardship as nearly all social welfare benefits were swept away.[12] The succession of mass popular uprisings against Sachs' program eventually culminated in the indigenous revolution that brought Evo Morales to power in 2006. From Bolivia, Sachs went on to pioneer the "shock program" of structural adjustment in Russia following the collapse of the Soviet Union, resulting in an overnight drop of 50 percent in the GDP, a tenfold increase in poverty and a spike of 75 percent in the mortality rate for workers). He as well drafted programs for the transition to capitalism in Poland and elsewhere in Eastern Europe, including overnight austerity and the wholesale transfer to private banks and corporations of large blocs of formerly state assets.

As global capitalism entered a period of stagnation that also saw renewed mass social struggle and a turn to political radicalism in the face of escalating inequalities at the turn of the twenty-first century these and other one-time apostles of neo-liberalism have framed the public agenda on global poverty and inequality. Their books have become bestsellers and standard texts in university courses.[13] They have helped to establish the hegemony of a mildly reformist discourse within this agenda that actually embraces the continuation of a campaign to open up the world to transnational capital within a new

---

direct health impact. Clearly trade in goods that embody aesthetic pollution concerns could be welfare enhancing. While production is mobile the consumption of pretty air is a non-tradable."

"The problem with the arguments against all of these proposals for more pollution in LDCs (intrinsic rights to certain goods, moral reasons, social concerns, lack of adequate markets, etc.) could be turned around and used more or less effectively against every Bank proposal for liberalization."

11   Lawrence Summers, "Why Isn't Capitalism Working?" *Reuters*, January 9, 2012, at http://blogs.reuters.com/lawrencesummers/2012/01/09/why-isnt-capitalism-working/ Accessed on November 8, 2015

12   See, for example, Kenneth Lehman, *Bolivia and the United States: A Limited Partnership*, (Athens: University of Georgia Press, 1999).

13   See Joseph Stiglitz, *Globalization and Its Discontents*, (New York: W.W. Norton, 2003); Jeffrey D. Sachs, *The End of Poverty*, (London: Penguin, 2005).

framework of transnational regulation and mild redistribution through taxation and limited social safety nets.

As case in point, Sachs serves as chief strategist for the United Nation's Millennium Development Goals (MDG). The UN's Millennium Development Goals were promulgated with much fanfare in 2000 at the United Nations Millennium Summit and with the participation of so-called civil society representatives. The Millennium Development Goals put forth a set of eight development goals to be achieved by 2015, among them: a reduction by half the proportion of people living in extreme poverty and who suffer from hunger; universal primary education; a reduction by two-thirds the mortality rate among children under five and by three quarters the maternal mortality rate, halt and reverse the incidence of major diseases, promote gender equality and the empowerment of women, and so on. However, the prescription put forth to achieve these lofty goals was based on a more thoroughgoing privatization of health and educational systems, further freeing up of the market from state regulations, greater trade liberalization and more structural adjustment, and the conversion of agricultural lands into private commercial property—in other words, an intensification of the very capitalist development that has generated the social conditions to be eradicated (see, e.g., Amin, 2006).[14]

The ranks of the reformists among the transnational elite and intelligentsia have been expanding rapidly since the 2008 global financial collapse. Many of these responded to the collapse and even prior to it by pushing for a neo-Keynesianism. These elites articulated a project involving a shift from neo-classical to institutional economics, a limited re-regulation of global market forces, tax reform (such as the Tobin Tax), limited redistribution, and multi-trillion dollar state intervention programs to bail out transnational capital. The role of the state is to assist transnational capital to accumulate even against its will, by raising demand and attenuating radical challenges without disputing the prerogative of capital or altering the fundamental structure of private property. What is called the "new institutionalism" is a research agenda spanning the social sciences whose principal theoretical claim is that institutions have an independent and formative influence on politics, economics, and social structure. As well, prior institutional development establishes paths that shape and circumscribe present and future political,

---

14   Samir Amin, "The Millennium Development Goals: A Critique from the South," *Monthly Review*, vol. 57 (10) 2006, published online at http://monthlyreview.org/2006/03/01/the -millennium-development-goals-a-critique-from-the-south.

economic, and social processes ("path dependence").[15] Reformists among global elites such as Joseph Stiglitz, Jeffrey Sachs, Kofi Annan, and George Soros, among others—all previously adherents to the neo-liberal "Washington consensus"—espouse institutional over neo-classical economics as the intellectual scaffolding of a post-neo-liberal global capitalist order.[16] If neo-classical economics provided the theoretical and ideological foundation for the neo-liberal program then institutionalism along with neo-Keynesianism is likely to provide such a foundation for reformist projects from above.

There is a contradiction between a globalizing economy within a nation-state based system of political authority. Transnational state apparatuses are incipient and unable to impose enough authority to reign in on the power of transnationally mobile capital, especially finance capital that moves seamlessly through the digital circuits of the global economy. Many among the transnational elite have been clamoring for a more effective TNS apparatus that could impose some international regulation and reign in on the anarchy of the global market, especially the global financial systems. This contradiction has Piketty and other reformers troubled. Indeed, Piketty's call for a "global tax on capital" hinges on the ability of transnational state institutions, starting with the European Union, to impose international financial transparency.[17]

Piketty beyond the Hype

This newfound critique of the model of free market global capitalism among one-time technocrats and intellectuals of neo-liberalism finds resonance and perhaps analytical legitimation in Piketty's study. Intellectual labor is always organic; it is always for or against one or another historical project

---

15   Perhaps the most well known academic associated with the New Institutional Economics is Douglass C. North, *Institutions, Institutional Change and Economic Performance*, (Cambridge: Cambridge University Press, 1990). See also John Harris, Karen Hunter, and Colin M. Lewis (eds), *The New Institutional Economics and Third World Development*, (New York: Routledge, 1997).

16   See, Joseph E. Stiglitz, *Globalization and its Discontents* (New York: W.W. Norton, 2003). To his right is Jeffrey D. Sacks, *The End of Poverty: Economic Possibilities for Our Time* (New York: Penguin Books, 2006).

17   Piketty states: "The difficulty is that this solution, the progressive tax on capital, requires a high level of international cooperation and regional political integration. It is not within reach of the nation-states in which earlier social compromises were hammered out." p. 573

and subjective standpoint *vis-a-vis* antagonistic social forces and interests. Theory is never neutral. It does not appear in a vacuum and can be positively correlated with distinct social projects in competition and conflict. Piketty's "theory" (actually his work is pre-theoretical) can be positively correlated to the agenda of reformist elements among the transnational elite and their growing concern, even alarm, over the political dangers to global capitalism of rapidly expanding world inequalities. Piketty is responsive to elite concerns yet his study is accommodating to capital, not a radical critique. Claims by such admirers of Piketty to the contrary,[18] his study is *decidedly not* a "dialogue with Marx"; in fact, Marx is largely written off, and Piketty admitted in an interview with the *New Republic* that he has not read Marx' *Capital*.[19] If Milton Friedman was the poster child of neo-liberalism Piketty may become a poster child of the emerging post-neo-liberal era in which states are to play a limited role in a mild reregulation of capital and effect a limited redistribution through transfer payments, more progressive income tax, and a tax on capital.

Some of the critique of *Capital in the Twenty-First Century* is well known. His study is based on just a handful of countries: some 20 are brought in, only five of which figure in any prominence (France, Germany, the United States, Japan and the United Kingdom), and only two constitute detailed case studies, France and the U.K. Capital in Piketty's definition is neither a social relation nor a process of accumulation; it is defined as anything at all that can theoretically have a commercial value—the instruments and the means of production as well as goods themselves. There is a conflation of capital with personal property and with anything that has any use to human beings. Capital by this definition is not specific to capitalism as a system. It includes factories and machinery, money itself, buildings, (including all individual dwellings), roads, jewelry, the clothes we wear, and also everything found in nature (Piketty defines nature itself as "natural capital"), even a cave where stone-age people may dwell and the spears they may use.[20]

---

18 See Timothy Shenk, "Thomas Piketty and the Millennial Marxists on the Scourge of Inequality," *The Nation*, April 14, 2014. http://www.thenation.com/article/thomas-piketty -and-millennial-marxists-scourge-inequality/ Accessed on November 16, 2016.

19 In fact, in the interview he suggested that the only work by Marx he has read is *The Communist Manifesto*. See Isaac Chotiner, *New Republic*, May 5, 2014, at https://newrepublic .com/article/117655/thomas-piketty-interview-economist-discusses-his-distaste-marx Accessed on November 6, 2015.

20 "Capital is defined as the sum total of nonhuman assets that can be owned and exchanged on some market" (Thomas Piketty, *Capital in the Twenty-First Century* (Cambridge:

This conception is significant because it means that every human being in global capitalism owns capital so long as s/he wears an article of clothing, has a bicycle, a cow, a cup to drink out of, a wristwatch, or a can of beans. Taking the logic of this definition to the extreme, a shopping cart that a homeless person pushes around is to be considered capital. "Inequality of capital ownership" for Piketty is a matter of unequal distribution within a continuum of ownership. Piketty rests his analysis on the notion that capital generates income (so that those with more capital have more income, hence the roots of inequality in his construct). Never mind that this is never squared with his definition of capital as anything that theoretically can be given a value, so that this blatant contradiction is never resolved; a can of beans or the shirt on one's back, of course, does not generate income.

Piketty' study exhibits the same fatal flaw that Marx identified for the two fathers of classical political economy, Adam Smith and David Ricardo. These two made major contributions to our understanding of political economy but could not identify the genesis or the nature of capitalism as a social system (or capital as a social relationship) because they *took for given* the existence of capital itself and the prevailing property relations or distribution of capital. Primitive accumulation in Europe through the enclosures and around the world through colonialism and imperialism dispossessed millions— billions—of people, turning their land and resources into capital (property) of the capitalist class and turning them into proletarians. A class of owners and a mass of dispossessed is the pre-given and non-problematic starting point for Piketty as it was for Smith and Ricardo. Capital and private property are thus *naturalized*.

As a result, force and violence as a fundamental and constitutive social relation in the making of world capitalism are not part of the story; *power* is glaring absent from the entire Piketty construct. *Exploitation* is as well. "In all societies, there are two main way to accumulating wealth," affirms Piketty, "through work or inheritance" (pp. 379). In fact, I read all 577 pages of text and found that he used the word exploitation *exactly twice*, once in reference to the exploitation of natural resources and the other citing Marx in order to reject the significance of the concept. Inequality for Piketty is not a social relationship of power, domination, or exploitation; it is not antagonism among social groups or classes. These concepts are not part of his vocabulary. It is simply the

---

Belknap Press, 2014, p. 46). Later Piketty states: "Historically, the earliest forms of capital accumulation involved both tools and improvements to land (fencing, irrigation, drainage, etc.) and rudimentary dwellings (caves, tents, huts, etc.)" Thomas Piketty, *Capital in the Twenty-First Century* (Cambridge: Belknap Press, 2014), p. 213.

unequal distribution of resources stacked up as income brackets. He dismisses in a single sentence (pp. 252, under the heading "Class Struggle or Centile Struggle?") the concept of class in analyzing inequality in favor of deciles and centiles of income earners and capital ownership.

Since the existence of capital and the prevailing property relations are given as the starting point of analysis, Piketty does not—and *cannot*—explain why in the first instance there would be inequality in the capitalist system. Inequality flows from the unequal ownership of capital, yet this unequal ownership of capital is not, and cannot be explained by Piketty. His narrative begins with an already established regime of property. The best he can achieve is to analyze a series of *proximate* causes for rising inequality, such as the rise of "supermanagers" with mega-salaries (but why?), the decline in the minimum wage (but why?), and so on. Social and class struggle and the configurations of forces these struggles bring about are not a significant part of his narrative. The two world wars and the 1930s depression, for instance, are the result not of the *internal* workings of the system but of *external* and unexplained "shocks."

The crux of Piketty's argument is what he refers to as the capital-rate of growth ration. When r, as the rate of return on capital, is greater than g, the growth rate, then inequality will rise, expressed as $r>g$.[21] This is, on the one hand, in essence a neo-liberal argument: inequality is not the result of exploitation but of slow growth ("Decreased growth—especially demographic growth—is thus responsible for capital's comeback" [pp. 156]). Piketty places causal centrality on slow growth: it is not inequality that leads to slow growth but slow growth that leads of inequality. The notion that high inequality means that output cannot be absorbed (insufficient purchasing power) and thus growth (accumulation) stagnates—that is, in simplified terms, *overaccumulation*—cannot figure into the model. On the other hand, there is a certain

---

21 "The central thesis of this book is precisely that an apparently small gap between the return on capital and the rate of growth can in the long run have powerful and destabilizing effects on the structure and dynamics of social inequality. In a sense, everything follows from the laws of cumulative growth and cumulative returns" Thomas Piketty. *Capital in the 21st Century*. (Cambridge: Harvard University Press, 2014), p. 77. I cannot here, to reiterate, undertake a complete review of Piketty. However, it is worth noting that he adds to his central thesis the notion that greater population growth will have the effect of diminishing inequality whereas less population growth with increase inequality, yet he never presents any convincing evidence for this proposition. His logic is absolutely contorted: greater population growth decreases the importance of inherited wealth. He claims that with greater population growth there is greater distributed earnings and savings.

tautology here; there is inequality because returns on capital are high. Returns on capital are high because there is an unequal distribution of capital. In any event, the world is rife with examples of a sharp and sustained rise in inequality simultaneous to very high growth rates. Brazil and Mexico experienced some of the highest growth rates in the world in the 1960s and were routinely referred to in that decade as "miracle economies." Yet inequalities skyrocketed at that time in those countries, as Braun has shown, as it has in China in the 21st century period of phenomenally high growth rates.[22]

Next, Piketty's theory of inequality hinges on the capital-income ratio that he postulates, capital being the total market value of all assets (as previously mentioned, this includes by Piketty's definition someone's can of beans, car or personal dwelling; in this conception the capital stock need not be productive), and income being the quantity of goods produced and distributed in a nation in one year. If the capital stock grows quicker than output then inequality will rise. Inversely, high growth rates will lower inequality (*assuming* that greater output will raise income).

Yet this capital-income ratio on which Piketty's thesis hinges tells us very little; it is actually misleading. He contends that slow growth starting in the late 20th century (including slow demographic growth, which is only mathematically relevant for the model but not demonstrated to have any relevance for the real world in explaining inequality) as well as high savings is the prescription for increasing the capital stock relative to income and therefore for an increase in inequality. This is indeed the very crux of Piketty's thesis. But it explains remarkably little. Indeed, it is by Piketty's fiat a mathematical law but not a social law, meaning that if one postulates that inequality is the result of more going to the capital side than the income side of the ratio then by definition inequality will increase.

But neither slow growth nor high savings (nor for that matter the rate of demographic growth) can cause anything; they are not independent but dependent variables. They need to be explained in turn, not as exogenous to the model but as endogenous and caused by something else going on. What is this something else? Here Piketty does not provide any causal explanation, apart from simply suggesting that historically the social system (he takes us back to Antiquity) tends to grow slowly so that high growth in societies are the exception and not the norm; again, he provides observation but not explanation. What then may be the independent variable in this model, that is, what may

---

22   Dennis Braun, *The Rich Get Richer: The Rise of Income Inequality in the U.S. and the World*, (Belmont: Wadsworth, 1997).

cause slow growth and high savings? If we move beyond the conceptual con-straints of Piketty's model—and of neo-classical economics—we find that all Piketty is saying is that as investment opportunities dry up (*over-accumulation*) growth will slow and the over-accumulated capital is expressed as growing piles of capitalists' wealth.

Once we step out of the neo-classical box we can see the circular reason-ing in this thesis. Circular reasoning is when one explanation for a condition or phenomenon is itself said to be caused by that condition or phenomenon. Heightened inequalities from 1970 to 2010 are said to be caused by slow growth and continued high savings. Slow growth and continued high savings are caused by the increase in capital stock relative to income in the capital-income ratio. Yet this increase in capital stock relative to income is caused by slow growth and high savings. Stepping outside this box, "continued high savings" in the capitalist economy, suggests that capitalists are accumulating capital that they cannot reinvest and thus expand the income side of the equa-tion. The ever-greater concentration of wealth leads to slow growth and "high savings" or to stagnation in the face of over-accumulated capital. Slow growth is the effect of inequality in this framework, not the cause.

Another serious problem in Piketty's narrative is the lack of distinction between real and fictitious capital. Fictitious capital is money thrown into circulation without any base in commodities or in production. He calculates as increases in capital the tremendous inflation of asset values (e.g., housing and stock markets) even though this rise in value does not necessarily (and in recent decades *has not*)[23] represent the expansion of real material production and services, e.g., more housing or industrial and service output. To be sure, these inflations *do* represent an increase in the social power of capital but they cannot explain the rise in inequality consistent with Piketty's hypothetical for-mulation. This leads him to claim that the increase in asset prices from 1950 to 2010 "is now complete" and that asset prices will now rise at "the exact same pace as consumer prices." (pp. 188).

I am reminded here of the following joke: A chemist, a physicist, and an economist are stranded on a desert island and have a can of beans they need to open. The chemist suggests they combine seawater and other mineral deposits on the island to generate a chemical response that will dissolve the tin. The physicist suggests they climb on to a palm tree and drop the can at a precise angle on to a sharp rock to open it. Then the economist declares: "I know, let us assume we have a can opener."

---

23   See inter-alia, William Robinson, *Global Capitalism and the Crisis of Humanity*, (Cambridge: Cambridge University Press, 2014).

Piketty calls for transfers programs (health, education, and pensions), progressive income tax, and a "global tax on capital" in order to resolve the problem of escalating inequalities. This call for a "global tax on capital" has sparked considerable interest among commentators. However, it is important to be clear on what he means by this. One would think typically of a "tax on capital" as corporate tax. But this is *not* a call for a tax on corporate profits. Recall Piketty's definition of capital as any asset that has a value. Although he mentions taxing foundations and financial institutions, by a "global tax on capital" he is referring to taxing individuals in accordance with the value of their assets and in the order of a few percentage points. "An 0.1 percent tax on capital would be more in the nature of a compulsory reporting law than a true tax," concedes Piketty. "Everyone would be required to report ownership of capital assets to the world's financial authorities in order to be recognized as the legal owner, with all the advances and disadvantages thereof" (pp. 519). This "global tax on capital" would amount to extending to all people's assets what in many countries is currently a property tax.

Piketty's proposed remedies for rising inequality do not involve control over capital but rather the capture of small amounts of its accumulated surplus. However important this may be, his reform agenda is considerably milder, in fact, than controls over capital that states imposed during the Fordist-Keynesian era or what many around the world are now demanding. He does not call for restraining "free trade," that is, the free movement of transnational capital across borders as epitomized in most recently in the Transnational Pacific-Partnership, or TPP, agreement. Such measures as nationalizing banks or rebuilding public sectors are simply not on his agenda.

Finally, Piketty does not really address truly *global* inequalities. There are two omissions of great significance in terms of his conception of global inequalities as well as the political significance of these inequalities. One is the lack of any historical or analytical treatment of the great North-South or center-periphery divide brought about by colonialism and imperialism. Modernization theory is recycled; the underdeveloped countries are seen by Piketty to be in a process of catching up. The second is the omission of inequality seen in terms of the global population as a whole, beyond the top centile and the billionaire class, such as that discussed by the Oxfam reported cited at the start of the present essay. According to that report, 52 percent of global wealth not owned by the richest one percent of humanity is owned by the richest 20 percent, while 80 percent of humanity has to make do with just 5.5 percent of global wealth. This is the new global social apartheid. A necessary step in overthrowing global apartheid is a critique of its elite critics.

CHAPTER 14

The Piketty Challenge:
Global Inequality and World Revolutions

Christopher Chase-Dunn and Sandor Nagy

Introduction

This chapter discusses those changes in the magnitude of wealth and income inequality within developed countries that have been revealed by Thomas Piketty's research as a context for considering the world history of social movements. Social movements and world revolutions have restructured global governance institutions over the past several centuries. The rebellions, protests and counter-hegemonic national regimes that have emerged since the 1990s need to be compared with earlier world revolutions in order to assess the prospects for the emergence in the next few decades of a more coherent effort to transform the capitalist world-economy into a democratic and collectively rational global commonwealth.

Thomas Piketty's[1] path-breaking research on changes in the magnitude of wealth and income inequalities within several core countries over the past 200 years is a major contribution to the study of economic inequalities because he uses data from tax returns that are more reliable and have greater temporal depth than the more usual household income surveys that have been used to study economic inequality. Also the tax returns allow the close study of the wealth and incomes of the very rich, which tend to be invisible in income surveys. Piketty's results show a long-term trend toward lesser and then greater economic inequality within core countries (the so-called "great u-turn") as well as important similarities and differences among these countries. He shows that the returns to wealth and labor have changed greatly as a result of the rise, and partial demise, of the welfare state. He also discusses the issue of distributive justice within national societies, and he argues in favor of a global progressive tax on wealth that would help to redistribute income.

The main lacunae in Piketty's work are the lack of attention to the role that social movements have played in the causation of the inequality trends and

---

1   Thomas Piketty. *Capital in the 21st Century*. (Cambridge, MA: Harvard University Press, 2014).

the possibilities for social movements to once again challenge the growing inequality trends of the past several decades. Piketty's analysis, despite the provocative title of his book (*Twenty-first Century Capitalism*), does not get at the roots of the problems of global capitalism. The most important political and analytical task is to distinguish between those institutional and structural aspects of the contemporary capitalist world-system that are congruent with a more egalitarian and sustainable future global society and those that are not.

The World-Systems Perspective

The world-systems perspective presents a structural interpretation of the cycles and trends that have constituted the expansion and evolution of global capitalism.[2,3,4] This holistic structural approach allows us to grasp both the similarities and the important differences between the current world historical period and earlier periods that were similar in some ways but different in others. The expansion and deepening of capitalism has occurred in the context of the rise and fall of hegemonic core powers, waves of colonization in which European powers subjugated and exploited most of Asia, the Americas and Africa, and the waves of decolonization that extended the European system of formally sovereign states to the non-core. The expansion and deepening of capitalist accumulation and the increasing size of the nation-states that played the role of hegemons were driven and made possible by movements of resistance that were located both within core polities and, importantly, in the non-core. Each of the hegemons (the Dutch in the 17th century, the British in the 19th century and the United States in the 20th century) were formerly semiperipheral states that rose to core status in struggles with contending great powers. Their successes were partly based on their abilities to deal with resistance from below more effectively than their competitors.[5]

---

2   Immanuel Wallerstein, *The Modern World-System, Volume 4: Centrist Liberalism Triumphant, 1789–1914,* (Berkeley: University of California Press, 2011).

3   Giovanni Arrighi, *The Long Twentieth Century,* (London: Verso, 1994)

4   C. Chase-Dunn and Bruce Lerro, *Social Change: Globalization from the Stone Age to the Present,* (Boulder: Paradigm, 2014).

5   Immanuel Wallerstein, "The three instances of hegemony in the history of the capitalist world-Economy," pp. 100–108 in *Current Issues and Research in Macrosociology International Studies in Sociology and Social Anthropology,* Vol. 37 ed. Gerhard Lenski, (Leiden: E.J. Brill, 1984).

It is important to accurately grasp both the structural similarities and differences between the current world historical period and earlier periods that were similar but also importantly dissimilar. The United States has been in decline in terms of hegemony in economic production since 1945 and this has been similar in many respects to the decline of British hegemony in the late 19th and early 20th centuries.[6] Giovanni Arrighi noted that the period of British hegemonic decline (1870–1914) moved rather quickly toward conflictive interimperial rivalry because economic competitors such as Germany and Japan were able to develop powerful military capabilities that could be used to challenge the British.[7] The U.S. hegemony has been different in that the United States ended up as the single superpower after the demise of the Soviet Union. Some economic challengers (Japan and Germany) cannot easily play the military card because they are stuck with the consequences of having lost the last World War. This, and the immense size of the U.S. economy, will probably slow the process of hegemonic decline down compared to the rate of the British decline.

The post-World War II wave of trade globalization and financialization faltered in 2008 but seems to have recovered since then. A future trough of trade deglobalization similar to what happened in the 1930s could happen if a perfect storm of calamities and resistance to further economic globalization should emerge. The declining economic and political hegemony of the U.S. poses huge challenges for global governance. Newly emergent national economies such as India and China need to be fitted in to the global structure of power. The unilateral use of military force by the Bush administration further delegitimated the institutions of global governance and provoked resistance and challenges. A similar bout of "imperial over-reach" in the late 19th and early 20th centuries on the part of Britain (the Boer Wars) preceded and led to a period of interimperial rivalry and world war. Such an outcome is less likely now, but not impossible.

These developments parallel, to some extent, what happened a century ago, but the likelihood of another "Age of Extremes" or a Malthusian correction such what occurred in the first half of the 20th century could be exacerbated by some new twists. The number of people on Earth was only 1.65 billion when the 20th century began, whereas at the beginning of the 21st century there were 6 billion. Moreover, fossil fuels were becoming less expensive as oil

---

6   Chris Chase-Dunn *et al.*, "Last of the hegemons: U.S. decline and global governance," *International Review of Modern Sociology* 37 (2011): 1–29. http://irows.ucr.edu/papers/irows65/irows65.htm

7   Giovanni Arrighi, *Adam Smith in Beijing*, (London: Verso, 2006).

was replacing coal as the major source of energy.[8] It was this use of inexpensive, but non-renewable, fossil energy that made the geometric expansion and industrialization of humanity possible.

Now we are facing global warming as a consequence of the spread and rapid expansion of industrial production and energy-intensive consumption. Energy prices have temporarily come down because of fracking and overproduction by countries that are dependent on oil exports, but the low hanging "ancient sunlight" in coal and oil has been picked. "Peak oil" is approaching. "Clean coal" and controllable nuclear fusion remain dreams. The cost of energy will probably go up no matter how much is invested in new kinds of energy production.[9] None of the existing alternative technologies offer low cost energy of the kind that made the huge expansion possible. Many believe that overshoot has already occurred in terms of how many humans are alive, and how much energy is being used by some of them, especially those in the core. Adjusting to rising energy costs and dealing with the environmental degradation caused by industrial society will be difficult, and the longer it takes the harder it will become. Ecological problems are not new, but this time they are on a global scale. Peak oil and rising costs of other resources are likely to cause more resource wars that exacerbate the problems of global governance. The war in Iraq was both an instance of imperial over-reach and a resource war because the u.s. neoconservatives thought that they could prolong u.s. hegemony by controlling the global oil supply. The Paris Agreement on greenhouse gas emissions reached in December of 2015 is good news, but compliance will be difficult, especially for non-core countries.

The first decade of the 21st century has seen a continuation of many large-scale processes that were under way in the last half of the 20th century. Urbanization of the Global South continued as the policies of neoliberalism gave powerful support to the "Live Stock Revolution" in which animal husbandry on the family ranch was replaced by large-scale production of eggs, milk and meat. This, and industrialized farming, were encouraged by the export expansion policies of the International Monetary Fund-imposed Structural Adjustment Programs (SAPS). One consequence was the ejection of millions of small farmers from the land. These rural residents had been producing a lot of their own food rather than buying it. A good part of the "increased income" that is counted as poverty reduction in the Global South is due to the monetization of what was formerly agrarian subsistence production. Money incomes and purchases went

---

8   Bruce Podobnik, *Global Energy Shifts: Fostering Sustainability in a Turbulent Age*, (Philadelphia: Temple University Press, 2006).

9   Richard Heinberg, *Powerdown*, (Gabriola Island: Island Press, 2004)

up but slum-dwellers are no longer able to produce as much of their own food as they did before they migrated to the city. This is one reason why counting monetized income and consumption alone is an imperfect way to study inequality.

For most of these former rural residents, migration to megacities meant moving to huge slums and gaining a precarious living in the "informal sector" of services and small-scale production. These huge slums lack adequate water or sewage infrastructure. The budget cuts mandated by the SAPs, required by the International Monetary Fund as a condition for further loans, have often decimated public health systems. And so the slums have become breeding grounds for new forms of communicable diseases, including new strains of avian flu, that pose huge health risks to the peoples of both the core and the non-core. These diseases are rapidly transmitted by intercontinental air travel. Many public health experts believe that a flu pandemic similar in scope and lethality to that of the infamous 1918 disaster is highly likely to occur in the near future.[10] Most of the national governments have failed to adequately prepare for such an eventuality, and so a massive die-off could easily occur. Like most disasters, the lethality would be much greater among the poor, especially in the megacities of the Global South.[11]

In addition to the lack of attention to the roles of past and future social movements, there are other lacunae in Piketty's analysis as well as his prescriptions. Whereas he mentions *global* inequality, his actual research is about trends within core societies. This is because taxation data over long time periods is not currently available for most of the non-core countries. But there is a large and contentious research literature about inequality trends in the global system as well as an important and consequential set of publically held assumptions about these trends. Many, including Bill Gates,[12] simply assume that global inequality has decreased because of rapid economic growth in China and India in the past several decades. Many critics of capitalist globalization assume that global inequality must be going up over the past decades because of Piketty's findings and because problems of poverty and dispossession in the Global South are well-known. The problem is that both within-country and between-country

10   Alfred W. Crosby, "Infectious Diseases as Ecological and Historical Phenomena, with Special Reference to the Influenza Pandemic of 1918–1919" pp. 280–287 in *The World System and the Earth System: Global Socioenvironmental Change and Sustainability since the Neolithic* edited by A. Hornborg and C. Crumley. (Walnut Creek: Left Coast Press: 2007).

11   Mike Davis, *Monster At Our Door: The Global Threat of Avian Flu,* (New York: New Press, 2005).

12   Bill Gates, "Why inequality matters" *gatesnotes* 2014. https://www.gatesnotes.com/Books/Why-Inequality-Matters-Capital-in-21st-Century-Review

trends need to be taken into account in order to know the true trend in income distribution for the whole population of the Earth. And there are difficult issues regarding the conversion of national currencies into a single global metric (usually U.S. dollars). A conservative estimate based on the contentious quantitative literature on trends in global income inequality is that global inequality increased greatly during the 19th century industrial revolution and it has remained at about the same high level or possibly decreased slightly since then.[13] Though the magnitude of global income inequality expanded in the 19th century, there were already important amounts of political inequality that had emerged between the core and the periphery as a result of European colonialism. And these structures were both outcomes of, and causes of, resistance and rebellions that occurred within the European core and in the colonized regions.

World Revolutions

The institutional changes that have occurred with the rise and fall of the hegemonic core powers over the past four centuries have constituted a sequence of forms of world order that evolved to solve the political, economic and technical problems of successively more global waves of capitalist accumulation. The expansion of global production required accessing raw materials to feed the new industries, and food to feed the expanding populations.[14] As in any hierarchy, coercion is a very inefficient means of domination, and so the hegemons sought legitimacy by proclaiming leadership in advancing civilization and democracy (the Gramscian side of hegemony). But the terms of these claims were also employed by those below who sought to protect themselves from exploitation and domination. And so the evolution of hegemony was produced by elite groups competing with one another in a context of successive powerful challenges from below. World orders have been contested and reconstructed in a series of world revolutions that began with the Protestant Reformation.[15,16]

13   Volker Bornschier, "On the evolution of inequality in the world system" pp. 39–64 in *Inequality Beyond Globalization: Economic Changes, Social Transformations and the Dynamics of Inequality*, ed. Christian Suter. (Zurich: LIT Verlag, 2010).

14   Stephen G Bunker and Paul S. Ciccantell, *"The Economic Ascent of China and the Potential for Restructuring the Capitalist World-Economy" Journal of World-Systems Research*, vol. 10 (3), 2004.

15   Terry Boswell and Christopher Chase-Dunn, *The Spiral of Capitalism and Socialism: Toward Global Democracy* (Boulder: Lynne Rienner, 2000), pp. 53–64.

16   Peter Linebaugh and Marcus Rediker, *The Many-Headed Hydra: Sailors, Slaves, Commoners and the Hidden History of the Revolutionary Atlantic.* (Boston: Beacon, 2000)

The idea of world revolution is a broad notion that encompasses all kinds of acts of resistance to hierarchy, regardless of whether or not they are coordinated with one another, but that occur relatively close to one another in time. Usually the idea of revolution is conceptualized on a national scale in which new social forces come to state power and restructure social relations. When we use the revolution concept at the world-system level a number of changes are required. There is no global state (yet) to take over. But there is a global polity, a world order, which has evolved as outlined above. It is that world polity or world order that is the arena of contestation within which world revolutions have occurred and that world revolutions have restructured.

Boswell and Chase-Dunn[17] focused on those constellations of local, regional, national and transnational rebellions and revolutions that have had long-term consequences for changing world orders. World orders are those normative and institutional features that are taken for granted in large-scale cooperation, competition and conflict. Years that symbolize the major world revolutions after the Protestant Reformation are 1789, 1848, 1917, 1968 and 1989. Arrighi, Hopkins and Wallerstein[18] analyzed the world revolutions of 1848, 1917, 1968 and 1989.[19,20,21] They observed that the demands put forth in a world revolution do not usually become institutionalized until a later consolidating revolt has occurred. So the revolutionaries appear to have lost in the failure of their most radical demands, but enlightened conservatives who are trying to manage hegemony end up incorporating the reforms that were earlier radical demands into the current world order in order to cool out resistance from below. It is important to tease out the similarities and the differences among the world revolutions in order to be able to accurately assess the contemporary situation and to learn from the past. The contexts and the actors have changed from one world revolution to the next.

This view of the modern world-system as constituting an arena of political struggle over the past several centuries implies that global civil society has

---

17   Terry Boswell and Christopher Chase-Dunn, *The Spiral of Capitalism and Socialism: Toward Global Democracy* (Boulder: Lynne Rienner, 2000)

18   Giovanni Arrighi, Terence K. Hopkins, and Immanuel Wallerstein, *Antisystemic Movements.* (London and New York: Verso, 2011)

19   Colin J. Beck, "The world cultural origins of revolutionary waves: five centuries of European contestation," *Social Science History* vol. 35 (2) 2011, pp. 167–207.

20   Sandor Nagy, "The evolution of revolution: a comparative analysis of world revolutions from 1789 to 2011" (Honors Thesis: University of California-Riverside, 2016).

21   Arguably 1955, the year of the Bandung Conference, should be included to represent the great wave of decolonization that occurred after World War II.

existed all along.[22] Global civil society includes all the actors who consciously participate in world politics. In the past it has consisted primarily of statesmen, religious leaders, scientists, financiers, and the owners and top managers of chartered companies such as the Dutch and British East India Companies. This rather small group of people already saw the global arena of political, economic, military and ideological struggle as their arena of contestation.[23] There has been a "global left" and transnational social movements involving non-elite actors at least since the world revolution of 1789.[24] While global civil society is still a small minority of the total population of the earth, the falling costs of communication and transportation have enabled more and more non-elites to become transnational political actors.

Our discussion below focuses on what has called the New Global Left and compares it with earlier incarnations of the global left.[25] This is part, but not all of global civil society. Other important actors are the forces organized around the World Economic Forum, the new conservative and neo-fascist elements,[26] the BRICS,[27] and the jihadists.[28]

We are in the midst of another world revolution now. Chase-Dunn and Niemeyer have called it the world revolution of 20xx (because it is not yet clear what the key symbolic year should be).[29] They claim that it began with the anti-International Monetary Fund riots in the 1980s and the Zapatista revolt in Southern Mexico in 1994.[30]

---

22   Mary Kaldor, *Global Civil Society*, (Malden: Polity Press, 2003).

23   Christopher Chase-Dunn and Ellen Reese, "Global party formation in world historical perspective" pp. 53–91 in Katarina Sehm-Patomaki and Marko Ulvila, Eds. *Global Party Formation*. (London: Zed Press, 2011)

24   Immanuel Wallerstein's *The Modern World-System* tells the story of politics in the geo-culture since the French Revolution. In *The Modern World-System IV; Centrist Liberalism Triumphant, 1789–1914*. (Oakland: University of California Press, 2011).

25   Boaventura de Sousa Santos, *The Rise of the Global Left*, (London: Zed Press, 2006).

26   Perry Anderson, *Spectrum*. (New York: Verso, 2005).

27   Patrick Bond, ed., *Brics in Africa: anti-imperialist, sub-imperialist of in between?* (Durban: University of Kwa-Zulu-Natal, 2013).

28   Valentine M. Moghadam, *Globalization and Social Movements: Islamism, Feminism and the Global Justice Movement*, (Lanham: Rowman and Littlefield, 2009).

29   Chris Chase-Dunn and R.E. Niemeyer, "The world revolution of 20xx" pp. 35–57 in *Transnational Political Spaces* in Mathias Albert et al. (ed.) (Campus Verlag: Frankfurt/New York, 2009).

30   Paul Mason also compares the current global justice movement with earlier world revolutions, sees it as having begun with the Arab Spring and anti-austerity movements in 2011. See Paul Mason, *Why Its (Still) Kicking Off Everywhere: The New Global Revolutions* (London: Verso, 2013).

World revolutions are hard to study and difficult to compare with one another because they are complex constellations of events. The time periods and places to include (and exclude) are hard to judge. They each have had different mixes of social movements, rebellions and revolutions, including reactionary movements, and have occurred unevenly in time and space. What have been the actual and potential bases for cooperation and competition across the progressive (antisystemic) movements? How did some of the movements affect the others? And how did they relate to the similar and different terrains of power and economic structures in the world-system at the time that they emerged? And how have they affected the struggles among elites in their efforts to maintain their positions or gain new advantages?

The World Revolution of 20xx

It is difficult to pick a symbolic year that expresses the main characteristics of the current world revolution because it is still in formation and it is not clear which characteristics to pick. The wave of protests that began with the Arab Spring in 2011 demonstrated some coherence with regard to their local and global causations, and so some have concluded that 2011 is a good choice. The Arab Spring was followed by an anti-austerity summer in Greece and Spain and then the Occupy movement in the Fall. But it is probably too soon to pick a symbolic year for the current world revolution.

Some claim that the anti-International Monetary Fund riots of the 1980s[31] were the first skirmishes of the revolts and rebellions against neoliberal corporate capitalism.[32] The Zapatista rebellion of 1994 was the first to name neoliberalism as the enemy. The "Battle of Seattle" in 1999 brought the "antiglobalization movement" to the attention of large numbers of people. The founding of the World Social Forum (WSF) in 2001, a reaction to the exclusivity

---

31   John Walton and David Seddon, *Free markets and food riots: the politics of global adjustment,* (Cambridge: Blackwell, 1994).

32   World revolutions have become more frequent and so they now seem to overlap one another. The anti-IMF riots occurred during what some have called the World Revolution of 1989, which was also a rebellion against one-party rule in Russia, Eastern Europe and China. These rebellions allowed Reagan and Thatcher to declare that the West had won over collectivism and that there was no alternative to the neoliberal globalization project. But the rebels of 1989 also asserted the importance of political rights, and this was not lost on the emerging New Global Left. See Mary Kaldor, *Global Civil Society,* (Malden: Polity Press, 2003).

of the World Economic Forum held in Davos, Switzerland since 1971, provoked the coming together of a movement of movements focused on issues of
global justice and sustainability. The social forum process has spread to all the
regions of the world despite, and because of, the events of September 11, 2001
and subsequent military adventures carried out by the neoconservative Bush
regime in the United States.

Many of the participants in the contemporary movement of movements
are unaware, or are only vaguely aware, of the historical sequence of world
revolutions. But others are determined not to repeat what are perceived to have
been the mistakes of the past. The charter of the World Social Forum does not
permit participation by those who attend as representatives of organizations
that are engaged in, or that advocate, armed struggle. Nor are governments or
political parties supposed to send representatives to the WSF.[33] There is a great
emphasis on diversity and on horizontal, as opposed to hierarchical, forms
of organization. And the wide use of the Internet for communication and
mobilization makes it possible for broad coalitions and loosely knit networks
to engage in collective action projects. The movement of movements at the
World Social Forum engaged in a manifesto/charter-writing frenzy as those
who sought a more organized approach to confronting global capitalism and
neoliberalism attempted to formulate consensual goals and to put workable
coalitions together.[34]

One continuing issue has been whether or not the World Social Forum itself should formulate a political program and take formal stances on issues.
The Charter of the WSF explicitly forbids this and a significant group of participants strongly supports maintaining the WSF as an "open space" for debate
and organizing. A survey of 625 attendees at the World Social Forum meeting
in Porto Alegre in 2005 asked whether the WSF should remain an open space
or should take political stances. Exactly half favored the open space idea.[35] So
trying to change the WSF Charter to allow for a formal political program would
be very divisive.

---

33   The World Social Forum Charter of Principles is at http://www.colorado.edu/AmStudies/
     lewis/ecology/wsfcharter.pdf. Accessed Dec 2, 2016.

34   Immanuel Wallerstein, "The World Social Forum: from defense to offense," modified
     2007. http://www.sociologistswithoutborders.org/documents/WallersteinCommentary
     .pdf. Accessed Dec 10, 2016.

35   Christopher Chase-Dunn et al., "North-South Contradictions and Bridges at the World
     Social Forum" pp. 341–366 in North and South In the World Political Economy, ed. Rafael
     Reuveny and William R. Thompson. (Malden, Oxford and Carlton: Wiley-Blackwell,
     2008).

But this is not necessary. The WSF Charter also encourages the formation of new political organizations. So those participants who want to form new coalitions and organizations are free to act, as long as they do not do so in the name of the WSF as a whole. In Social Forum meetings at the global and national levels the Assembly of Social Movements and other groups have issued calls for global action and political manifestoes. At the end of the 2005 meeting in Porto Alegre a group of nineteen notable intellectuals and activists issued a statement that was purported to be a consensus of the meeting as a whole. At the 2006 "polycentric" meeting in Bamako, Mali a somewhat overlapping group issued a manifesto entitled "the Bamako Appeal" at the beginning of the meeting. The Bamako Appeal was a call for a global united front against neo-liberalism and United States neo-imperialism.[36] And Samir Amin, the famous Egyptian Marxist economist and one of the founders of the world-systems perspective, wrote a short essay entitled "Toward a fifth international?" in which he briefly outlined the history of the first four internationals.[37] Peter Waterman[38] proposed a "global labor charter" and a coalition of women's' groups meeting at the World Social Forum have produced a feminist global manifesto that tries to overcome divisive North/South issues.[39,40]

There has been an impasse in the global justice movement between those who want to move toward a global united front that could mobilize a strong coalition against the powers that be, and those who prefer local prefigurative, horizontalist actions that abjure formal organizations and refuse to participate in "normal" political activities such as elections and lobbying. Horizontalism abjures hierarchical organization and prefers flexible networks without formal organization.[41] Prefiguration is the idea that individuals and small groups can willfully constitute more humane and egalitarian social relations in the

---

36   Jai Sen *et al., A Political Programme for the World Social Forum?: Democracy, Substance and Debate in the Bamako Appeal and the Global Justice Movements* (Durban: Indian Institute for Critical Action: Centre in Movement (CACIM), New Delhi, India & the University of KwaZulu-Natal Centre for Civil Society (CCS), 2007.

37   Samir Amin, "Towards the fifth international?" pp. 121–144 in *Democratic Politics Globally* ed. Katarina Sehm-Patomaki *et al.* (Tampere: Network Institute for Global Democratization, 2006).

38   Peter Waterman, "Toward a Global Labor Charter Movement?" Modified 2006. http://wsfworkshop.openspaceforum.net/twiki/tiki-read_article.php?articleId=6

39   Valentine M. Moghadam, *Globalizing Women,* (Baltimore: Johns Hopkins University Press, 2005).

40   Moghadam, *Globalization and Social Movements.*

41   Moreover, see Jo Freeman, "The tyranny of structuralessness," 1970. http://www.jofreeman.com/joreen/tyranny.htm. Accessed Dec 21, 2016.

present. It has a long history as utopian socialism[42] and communes, and was an important component of the Occupy movement's construction of face-to-face participatory democracy[43] and has strong support in the social forum process.[44,45] Some of this horizontalism and prefiguration was inherited from similar tendencies in the world revolution of 1968. Arrighi, Hopkins and Wallerstein pointed out that the New Left of the sixties embraced direct democracy, attacked bureaucratic organizations, and was itself resistant to the creation of new formal organizations that might act as instruments of revolution.[46] These organizational predilections were seen as the important lessons learned from earlier waves of class struggle and decolonization. As Arrighi, Hopkins and Wallerstein pointed out:

> ... the class struggle "flows out" into a competitive struggle for state power. As this occurs, the political elites that provide social classes with leadership and organization (even if they sincerely consider themselves "instruments" of the class struggle) usually find that they have to play by the rules of that competition and therefore must attempt to subordinate the class struggle to those rules in order to survive as competitors for state power.[47]

In later years, many 68ers joined prefigurative communes or formed new Leninist organizations, some which have survived.[48] The resistance to politics as usual, especially competing for state power, has been very salient in the world revolution of 20xx. These proscriptions are based on the critique of the practices of earlier world revolutions in which labor unions and political parties became bogged down in short-term and self-interested struggles that then reinforced and reproduced the global capitalist system and the interstate system.

42   Frederick Engels, *Socialism: Utopian and Scientific*, (Chicago: Charles Kerr, 1918).

43   David Graeber, *The Democracy Project: A History, A Crisis, A Movement*, (New York: Spiegel and Grau, 2013)

44   Jeffrey S. Juris, *Networking Futures: the Movements Against Corporate Globalization*, Durham: Duke University Press, 2008.

45   Geoffrey Pleyers, *Alter-Globalization*, (Cambridge: Polity, 2010).

46   Giovanni Arrighi, Terrence Hopkins, and Immanuel Wallerstein, *Antisystemic Movements*, (New York: Verso. 1989). pp. 37–38.

47   Giovanni Arrighi, Terrence Hopkins, and Immanuel Wallerstein, *Antisystemic Movements*, (New York: Verso. 1989). p. 64.

48   See the Revolutionary Communist Party, *Constitution for the New Socialist Republic in North America*, (Chicago: RCP Publications, 2010).

This abjuration of formal organizations and participation in institutionalized political competition is strongly reflected in the constitution of the World Social Forum as discussed above. And the same elements were robustly present in the Occupy movement as well as in the several popular revolts that have constituted the Arab Spring and the other anti-austerity movements.[49]

Journalist Paul Mason[50] spent the last decade doing ethnographic immersion in the wave of protests that occurred in the Middle East, Spain, Greece, Turkey and the Occupy movement. His sympathetic analysis of the current world revolution contends that the social structural basis for horizontalism and anti-formal organization, beyond the reaction to the reformist outcomes of earlier efforts of the Left, is due to the presence of a large number of middle-class students in the protests that were building in the first decade of the 21st century.[51,52,53] Of course, the world revolution of 1968 was also composed of an activist element within the large stratum of college students who had emerged on the world stage with the global expansion of higher education since World War II.[54]

Precariat Fractions

Mason makes an interesting comparison of the recent protest wave with the world revolution of 1848, in which a large number of the activists were also educated, but underemployed, students.[55] He notes that the participants in the

---

49   Paul Mason, *Why Its (Still) Kicking Off Everywhere: The New Global Revolutions,* (London: Verso, 2013).

50   Ibid.

51   Andre V. Korotayev and Julia V. Zinkina, "Egyptian Revolution: A Demographic Structural Analysis" *Entelequia, Revista Interdisciplinar,* vol. 13, 2011.

52   Ruth Milkman, Stephanie Luce and Penny Lewis, "Changing the subject: a bottom-up account of Occupy Wall Street in New York City" (Paper, CUNY: The Murphy Institute, 2013).

53   Michaela Curran, *et al.,* "The Occupy Movement in California" in *What Comes After Occupy?: The Regional Politics of Resistance* ed. Todd A. Comer. (Cambridge: Scholars Publishing, 2014)

54   John W. Meyer (2009) explains the student revolt of the 1960s as analogous to earlier waves of expansion and incorporation into the political process. Men of no property and women had protested and been incorporated into the formal processes of democracy (suffrage) in the 19th and 20th centuries. After World War II higher education was greatly expanded across the world, creating a large, but politically unincorporated, interest group— college students.

55   Paul Mason, *Why Its (Still) Kicking Off Everywhere: The New Global Revolutions,* (London: Verso, 2013).

recent wave of protests were heavily composed of highly educated young people who were facing the strong likelihood that they will not be able to find jobs that are commensurate with their skills and certification levels. Many of these "graduates with no future" have gone into debt to finance their education, and they are alienated from politics as usual and enraged by the failure of global capitalism to continue the expansion of middle-class jobs. Mason notes that the urban poor, especially in the Global South, and workers whose livelihoods have been attacked by globalization, have also been important constituencies in the protests. And he points to the significance of the Internet, social media and cell phones for allowing disaffected digital youth to organize large protests. He sees the netizens' "freedom to tweet" as an important element in a strong desire for individual freedom that is an important driver of those middle class graduates who have enjoyed confronting the powers-that-be. This embrace of individuality may be another reason why the movements have been reticent to develop their own formal organizations and to participate in traditional organized political activities.

Guy Standing[56] has undertaken a broad consideration of how the neoliberal globalization project has affected global class relations and the nature of work. Standing does not focus on the nature of the recent protest wave, but his observations and claims overlap with, and in some ways diverge from, those of Paul Mason. Standing claims that the reorganization of production that David Harvey [57] calls flexible accumulation has produced the recent rise of what he calls the precariat. Standing sees the rise of precarious labor as constituting a new class, the precariat, which is significantly different from the proletariat. Employment is increasingly temporary and workers have little identification with their jobs or the firms that pay them. The increasing power of capital, deindustrialization of the core and attacks on labor unions have produced a reorganization of the global class structure around precarious work. Standing notes that there are important differences between different sectors of the precariat. The slum-dwellers in the informal sector in megacities of the Global South have long been exposed to precarious labor, though this group has expanded as a result of the neoliberal transformation of agriculture discussed above. The over-educated, underemployed are young people from working class and middle class backgrounds who also face a precarious livelihood, but with rather different tastes and interests from the folk of the planet of slums. They are individualistic and difficult to organize using the methods that worked fairly well for the industrial proletariat.

Standing wants to forge political alliances among these different groups in order to press for workers rights and greater protections from states, but he

---

56   Guy Standing, *The Precariat: The New Dangerous Class,* (London: Bloomsbury, 2011)

57   David Harvey, *The Condition of Postmodernity,* (London: Blackwell, 1989)

recognizes that this effort faces very difficult obstacles. Standing also has a very different attitude toward the "freedom to tweet" than does Mason. He believes that the short attention span produced by constant exposure to electronic communications makes it difficult for the young to develop an understanding of the larger historical context in which the precariat is emerging. Tweeting makes you stupid, according to Standing. He is rather less sympathetic with these aspects of the millennials than is Mason, but they both agree that these are important characteristics that need to be taken into account in projects that seek to build larger alliances in order to fight for workers' rights.

The Multicentric Network of Leftist Movements

Just as world revolutions in the past have restructured world orders, the current one might also do this. But in order for this to happen a significant number of activists who participate in the New Global Left would need to agree on several complicated matters:

- the nature of the most important contemporary problems,
- a vision of a desirable future and
- judgments about appropriate tactics and forms of movement organization.

The Transnational Social Movements Research Working Group at the University of California-Riverside performed a network analysis of movement ties based on the responses to a survey of attendees that was conducted at the 2005 World Social Forum meeting in Porto Alegre, Brazil.[58] This study examined the structure of overlapping links among movement themes by asking attendees with which of 18 movement themes they were actively involved. The choices of those attendees who declared that they were actively involved in two or more movement themes were used to indicate the overlaps among movements. The results show a multi-centric network of movement links.[59]

All the movements had some people who were actively involved in other movements. The overall structure of the network of movement linkages reveals

---

58   The survey and other results are available at http://www.irows.ucr.edu/research/tsmstudy.htm

59   Christopher Chase-Dunn et al., "North-South Contradictions and Bridges at the World Social Forum" pp. 341–366 in North and South In the World Political Economy, ed. Rafael Reuveny and William R. Thompson. (Blackwell, 2008) 8, Fig. 1.

a multi-centric network organized around five main movements that served as bridges linking other movements to one another: peace, anti-globalization, global justice, human rights and environmentalism. These were also the largest movements in terms of the numbers of attendees who professed to be actively involved. While no single movement was so central that it linked all the others, neither was the network structure characterized by separate cliques of movements that might be easily separated from one another.

Chase-Dunn and Kaneshiro compared the movement network results found at the 2005 Porto Alegre meeting with the results of a very similar survey carried out at the World Social Forum meeting in Nairobi in 2007.[60] Their findings show a few changes but the main network structure was very similar to that found in Porto Alegre. This suggests that the New Global Left contains a rather stable global network structure of movement interconnections that is largely independent of the location of the meetings. Rather similar network structures were also found at meetings of the U.S. Social Forum in Atlanta in 2007 and in Detroit in 2010[61] indicating that the network links among movements seem to be quite similar at the global and national levels, at least for the case of the United States.

This structure means that the transnational activists who participate in the World Social Forum process share many goals and support the global justice framework asserted in the World Social Forum Charter. It also means that the network of movements is relatively integrated and is not prone to splits. A global justice united front that is attentive to the nature of this network structure could mobilize a strong force for collective action in world politics. But there are some obvious problems that need attention.

Global North-South Challenges

Thomas Piketty's[62] empirical contribution was to the study of changes in the magnitude of within-country inequalities, but his prescriptions for solutions

60   C. Chase-Dunn and Matheu Kaneshiro, "Stability and Change in the contours of Alliances Among movements in the social forum process," pp. 119–133 in *Engaging Social Justice* ed. David Fasenfest. (Leiden: Brill, 2009)

61   Christopher Chase-Dunn and Ian Breckenridge-Jackson, "The Network of movements in the U.S. social forum process: Comparing Atlanta 2007 with Detroit 2010," Submitted for publication. Institute for Research on World-Systems, 2013. http://irows.ucr.edu/papers/irows71/irows71.htm.

62   Thomas Piketty. *Capital in the 21st Century*. (Cambridge: Harvard University Press, 2014).

included considerations of inequalities at the global level. The focus on global justice and north/south inequalities and the critique of neoliberalism provide strong orienting frames for the transnational activists of the New Global Left.[63,64] But there are difficult obstacles to collective action that are heavily structured by the huge global inequalities that exist in the contemporary world-system and these issues must be directly confronted.[65]

Our survey of the attendees of the 2005 World Social Forum in Porto Alegre found several important differences between activists from the core, the periphery and the semiperiphery.[66] Those from the periphery were proportionately fewer, older, and more likely to be men. In addition, participants from the periphery were more likely to be associated with externally sponsored NGOs, rather than with self-funded Social Movement Organizations (SMOs) or unions. NGOs have greater access to travel funds and were able to bring more representatives from the peripheral countries. Survey respondents from the Global South (the periphery and the semiperiphery) were significantly more likely than those from the Global North (the core) to be skeptical about creating or reforming global-level political institutions and were more likely to favor the abolition of existing global institutions such as the International Monetary Fund and the World Bank.[67]

This skepticism probably stems from the historical experience of peoples from the non-core with colonialism and global-level institutions that claim to be operating on universal principles of fairness, but whose actions have either not solved problems or have made them worse. These "new abolitionists" pose strong challenges to both existing global institutions and to efforts to reform or replace these institutions with more democratic and efficacious ones.

George Monbiot's *Manifesto for a New World Order*[68] is a reasoned and insightful call for radically democratizing the existing institutions of global

---

63   Scott C. Byrd, "The Porto Alegre Consensus: Theorizing the Forum Movement" *Globalizations*, vol. 2(1) (2005).

64   Manfred Steger, James Goodman and Erin K. Wilson, *Justice Globalism: Ideology, Crises, Policy*, (Thousand Oaks: Sage, 2013).

65   J. Timmons Roberts and Bradley Parks, *A Climate of Injustice: global inequality, North/South politics and climate policy*, (Cambridge: MIT Press, 2007).

66   Christopher Chase-Dunn et al., "North-South Contradictions and Bridges at the World Social Forum" in North and South In the World Political Economy, ed. Rafael Reuveny and William R. Thompson. (Blackwell, 2008, pp. 341–366).

67   *Christopher Chase-Dunn et al., "North-South Contradictions and Bridges at the World Social Forum" in* North and South In the World Political Economy, *ed. Rafael Reuveny and William R. Thompson. (Blackwell, 2008, pp. 341–366).*

68   George Monbiot, *Manifesto for a New World Order*, (New York: New Press, 2003).

governance and for establishing a global peoples' parliament that would be directly elected by the whole population of the Earth.[69] Monbiot also advocated the establishment of a trade clearinghouse (first proposed by John Maynard Keynes at Bretton Woods) that would reward national economies with balanced trade, and that would use some of the surpluses generated by those with trade surpluses to invest in those with trade deficits.[70] And Monbiot proposed a radical reversal of the World Trade Organization regime, which imposes free trade on the non-core but allows core countries to engage in protectionism—a "fair trade organization" that would help to reduce global development inequalities. Monbiot also advocated abolition of the u.n. Security Council, and shifting its power over peacekeeping to a General Assembly in which representatives' votes would be weighted by the population sizes of their countries.

Monbiot also noted that the current level of indebtedness of non-core countries could be used as formidable leverage over the world's largest banks if all the debtors acted in concert. This could provide the muscle behind a significant wave of global democratization. But in order for this to happen the global justice movement would have to organize a strong coalition of the non-core countries that would overcome the splits that tend to occur between the periphery and the semiperiphery. This is far from being a utopian fantasy. It is a practical program for global democracy.

The multiple local, regional and largely disconnected human interaction networks of the past have become strongly linked into a single global system. The treadmill of population growth has been stopped in the core countries, and is slowing in the non-core. The global human population is predicted to peak and to stabilize in the decades surrounding 2075 at somewhere between nine and twelve billion. Thus, population pressure will continue to be a major challenge for at least another century, increasing logistical loads on governance institutions. The exit option is blocked off except for a small number of pioneers who may move out to space stations or try to colonize Mars. Thus, a condition of global circumscription exists. Malthusian corrections may not be only a thing of the past, as illustrated by continuing warfare and genocide. Famine has been brought under control, but future shortages of clean water, good soil, non-renewable energy sources, and food might bring that old horseman back.

---

69   Ulrich Beck's call for "cosmopolitan realism" supported the formation of global democratic institutions. Ulrich Beck, *Power in the Global Age,* (Malden: Polity Press, 2005).

70   The current u.s. trade deficit might qualify it for global welfare, but the balance of payments and ability to print world money would also need to be taken into account.

As we have already noted above, huge global inequalities complicate the collective action problem. First world peoples have come to feel entitled, and non-core people want to have their own cars, large houses and electronic gadgets. The ideas of human rights and democracy are still contested, but they have become so widely accepted that existing institutions of global governance are illegitimate even by their own standards. The demand for global democracy and human rights can only be met by reforming or replacing the existing institutions of global governance with institutions that have some plausible claim to represent the will and interests of the majority of the world's people. That means democratic global state formation,[71] although most of the contemporary protagonists of global democracy do not like to say it that way.

Individualism in the World Revolution

The relationship between individualism, sociocultural evolution and modernity is a long story, but Paul Mason's[72] claim that a new level of individual freedom is an important element in the recent global wave of protests brings this issue once again to the center of the discussion about the nature of the New Global Left.[73] It is also raised by David Graeber's[74] assertion of the individual's right to self-assess the question of social debt and by Mary Kaldor's[75] defense of the individual's right to not participate in politics. Many would agree with the horizontalists and anarchists that the attack on individualism that was waged by communists and some socialists in the world revolution of 1917 and its aftermath was a mistake. Individualism is rightly associated with capitalist modernity, but arguably it is one of the good things that modernity has brought. The rise of a global human rights regime since World War II and the

---

71   Christopher Chase-Dunn and Hiroko Inoue, "Accelerating democratic global state formation." *Cooperation and Conflict*, vol. 47(2) 2012, pp. 157–175. http://cac.sagepub.com/content/47/2/157 Accessed March 22, 2015

72   Paul Mason, *Why Its (Still) Kicking Off Everywhere: The New Global Revolutions*, (London: Verso, 2013)

73   We should recall that glorification of the individual self was already seen in the world revolution of 1968's maxim to "do your own thing."

74   David Graeber, *Debt: The First 5000 Years*, (Brooklyn: Melville House, 2011).

75   Mary Kaldor, *Global Civil Society*, (Malden: Polity Press, 2003)

76   Alyson Brysk, "Global Good Samaritans? Human Rights Foreign Policy in Costa Rica," *Global Governance: A Review of Multilateralism and International Organizations*: Vol. 11 (4) 2005.

77   John W. Meyer, *World Society*, (New York: Oxford University Press, 2009).

centrality of the human rights movement theme within the network of movements found at the World Social Forum also indicate the importance of the
issue of individualism in contemporary world politics.[76,77]

Of course there are many kinds of individualism, and it has been emerging
since the birth of the world religions, and before.[78] Norman Cohn's study of
European medieval millenarianism describes the Free Spirits, a movement of
self-deification in which individual mystics became convinced that they had
attained omniscience and omnipotence and were thus entitled to do whatever
they wanted, irrespective of the consequences of their acts for others.[79] Ethical
egoism denies any obligation to act in the interests of others.[80] The freedom
to express one's unique self in artistic works and in consumer choices are the
relatively mild forms of individualism that have become widely accepted by
both those who have opportunities to express themselves and by most of those
who wish that they could. Individualism that allows great choice, but that does
not countenance harming or constraining the actions of others, is not a bad
thing whether or not it is engrained in biological human nature, as the evolutionary psychologists believe.[81] The construction of more effective forms of
collectivism need not attack the individualisms that serve as legitimations for
capitalism, nor the forms of individualism that are supported by many of the
activists in the emerging New Global Left.

David Graeber's individualism asserts the right of each person to decide regarding the issue of social debt—what one owes others, society and nature.[82]
Graeber points out that socialists and communists (and almost all other authorities) set up systems that justified policies of distribution and power based

---

78   Christopher Chase-Dunn and Bruce Lerro, *Social Change: Globalization from the Stone Age
      to the Present* (New York: Routledge, 2016).

79   Norman Cohn, *The Pursuit of the Millennium,* (New York: Oxford University Press, 1970).

80   See for example Ayn Rand, *Atlas Shrugged,* (New York: New American Library, 1957).

81   Susan McKinnon, *Neoliberal Genetics: the Myths and Moral Tales of Evolutionary Psycholo-
      gy,* (Chicago: Prickly Paradigm Press, 2005).

82   As David Graeber put it, "If one were looking for the ethos for an individualistic society
      such as our own, one way to do it might well be to say: we all owe an infinite debt to
      humanity, society and nature, or the cosmos (however one prefers to frame it), but no
      one else could possibly tell us how we are to pay it. ... it would actually be possible to see
      almost all systems of established authority—religion, morality, politics, economics, and
      the criminal-justice system—as so many different fraudulent ways to presume to calcu-
      late what cannot be calculated, to claim the authority to tell us how some aspect of that
      unlimited debt ought to be repaid. Human freedom would then be our ability to decide
      for ourselves how we want to do so." *Debt: The First 5000 Years*, Brooklyn: Melville House
      Publishing, 2011, p. 68).

on assumptions about debt. Graeber rejects these, and many would agree with him. Beyond this assumption of individual authority over the matter of debt, Graeber presumes natural human tendencies toward sociability, sharing and friendship. And he contends that the techniques of direct decision-making that constituted the processes developed by the Occupy movement are good guarantees of individual rights in collective decision-making.[83] This is a sympathetic view of human nature and an attractive version of individualism that acknowledges the importance of social life, but leaves participation up to the person.

A Global United Front?

As mentioned above, Paul Mason stressed the importance of unemployed, but educated, youth in the world revolutions of 1848 and 20xx.[84] Of course scholars of social movements have long known that oppressed people are usually led by disaffected members of the middle or upper classes who have some education and resources that can be devoted to the tasks of movement leadership. But is there more than this to Mason's claim? He notes that many middle class radicals in earlier world revolutions turned against the urban poor and workers when they posed a strong and radical challenge. Mason attributes part of the defeat of the revolutionaries in 1848 to the students' betrayal of the radical workers in European cities. Mason contends that one reason why the middle-class radicals in the current wave of global protest have mainly kept their radicalism is because the urban poor and workers have been relatively quiescent, at least so far.

We may also wonder how the differences between now and 1968 will affect the politics of middle class students. Perceptions of the availability of future middle class jobs have changed greatly. Most of 68ers were able to find middle class jobs if they wanted them, whereas the current crop of highly educated youth are facing a much more constrained job market as well as mountains of debt incurred in getting their degrees. Mason sees this as a cause of activism, but others surmise that educational indebtedness may undermine rebellious courage.

---

83   David Graeber, *The Democracy Project*. (New York: Spiegel & Grau, 2013)

84   Paul Mason, *Why It's (Still) Kicking Off Everywhere: The New Global Revolutions* (Brooklyn: Verso, 2013)

85   Paul Mason, *Why It's (Still) Kicking Off Everywhere: The New Global Revolutions* (Brooklyn: Verso, 2013)

In 2013 Mason[85] guessed that the wave of protests would likely melt away if the global economy was successfully reflated, which is what has happened to some extent (see below). Mason also recounted the story of the 1930s, when the Global Left started off as a squabbling bunch of ideological purists, but was driven to make broad alliances in the popular front by the rise of fascism. Mason saw horizontalism and prefiguration as going nowhere. But he suggested that the Left might be driven to form a new united front by the emergence of new economic fiascos, global environmental disasters and by the further rise of neofascism. Mason said:

> Up to now, in today's crisis, protest has been driven by narratives of hope and outrage, not of fear. The horizontalists' self-isolation, indeed self-obsession, is not the result of a dictated party line, as in the 1930s, but of something equally strong in today's conditions; the inner zeitgeist.... As austerity pushes parts of Europe towards social meltdown, as fascism revives there and as democracy is eroded, maybe it is this that drives the worker's movement beyond the one-day strike and the social movements beyond the temporary occupation of space, as well as goading the existing parties beyond the comfort zone dictated by the global order.[86]

At the World Social Forum a somewhat less ideological approach could involve a greater willingness to collaborate with progressive national regimes such as that in Bolivia. Mason called for the radicals to engage in "physical politics," by which he meant contention for power within existing institutions. Arguably this is what the New Global Left must do if it is to have an important impact on the human future. But this could be done without completely abandoning some of concerns of the 68ers and the current generation of activists. The new individualism and participatory democracy could be embraced while also inventing or reinventing more humane and sustainable forms of collectivism and new modes of participation in institutional politics. The enhanced ability to swarm, using social media and the Internet, is a tactic that appeals to the millennials and that could be coordinated with more populist forms of participation in electoral politics.

And with regard to bureaucratization, the oligarchical tendencies of political parties and all other formal organizations are well known to sociologists of

---

86   Paul Mason, *Why It's Kicking Off Everywhere: The New Global Revolutions* (Brooklyn: Verso, 2012), pp. 295–6.

87   Indeed, every undergraduate at Harvard is expected to found a business or an NGO before graduation.

organization. But we should recall that it was Thomas Jefferson, an 89er, who said that a revolution is needed about every 20 years. Voluntary associations have gotten much easier to start since Jefferson's time.[87] Many global activists carry neonatal NGOs around with them in their backpacks. So if the organization you are currently working with seems to have gotten ossified, you can start a new one. This is the part of horizontalism and network organizing that solves the problem of ossified parties and unions. But it also leads to the proliferation of specialized organizations at a time when the main challenge is to weave different movements into a larger organizational instrument with enough muscle to challenge the global powers that be—a party-network.

The wave of protests that built up in the last few decades peaked in 2011 and has declined somewhat since then.[88,89] The protest intensity measure assembled from web sources by GDELT[90,91] shows successive waves of global protests from 1979 to 2014.[92]

The partial decline since 2011 is probably due, in part, to reflation of the global economy since the crash of 2008. But the decline probably also reflects the debacles that have ensued since the Arab Spring, which have understandably reduced the enthusiasm of idealistic democracy protestors in war zone countries. The Green Revolution in Iran was suppressed. The tragic events in Egypt and Syria have been especially disheartening. Horizontalism and prefiguration seem to presume a Habermasian world of legitimate and protected political discourse that does not exist in many world regions. Military coups and contending mass parties like the Muslim Brotherhood leave little room for the protests of the precariat to influence political discourse. All world revolutions have gone through cycles of activism and quiescence.

---

88   Savan Savas Karatasli *et al.*, "Class crisis and the 2011 protest wave: cyclical and secular trends in global labor unrest" pp. 184–200 in *Overcoming Global Inequalities* ed. Immanuel Wallerstein et al. (Boulder: Paradigm Publishers, 2015).

89   Thomas Carothers and Richard Youngs, *The Complexities of Global Protests,* (Washington: Carnegie Endowment for International Peace, 2015).

90   GDELT Project. http://gdeltproject.org/

91   Kalev Leetaru, "Did the Arab Spring Really Spark a Wave of Global Protests?" *Foreign Policy,* May 30, 2014, accessed June 1, 2014. http://foreignpolicy.com/2014/05/30/did-the-arab-spring-really-spark-a-wave-of-global-protests/?wp_login_redirect=0

92   GDELT's measure of "protest intensity" is calculated as the number of protests in a given month divided by the total number of all events recorded that month. GDELT's event coding methodology has been criticized for double-counting, but it is not known how much variation there is in this measurement error over time. If double-counting is constant, the trends would still be fairly accurate.

The protests mounted by the global justice and anti-austerity movements have changed the political discourse about inequality and have helped set the stage for Thomas Piketty's research to be widely read and discussed. The current U.S. presidential election campaign has the Democrats vying with one another over how much to crack down on Wall Street. Podemos, an anti-austerity party in Spain led by former autonomist Pablo Iglesias Turrion, developed a wide following and gained important representation in the Spanish election of December 2015. But the debacle of Syriza in Greece, concluding an austerity compromise despite a popular mandate to stand up against global finance capital, presents an object lesson for those who have preached the dangers of institutional politics. The quote above from Arrighi, Hopkins and Wallerstein seems particularly apt.[93] A valuable opportunity was missed in Greece to show that indeed there are progressive alternatives to neoliberal capitalist globalization.

Will the current world revolution eventually develop enough muscle to challenge neoliberal capitalism and to provoke enlightened conservatives to usher in a new era of global Keynesianism that is more sustainable and less polarizing than the capitalist globalization project? Or will a perfect storm of environmental disaster, hegemonic decline, mass migrations, interimperial rivalry, ethnic violence, and neo-fascism produce so much chaos that a United Front of the New Global Left will have an opportunity within the next few decades to fundamentally transform the capitalist world-system into a democratic and collectively rational global commonwealth? Both of these options would require a United Front that brings the progressive movements, parties and regimes together.

---

93   Giovanni Arrighi, Terence K. Hopkins, and Immanuel Wallerstein *Antisystemic Movements,* (New York City: Verso Books, 2012), p. 64.

CHAPTER 15

Global Inequality, Competition, Uncertainty, and the Legitimation Crisis of Neoliberalism

Alessandro Bonanno

Introduction

Thomas Piketty's *Capital in the 21st Century*[1] probes the historically relevant theme of the relationship between capital accumulation and distribution of wealth. His inquiry simultaneously addresses the classical Marxist tenet that affirms that the expansion of capitalism concentrates wealth in the hands of the upper class and impoverishes the masses and the opposing Neoliberal view that maintains that through market competition inequality is reduced and greater harmony among the classes is generated. After producing the richest data set and analysis of economic inequality to date, he provides an answer that clearly stands on the side of the Marxist camp. While Piketty is not a Marxist, he joins Marx and the Marxist tradition in arguing that there is a structural tendency for capital to generate unsustainable levels of inequality. These levels of inequality, however, can be mitigated by state generated wealth redistribution policies, such as those implemented during the first three post WWII decades. In the absence of these policies, inequality tends to grow and to become particularly acute in periods of economic recession.

Piketty further contends that inequality undermines the meritocratic values that constitute the foundation of democratic societies. Departing from the Marxist revolutionary argument, Piketty argues that there are ways in which capitalism can be democratized and this process requires postures that would transcend reliance on the simple free functioning of the market and the adoption of formal democracy. In this context, he emphatically insists in reversing the recent tendency to conflate formal with substantive democracy and calls for ways to democratically control capital. Accordingly, he proposes measures that would redistribute wealth downward and restore the post-WWII Fordist social state in all its fundamental components. This neo-Fordist proposal finds

---

1 Thomas Piketty, *Capital in the Twenty-First Century*. Translated by Arthur Goldhammer. (Cambridge: The Belknap Press of Harvard University, 2014).

him on the same camp with a number of progressive intellectuals that have recently argued about a return to some form of regulated capitalism. However, and calling his proposed global tax on capital "utopian," Piketty remains skeptical of any real possibility of short-term change and contends that the historical forces that could challenge the dominance of capital and reverse the trend toward greater inequality are lacking.

Dwelling on Piketty's contention about the concentration of wealth and the growth of inequality under contemporary capitalism and briefly presenting core arguments of classical neoliberals such as F.A. Hayek, Milton Friedman, and Ludwig von Mises, in this chapter I maintain that Neoliberalism faces a crisis of legitimation. This crisis results from the neoliberal proposal of addressing the repeated market failures that characterize the recent evolution of the economy and society through the further liberalization of markets while the actual solution of market failures has systematically required the intervention of the state. I also contend that Neoliberalism considers inequality but also uncertainty desirable and necessary conditions for the functioning of the economy and society: a situation that is opposed and further destabilizes society. Because state intervention is needed to address the contradictions of Neoliberalism but it is also advocated to redistribute wealth and protect society from the unwanted consequences of capitalism, I conclude that the state has emerged as an important contested terrain in contemporary capitalism.

Inequality, Uncertainty, and the Legitimation Crisis between Fordism and Neoliberalism

Writing in the early 1970s, Jürgen Habermas[2] illustrated the emerging conditions that would have ended Fordism, the regime of accumulation and social regulation that dominated the first three post-World War II decades. Anticipating a wealth of analytical contributions that would have dissected this regime's crisis[3], but also hoping for the substantive democratization of capitalism, Habermas contended that the inability of the state to fulfill the claims of economic expansion, social stability, equality, and social inclusion engendered

---

2   Jürgen Habermas, *The Legitimation Crisis.* (Boston: Beacon Press, 1975).

3   See among others Michel Aglietta, *A Theory of Capitalist Regulation.* (London: New Left Books, 1979); David Harvey, *The Condition of Postmodernity.* (Oxford: Basil Blackwell, 1989); Alan Lipietz, *Towards a New Economic Order: Post-Fordism, Ecology, and Democracy.* (New York: Oxford University Press, 1992).

a crisis of legitimation of this regulated post-war form of capitalism (*spätka-pitalismus*). In essence, for Habermas a crisis of legitimation emerges when the instruments that the state can mobilize to address existing problems are ineffective. The failure of earlier laissez-faire arrangements, and most importantly, the horrific inter-war totalitarian experiences of Fascism and Stalinism allowed the emergence of the Fordist organized capitalism. Under Fordism, the continuous tension between the claims of equality and justice that have accompanied modernity and bourgeois democracy and the existence of inequality and unresolved uncertainty that have characterized capitalism were addressed through high state regulation. According to Habermas, therefore, at the core of the crisis there was the inability of the state to provide the great majority of people with the necessary security and instruments to successfully pursue established social goals.

At the time, state intervention was justified by converging theories on the importance of regulating the economy and society. While Marxist positions had traditionally contemplated state planning and organization of economic activities, liberal postures had strongly advocated economic and social *laissez faire*. Yet, at the outset of the 20th Century, the growing concentration of wealth and political power in the hands of the upper class, the emergence of monopolies, and the continuous precarious socio-economic conditions of the working masses prompted liberals to advocate substantive forms of state intervention that would foster equality, security, and economic wellbeing. In his seminal essay "Liberalism and Social Action," John Dewey[4] contended that the era Liberalism signified "liberation from material insecurity and from the coercion and repression that prevents multitudes from participating in the vast cultural resources that are at hand."[5] Providing the theoretical justification for the New Deal and post-World War II reconstruction policies and programs, this version of Liberalism shaped political discourses and social and economic policies of the time.

This type of understanding of Liberalism had previously allowed Harry Ford[6] and John M. Keynes[7] to theorize that the broader participation of the lower and middle classes in the functioning of society and the economy is a fundamental condition for social stability and economic growth. Addressing a similar point—albeit from a Marxist point of view—Antonio Gramsci

---

4 John Dewey, *Liberalism and Social Action*. (New York: Capricorn Books, 1963 [1935]).

5 John Dewey, *Liberalism and Social Action*. (New York: Capricorn Books, 1963 [1935]), p. 48.

6 Henry Ford, *Today and Tomorrow*. (New York: Productivity Press, 1988 [1926]).

7 John Maynard Keynes, *The General Theory of Employment, Interest and Money*. (New York: Harvest Books, 1964 [1936]).

predicted the American post-war economic expansion, social stability, and hegemonic social control as results of the state-regulated integration of the lower classes into the capitalist system. While uncertainty and risk remained constantly present, they were viewed as entities that could have been controlled through enhanced calculability and the deployment of political and economic instruments designed to mitigate their negative effects. The state was viewed as the guarantor of, and also ultimately responsible for, the socio-economic security of its citizens. In essence, it was the duty of the state to promote equality, reduce uncertainty, control capitalism, and steer it toward growth.

In the Fordist era, the protection of the economic activities of large corporations was accompanied by the buffering of the unwanted consequences of the functioning of capitalism, the downward redistribution of economic resources, and the creation of opportunities for upward social mobility. While, and as Piketty aptly documents, the economic distance between the lower and upper classes never significantly diminished, inequality was at historical lows in the US and other major advanced societies. Additionally, a number of important spheres of society were partially de-commodified. Education, health, social services, and retirement were, in various ways and degrees, supported through public spending to the benefit of the middle and lower classes and minorities. The creation and development of an expanded "social state" marked the historical relevance of Fordism and the success of planning.

While Talcott Parsons and likeminded theorists of the regime argued that crises sooner or later would melt into renewed equilibrium and prosperity, advanced processes of rationalization and normalization limited substantive equality and democratic participation for the middle and working classes. The rosy accounts of the effectiveness of Fordist measures only partially resembled a much more complex and discriminating reality, but their implementation pacified and stabilized society, offered unprecedented "security" to its members, and transformed the obedient masses into even more obedient and happier consumers. Yet, and promoted by the actions of strong labor unions, employment was stable and lifelong, working class wages and middle class salaries grew and were at a historical high, education led to better employment, and retirement was supported by established pension systems and lifelong payments. For many senior citizens of the time, retirement was a predictable experience and one that greatly differed from the uncertain and often unattainable phenomenon of the neoliberal era. Similarly, for many workers, employment often meant working full time for the same firm without many worries about losing one's job, furloughs, and/or the introduction of unstable and under-remunerated contractual work.

Criticizing the limits of the emancipatory claims of the Fordist project, the intellectual and political left denounced the growth of new and more sophisticated processes of control and domination and the contradictions generated by the intervention of the Fordist state. The unfulfilled promises of substantive emancipation, the cultural and economic subjugation of the working class and the persistent underdevelopment of societies of the South became symbols of the critique and opposition of the left. Mass media manipulation, elite planning, the exploitation of marginalized social groups (i.e., immigrants and people of color, women), depoliticization, and consumerism were among the key elements employed by the left to denounce the limits and class nature of Fordism. Assessing the contradictory dimension of state intervention in the social and economic spheres, critical theorist Claus Offe[8] commented that the lower classes were transformed into "clients" of the state and their participation in the welfare state required ultimate obedience to authority.

This sharp critique of the left dwelled also on the fiscal unsustainability of the Fordist project.[9] State intervention signified primarily the economic, political, and military support of multinational corporations domestically and internationally. In this context, the state claims of autonomy and pro-lower classes social spending concealed its actual subordination to corporate interests and the growth of private profit. While corporate success was presented as a national achievement, the popularity of the saying "What is good for GM is good for America" obscured the reality of a socio-economic system that prioritized profit over people and corporations over communities. Simultaneously, the post-World-War II Bretton Wood agreement and inadequate fiscal policies could no longer provide solutions to fiscal crises of the Fordist state in the US and all the other social democracies of the advanced world.

The economic and political instability of the Fordist regime gave impetus to criticisms from the right. Stressing the distorting and unsustainable dimensions of state interventionism, conservative critics underscored that state interventionism not only curtailed the search for profit but also limited the aspiration of the lower and middle classes. Employing populist-sounding pronouncements, they contended that wealth redistribution policies achieved results that were often opposite to the intended goals, penalized hard-working citizens, and created unsustainable national deficits. They called for an end of state regulation of the economy and proposed a return to the free market—that they named Neoliberalism—as the ultimate form for the resolution not only

8   Claus Offe, *Disorganized Capitalism*. (Cambridge: MIT Press, 1985).
9   James O'Connor, *The Fiscal Crisis of the State*. (New York: St. Martin's Press, 1974).

of economic but also political and social problems. Originally formulated in the immediate pre-World War II years,[10] gaining organizational strength in the late 1940s,[11] and departing from classical economic and political Liberalism, Neoliberalism offered a view that made inequality and uncertainty permanent and, ultimately necessary, elements of the organization of society.

Stressed by Ludwig von Mises, F. A. Hayek, and Milton Friedman alike, the claim of the impartiality of the market was employed to criticize the politically negotiated, and therefore considered biased, nature of state intervention. These classical neoliberals contended that no group of humans could understand, let alone predict, the behavior of the factors that affect economic processes and their outcomes. Accordingly, any form of "intelligent design" (state intervention and planning) is inherently inadequate and destined to failure. Conversely, the spontaneous free functioning of the market allows for the determination of the actual value of commodities (price), and because the market is apolitical and does not privilege the interests of any particular class or group, its free functioning generates the most desirable outcomes for the entire society. Endowed with impartiality, the market is the highest possible democratic arena that permits the pursuit of individual interests while allowing the triumph of efficient enterprises and the elimination and/ or restructuring of poor performing ones. This impartiality and the associated political neutrality, they continued, make the market the best instrument to deliver private and public goods. As the crisis of Fordism opened the way for alternatives, this neoliberal thinking became appealing and gained popular support.[12]

Neoliberalism and the Legitimation of Inequality, Competition, and Uncertainty

The elections of Ronald Reagan (1980) and Margaret Thatcher (1979) are often employed to symbolize the establishment of Neoliberalism as the dominant

---

10   The conference honoring Walter Lippmann in Paris in 1938 is considered the first formal gathering of Neoliberal intellectuals.

11   Formed in 1947, the Mont Pelerin Society is considered the first organization of neoliberal thinkers.

12   Colin Crouch, *The Strange Non-Death of Neoliberalism*. (Cambridge: Polity Press, 2011). Philip Mirowski, *Never Let a Serious Crisis Go to Waste*. (London: Verso, 2014). Daniel Stedman Jones, *Masters of the Universe*. (Princeton, NJ: Princeton University Press, 2012).

social, political, and economic ideology of our times. Since then, Neoliberalism has not only inspired the functioning of the economy and economic institutions but has also emerged as the dominant rationality in political and social life.[13] As underscored by Michel Foucault in his lectures at the College de France in 1979,[14] Neoliberalism is a governing rationality that has introduced a new form of normative reasoning. It has transformed the tenets of Classical Liberalism into a different brand of Liberalism that reflects the financialization of the economy, the individualization of society, and the economization of politics. Employing Gary Becker's theory of human capital, Foucault documented the application of the free market rationality (supply and demand) to all spheres of society. The importance of Foucault's analysis for this discussion rests on its emphasis on the replacement of the society's central objectives of exchange among equals, equality, and security with competition, inequality, and uncertainty.

Foucault[15] stressed that Neoliberalism is different from all pre-existing forms of Liberalism. In Classical Liberalism the free functioning of the market is based on the assumption of the free exchange between equals. Because this process of exchange is free and equal, it determines the true value of goods. Simultaneously, the free functioning of the market would provide validity to the exchange. The ultimate role of the state is to supervise the smooth running of the market and prevent the development of obstacles to this free exchange. The state does not have to intervene in the market. Conversely, according to Neoliberalism, Foucault continued, the central dimension of the market is competition, for through competition it is possible to determine the actual prices of goods and services. This is one of the most fundamental points proposed by Hayek and his theory of price that allowed him to win the Nobel Prize in Economics in 1974. Rejecting Marx's theory of value, for Hayek free competition is the only condition that allows for the accurate and fair determination of the value of commodities and work.[16]

The focus on competition over exchange altered the view of the relationship between the market and the state. For Foucault, both eighteenth- and

---

13   Wendy Brown, *Undoing the Demos. Neoliberalism Stealth Revolution.* (New York: Zone Books, 2015).
      Colin Crouch, *The Strange Non-Death of Neoliberalism.* (Cambridge, UK: Polity Press, 2011)
      Philip Mirowski, *Never Let a Serious Crisis Go to Waste.* (London: Verso, 2014).
14   Michel Foucault, *The Birth of Biopolitics.* (New York: Picador, 2004).
15   Michel Foucault, *The Birth of Biopolitics.* (New York: Picador, 2004), pp. 118–19.
16   Frederick A. Hayek, *The Constitution of Liberty.* (Chicago: University of Chicago Press, 2011 [1960]).

nineteenth-century liberals saw the state as the protector of free exchange and competition and called for state intervention to eliminate obstacles to the functioning of these two processes such as the growth of monopolies and extreme poverty. In the case of Neoliberalism, the idea that free exchange and competition are parts of an original "state of nature" is rejected as "naïve naturalism".[17] Free competition is not a spontaneous product of nature, but it is constructed and the result of deliberate efforts on the part of the state. The state, under Neoliberalism, is called to create and defend the conditions that allowed for competition to be instituted and maintained. The state "must govern for market rather than because of the market."[18] Competition, however, is not, like in the case of Classical Liberalism, a contradictory entity that through its functioning tends toward the creation of monopolies. Monopolies and the emergence of large corporations are not dysfunctions of the free market. Conversely, they are positive results of competition. Milton Friedman[19] argued that, because of the impartial nature of competition, the emergence of large corporations and monopolies indicates the good functioning of the market and, above all, the achievement of economic efficiency. Friedman, Hayek, and Ludwig von Mises[20] alike contended that these types of monopolies are not very common while the most frequent instances of monopolies are state created such as the case of utilities and public services. These are inefficient occurrences that need to be corrected through privatization.

The centrality of competition in the Neoliberal understanding of the market provides legitimation to the existence of inequality. Departing from 20th Century Liberalism that identified in the elimination of inequality one of the normative dimensions of contemporary society, neoliberals justify inequality as one of the necessary and beneficial products of competition. Friedman[21] explained the importance of the existence of social inequality through two points. First, state intervention through redistributive and social welfare measures adds to inequality as these measures are largely ineffective and unfair. Their ineffectiveness is based on the fact that results often generate advantages to unintended and usually better-off groups. Their unfairness rests on the fact

---

17   Michel Foucault, *The Birth of Biopolitics*. (New York: Picador, 2004), p. 120.

18   Michel Foucault, *The Birth of Biopolitics*. (New York: Picador, 2004), p. 121.

19   Milton Friedman, *Capitalism and Freedom*. (Chicago: University of Chicago Press, 1982 [1962]).

20   Ludwig Von Mises, *Socialism. An Economic and Sociological Analysis*. (Auburn: The Ludwig von Mises Institute, 2009 [1951]).

21   Milton Friedman, *Capitalism and Freedom*. (Chicago: University of Chicago Press, 1982 [1962]).

that those that are supposed to be helped receive only limited assistance. He illustrated his point employing a number of examples, including the then and now popular policy of price support program for agricultural commodities. Designed to support the income of family farm holders, these programs are based on size (normally volume of production and/or acreage employed) and, therefore, automatically and disproportionally benefit larger operations over the intended family farms. Moreover, they add an unnecessary burden to the state budget as the protection of these commodities and groups prevents the outflow of resources and labor to more efficient utilizations. In essence, state intervention should be eliminated for it worsens the conditions of groups most affected by inequality. The second point made by Friedman refers to the claim that inequality is beneficial to the economy and society. Friedman maintained that politically negotiated solutions to problems are always limited. Solutions to problems should be removed from the political arena and addressed by the impartiality and effectiveness of the market. The market allocates available resources in the most efficient and impartial manner and rewards those economic actors who work harder and risk the most. As competition impartially declares winners and losers, the ensuing inequality is nothing more than the just and efficient outcome of the desirable functioning of the market.

The justification of inequality made by Friedman is also proposed by other classical neoliberals. Hayek,[22] for instance, contended that not only state intervention distorts the consequences of the necessary existence of inequality, but also the actions of other institutions alter free competition and achieve equally negative outcomes. This is the case of trade unions that, he maintained, rather than helping, penalize workers. He explained his point through a number of factors. First, higher wages created by the actions of unions increase unemployment as they limit the number of workers that can be hired in any given industry. Second, the actions of unions create inflation and limit the growth of real wages. As higher wages are negotiated, production costs increase along with the prices of goods and services. Accordingly, inflation is triggered and, with it the actual value of wages (real wages) declines. Third, the creation of protected segments of the working class discriminates against other workers employed in less protected and/or unprotected sectors. Disregarding the historical significance of the success of unions in negotiating higher wages, better working conditions, and stability of employment, he maintained that this common occurrence in Western countries in the post-World War II

---

22   Frederick A. Hayek, *The Constitution of Liberty.* (Chicago: University of Chicago Press, 2011[1960]), pp. 391–393.

decades is nothing more than a strategy employed by unions and governments to prevent, rather than promote, the growth of real wages. Finally, the collusion between unions and firms leads to the creation of monopolies that prevents competition, technical and technological innovation, and, ultimately, development. The essential point of this neoliberal reasoning is that efforts to correct inequality at the political level through state intervention and the actions of unions are destined to failure and create distortions. The solution is to allow the free market and competition to allocate resources in an optimal way and with it to allow the necessary amount of inequality to exist. Inequality is the condition, therefore, for the better functioning of the economy and society.

As the market and competition dominate society and are the mediators between social life and the imperative of capital accumulation, there is very little room for any sense of certainty. Uncertainty has emerged as one of dominant social features under Neoliberalism. Replacing the Fordist, but also modern, claim that the state is charged with the protection of its citizens and should establish instruments to control the unwanted consequences of capitalism, the neoliberal preference for unregulated competition places individuals at the mercy of the outcomes of market adjustments. As individuals compete, they have no guaranty of security, for their employment, careers, future perspectives and retirement are all affected by the volatility of market competition. Uncertainty dominates and replaces past understandings and practices of calculated risk.

While some accounts explain this increased uncertainty in terms of the establishment of a second modernity,[23] Foucault made clear that the ascendance of Neoliberalism as a governing rationality implies open competition among individuals that are responsible for their actions and the augmentation of the value of their human capital. The view of people as human capital mandates that the substantive dimension of each human action is replaced by the understanding of humans as enterprises operating in a system dominated by financialization. It is not the simple search for profit that characterizes Neoliberalism, Foucault contended, but it is the transformation of each individual into capital whose value must be increased.[24] Importantly, however, individuals do not simply compete among themselves, but they act in a context in which other and larger entities, such as firms, corporations and states, also compete. As these entities make their moves and pursue their competitive strategies, even the most responsible individuals are not immune from

23   Ulrich Beck, *World at Risk.* (Malden: Polity Press, 2009).
24   Michel Foucault, *The Birth of Biopolitics.* (New York: Picador, 2004), p. 226.

the unforeseeable and abrupt consequences of this all-encompassing market competition.[25] Additionally, the unmet assumption that individuals are always rational actors and always select the best conduct of action adds to the inaccurate view of competition presented by neoliberals.[26]

Inequality, Uncertainty, and the Legitimation Crisis of Neoliberalism

The neoliberal proposal is to accept inequality and uncertainty as inevitable and, in fact, as desirable consequences of the functioning of the market. It maintains that their existence along with the use of the market as the locus for the determination of solutions to socio-economic problems permit a better functioning of the entire society. This situation, it is concluded, avoids the errors and compromises generated by political solutions and ends the divisiveness and ambiguities of politics. However, and despite the many accounts of the power of this ideology and regime, Neoliberalism is resisted. More importantly, the consequences of this regime's growth are viewed as important social problems. Social inequality, wealth concentration, the instability of the economic system, the volatility and structural fragility of financial markets and institutions, the uncertain and difficult labor market, the very serious climate change, and environmental crisis remain problems whose solution is requested from all parts of the political and ideological spectrum.

As solutions are sought, however, it has been impossible to address these problems through the simple free functioning of the market and competition as maintained by neoliberals. In all these and other relevant instances, the state has been called to intervene. Differing for traditional neoliberal calls for de-regulation, this state intervention has been directed at correcting and assisting markets. From this point of view and following Habermas, Neoliberalism is facing a crisis of legitimation as the instruments that it proposes cannot address existing problems. Neoliberals react to this contradiction in at least two interrelated ways. First, they claim that there are interferences to the

---

25 Wendy Brown, *Undoing the Demos. Neoliberalism Stealth Revolution.* (New York: Zone Books, 2015), p. 37.

26 David Kotz, *The Rise and Fall of Neoliberal Capitalism.* (Cambridge: Harvard University Press, 2016).

free functioning of the market that prevent it from achieving the necessary adjustments. These interferences are engendered by the above-mentioned calls for the state to regulate the market. The second refers to the need to establish new markets to solve these problems. Market problems, in other words, are to be corrected by the creation of more markets. The theoretical weaknesses of these arguments rests primarily—albeit not exclusively—on their tautology and teleology. This explanation is tautological because the assumption that the market always achieves the perfect allocation of resources is automatically transformed into "the conclusion." It is teleological because state-generated distortions are identified as the *a priori* reasons for market failure in a context in which other possible explanations are not considered. More importantly, however, it is at the historical level that this posture is particularly problematic. The revival of free-market solutions that have failed and that had to be corrected by state intervention is promoted by the same actors (i.e., corporations, financial institutions and conservative political groups) that also advocate further market liberalization. In essence, the evolution of the neoliberal regime implies, and simultaneously calls for, the continuous liberalization and creation of markets and state intervention to regulate the unwanted consequences of the functioning of the market. As this intervention is almost exclusively benefitting large corporations, financial institutions and the social elites, it does very little to address the problems mentioned above and carries little credit within broader segments of society. Following this analysis, I contend that society *has entered a phase of the evolution of the neoliberal regime in which state intervention has shifted from the exclusive liberalization of markets and market creation to decisive and systematic intervention to correct the problematic consequences of the functioning of the market. Moreover, and at the historical level, this state intervention is seen as necessary for the reproduction of this regime by neoliberal forces.*[27]

Importantly, calls for state intervention have also characterized proposals that oppose Neoliberalism. These are primarily Neo-Fordist or Post-Neoliberal

---

27   Despite the rhetoric of the desirability of the free functioning of the market, the acceptance of the discourse stressing that large corporations and financial institutions are "too large to fail" has been identified as one of the most important "successes" of Neoliberalism. Therefore, negative consequences that affect the upper class and corporations continue to involve calls for robust state intervention. The instance of "quantitative easing" that has dominated the economic policy of the most advanced countries world-wide in the 2010s is a case in point. From the point of view of those in the progressive camp, this contradictory position in regard to state action represents an important weakness of the neoliberal regime.

schemes that contemplate the renewal of Keynesian policies, state-directed wealth redistribution measures, the control of the financial and banking systems, and a return to a robust welfare state.[28] Piketty's proposal of a global tax on capital and progressive policies aimed at revamping the social state fits this camp's state-centered ideology and social democratic political vision. Paradoxically, therefore, state intervention is advocated simultaneously by opponents and proponents of the Neoliberal regime. While the divergent nature of these proposals is clear, these calls for state intervention give the state renewed importance and make it a politically relevant and contested terrain.

This renewed political relevance of the state certainly does not diminish the importance of calls that place opposition to Neoliberalism primarily at the level of the civil society.[29] Yet, it suggests that the promotion of actions that focus on the role of the state deserves attention among those who oppose Neoliberalism. Accordingly, and while Piketty's own definition of "utopian" is telling of the difficulties of the implementation of state-sponsored measures designed to control the concentration of wealth and global capital, this and similar proposals are all indications of the contemporary centrality of the role of the state. Two final considerations should be briefly mentioned as the role of the contemporary state is considered. The first refers to the limits of the historically available forms of the state under Neoliberal Globalization. The ability of corporate actors to by-pass nation state measures that oppose their interests has accompanied the state establishment of pro corporate policies. Accordingly, the redirecting of the actions of the nation state would not necessarily address the transnational scope of neoliberal capitalism. As Piketty's analysis implies, anti-neoliberal strategies require state forms that transcend the nation state. Second, the social forces and political coalitions that would generate the necessary conditions for the redirecting of state action are not currently available. The movement to the center that since the 1990s has characterized parties and organizations of the historical left has often subordinate political alternatives to the same logic of financialization, individualization, and responsibilization that guides Neoliberalism. Accordingly, and despite the recent growth of anti-establishment sentiments world-wide, it is difficult to

---

28   See Paul Krugman, *End This Depression Now*. (New York: W.W. Norton, 2012); Joseph.
      E. Stiglitz, *The Price of Inequality*. (New York: W.W. Norton, 2012)

29   See, Colin Crouch, *The Strange Non-Death of Neoliberalism*. (Cambridge, UK: Polity Press,
      2011)

imagine a progressive redirection of state intervention that would overcome the contradictions that engendered the crisis of the Fordism regime. These problems notwithstanding, the limits of the neoliberal regime, the unsustainability of its consequences and the importance of the role of the state require immediate attention and action. From this point of view, Piketty's analytical contribution remains fundamental.

CHAPTER 16

The Piketty Thesis and the Environmental Wall: Rentier Society, Post-Carbon Democracy, or Apocalyptic Ruin?[1]

Robert J. Antonio

Without a radical shock it seems fairly likely that the current equilibrium will persist for quite some time. The egalitarian pioneer ideal has faded into oblivion and the New World may be on the verge of becoming the old Europe of the twenty-first century's globalized economy.[2]

Introduction

In *Capital in the Twenty-First Century*, Thomas Piketty contends that major sociopolitical and socioeconomic "shocks" ultimately drove the twentieth century's great income convergence and helped spur the enormous post-World War Two economic expansion. As he implies above, new shocks hopefully could disrupt and help reverse the pattern of ever sharper income divergence that has followed the postwar era's "glorious" decades. However, as history attests, substantial social shocks have contingent and often infelicitous outcomes. Although discussion and debate over Piketty's tome has been very wide-ranging, his comments about climate change and environmental resource issues have been ignored. This is hardly surprising because his only 'sustained' commentary on the topics takes place in a few pages near the book's end. Yet he asserts that major climate change impacts and erosion of the globe's stock of natural resources, likely within a century, are "clearly the world's principal long-term worry."[3] Substantial ecological risk is an exceptionally important topic relevant to Piketty's ideas about shock and its disruptive impacts on a social formation's 'structure of accumulation' or its array of institutions that insure a steady,

---

1 Thanks to Alessandro Bonanno, Riley Dunlap, Joane Nagel, and David Norman Smith for critical comments.

2 Ibid., p. 514.

3 Thomas Piketty, *Capital in the Twenty-First Century* (Cambridge, MA: Belknap Press of Harvard University Press, 2014), pp. 567–69.

positive rate of return on capital. Undercutting or possibly even terminating the Holocene's Epoch's unusual climatic stability that has facilitated the rise of complex cultures, urban concentrations, and unparalleled human population growth, climate change threatens the biophysical foundations of the economy, civilization, and life forms as we have known them.[4] However, Piketty does not analyze ecological shock and its potential impacts on today's neoliberal regime or capitalism per se. He also does not theorize robustly capitalism and its growth imperative, a primary nexus of contradictory political economic and ecological relations that are eroding the social and material conditions necessary for system reproduction. In light of recent scientific work on climate change and other global environmental problems, this essay addresses possible ecological shock and its relevance for Piketty's hopes about averting a return to rentier society and reasserting "democratic control of capitalism."

Piketty's Core Argument about Shock and Rentier Society

Before the twentieth century, Piketty argues, the average rate of return on capital (r) usually substantially exceeded the rate of growth (g).[5] Yet even a small gap between the two in the long-run, he says, produced enduring, sharp income divergence and oligarchic societies dominated by inherited wealth and steep, rigid socioeconomic hierarchy (as portrayed vividly by writers such as Jane Austen). Piketty states flatly that: "The inequality $r>g$ is the basis of a society of rentiers."[6] In these societies, he explains, kinship and strategic marriage

---

4   Will Steffen, Åsa Persson, Lisa Deutsch, Jan Zalasiewicz, Mark Williams, Katherine Richardson, Carole Crumley, Paul Crutzen, Carl Folke, Line Gordon, Mario Molina, Veerabhadran Ramanathan, Johan Rockström, Marten Scheffer, Hans Joachim Schellnhuber, Uno Sved in, "The Anthropocene: From Global Change to Planetary Stewardship."*Ambio* vol. 40 (7) 2011, pp. 739–61.

5   Thomas Piketty, Capital in the Twenty-First Century (Cambridge, MA: Belknap Press of Harvard University Press, 2014), pp. 25–27, 77.

6   Ibid., p. 564. In rentier societies, r usually has ranged from 4–5 percent and g below 1 percent; Piketty says that economic growth was not "a tangible, unmistakable reality for everyone" until the twentieth century, when it averaged 1.6 percent. From antiquity to the 1600s, *g* never exceeded 0.1–0.2 percent for long, while *r* averaged 4–5 percent. Even from 1700–2012 global *g* averaged only 0.8 percent (Ibid., pp. 86–87, 94–96). The upper decile usually owned about 90 percent of the wealth and top centile half of it (Ibid., p. 264). In today's U.S., the upper decile owns about 77 percent and top 1 percent about 42 percent of the wealth Gabriel Zucman, "Wealth Inequality." *Pathways: The Poverty and Inequality Report* (Palo Alto The Stanford Center on Poverty and Inequality, 2016), p. 42. http://inequality.stanford.edu/sites/default/files/Pathways-SOTU-2016-Wealth-Inequality-3.pdf. Accessed July 2, 2016.

trump "study, talent, and effort."[7] He sees the twentieth century income convergence and eclipse of rentier society to be "accidental" events driven by exceptional shocks (e.g., Bolshevik Revolution, World Wars One and Two, Great Depression) and unusually strong, innovative political actions in response (e.g., major pressure from organized labor, confiscatory taxation; capital controls, welfare state policies), which shrank inherited wealth and labor income gaps. The adjustments to the shocks culminated in post-World War Two economic and sociopolitical democratization, which instituted varying levels of social democratic control of capitalism in wealthy nations.[8]

Piketty argues that the later twentieth and early twenty-first century U-turn reversed the postwar egalitarian trajectory and greatly increased income divergence. He warns that continuing divergence and slow growth are producing sharp r>g and sociopolitical conditions that threaten to give rise to a new version of the ancient régime.[9] Piketty asserts that there is "no natural or spontaneous process" preventing highly inegalitarian trends from "prevailing permanently."[10] His tome became an unexpected U.S. bestseller and bane to conservative critics, because his rentier society thesis resonated with growing public fears that the 'great reversal' or roughly thirty-five year erosion of substantive equal opportunity, social mobility, and economic security and absence of democratic political alternatives to hegemonic neoliberal governance constitute a 'new normal' destined to harden into an enduring polarized, top-down regime. Public pessimism was in part motivated by the top centile's capture of most all income gains after the 2007–2009 financial and economic crises and its enormous political clout (facilitated by the entrenched neoliberal political policy regime, favorable court decisions, and the suffusion of deregulated political money and very powerful and influential corporate lobbyists and "wealth-protection" law firms representing the 1 percent's wealthiest fractions).[11]

---

7   Thomas Piketty, Capital in the Twenty-First Century, (Cambridge, MA: Belknap Press of Harvard University Press, 2014), pp. 238–40.

8   Although fundamental to the book's core argument and discussed at various junctures (Ibid., e.g., pp. 13–15, 146–55, 274–76, 284–94, 321–25), Piketty does not provide a sustained analytical discussion of shock per se.

9   Ibid., 13, 146–50, 274–78. Peak global g of nearly 4 percent from 1950–2012 was exceptionally robust, but it slowed sharply after the postwar boom. Piketty projects global r to rise from 4–4.5 percent and g to slow to about 1.5 percent this century as population growth declines and emerging nations catch up technologically and end their growth spurts (Ibid., pp. 354–58, 375).

10   Ibid. p. 21.

11   Emmanuel Saez, "Striking it Richer: The Evolution of Top Incomes in the United States." January 25, 2015. https://eml.berkeley.edu/~saez/saez-UStopincomes-2013.pdf.

Piketty rejects critics' charges that his $r>g$ and rentier society theses are excessively pessimistic and deterministic. Warning against "economic determinism," he asserts that income inequalities are irreducible to "purely economic mechanisms." Piketty stresses the vital role of "history, sociology, anthropology, and political science" in inquiries about economic inequality and class structure and formation of related public policies.[12] He sees $r>g$ to be divergence's "fundamental force" and capitalism's "central contradiction," but he implies that this inequality is shaped by social drivers, which justify wealth and generate, reproduce, unravel, and reconstitute political economies. He holds that the distribution of power, sociopolitical struggles, and beliefs about justice are vital forces shaping economic inequality. Piketty argues that "the history of inequality has been chaotic and political, influenced by convulsive social changes and driven not only by economic factors, but by countless social, political, military, and cultural phenomena as well."[13] Twentieth century income convergence and democratization exemplify his view that the distribution of wealth is "deeply political" and that shocks of variable intensity and reach can stir downward or upward mobility and sociopolitical responses that increase or diminish the trends and harden or undercut political economic regimes.[14] Although rentier societies have dominated historically and threaten to remerge again, Piketty holds, various institutional forces favor increased convergence as well as greater divergence. He says he wants to believe that people can learn from past crises and forge collective action to strengthen democratic institutions and to "someday regain control of capitalism." He implies that moderate shocks could open opportunities for democratic collective action and reform.

Accessed July 7, 2016. On Americans' concern and pessimism about inequality, see "New York Times/CBS Poll: Americans' Views on Income Inequality and Worker's Rights." *New York Times*, June 3, 2015. hhtp://www.nytimes.com/interactive/2015/06/03/business/income-inequality-workers-rights-international-trade-poll.html. Accessed June 6, 2016.

12   Thomas Piketty, *Capital in the 21st Century* (Cambridge, MA: **Belknap Press of** Harvard University Press, 2014), p. 33. Piketty rejects neoclassical economists' claims that their work is genuinely 'scientific' and that the 'soft' social and historical sciences have little to say about 'economic' problems and related public policy (Ibid., pp. 30–33; 571–75). See Thomas Piketty, "Dynamics of Inequality" [Interview]. *New Left Review* 85 (2014): pp. 108–11; Thomas Piketty, "Putting Distribution Back at the Center of Economics: Reflections—On *Capital in the Twenty-First Century*." *Journal of Economic Perspectives* 29, no. 1 (2015), pp. 67–88; Thomas Piketty, "About Capital in the Twenty-First Century." *American Economic Review: Papers & Proceedings*. vol. 105 (5) (2015), pp. 48–53.

13   Thomas Piketty, *Capital in the 21st Century* (Cambridge **Belknap Press of** Harvard University Press, 2014), p. 274.

14   Ibid., pp. 20, 25.

Cognizant of financial elites' power to shape law and taxation, however, Piketty fears that only extreme shock can reverse the drift toward oligarchy and thus expresses pessimism about democracy's future.[15]

Piketty on Climate Change: Discounting Ecological Risks

By holding that ecological degradation is the globe's primary "long-term worry," Piketty implies that it could generate major social shocks. However, he focuses narrowly on the much discussed disagreement between economists Nicholas Stern and William Nordhaus over discount rates for climate change mitigation.[16] Warning of climate change's likely very high future economic costs (5 to 20 percent of Gross Domestic Product [GDP]), Stern held that enormous risk dictates immediate collective action (e.g., costly regulatory and tax measures to reduce greenhouse gas [GHG] emissions). He called for a low discount rate close to the growth rate and substantial investment to mitigate climate change because it poses a severe threat to future generations' well-being. By contrast, Nordhaus presumed that they will enjoy more wealth than people today and suffer only modest damages from climate change this century. He acknowledged possibility of longer-term severe damages, but considered them too uncertain to demand costly action now. He and other neoclassical critics saw Stern's low interest rate to be a wasteful 'radical' move.[17] Nordhaus called for a high discount rate close to the rate of return on capital, and did not support immediate efforts to mitigate climate change at public expense. Benefitting from preceding wealth creation, scientific and technical innovations, and consequent enriched sociocultural resources, he argued, future generations would

---

15 Thomas Piketty, "Dynamics of Inequality" [Interview]. *New Left Review* 85 (2014), p. 116; Thomas Piketty, *Capital in the 21st Century* (Cambridge Belknap Press of Harvard University Press, 2014), pp. 514, 571.

16 Thomas Piketty, "Dynamics of Inequality" [Interview]. *New Left Review* 85 (2014), pp. 567–69, 654.

17 Discounting is based on normative as well as empirical judgments about the relative weight given to the welfare of current versus future generations, likelihood of continued growth of wealth in light of potential ecological damages, and distribution of impacts among different classes and groups. Discount rates are "strongly nonlinear"—e.g., discounting at "1 percent [approximating Stern's rate], the discounted value of $1 million 300 years hence is around $50,000 today," while discounting over the same period at "5 percent [approximating Nordhaus's rate], the discounted value is less than 50 cents" (Thomas Sterner and U. Martin Persson, "An Even Sterner Review: Introducing Relative Prices into the Discounting Debate." *Review of Environmental Economics and Policy*. Vol. 2 (1) 2008, p. 62.

adapt to unavoidable climate change impacts and likely curtail or eliminate more severe, long-term, future damages.

Siding with Stern, Piketty holds that Nordhaus underestimated likely serious, irreparable damage to natural capital and that his 'go slow' approach mirrors U.S. unwillingness to regulate carbon emissions. Moreover, Piketty asserts that the "abstract debate over discount rates" does not come to terms with the most pressing problems. He says that public discussion in many nations has begun to acknowledge the need for clean technologies and alternative forms of energy and, in Europe, for an ecological stimulus. If Stern is correct about climate change risk, Piketty states, its damages and curtailment will require vaster public investment by rich nations than ever before, which provokes the question—how can we spur such investment and enact such costly regulatory measures when the essential mechanisms, broad public support, and political vision is now lacking in so many nations? Piketty holds that coping with these problems requires democratic control of capital and new forms or property, participation, and governance. He does not explain these fundamental changes, but implies that they would reverse today's hegemonic market-centered deregulating, privatizing, financializing strategies, which preclude his proposals for expansive investment in educational capital, confiscatory upper bracket taxation (e.g., 80% top marginal rate), and much increased financial transparency (e.g., via a progressive global tax on capital). Similar blockages prevent regulatory action and public investment to mitigate climate change. Climate change inaction manifests what Piketty identifies as absent democratic control of capital, the erosion of which has been driven by the same sociopolitical forces that have sharply reduced upper bracket tax rates, decreased financial transparency, stripped down the social state, and greatly increased economic inequality.

Understating Climate Change Urgency

Piketty's critical points about Nordhaus's position and the limits of discount rates per se converge with the views of climate scientists deeply concerned about ecological risk. Had Piketty addressed climate science discourse after the 2006 *Stern Review* and Nordhaus critique, he might have seen climate change as an imminent threat rather than exclusively a long-term one. Major climate findings and debates, like that between Stern and Nordhaus, are now widely reported in major newspapers of record. In 2008, Stern warned that GHG emissions and climate change were increasing much faster than he estimated just two years before and that 'business as usual' would likely produce a 4–5°Celsius (C) increase above the preindustrial average global surface temperature and catastrophic impacts. Stressing emphatically the urgent need to begin serious mitigation efforts, he doubled his earlier estimate of the percentage of GDP that needs to be invested now to avert climate disasters.[18] The Intergovernmental Panel on Climate Change (IPCC) Fourth Assessment Report (AR4 [2007]) also had expressed this sense of urgency, and AR5 (2014) held that climate change is underway and costly and already has had terrible impacts in the most vulnerable, poor parts of the world.[19] The IPCC reports are the most reliable, comprehensive, transparent reportage on the overall state of climate science, but they have tended to err on the side of caution; the science following the reports has suggested faster moving, more severe climate change impacts.[20] That the current 1°C (1.8° Fahrenheit) rise likely has begun a long-term irreversible collapse of the West Antarctic Ice Sheet, caused major instabilities and shrinkage of the Greenland Ice Sheet and Arctic summer ice, worldwide retreat of mountain glaciers, and substantial sea level rise (e.g., already forcing resettlement of some island peoples and sharply increasing storm surge risks in many more coastal areas) is a sobering warning of about the more severe consequences of a climate future that rises to 3–4°C or higher.

A United Nations Environmental Program report holds that major mitigation efforts must begin soon because much of the carbon budget to limit climate change to 2°C above preindustrial levels already has been used and that

---

18 Juliette Jowit and Partrick Wintour, "Cost of tackling climate change has doubled, warns Stern." *The Guardian* June 26, 2008. http://www.theguardian.com/environment/2008/jun/26/climatechange.scienceofclimatechange. Accessed June 8, 2015.

19 *Fourth Assessment Report: Climate Change: Synthesis Report Summery for Policymakers.* Intergovernmental Panel on Climate Change (2007), https://www.ipcc.ch/publications _and_data/ar4/syr/en/spm.html. Accessed June 13, 2015. *Fifth Assessment Report: Climate Change: Synthesis Report Summery for Policymakers* (2014). Intergovernmental Panel on Climate Change. http://www.ipcc.ch/pdf/assessment-report/ar5/syr/AR5_SYR_FINAL _SPM.pdf. Accessed June 13, 2015.

20 AR5 underestimated substantially rising global temperatures since 1997, aiding skeptic claims about a 'climate change pause,' which since has been debunked. See e.g., Carolyn Gramling, "Lost and found: Earth's missing heat." *Science*, vol. 348 (6239) (2015), pp. 1066–67. Under-prediction in IPCC reports has occurred far more often than over-prediction. This tendency is likely in part due to the fact that IPCC Reports must be vetted and approved by government representatives as well as by scientists. Also, climate scientists usually avoid immoderate sounding tones, and are reluctant to discuss publically dangerous climate change impacts and costs. See Keynyn Brysse, Naomi Oreskes, Jessica O'Reilly, and Michael Oppenheimer. "Climate change prediction: Erring on the side of least drama?" *Global Environmental Change* 23 (2012), pp. 327–37; William R. Freudenburg and Violetta Muselli "Reexamining Climate Change Debates: Scientific Disagreement or Scientific Certainty Argumentation Methods (SCAMs)." *American Behavior Sciences* vol. 57 (6) 2013, pp. 777–95.

'business as usual' will likely reach that level around mid-century and possibly 4°C or higher by 2100 or before.[21] The report says that staying at or below the 2°C limit requires about a 55% percent GHG emissions reduction below 2010 levels by midcentury and zero by 2080 to 2100. Vulnerable nations have called for a 1.5°C limit to avoid catastrophe, but wealthy nation policymakers have seen that target to be 'infeasible' and blocked it.[22] Tyndall Center climate scientists Kevin Anderson and Alice Bows argue that 2°C may be already out of reach and that likely impacts of that level increase have been sharply understated (e.g., much of Earth's surface is covered by cooler large water bodies, but average land temperatures are warmer and in some regions far warmer).[23] Most policy frameworks, Anderson and Bows say, call for accepting a "high probability of extremely dangerous climate change" rather than implementing needed costly emissions reductions. Climate scientists warn of approaching 'tipping points' that, if breached, will cause irreversible qualitative changes of earth subsystems (e.g., Arctic summer ice) and possibly upset overall naturalistic interdependence. Accelerating anthropogenic global forcings (e.g., energy usage, population growth, resource usage, habitat destruction) threaten a global 'state shift' that could end mild Holocene conditions (which heretofore have sustained complex civilizations) and insure a 'sixth great extinction.' Climate change and other anthropogenic, global ecological problems (e.g., desertification and land degradation, biodiversity loss; fresh water shortages, ocean acidification, toxic pollution, disruption of the nitrogen and phosphorous cycles) have motivated scientists to entertain whether we have entered a new climatically unstable Anthropocene Epoch in which human activity has become the main driver of overall ecological change.[24]

---

21   "The Emissions Gap Report: Synthesis Report." United Nations Environment Program November, 2014. http://www.unep.org/publications/ebooks/emissionsgapreport2014/portals/50268/pdf/EGR2014_LOWRES.pdf. Accessed June 18, 2015.
      Set at the 2010 Cancun Climate Conference (U.N. Framework Convention on Climate Change), the 2°C limit was supposed to provide a rough benchmark to motivate avoidance of climate change's most dangerous, irreversible impacts. See John Tollefson, "Global-warming limit of 2° hangs in the balance." *Nature* vol. 520 (7545) (2015), pp. 14–15.

22   John Tollefson, "Global-warming limit of 2° hangs in the balance." *Nature* vol. 520 (7545) 2015.

23   Kevin Anderson and Alice Bows, "Beyond 'dangerous' climate change." *Philosophical Transactions of the Royal Society* vol. 369 (1934) (2011), pp. 40–41.

24   Will Steffen, Åsa Persson, Lisa Deutsch, Jan Zalasiewicz, Mark Williams, Katherine Richardson, Carole Crumley, Paul Crutzen, Carl Folke, Line Gordon, Mario Molina, Veerabhadran Ramanathan, Johan Rockström, Marten Scheffer, Hans Joachim Schellnhuber, Uno Sved in, "The Anthropocene: From Global Change to Planetary Stewardship," *Ambio* vol. 40 (7) 2011.

The Deep Decarbonization Pathways Project states that nations would have to institute a "profound transformation of energy systems by midcentury" to meet the 2°C target and that this would require "unprecedented global co-operation." Few nations' policymakers have even considered how they would contribute to such a project or what it would entail. Achieving this goal, would be enormously complex technically, institutionally, and politically for it requires massive changes and costs and major technology and financial transfers from wealthy to poor nations.[25] Some climate scientists hold that avoiding a 'disaster scenario' calls for a 1.5°C. or less increase and that atmospheric carbon dioxide must not exceed 350 parts per million (ppm).[26] We are already over 400 ppm, and carbon emissions are still rising globally. Considering the huge costs and complexity of rapidly decarbonizing the path-dependent carbon-based economic, technological, and sociocultural complex and very powerful interests opposed to this strategy, sociologist John Urry asserted that likely "nothing can be done except to *prepare* for various catastrophes."[27] In the last substantive chapter of the fourth and final volume of the magisterial *The Sources of Social Power*, Michael Mann stresses the extreme difficulty of the needed turnabout; the leading social actors of our time, capitalists, political leaderships, and consumers drive climate change and are resistant to the "international collectivism" required to orchestrate mitigation.[28] In his view, climate catastrophe and major sociopolitical shock are clearly possible absent an unexpected cultural and political about-face or an equally unlikely sudden, profound technological breakthrough (e.g., carbon extraction). Mann warns that runaway climate change may cause us to be "overwhelmed by wars, massive refugee flows, chaos, and extremist ideologies."[29] Concerns about such major ecological shocks appear in recent World Economic Forum [WEF] Risk Reports and national security agencies' assessments.[30] Piketty acknowledges serious environmental risk, but does not entertain ecological shock or its catastrophic impacts.

25 "Pathways to Deep Decarbonization: Executive Summary." The Deep. Decarbonization Pathways Project September, 2014, III. http://undsn.org/what-we-do/deep-carbonization-pathways/. Accessed June 21, 2015.

26 James Hansen, *Storms of My Grandchildren* (New York: Bloomsbury, 2009), pp. 140–171.

27 John Urry, *Climate Change & Society* (Malden: Polity, 2011), p. 166.

28 Michael Mann, *The Sources of Social Power, Vol. 4: Globalizations 1945–2011* (New York: Cambridge University Press, 2013), pp. 361–99.

29 Ibid., p. 432.

30 "The Global Risk Landscape." *Nature Climate Change* 5, March (2015), p. 175.

Undertheorizing Capitalism: The Growth
Imperative and Ecological Wall

Piketty mentions "liberalization" in passing, but does not address directly or deeply the neoliberal regime of accumulation or capitalism per se. Growth is central to his argument, but he does not theorize its distinct role within capitalism.[31] Piketty's truncated analysis of the political economic regime may follow from his desire to avoid straying from his core focus on long-term trends in income inequality or being locked into the capitalism and socialism binary and identified as Marxist.[32] Whatever the reason, he stops short of doing a full-throated critique of neoclassical economics and neoliberalism and illuminating the ultimate political economic mechanisms that drive climate change and other global ecological problems, undercut the material and social relations that sustain economy and society, and open the way for serious ecological shock. Neoclassical economists share an unyielding commitment to an all-important normative and theoretical presupposition and core structural principle of capitalism, its *growth imperative*, valorizing exponential, unplanned economic growth or the virtue of ever-increasing production and ever-growing consumer numbers and appetites in service of ever-expanding capital accumulation. The aggregated market value of a nation's final goods and services, GDP is the conventional standard for measuring growth. Ignoring economic inequality, human well-being, and ecological sustainability, GDP expansion is equated with 'development' and 'wealth' per se.[33] Embracing

---

31   Piketty's failure to address capitalism more deeply results in theoretical ambiguities in
        his overall argument. For example, he speaks of r>g as "the central contradiction of cap-
        italism" and two related core theorems ($\alpha = r \times \beta$ and $\beta = s/g$) as "fundamental laws of
        capitalism," but he employs them in analyses of rentier societies that precede capitalism
        (Ibid., pp. 31, 52, 166, 571).

32   Thomas Piketty, *Capital in the 21st Century*, (Cambridge: Belknap Press of Harvard Uni-
        versity, 2014), pp. 7–11, 31, 227–30, 576, 655, ftn. 2.

33   On the growth imperative, see Herman E. Daly, "Economics in a Full World." *Scientific
        American* September (2005), pp. 100–07; James Gustave Speth, *The Bridge at the End of
        the World* (New Haven: Yale University Press, 2008); Robert J. Antonio, "Climate Change,
        the Resource Crunch, and the Global Growth Imperative." in *Current Perspectives in Social
        Theory*, Vol. 26, ed. Harry F. Dahms (Bingley: Emerald 2009), pp. 3–73. Aware of unre-
        stricted growth's social costs, Keynesian and other progressive economists usually have
        qualified their versions of the growth imperative. By contrast, 'ecological economists'
        frame heterodox ecofriendly approaches cognizant of the limits to growth and costs of
        exceeding the planet's carrying capacity (e.g., Herman E. Daly and Joshua Farley, *Ecologi-
        cal Economics* (Second Edition). (Washington DC: Island Press, 2011), pp. 61–76, 261–84.

neoclassical economic ideas, neoliberal political, intellectual, and business elites, fashioned their new regime to overcome a profit squeeze and other crises of what Piketty calls the postwar "social state" and "democratic capitalism."[34] Maximizing capital accumulation by eliminating regulatory, redistributive, and other social constraints on the growth imperative is the sine qua non of neoliberal policymaking and key driver of global ecological problems as well as of trends toward de-democratized capitalism and rentier society.

The postwar capitalist expansion started a 'Great Acceleration' of unparalleled resource usage and mass consumption, but later twentieth and early twenty-first century globalization spread capitalism worldwide and neoliberal policies far beyond their Anglo-American heartland, increasing enormously the global economy's physical size relative to the biosphere and spreading afar the gospel of unregulated growth. The new global capitalism sharply accelerated the speed and volume of natural resource throughput and waste production, intensifying the contradiction between unplanned, exponential growth and the planet's biophysical carrying capacity, producing 'uneconomic growth' (disutility exceeding utility), and depleting the biosphere in which capitalism is embedded and on which it depends. The growth imperative was formulated when the global economy was tiny relative to the biosphere and waste absorption capacities seemed infinite so that earlier modern social and economic thinkers, who at least tacitly embraced it, did not engage the problem of scale and planetary carrying capacity.[35]

Most climate scientists are hesitant to speak publically about the political economic drivers of climate change, its speed and scope, and its likely or possible social impacts. American climate scientists who have addressed these matters vocally in public arenas have often been subject to political attacks.[36] The

---

34   On the theory and politics of neoliberalism, see Philip Mirowski, "Postface: Defining Neoliberalism." in *The Road from Mont Pèlerin*, ed. P. Mirowski, and D. Plehwe (Cambridge: Harvard University Press, 2009), 417–55; Daniel Stedman Jones, *Masters of the Universe* (Princeton: Princeton University Press, 2012).

35   Herman E. Daly, "Economics in a Full World." *Scientific American* September (2005), 100–07; Will Steffen, Åsa Persson, Lisa Deutsch, Jan Zalasiewicz, Mark Williams, KatherineRichardson, Carole Crumley, Paul Crutzen, Carl Folke, Line Gordon, Mario Molina, Veerabhadran Ramanathan, Johan Rockström, Marten Scheffer, Hans Joachim Schellnhuber, Uno Sved in, "The Anthropocene: From Global Change to Planetary Stewardship."*Ambio*, vol. 40 (7) 2011.

36   Scientists' hesitation to speak in public venues about politically controversial, scientific issues, in part, reflects their observance of norms of 'objectivity' and 'scientific reticence.' Their tendency to be sober and cautious about claims and findings is manifested in the

comprehensive, mandatory, global regulatory regime needed to deal seriously with climate change contradicts directly and profoundly neoliberal first principles, policy frameworks, and visions of capitalism. Ideas of ecological 'limits' and public 'planning' must be accepted more widely than ever before and shape policy formation to initiate climate change adaptation and mitigation. Consequently, neoliberals have generally resisted doggedly the idea of anthropogenic climate change and have charged that proposed nonmarket methods to decarbonize society and otherwise regulate economic activities echo the old communist regimes ("green on the outside, red on the inside"). Deploying neoclassical economic principles, they have stressed emphatically the fatal threats aggressive mitigation programs pose to 'growth' and consequently 'jobs' and 'liberty.' By contrast, Anderson and Bows charge that the growth imperative dominates climate change policy and even permeates, distorts, and mutes, via political threat and self-censorship, climate science estimates and reports. Asserting that "collective acquiescence" leaves the "elephant in the room undisturbed," Anderson and Bows contend that in the absence of intense mitigation efforts, business as usual will likely drive a 4°C or more temperature rise this century and devastate the biosphere and undercut economic growth. They advocate liberating climate science from neoclassical economics and neoliberal finance and their political enablers so that climate science research findings

---

much higher statistical confidence limits set for Type 1 errors (holding that a condition is true when it is false) than for Type 2 errors (failing to confirm a condition that is true). Yet Type 2 errors can be disastrous in ecological matters like climate change, which motivates the 'precautionary principle' (stressing preventative actions despite uncertainty). In the U.S., intense political polarization over climate change and climate science has intensified scientists' reticence and caution. Vocal climate scientists have been charged with malfeasant 'alarmism' and 'conspiracy' and purveyance of 'junk science,' 'pseudo-science,' or simple 'lies' by right-wing bloggers, newspaper op-ed writers, and politicians. They have sometimes even had to cope with political and legal threats from conservative organizations and public officials. See Keynyn Brysse, Naomi Oreskes, Jessica O'Reilly, and Michael Oppenheimer. "Climate change prediction: Erring on the side of least drama?" Global Environmental Change 23 (2012), 327–37; William R. Freudenburg, Robert Gramling, and Debra J. Davidson. "Scientific Certainty Argumentation Methods (SCAMS)." Sociological Inquiry, vol. 78 (1) 2008, pp. 2–38; James Hansen, Storms of My Grandchildren (New York: Bloomsbury, 2009), pp. 70–89, passim; Michael E. Mann, The Hockey Stick and the Climate Wars (New York: Columbia University Press, 2012); Naomi Oreskes and Erik M. Conway, Merchants of Doubt (New York: Bloomsbury, 2010). John H. Richardson, "When the End of Civilization is Your Day Job." Esquire July 7, 2015. http://www.esquire.com/news-politics/a36228/ballad-of-the-sad-climatologists-0815. Accessed July 8, 2015.

and projections could be addressed frankly to the public and policymakers and stir visions of "alternative futures."[37]

Piketty understands that substantial population growth requires clean, renewable energy and a radically reduced carbon footprint, but he seems unaware how fast decarbonization has to occur to avoid climate catastrophe. He projects a slowing of population growth and economic growth after emerging nations catch up with rich ones around mid-century. But how could the robust economic growth needed for 'catch up,' especially in very populous nations and with a global population estimated to reach more than 9 billion by midcentury, be harmonized with urgent mitigation targets and other needed regulatory policies to avert severe environmental damages and exceeded tipping points that threaten irreversible ecological changes? Absolutizing the growth imperative to maximize accumulation, neoliberal restructuring extends unrestricted market logic across social life, removing regulatory constraints, eviscerating the public realm, and constituting the essence of what Piketty identifies as democracy's relinquished control of capitalism. Piketty contends that high economic growth rates help stem movement toward rentier society, but he is definitely *no* cheerleader for the growth imperative. He asserts that growth is used to "justify inequalities of all sorts" and attribute "winners ... every imaginable virtue" and that it cannot bring forth on its own a more democratic or just society. He does not believe that we need high growth rates to live well and advance culturally.[38]

Still Piketty has not addressed capitalism, neoliberalism, and growth in sufficient depth or entertained the most serious but necessary question—can climate change and other serious growth related global environmental catastrophes be avoided within a capitalist regime of any sort. *If* capitalism per se depends on the growth imperative, then dealing with economic inequality and climate change may require thinking beyond capitalism as we have known it? And the same may hold for socialism. Had Piketty addressed this question, he might have probed even more deeply the neoliberal era's accelerated $s>v$, great income divergence, and drift toward rentier society and engaged the drivers of climate change and potentialities for ecological shock. The networks of social factors that drive and condition the growth imperative constitute the nexus of capitalism's contradictory political economic and ecological relations. The consequent tendency even of many well-informed scientists, economists, and policymakers to see

37   Kevin Anderson and Alice Bows, "A new paradigm for climate change." *Nature Climate Change* 2, September (2012), p. 640. http://www.environmentportal.in/files/file/paradigm%20for%20climate%20change.pdf. Accessed April 8, 2015.

38   Thomas Piketty, *Capital in the Twenty-First Century* (Cambridge Belknap Press of Harvard University Press, 2014), pp. 83, 85, 95–96.

income polarization and climate change as "wicked problems," which can never be resolved because of their complexity, contradictory features, and indeterminacy, precludes visionary alternatives and insures eventual shocks.[39] As Fredric Jameson declared and others have repeated variously, today "it is easier to imagine the end of the world than to imagine the end of capitalism."[40]

Averting Apocalyptic Shock: An Authoritarian or Substantive Democratic Turn?

If democracy is someday to regain control of capitalism, it must start by recognizing that the concrete institutions in which democracy and capitalism are embodied need to be reinvented again and again.[41]

Piketty could have enriched his idea of shock by elaborating the authoritarian responses and possibilities of the chaotic events in the years spanning the two world wars. Appreciating historical contingency, he knows that a few turnabouts of key military and political events could have resulted in the opposite of the *Trente Glorieuses*. Similarly, ecological shock could harden and militarize incipient rentier society as well as unravel it. The idea of ecological catastrophe driven by corporate power run amuck and productive of chaos, authoritarianism, and social decline has long been a leitmotif of post-apocalyptic cinema (e.g., *Soylent Green*, *Silent Running*, *Blade Runner*, *Mad Max*, *Waterworld*, *The Day After Tomorrow*, Wall*E). Potential catastrophic shock, generated by unplanned growth and ecological overshoot, likely has been a subliminal collective fear more easily dealt with in fantasy than scientific projections. Historians of science, Oreskes and Conway employ their knowledge of medium to worst case scenarios of business as usual climate policies in a futuristic portrayal of runaway climate change. Their narrator reports major ecological shocks that begin in the 2040s, generate social dissolution in the 2050s, and cause a collapse of Western civilization in 2093. The narrator says that China's highly centralized polity responded more quickly and effectively to climate crisis than the U.S. neoliberal regime, whose antiregulatory policies opened way for more extreme ecological shock, left the nation unprepared to deal with the

---

39   Mike Hulme, *Why We Disagree About Climate Change* (Cambridge: Cambridge University Press, 2009), pp. 335–37.

40   Fredric Jameson, "Future City." *New Left Review* 21 May-June (2003), p. 76. https://newleftreview.org/II/21/fredric-jameson-future-city

41   Thomas Piketty, Capital in the Twenty-First Century (Cambridge, MA: Belknap Press of Harvard University Press, 2014), p. 570.

impacts, and in the face of chaos 'necessitated' a massive government response that ended democracy.[42] Climate scientists Anderson and Bows' warn of panic scenarios, geoengineering, and authoritarianism in response to climate change shock, and Speth, Urry, and Mann suggest possible "fortress worlds," plagued by repressive militarized regimes, forced migrations, interstate conflicts, and internecine battles between retainers of gated wealthy enclaves and desperate vulnerable masses.[43] A central theme in dystopian fantasies, frightful feedbacks between ecological shocks and extreme economic inequalities have now become plausible risks of business as usual as assessed by national security agencies and other concerned public and international organizations.

Ecological shock and authoritarianism are speculative possibilities, but neoliberal sociopolitical forces, empowered by concentrated wealth, have fueled de-democratization, which easily could be hardened by responses to runaway climate change. The 2016 wave of right-wing populism in Europe and the u.s., and parallel neo-tribal populist uprisings in other parts of the world in response to the economic strains, refugee crises, and religious and ethnic conflicts provide hints of chaotic, violent forces that could be unleashed in far more powerful ways than Brexit, Trump Presidential politics, or resurgent nationalist parties if the trends toward sharp economic inequality and environmental devastation continue and produce serious ecological, food, employment, and socio-political crises. Wealthy strata have economic and political resources to adapt effectively to earlier stages of catastrophe and block the heavy progressive taxation, regulation, and restrictions on property rights necessary for socially just adaptation and mitigation strategies. Regardless of equating oppression with state intervention and advocating rollback, neoliberals have not hesitated to justify and participate in expanding and imposing state power in service of 'liberal principles' (especially property rights).[44] Oreskes and Conway's narrator explains that early

---

42   Naomi Oreskes, and Erik M. Conway, *The Collapse of Western Civilization* (New York: Columbia University Press, 2014).

43   Kevin Anderson and Alice Bows, "Beyond 'dangerous' climate change: emission scenarios for a new world." *Philosophical Transactions of the Royal Society* A. vol. 369 [2010] 2011, pp. 20–44; James Gustave Speth, *The Bridge at the End of the World* (New Haven: Yale University Press, 2008), p. 43; John Urry, *Climate Change & Society* (Cambridge: Polity, 2011) pp. 148–50; Michael Mann, *Sources of Social Power* (New York: Cambridge University Press), pp. 396–99.

44   F. A. Hayek and Chicago School economists advised General Pinochet's authoritarian dictatorship and helped guide his "Chilean Miracle." See e.g., Philip Mirowski, "Postface: Defining Neoliberalism." in The Road from Mont Pélerin, ed. P. Mirowski, and D. Plehwe (Cambridge, MA: Harvard University Press, 2009), before pp. 434–36.

twenty-first century neoliberal erosion of "actionable freedom" (i.e., Piketty's view of de-democratization) paved the way for later authoritarian responses to shock.[45]

Speaking of the enormous divide between public views and scientific knowledge about climate change, James Hansen warns that, without a fundamental change of course soon "we may well pass the point of no return."[46] Climate science reportage in 2015 and 2016 suggest that we are substantially further along that dangerous path than when Hansen spoke. However, Mann says that the major risks generated by neoliberalism and climate change "remain abstract" or distant from average folks' daily experience (especially less vulnerable people in rich nations) and that an "imaginative social movement" is needed to bridge the gap between mounting catastrophic risk and everyday life.[47] Hoping to ignite such a movement from an unlikely perch, Pope Francis' remarkable *Laudato Sí* speaks of the profound threats climate change pose to "our common home" and great political economic and cultural transformation it cries out for. Pope Francis stresses emphatically that the poorest, most vulnerable people and other creatures with which we share the Earth have suffered most from ecological degradation, driven mainly by rich nation resource consumption and waste production and by unrestricted market liberalism and its unleashed growth imperative. In Pope Francis' view, avoiding climate catastrophe calls for ending the neoliberal regime and reversing the inegalitarian trends that Piketty articulates.[48]

Addressing capitalism and shock more deeply would have extended the reach of Piketty's book, but his work still illuminated basic tensions of neoliberal capitalism at a moment when its legitimacy was starting to be challenged on multiple fronts. His book and related work with his collaborators on income inequality and the ultra-rich have generated substantial critical

45   Naomi Oreskes and Eric. M. Conway, *Collapse of Western Civilization; A View from the Future* (New York: Columbia University Press, 214), pp. 48–49.

46   James Hansen, *Storms of My Grandchildren* (New York: Bloomsbury, 2009), p. 171.

47   Michael Mann, *The Sources of Social Power, Vol. 4: Globalizations 1945–2011* (New York: Cambridge University Press, 2013), p. 399.

48   Pope Francis, *Laudato Sí (Encyclical Letter of the Holy Father on Care for our Common Home)*. 2015. The Vatican. June 18, 2015. http://w2.vatican.va/content/dam/francesco/pdf/encyclicals/documents/papa-francesco_20150524_enciclica-laudato-si_en.pdf. Accessed July 12, 2015. See *Nature Climate Change's* (October 2015) editorial and special section commentaries on the significance of the Pope's intervention, http://www.nature.com/nclimate/archive/issue.html?year=2015&month=10.

discourse and policy debate and constitute an exceptionally important contribution to public life.[49] The book's primary analytical and empirical focus on
very long-term trends in income inequality likely ruled out detailed treatment
of the neoliberal conjuncture, and in-depth exploration of ecological shock
would have been even a greater detour in an already long, complicated tome.
My critical comments mainly extend his argument. Piketty declares that "if we
are to regain control of capitalism, we must bet everything on democracy...."[50]
He poses reforms to defend what remains of postwar European social states'
egalitarian facets, but implies a wider project of 'reinventing democracy'—a
daunting, uncharted path and more fundamental transformation. Its fate rides
on transforming conditions that give priority to accumulation of finance capital or 'abstract wealth,' which concentrates especially amongst tiny fractions
of 'the 1%,' empowers them, and propels the drift toward rentier society and
possibly worse catastrophes.

In more recent work, Piketty addresses the connection between ecological
inequality and economic inequality more broadly and proposes a progressive
carbon tax to fund climate change adaptation.[51] However, his call for a democratic imperative, in the face of today's plutocratic income and power divide
and grave ecological risks requires radically rethinking and reconstructing our
economic life, our relation to nature, and our obligations to other peoples and
creatures with which we share the planet. We must face this daunting task of
reimagining and perhaps transcending capitalism before the de-democratizing
force of income divergence and dispossession and looming threat of fast moving, catastrophic climate change overtake us. The upside of the sweeping,
costly changes required to decarbonize society and avoid ecological shock is
that they require benign growth of 'real wealth' serving our collective well-
being and that of life on the planet and hopefully providing time and building

---

49   See the Piketty circle's World Wealth and Income Database http://www.wid.world/;
      Robert J. Antonio, "Piketty's Nightmare Capitalism: The Return of Rentier Society and
      De-democratization," review of *Capital in the Twenty-first Century* by Thomas Piketty.
      Contemporary Sociology, vol. 43 (6) 2014, pp. 783–90.

50   Thomas Piketty, *Capital in the Twenty-First Century* (Cambridge Belknap Press of Harvard
      University Press, 2014), p. 573.

51   Lucas Chancel and Thomas Piketty. "Carbon and inequality: from Kyoto to Paris."
      Paris School of Economics November 3, 2015. http://piketty.pse.ens.fr/files/
      ChancelPiketty2015.pdf. Accessed January 20, 2016.

cultural and political resources needed to create a sustainable, just ecology and society. Such fundamental change may seem farfetched but is necessary to avoid fateful extreme economic inequality and collision with the ecological wall, which could plunge the world into shocks, chaos, and worse.

CHAPTER 17

The Adventures of Professor Piketty: In Which We Meet the Intrepid Data-Hunter Thomas Piketty and Hear His Startling Story

David Norman Smith with art by *Tom Johnson*

It all began in March 2014. Thomas Piketty's book *Capital in the 21st Century* was published by Harvard University Press – and in just a matter of weeks it was a bestseller and a publishing phenomenon. Before long, it was positively raining critical reviews and mass media headlines...

Piketty fever

Bigger than Marx

Kapital for the Twenty-First Century?

Thomas Piketty Revives Marx

Capitalism and its critics

A modern Marx

Thomas Piketty Pens Communist Manifesto for 21st Century

The New Marxism

Capital for the Masses

Class warfare justified?

150 Years After Marx, 'Capital' Still Can't Shake Loose Of 'Das Kapital'

But I knew little about any of this until I was lucky enough to meet with the author...

David Smith is the author of *Marx's Capital Illustrated*, which was published in July 2014 by Haymarket Books. Tom Johnson is a concept artist whose work is featured in films and video games. For creative input we thank Laura Bennetts, Daniel Smith, and Robert J. Antonio – whose essay "Piketty's Nightmare Capitalism," *Contemporary Sociology*, 43 (6), pp. 783-90. is an outstandingly insightful commentary on Piketty's important work.

I had waited nearly an hour when the suddenly famous Thomas Piketty arrived at the café, breathless and apologetic. "I'm sorry to be so late. My life has been wild lately. I can hardly believe that it's been just months since my book on 21st century capitalism came out. It feels like years.... Who would ever have guessed that a 700-page study by an economist, with data and charts, would get so much attention?"

"Well, yes," I said, "but your book does have the word *Capital* in the title. Marx's *Capital* is even longer and harder, and it's one of the most famous books ever written." "Agreed," Thomas replied, "but I really don't think that explains it. Marx predicted an apocalypse with a happy ending, and that kind of thing fascinates people. But I barely discuss Marx, I focus mainly on long-term trends, and my predictions are pessimistic – a society increasingly dominated by an oligarchy of the ultra-rich. And yet, I've been absolutely mobbed by the media!"

"It's been just crazy. I feel like I've been running a gauntlet, with *Wonks* and *Speed Readers* on one side and *Pundits* on the other. Nearly as soon as the book came out, it was reviewed and hotly debated. The attention has been incredible! Of course, I'm pleased, but..."

Thomas hesitated, and gave me an inquiring look. "Is this something you already know about?" "Not really," I answered. "I know you've studied inequality for many years, and I know your colleagues were excited when your big book finally appeared. I've seen you on a lot of television shows and magazine covers. But I'm still not quite sure how all that came together, and how you morphed into a celebrity."

A dreamy look spread over his face. "It all began," Thomas reminisced, "when I was deep in the archives, collecting tax data. Everyone has heard that '*the rich get richer and the poor get poorer*,' but I wanted to get the hard facts, across centuries and countries. I spent long hours, working with Emmanuel Saez and others, lost in thought and buried in numbers.

One day, I saw light at the end of the archive…"

"I went into the light. At first I was blinded, but soon I knew that I had
found what I was searching for. The numbers came together, and took
shape as pyramids..."

"Everywhere, I saw the wealthiest 1% at the top of the pyramid, with
just a few others near them, and everyone else below...often far below.
And I saw more than that. The pyramids of wealth were steep in the
early 20th century, but then, when welfare states emerged from the Great
Depression of the 1930s, the pyramids flattened out a lot."

"In the 1970s and 1980s everything changed, again, when 'globalization' took off. Multinational corporations searched the globe for low-wage investments, leaving shuttered factories behind, and the pyramids of wealth soared even higher."

"That's the reality we face today. Inherited wealth is increasingly powerful, politically as well as economically. But jobs, wages, and services have been sharply cut since the Great Recession, and they're still being cut, so people without profits or trust funds aren't faring well."

"Overall, the trend throughout history seems to be that wealth grows faster than productivity – and that's certainly true today. That's what I mean by the equation $R > G$. The best solution I can picture is a world-wide wealth tax, which would reduce inequality and put some of that accumulated capital to good use."

"I can see," I said drily, "why so many business journalists are calling you the new Marx." "But I'm not Marx!" Thomas protested. "I'm not anti-capitalist, I haven't read Marx carefully, and I'm not even against all forms of inequality. I'm just trying to find a way to leverage the wealth of our society, so that we *all* get richer, not just the rich."

At this point, a curious sight interrupted us. A nearby fortune telling machine began creaking and shaking. The fortune-teller, remarkably, appeared to be none other than Karl Marx himself.

*HTTP://TOPINCOMES.G-MOND.PARISSCHOOLOFECONOMICS.EU/

"If each industrial investment yields a progressively smaller return, industry becomes folly. Even the richest capitalists will hesitate to invest in manufacturing if they see returns diminishing to the zero point – and that is increasingly what tends to happen.

As business competition drives down production costs, the profit per commodity tends to fall. Ultimately, a commodity that once earned the capitalist a dollar will earn only pennies. If even those pennies are not guaranteed, the investor might invest *speculatively* instead of *productively*.

That, too, is now happening – and on a vast scale. The net result is that investment is moving away from production, and people are increasingly left jobless. That puts the very *legitimacy* of the system in question."

BUT THE RICH ARE SO INCREDIBLY RICH... AND THEIR CHILDREN INHERIT NOT ONLY THEIR WEALTH, BUT THEIR POWER. CAN THEY REALLY BE CHALLENGED?

YES, THE RULING CLASS RULES.

BUT WEALTH THAT INCREASINGLY CONSISTS OF STOCKS, BONDS AND DEBT CAN FALL LIKE A HOUSE OF CARDS. STOCKS ARE WORTH ONLY WHAT SOMEONE WILL PAY FOR THEM. SO IF THE STOCK MARKET FALTERS, OR IF WE SINK INTO A GLOBAL DEPRESSION, TODAY'S VAST WEALTH COULD BE TOMORROW'S WORTHLESS PAPER.

THEN THE TOP 1% WOULD BE JUST AS POOR AS EVERYONE ELSE?

RIGHT, BUT THAT POVERTY WOULD ONLY BE A SHORTAGE OF *MONEY*. THE SUN IS STILL SHINING, THE LAND IS STILL FERTILE, WE STILL HAVE PLENTIFUL RESOURCES. IF WE REBUILD SOCIETY AND SHARE EQUALLY, WITHOUT WORRYING ABOUT MONEY – AND CAPITAL IS JUST MONEY CHASING MONEY– WE WOULD ALL HAVE ENOUGH OF WHAT COUNTS: FOOD, SHELTER, FUN, ART, EDUCATION, MEDICAL CARE, IN THAT CASE THERE *WOULD* BE NO CAPITAL IN THE 21ST CENTURY. *PYRAMIDS* AND *INEQUALITY* WOULD BECOME A DISTANT MEMORY...

AND THEY CALL ME UTOPIAN! I'M JUST PROPOSING REFORMS.

THE REAL UTOPIANISM... IS THINKING THAT CAPITAL HAS A BRIGHT FUTURE. IN REALITY, THE PURSUIT OF CAPITAL AND MORE CAPITAL BLOCKS EQUALITY, DEMOCRACY, AND PRODUCTION – AND THREATENS OUR VERY SURVIVAL.

YIKES!

YIKES, INDEED.

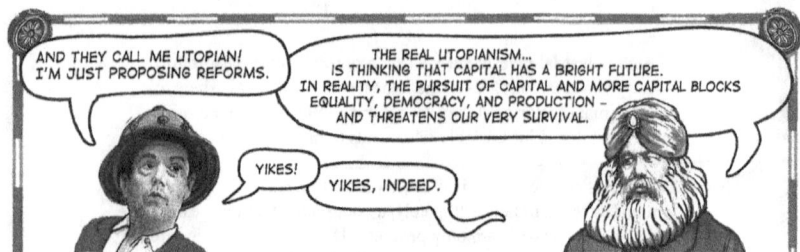

Suddenly, just as suddenly as it had begun, the clanking and hissing of the mechanical fortune-teller subsided. A haze of mist dissipated, as Thomas and I exchange puzzled glances. "What was that?" Thomas asked incredulously. "A dream? A nightmare?"

We found ourselves standing amid fallen headlines, as if autumnal trees were shedding their leaves.

WELL, IF IT WAS A NIGHTMARE, IT WASN'T ONLY YOURS. SOCIETY HAS BEEN IN CRISIS SINCE THE WORLD PLUNGED INTO GLOBAL RECESSION IN 2008, AND YOUR NEW *CAPITAL* REMINDS EVERYONE OF THE DARK PREDICTIONS THEY ASSOCIATE WITH *DAS KAPITAL*.

I CAN LIVE WITH THAT. I MAY NOT BE INSPIRED BY MARX MYSELF... BUT I'LL BE ENCOURAGED IF PEOPLE TAKE THE DANGERS OF WEALTH INEQUALITY SERIOUSLY.

THE SUCCESS OF YOUR BOOK SEEMS TO INDICATE JUST THAT.

LET'S HOPE SO!

CHAPTER 18

21st Century Capital:
Falling Profit Rates and System Entropy
Postscript to "The Adventures of Professor Piketty"

David Norman Smith

Imagine a physicist who declined to study Einsteinian relativity theory because it was hard to understand—and then alleged that Einstein paid too little attention to gravity. That is, in effect, Piketty's position with respect to Marx's theory of capital and capitalism. In an interview, he casually admitted that reading Marx was beyond him,[1] while, in *Capital in the Twenty-First Century*, he said that "Marx totally neglected the possibility of durable technological progress and steadily increasing productivity."[2] In fact, Marx's account of capital accumulation pivots around increasing productivity in every volume of *Capital*. The main source of that productivity dynamic is precisely technological progress, which Marx discusses under the rubric of the "rising organic composition of capital"—that is, the steadily increasing ratio of capital goods to labor in the capitalist production process. Every new phase of capital accumulation brings further refinements in the sophistication of the means of production, which include, above all, the machines that power what Marx calls "machinofacture." It is this very process, further, that drives capitalism into crisis, since profit rates decline, Marx says, as production becomes increasingly high-tech.

Marx, in short, could hardly have paid more attention to the steadily increasing productivity at the heart of modern capitalism. As early as 1848, in *The Manifesto of the Communist League,* he said, with Engels, that capitalists are compelled by competition to "continuously revolutionize" the means of production. That claim remained central to all of his subsequent analysis.

---

1 Interviewer: "Can you talk a little bit about the effect of Marx on your thinking and how you came to start reading him?" Piketty: "Marx?" Interviewer: "Yeah." Piketty: "I never managed really to read it. I mean I don't know if you've tried to read it. Have you tried?" "Thomas Piketty: I Don't Care for Marx: An interview with the left's rock star economist" by Isaac Chotiner, *The New Republic*, online at *http://www.newrepublic.com/article/117655/thomas-piketty -interview-economist-discusses-his-distaste-marx*. Accessed May 5, 2014

2 Thomas Piketty, *Capital in the Twenty-First Century*, translated by Arthur Goldhammer (Cambridge, MA: The Belknap Press of Harvard University Press, 2014), p. 10.

But he complicated that claim by observing, in the *Grundrisse* (1857–58) and *Capital* (1867–1894) that the rising organic composition of capital is not only pivotal to successful accumulation but is, at the same time, the Achilles' heel of capitalism as a system. Marx ultimately concluded that surplus value, and hence (by his logic) profit, derives exclusively from the exploitation of living labor, not from the purchase and use of capital goods—which, he says, transfer their value to the final product, but do not endow that product with additional value. That conclusion, although sharply controversial, is argued with force and nuance in countless pages of *Capital* and in Marx's many corollary texts. It is, furthermore, profoundly significant for anyone seriously interested in the fate of capitalism, since, if Marx's analysis is correct, profit rates are destined to fall even as capital accumulates ever more massively. The likely consequence, Marx says, is that capitalism will be deeply and repeatedly shaken, and may ultimately collapse.

This argument can and should be questioned, but it should not be ignored. No one can doubt, after 1929 and 2008, that capitalism is susceptible to seismic shocks. Nor has anyone yet produced a theory of capitalism to match the breadth and depth of Marx's theory. The best contemporary research, by Andrew Kliman, shows that profit rates in the United States have fallen significantly,[3] much as Marx anticipated. Innumerable investors have fled the realm of production altogether, gambling that increasingly exotic speculative spending will outstrip the profitability of industrial investment. As the McKinsey Global Institute has shown, many trillions of dollars that, in 1975, would have been invested in production, had fled by 2005 to the ostensibly greener pastures of speculation.[4] Rates of industrial investment have plunged in many places, now even including China; and it is not fanciful to think that falling profit rates might be substantially driving this epochal shift.[5]

---

3   See Andrew Kliman, *The Failure of Capitalist Production: Underlying Causes of the Great Recession* (London: Pluto Press, 2012), especially Chapter 5.

4   See the epilogue, "The Crash and After," in David Norman Smith, *Marx's Capital Illustrated*, illustrated by Phil Evans (Chicago: Haymarket, 2014). See also David Norman Smith, "Mapping the Great Recession: A Reader's Guide to the First Crisis of 21st-Century Capitalism," *New Political Science*, vol. 34 (4), 2011, 577–83, with appended book reviews by 13 collaborators, pp. 583–601.

5   On profit tendencies outside the United States—about which Kliman is cautious, on the ground that reliable data are seldom available—see Elias Ioakimoglou and John Milios: "Capital Accumulation and Over-Accumulation Crisis: The Case of Greece (1960–1989)," *Review of Radical Political Economics*, vol. 25 (2), 1993: 81–107; and "Capital Accumulation

Piketty is free, if he wishes, to ignore Marx, but he does so at the risk of failing to grasp even his own findings. His work is a major empirical achievement, but he falters at the threshold of interpretation. Take, e.g., the vexed question of "capital" in relationship to inequality. Piketty seems to think that inequality is simply a matter of unequal wealth and that wealth is simply money. But is money always wealth? Is wealth always power? The conventional wisdom is that today's super-rich are powerful in direct proportion to their money holdings—and since they now have towering sums of money (that is, many zeros in their bank accounts), they must be vastly powerful. It thus seems that capital in the twenty-first century is flourishing. But capital, as Marx explained, is not just money. What makes the world go 'round is not just money, but money invested *in production*. Gambling produces nothing but (as the poets tell us) heartache; speculation is a hall of mirrors. Hence the wealthy who chase money without investing in production are not capitalists but pseudocapitalists. They neither hire workers nor realize industrial profits. Their wealth is money, but it does not act as capital.

How much does this matter? A great deal. Since 2008, global production has slowed tremendously. Consumer demand has fallen precipitously, and in many places (Greece, South Africa, elsewhere) unemployment has persisted at record levels, often in excess of 25 percent. The wealthy have more money than ever before and the public is increasingly money-starved—to that extent, at least, Piketty's vision is empirically right. But money in the twenty-first century is far from flourishing. The jobless and wage-poor have reduced buying power, so the rich have a reduced incentive to invest in production. Instead they speculate; but even this is proving problematic. Once lucrative speculative investments (e.g., government bonds) now often seem just as risky as subprime mortgages and junk bonds. Speculation *per se* increasingly seems to be entering a subprime phase. Even the speculative rate of profit appears to be falling.

---

and Profitability in Greece (1964–2004)," 2005, online at *http://users.ntua.gr/jmilios/ JMiliosJoakim91EnglFin.doc*. See also: Seongjin Jeong, "Trend of Marxian Ratios in Korea: 1970–2003," in Martin Hart-Landsberg, Seongjin Jeong, and Richard Westra, eds., *Marxist Perspectives on South Korea in the Global Economy* (Aldershot, UK: Ashgate), 2007: 35–64; Anwar M. Shaikh and E. Ahmet Tonak, *Measuring the Wealth of Nations* (Cambridge and New York: Cambridge University Press, 1996); and Andrew Kliman and Nick Potts, eds., *Is Marx's Theory of Profit Right?* (Lanham, MD: Lexington, 2015). Also helpful is Fred Moseley, "The Development of Marx's Theory of the Falling Rate of Profit in the Four Drafts of *Capital*," 2014, available online at: *https://thenextrecession.files.wordpress.com/2015/01/ moseley-piketty.doc*.

If so, money is truly at an impasse. Money that cannot be productively invested is not capital—and money that stalls or misfires in the sphere of speculation is a failure even as pseudocapital.

The "wealthy," in other words, may have astronomical masses of accrued profit, but they are increasingly destitute of opportunities to amass further profit. The rest of us, meanwhile, suffer from the inverse problem—namely, that opportunities to collect *wages* are declining. Money owners hire fewer workers because consumer demand is down and consumer demand falls even farther because employment is down. It's a vicious circle, and unsustainable.

System Entropy

Piketty sees the obvious—that amassed profits are higher than ever. What he does not see is that, as Marx explained, mountains of profit can coexist with declining profit *rates.* A semblance of vast wealth can mask a sclerotic reality of increasing economic paralysis.

To explore this possibility, Piketty would have to consider whether profit rates are falling. That, it seems, is beyond his purview, though without an answer to that question we remain largely in the dark about the very phenomenon he documents. Paul Krugman, for example, recently expressed bafflement over the fact that corporations have a rising profit share but weak investment[6]—but Piketty assumes that Marx's theory is not only difficult but also irrelevant.

Piketty is not alone in dismissing Marx. Rosa Luxemburg, who was otherwise among Marx's most gifted disciples, belonged to a founding generation of self-declared Marxists who derived their crisis theory from Vol. 2 of *Capital,* which Engels published in 1885, just two years after Marx's death.[7] In that volume, Marx offered a complex approach to the interconnectedness of the major "departments" of capitalist production (including Dept. 1, in which "the production of means of production" occurs, and Dept. 2, in which means of consumption are produced). Influential commentators in the 1890s and after—above all Mikhail Tugan-Baranovsky—took that analysis as the starting point for inquiry into the extent to which inter-departmental "disproportionalities" could

---

6   Paul Krugman, "Challenging the Oligarchy," *The New York Review of Books,* December 17, 2015, p. 20.

7   Rosa Luxemburg, *The Accumulation of Capital,* translated by Agnes Schwarzschild and edited by Joan Robinson (London: Routledge and Kegan Paul, [1913] 1951).

lead to crisis.[8] Tugan-Baranovsky held that this was indeed possible, but that prudent state planning could secure stability by harmonizing the departments. Many subsequent economists have echoed this claim, including prominent Marxists (Bauer, Hilferding) and equally eminent non-Marxists (Keynes, Hansen). Luxemburg, who ardently criticized Tugan-Baranovsky, held that crises could not be held indefinitely at bay by harmonist state planning. But even she was so engrossed by Vol. 2 that she curtly dismissed the notion that crises can be explained in terms of the general tendency of the rate of profit to fall. Marx had argued this position at length, and brilliantly, in Vol. 3 of *Capital;* but by the time Engels brought this volume into print in 1894, Marxian "orthodoxy" had already fastened on the less relevant schematics of Vol. 2.

Not until 1929, when Henryk Grossman's monumental treatise on profits and crises appeared, did themes from Vol. 3 begin to infiltrate the thinking of Marxist crisis theorists.[9] And even then, Marx's symphonic and dialectical reasoning tended to fall on deaf ears. Grossman was affiliated with "the Frankfurt School," which is celebrated for its contributions to modernist Marxism. But even the leading figures in this school turned, for insight into the future of capitalism, not to Grossman but to Friedrich Pollock, who echoed Tugan-Baranovsky in a few slender essays.[10] Theodor Adorno, the most gifted of the

---

8   Michael Tugan-Baranovsky, "Studies on the Theory and the History of Business Crises in England, Part 1: Theory and History of Crises" (1901), translated by Alejandro Ramos-Martinez, in *Research in Political Economy,* vol. 18: *Value, Capitalist Dynamics, and Money,* 2001, pp. 43–110. On Tugan-Baranovsky's influence, see Lubomyr Marian Kowal, *Economic Doctrines of M. I. Tugan-Baranovsky* (Ph.D dissertation, University of Illinois, 1965); Vincent Barnett's articles "Calling Up the Reserves: Keynes, Tugan-Baranovsky and Russian War Finance" (*Europe-Asia Studies,* vol. 53 [1], 2001: pp. 151–69) and "Tugan-Baranovsky as a Pioneer of Trade Cycle Analysis" (*Journal of the History of Economic Thought,* vol. 23 [4] 2001: pp. 443–67); and Daniele Besomi, "'Marxism Gone Mad': Tugan-Baranovsky on Crises, Their Possibility, and Their Periodicity," *Review of Political Economy,* vol. 18 [2], April 2006: pp. 147–71.

9   See Henryk Grossman, *Das Akkumulations- und Zusammenbruchsgesetz des kapitalistischen Systems* (Leipzig: Hirschfield, 1929) and, in abbreviated form, *The Law of Accumulation and Breakdown of the Capitalist System,* translated by Jairus Banaji (London: Pluto, 1992). Rick Kuhn is preparing a complete English translation of this long neglected work. See also his book *Henryk Grossman and the Recovery of Marxism* (Urbana & Chicago: University of Illinois Press, 2007).

10   See especially Friedrich Pollock, "State Capitalism" (1941), in *The Essential Frankfurt School Reader,* edited by Andrew Arato and Eike Gebhardt (New York: Continuum, 1978), pp. 71–94. For a good overview of Pollock's economics see Jeremy Gaines, *Critical Aesthetics* (Ph.D dissertation, University of Warwick, 1985), Chapter 2.

Frankfurt thinkers and a defining figure in Marxian cultural critique, was able to say, in a late essay, that socialists who expect the falling rate of profit to consign capitalism to breakdown would be rewarded for their patience only *ad calendas Graecas*—that is to say, never.[11] Adorno treated this proposition as self-evident, requiring neither evidence nor argument.

The superficiality of this perspective, the degree to which even serious Marxists have allowed themselves to be complacent about falling profit rates, is strikingly revealed by Luxemburg's scathing reply to the "little expert" who had the temerity to challenge her book, *The Accumulation of Capital* (1912), in the *Dresdner Volkszeitung* on January 22, 1913. Luxemburg derides her critic's claim that capitalism will ultimately fail "because of the falling rate of profit":

> One is not too sure exactly how the dear man envisages this—whether the capitalist class will at a certain point commit suicide in despair at the low rate of profit, or whether it will somehow declare that business is so bad that it is simply not worth the trouble, whereupon it will hand over the keys to the proletariat. However that may be, this comfort is unfortunately dispelled by a single sentence of Marx's, namely the statement that 'large capitals will compensate for the fall in the rate of profit by mass production' [*für große Kapitale der Fall der Profitrate durch Masse aufgewogen.*] Thus there is still some time to pass before capitalism collapses because of the falling rate of profit, roughly until the sun burns out.[12]

---

11   The phrase *ad calendas Graecas* was a witticism credited to the emperor Augustus by his biographer, Suetonius. Unimpressed by debtor's promises, Augustus said he expected payment upon the arrival of the Greek calends—i.e., when pigs fly, since the Greek calendar, unlike the Roman calendar, did not include "calends." About profits, Adorno wrote: "Even if Marx's by no means unambiguous law of the falling rate of profit had turned out to be true, we would have to concede that capitalism has discovered resources within itself that have postponed its collapse until the Greek Calends." See Adorno, "Late Capitalism or Industrial Society?," translated by Rodney Livingstone, in Theodor Adorno, *Can One Live After Auschwitz?*, edited by Rolf Tiedmann (Stanford: Stanford University Press [1969] 2003), p. 112.

12   Rosa Luxemburg, "The Accumulation of Capital, or What the Epigones Have Made Out of Marx's Theory—An Anti-Critique," translated by George Shriver, in *The Complete Works of Rosa Luxemburg*, Vol. II: *Economic Writings 2*, edited by Peter Hudis and Paul Le Blanc (London: Verso [1915] 2015), p. 499, note 4. Peter Hudis, in an email, identifies the unnamed target of Luxemburg's criticism here as M. I. Nachimson, who was better known as M. Spektator. On this rarely discussed passage, see, e.g., Grossman, 1929,

This passage, confined to a footnote, is the entire sum and substance of what Luxemburg felt obliged to say about the falling profit rate in one of her principal economic texts. *The Accumulation of Capital* is a major work, illuminating and extending many themes drawn from Vol. 2 of *Capital.* In the anti-critical pamphlet in which this dismissive note appears, Luxemburg's argument is razor sharp and often highly enlightening. But, like Piketty, she takes for granted the strength of the profit dynamic. Capitalism is historically limited, she feels, not because its internal contradictions will ultimately "fetter" growth, as Marx held, but rather because the world is too small to permit capital to grow infinitely.

Marx, like Luxemburg's "little expert," held that the falling rate of profit poses an inner barrier to capital accumulation. Capital is its own worst enemy: "The true barrier to capitalist production is *capital* itself."[13] So Marx wrote in 1864–65, in the draft manuscript that Engels published, 30 years later, as Vol. 3 of *Capital.* Immediately afterwards, Marx offers the 'single sentence' that Luxemburg construes as proof that Marx, too, denied the system-shaking power of declining profit rates. But in fact, that sentence and the larger passage in which it appears show precisely the opposite. The point Marx makes here is that capitalists need to concentrate ever increasing masses of means of production and labor power if they hope to amass enough total profit to compensate for falling rates of profit. But concentration is costly. To stay ahead of the profit curve, capitalists must deploy state-of-the-art equipment and production techniques. They must spend, at spiraling levels, to keep profits growing faster in absolute terms (for the entire universe of commodities) than they fall, proportionally, per commodity.[14]

Capital, in short, must concentrate to counteract falling profit rates.[15] But this option is not available to all. To enter this path, capitalists must cross a

---

op. cit., p. 116, note 76, and Paul Mattick, "Die Gegensätze zwischen Luxemburg und Lenin," *Rätekorrespondenz*, 12, September 1935, *http://en.internationalism.org/ir/21/internationalisme-1952.*

13   Karl Marx, *Ökonomische Manuskripte 1864–65*, in *Marx/Engels Gesamtausgabe*, Section II, Volume 4/2 (Berlin: Dietz, [1864–65] 1992), p. 359.

14   To increase production and achieve "economies of scale," capitalists need armies of labor and concentrated means of production. As productivity increases, every labor hour yields more commodities. If, yesterday, an hour produced a single widget and today an hour produces two widgets, today's two widgets have the same amount of new value that one widget had yesterday. So production must double for the absolute mass of profits to remain unchanged.

15   By concentrating every larger masses of workers and equipment, capitalists seek to defy economic gravity and counteract what can be called Marx's law of profit entropy.

critical threshold, which Marx calls the 'capital-minimum'—they must be large enough to invest massively at escalating, profit-sustaining levels. Smaller, less concentrated firms are more immediately and acutely vulnerable to falling profit rates because they lack this *Kapitalminimum*. They are thus drawn, Marx says, to speculative and even criminal escapades, outside the realm of production.

This is the point at which, according to Luxemburg, Marx reassures his readers that "large capitals will compensate for the fall in the rate of profit by mass production."[16] But this is far from accurate. In fact, Marx says that falling profit rates threaten not only smaller firms, but also, ultimately, the capitalist class as a whole. Concentration is an antidote to profit bottlenecks only "within certain limits," when "a large capital with a lower rate of profit accumulates more quickly than a small capital with a higher rate of profit."[17] But the antidote is temporary; the apparent cure, the concentration of high-tech production, is the very poison that caused the profit rate to fall to start with. "This growing concentration leads, in turn, at a certain level, to a new fall in the rate of profit. The mass of small, disunited [*zersplitterten*] capitals are ... forced into risky adventures: speculation, credit swindles, share swindles, and the resulting crises."[18]

The underlying dilemma, Marx says, is that, relative to investment opportunities, capital finds itself superabundant.[19] What might appear to naïve observers as a new zenith of wealth becomes, in fact, a 'plethora' of capital. Relatively defenseless, non-concentrated capitals are the first to suffer. This is Marx's point elsewhere in this passage, which includes the fateful clause, tucked into the text, that Luxemburg ironically calls the "single sentence" that authorizes us to discount the ultimate significance of falling profit rates:

> The 'plethora' of capital is always basically reducible to a plethora of that capital for which the fall in the profit rate is not outweighed by its mass [*für das der Fall der Profitrate nicht durch seine Masse aufgewogen*

16   See Rosa Luxemburg, *Gesammelte Werke*, Bd. 5: *Ökonomische Schriften* (Berlin: Dietz, 1975), p. 446.

17   See *Marx's Economic Manuscript of 1864–1865*, translated by Ben Fowkes and edited by Fred Moseley (New York: Brill, 2015), p. 360. See especially Chapter 3: "The Law of the Tendential Fall of the General Rate of Profit > with the Advance of Capitalist Production," pp. 320–75.

18   Marx ([1864–65] 2015), ibid., p. 360. Here and elsewhere I have lightly edited the translation.

19   Marx adds that capital ultimately reaches a saturation point when even "the expanded capital produces only the same mass of surplus value as before < or even less—we are speaking here of the absolute mass, not the rate of profit" ([1864–65] 2015), ibid., p. 360.

wird]²⁰—and this is always the case with fresh offshoots of capital that are newly formed—or to the plethora of those capitals that depend for credit on the directors of the greater branches of business because they are unable to act autonomously.[21]

Luxemburg plucks only a line from this passage, while overlooking Marx's conclusion: that crises, rendering masses of capital and labor "superfluous," issue directly from this profit dialectic: "The plethora arises from the same causes that stimulate the production of a relative surplus population and it is thus a phenomenon that complements the latter, even though the two things stand at opposite poles—unoccupied capital on the one hand and an unemployed working population at the other."[22]

Marx does not predict a linear, teleological progression from crisis to collapse. Alongside the general tendency of the falling rate of profit, he posits many countervailing tendencies, some of which can, for a while at least, turn the tide in the opposite direction. One merit of the recent translation of Marx's 1864–65 manuscript, which Engels converted into Vol. 3 of *Capital*, is that these tendencies are vividly presented in Marx's unvarnished, unedited prose. It becomes clear that, though Marx was not optimistic about capitalism's future—not sharing *The Wall Street Journal's* serene conviction, as expressed in a recent editorial, that "what comes down must go up again"—he was even less mechanical and inevitabilist in his outlook than the version of Vol. 3 edited by Engels would suggest. In one key passage Marx says that, if countertendencies were not at work, capitalist production would "shake" (*Klappen*). Engels replaced "shake" with "breakdown" (*Zusammenbruch*).[23]

---

20   Luxemburg's paraphrase of this line omits the word "nicht."

21   Marx ([1864–65] 2015), op. cit., p. 360. In *Capital* Vol. 3, as edited by Engels, this passage appears as follows: "The so-called plethora of capital always applies essentially to a plethora of the capital for which the fall in the rate of profit is not compensated through the mass of profit (this is always true of newly developing fresh offshoots of capital) or to a plethora which places capitals incapable of action on their own at the disposal of the managers of large enterprises in the form of credit." Karl Marx, *Capital,* Vol. 3, translated by Ernest Untermann (Chicago: Charles H. Kerr & Company, [1894] 1909), available online at https://www.marxists.org/archive/marx/works/1894-c3/ch15.htm

22   Cf. Karl Marx, *Theories of Surplus Value,* "Chapter 17: Ricardo's Theory of Accumulation and a Critique of It. (The Very Nature of Capital Leads to Crises)," available online at *https://www.marxists.org/archive/marx/works/1863/theories-surplus-value/ch17.htm*

23   Marx ([1864–65] 2015), op. cit., p. 360.

A few pages later he added a full sentence, strengthening the impression that Marx saw collapse as inevitable: "In practice, however, the rate of profit will fall in the long run."[24] Marx did, in fact, envision recurring and worsening phases of "stagnation," "disruption," and capital annihilation. He saw no way for capital, in the long run, to sustain healthy rates of accumulation, employment, and demand.[25] But he did not predict automatic collapse. How long the stress placed on capitalists by the falling profit rate could be counteracted was an empirical question, and many contingencies entered into the equation. The general tendency was clear, but countertendencies were not to be underestimated.

When, periodically, the capitalist class *en bloc* does fall into crisis, the only solution, Marx says, is the "annihilation" of underachieving capital. That was what had happened in the Great Depression, when vast sums of overflow money, which had failed as capital, dissipated in waves of bankruptcy. But today—*note well*—that cyclical pattern is not being reproduced. Annihilation is seldom the fate of today's superabundant capital. Zombie banks and firms, regarded as "too big to fail," are kept on life support, and capital increasingly flees industry entirely. Sublimation of capital, into speculative pseudocapital, is today's apparent alternative to *both* capital accumulation and capital annihilation.

Capital Becomes Pseudocapital

Superficially, the shift to speculation resembles capital annihilation. In each case, capital vanishes from industry. But rather than dissipating, today's superabundant capital becomes pseudocapital. Manic, undying, this zombie capital chases at least a simulacrum of profit. But profit rates remain low, demand remains slack, and money continues to shy away from industry, as the allure of speculative "yield" fetters manufacturing still further. Superfluous as capital, today's plethora of money has become a means of speculation rather than a means of accumulation.[26]

---

24 Moseley, n. 17, in Marx ([1864–65] 2015), op. cit., p. 350.

25 Moseley, n. 19, in Marx ([1864–65] 2015), op. cit., p. 354.

26 See Marx ([1864–65] 2015), op. cit., pp. 361f. Here Marx specifically rules out the notion that Luxemburg credited to him—namely, that ever rising productivity would keep capitalism afloat "until the sun burned out." He said, on the contrary, that "if capital formation were to fall exclusively into the hands of a few existing big capitals, for whom the mass of profit outweighs the rate, the animating fire of production would be totally extinguished.

Luxemburg had asked, with what she thought was devastating rhetorical irony, "whether the capitalist class will at a certain point commit suicide in despair at the low rate of profit, or whether it will somehow declare that business is so bad that it is simply not worth the trouble, whereupon it will hand over the keys to the proletariat." We now know that, on a wide and growing scale, investors do indeed declare business to be so bad that speculation is preferable to old-style capital accumulation. "Awash" in money (in the favored idiom of *The Wall Street Journal*) corporations, sovereign wealth funds, and other bastions of overflow wealth increasingly see capital investment as folly. Capitalists verge, quite literally, on social suicide, as they shed their capitalist skins to reinvent themselves as swindlers and swashbucklers.

Twenty-first century swindling often takes the form of massive tax fraud, evasion and "inversion," as Piketty's associate Gabriel Zucman has shown in his excellent exposé, *The Hidden Wealth of Nations*.[27] Zucman calculates that roughly 8% of the world's money ($7.6 trillion) is stowed in tax havens—hidden from the tax authorities and, I would add, deflected from production.

Is this simply a problem of "inequality"? Is the dilemma we face that some people have too much money, while others have too little? That is the lesson many readers have drawn from Piketty's work. But for Marx the problem is that "wealth" in capitalist society simply *fails*. Capital accumulates by privileging profit over need. When it "succeeds," the result is a plethora of capital which, rendered superfluous by falling profit rates, ceases to act as capital and leaves workers wageless. The problem is not simply disparity in wealth but the fact that money itself is wealth only in the most peculiar and least humane sense. Capitalists, unable to spend money profitably, chase their own tails in financial markets, while workers, afflicted with austerity policies and wagelessness, are unable to consume adequately because their bank accounts are too small— when they have bank accounts. "Too much" money is *ineffectual* money. Too little money ... is tragic.

Money, in short, is the problem. Is it also the answer? That is what Piketty and other reformers imply when they call, e.g., for a global minimum wage or

---

It would cease blazing. The *rate of profit* is the driving agency in capitalist production..." ([1864–65] 2015), op. cit., p. 367.

27 Over time, it has come to seem that even the very largest businesses find it hard to reach the *Kapitalminimum*, which rises relentlessly, even as prices and profit rates fall. It begins to seem that, as Marx suspected, no amount of money, no level of concentration, ensures that capital will accrue faster *en masse* than it falls per commodity.

a global wealth tax.[28] But if capitalism yields a plethora of profit, a falling profit rate, unoccupied capital and unemployed workers, then asking capitalists to share the pain is unlikely to reverse the systemic trend toward entropy. Luxemburg showed, in *The Accumulation of Capital*, that consumption is limited on a global scale. Marx showed that production is limited as well. Money now has a fateful tendency to flow out of consumption, production and tax revenues. What we need, hence, is a solution that does not depend on money. That will require sharing and cooperation, rather than selling and competition – a prospect which, of course, sounds naive to people who pride themselves on their fact-facing realism. But there is a point at which realism becomes what C. Wright Mills called "crackpot realism." That point is reached when short-run solutions ensnare us even further in long-run traps. Marx's theory suggests that the quest for profit does ultimately entrap us, and that the wishful hope that profit can be redirected to rescue us is misguided.

Adorno, in an autumn 1965 lecture, derided Marx's call for a theory and practice of workers' self-emancipation, which he deemed "touchingly innocent." Philosophy, he said, not revolutionary praxis, is the true path for thought in late capitalist society:

> A revolutionary practice that has been endlessly postponed and has to be deferred further to the Greek calends, or else to be utterly transformed, can no longer act as the court of appeal that authorizes us to dismiss philosophy ...[29]

But philosophy, contra Adorno, will not save us. If we hope to find an antidote to system entropy, we need theoretically informed action. That action must steer by the actual stars in the social firmament. If the truth is that massed but unproductive profit is leading us into societal shipwreck, we need to change direction. Marx, even in the 21st century, remains the only thinker to squarely address that possibility.

Should data hunters, like Piketty and Zucman, explore Marx's theory to better understand the larger significance of their data? I leave the closing word on this subject to Marx, who said this about fluctuating global wage rates: "Only

---

28   For advocacy of a global minimum wage—largely, in this instance, as a means of spurring global demand—see Richard Duncan, *The Dollar Crisis*, revised second edition (New York: John Wiley & Sons, 2011).

29   Theodor W. Adorno, *Lectures on Negative Dialectics: Fragments of a Lecture Course 1965/1966*, translated by Rodney Livingstone and edited by Rolf Tiedemann (Cambridge: Polity, 2008), p. 46.

when the relationships that form the rate of profit have been understood will statisticians be able to undertake genuine analyses of wage-rates in different countries."[30] Let the studies begin!

---

30   Marx ([1864–65] 2015), op. cit., p. 343.

CHAPTER 19

From Inequality to Social Justice

Peter Marcuse

Introduction

Whatever else might be said about Piketty's *Capital in the Twenty-First Century*, he provoked a variety of discussions and critiques of inequality. Today, inequality is usually equated with the extent of the gap between the 1% and the 99% that that the Occupy movement brought to public attention-pointing to class structures and class differences usually avoided in American political discussions where everyone, save the homeless or those on welfare or billionaires were "middle class" or should we say "muddled class," as if a barista working at Starbucks was in the same class as a heart surgeon. More recently, Bernie Sanders highlighted the growing inequality by properly criticizing the distribution of wealth and income in the United States in which the 6 Walton heirs have almost 1/3 of the US wealth and a small cadre of billionaires provide a great deal of the funding of candidates. Piketty uses a definition of inequality benefitting most those most in need, akin to Rawls' definition of justice, but he writes that fuller discussion of the meaning of justice is beyond the scope of his tome, and it is well beyond the scope of this essay. But to simply regard inequality as unjust distributions of wealth and/or income is a mischievously facile definition of inequality. Some inequalities are in fact fair, and result from differences in talent, physical strength, luck, and commendable effort. And while gross disparities are a vivid indicator of a likely problem, they do not draw attention to its causes, which lie in critical social, economic, and political relationships. To focus on the gap itself and to address it with remedial measures aimed at narrowing its extent detracts attention from those causes. Thus we must more carefully scrutinize the nature of inequality and justice.

Inequality Just and Unjust: Why the Difference Matters

Equality and inequality are deceptively simple concepts. In the modern era they came into prominence with the French revolutionary slogan of *Liberté,*

Égalité, Fraternité,[1] where equality meant political and legal equality, equality of "rights," equality in relation to the State. Similarly, the United States Declaration of Independence declared that "All men are created equal" as to "certain inalienable rights."[2] Similarly, in considering "Rights" in the UN's Declaration of the Rights of Man, "Equality" did not mean equality in incomes or wealth or in the distribution of goods and services; equality in the distributions of those benefits was seen, if considered at all, as dependent on equality of legal and political rights. The right to property was specifically stricken in favor of the right to the pursuit of happiness. Equality in the material distributions of material goods in all of these documents was seen, if at all, as a concomitant of defined legal and governmental rights, a part of social justice, not its center.

Comparing equality as a goal with justice as itself a goal, brings the realization that not all inequality is unjust.[3] While some differences are unjust, others are not. Not all humans are of the same height or weight or prowess, not all people are the "equals" of Albert Einstein or Jackie Robinson or Serena Williams or Martin Luther King. We consider some inequality in the distribution of wealth and power fair. It may derive from natural inequalities, it may be earned by hard work, or by social contribution, what Piketty calls the "common utility," or be justified by different needs. In some cases unjust inequalities may be built on natural or earned "not-unjust" inequalities, but their extreme extent may then built on power, part of their wealth earned, another part not. Consider for example, Donald Trump? Hillary Clinton? Thomas Edison? Bill Gates? There is a balancing involved. Granted a Hollywood star or tennis champion or skilled artisan deserves to earn more than the average person, but how much more is just? This is tricky question, *but the answer can be one theoretically produced through democratic processes, and thus legitimated.* Democratic processes could, for instance, lead to decisions as to how progressive the tax structure should be. (But as we have seen, the economic elites have

---

1 The 1789 French Declaration of the Rights of the Right of Man begins with: "art. 1. Men are born and remain free and equal in rights." [http://www.hrcr.org/docs/frenchdec.html] considers *egalite* in terms of legal equality and merit-based entry to government (art. 6): [The law] "must be the same for all, whether it protects or punishes. All citizens, being equal in its eyes, shall be equally eligible to all high offices, public positions and employments, according to their ability, and without other distinction than that of their virtues and talents."

2 "... all men are created equal, that they are endowed by their Creator with certain unalienable Rights, that among these are Life, Liberty and the pursuit of Happiness.—That to secure these rights, Governments are instituted among Men."

3 As Susan Fainstein does in *The Just City,* for example, in a wide-ranging discussion; Fainstein, Susan. *The Just City.* (Ithaca and London: Cornell University Press, 2010).

managed to secure political power that has cut their taxes, while at the same time, keeping much of their wealth hidden in offshore accounts in the British Virgin Islands, the Bahamas or the Cayman Islands or perhaps Switzerland or Macau.) Similarly, a person who is ill, or suffering from a disability, or is limited by conditions beyond his or her control; s/he might be entitled to more governmental support than the average person, and again at what levels could be legitimately an appropriate subject for democratic decision-making, leading to decisions as to not unjust but yet unequal levels of welfare benefits reimbursement for health care expenses, and so forth.[4] There is thus "just inequality" and "unjust inequality." How does one generalize the difference?

Just and Unjust Inequality

Inequality is unjust, I propose, if unjust inequality derives from the exercise of power used for the exploitation or oppression of one person or group by another.[5] The resulting unequal distribution of goods and services, of wealth and income, the gap between the 1% and 99% is then unjust, not because of its size, but because of its origins. What is "just" is a matter that is socially defined—Rawls' definition of justice as fairness could be useful, what would be considered as fair by people acting behind a "veil of ignorance" as to how their own position would be affected by the outcome. The results of not-unjust inequalities in the distribution of goods and services can then be countered by appropriate public policies of redistribution of those goods and services, e.g. by taxes or public provision. But the results of unjust inequalities need to be addressed, I would argue, at their source in exploitation and oppression, as implemented in the social, political, and economic relations among individuals and groups which skew the distribution of goods and services, made possible by the skewed distribution of power. Acting on the results of just-inequalities can theoretically be guided by democratic procedures, debates on values, and the use of reason. Acting on the results of unjust-inequalities necessarily involves dealing with the distribution of power, and a durable consensus of those

---

4   John Rawls, *A Theory of Justice.* (Cambridge: Belknap Press, 1971). Here the definition of justice or fairness as what would be decided by people acting behind a veil of ignorance as to their own position is I believe consistent with this approach.

5   Thompson's chapter (10) in this volume makes a similar point that just distributions need to rest upon democratic processes and considerations of serving the public good, not, the power of elites.

benefiting from unjust inequality with those suffering from it should not be expected, and should not be an aim of public policy.

Justice is a moral formulation for the prevention of unjust inequalities. Politically, dealing with all forms of inequality, just and unjust alike, through redistribution of their results can be done by consensus reforms, and should be facilitated by democracy, but will have limited results. That is because the unjust component requires more than quantitative modification of its results; it requires dealing with power. This may have been the difference between Hilary Clinton's and Bernie Saunders' approach to inequality in the recent political campaign. The issues around inequality are complex for practice, as well as theoretically challenging; the answers make a significant difference in matters of immediate policy as well as in philosophy and world outlook.

What's the Answer? Conservative, Liberal, Progressive, Radical, Transformative Responses

The debate between the Democratic candidates in the United States election campaign also seemed at times to be between answers addressing, economic inequality on the one hand, a major theme for Bernie Sanders, and on the other hand, Hillary Clinton frequently emphasized racial and ethnic disparities. Black Lives Matter is often taken to hold that view. The choice of course depends on the analysis of the problem. If the suggestion of this essay is accepted, that the key definition of unjust inequality of wealth and income, lies not simply in their extent of the inequality but more fundamentally in whether or not it arises from the economic, political, and social relations of exploitation and oppression within the society, then that analysis might be applied as well to the issue of unjust non-economic inequalities. Exploitation and oppression divide groups not only by economic class but also by race, ethnicity, gender, age, religion between black and white, "native" born and immigrant, men and women, religious majorities and minorities, non-conformists generally, and by any characteristics that can be used by those exploiting and oppressing to serve their particular interests.

In fact, as the Marxist analysis has long argued, relations of exploitation and oppression, of economic and non-economic inequality, are historically opposite sides of the same coin. As to "race," slavery of course combined both oppression with exploitation. Today the attitudes toward immigrants do so as well, even if in different legal and social ways. The clear disparities in women's and men's wages are linked to patterns of sexist treatment that is both economic and social/cultural and the cultural provides legitimations for the subordination of women whether at work or at home. Patterns of social behavior, such as are embodied in religious codes as well as sexual and gender-related attitudes, play a role in supporting economic structures as well. When looking for concrete answers, then, for policies, programs and strategies to rectify these twin problems of exploitation and oppression, the key is to understand them as linked parts of a single pattern, and examine proposed answers with those linkages in mind. Looking at the details of conservative as opposed to liberal as opposed to radical current answers illustrates the point.

The Conservative Response

In the current debates represented by both the Trump and Cruz wings of the Republican Party and its establishment, inequality should not be a concern. Conservatives essentially see economic inequalities as both inevitable and necessary. While these views are held by those enjoying the benefits of others' lesser equality, conservative defend quantitative inequality by arguing that greater wealth or income is the result of differences in effort, ability, or a greater reward for innovation and hard work. If we were to end inequality, you would take away the incentives for an individual to work hard and to use the abilities they have to contribute to prosperity and growth. The poor are poor because they have lesser abilities and/or motivation. It is only poverty or its threat that makes them enter the labor market at all, where they are however needed to do the unskilled work that needs to be done. If the market at any point requires less unskilled work than there are unskilled workers, that's too bad. Charity requires that they not be left to starve to death on the streets, but they should not be given government support by a "nanny state" that provides programs that stifle ambition and to such an extent that their incentive to work disappears and they would spend their lives as takers—what Romney referred to as the 47% who were bums, moochers and parasite that would never vote for him.[6] Inequality is thus the inevitable accompaniment of different natural capabilities of ambitious, creative individuals and enforcing equality unfairly penalizes those with greater capabilities, who deserve to have more than less capable others. Equality would just be unfair. This view is of course primarily held by those that benefit from inequality and drive its formative

---

6   Included among his takers who lived off of the makers were those on social security who had paid into the funds, those on Medicare who also paid into the fund, students who borrowed money for college etc. Not included among the moochers are the various industries like banks and auto companies who were bailed out, nor big agra that receives huge subsidies, government research like what led to the Internet etc. This has been called socialism for the rich and capitalism for the poor.

processes. Such legitimating ideologies pay little attention to the hidden priv-ileges of race, gender and class background. Thus neither Romney, nor Trump, or Bush one or two, had come from more modest backgrounds.

For conservatives economic inequalities are directly linked to and justified by non-economic inequalities: the exploitation of subordinate groups is linked to oppression and its supportive culture and ideologies. Less pay for women is explained by sexist views of their work, lower pay for African-Americans is jus-tified by their work habits and/or hedonistic, if not pathological, value systems. The unconcern for living wages for immigrants, by a logical market reaction to their greater "willingness" to accept work undesired by natives. Non-economic inequalities are oppressive and painful to African-Americans, women (both married and unmarried, in different and overlapping ways), LGBT individu-als, foreigners speaking other languages as their native tongue, some artists, non-conformity of all sorts. Those subject to such oppressive treatment are admittedly unequal in the conservative view, but the difference is explained as a matter of voluntary choice of life style. The solution is simply individual adaptation to more dominant patterns of behavior of the "successful" higher classes. Those not conforming to middle-class values in their behavior are not entitled to claims for equal treatment, and may be forcibly repressed through police action and incarceration if they do not "behave." And altogether, the pressure for life-style conformity, even if leading to obvious unjust inequality, is part of a societal pattern accepted as desirable and functional for society, even if criticized as one-dimensional by some. Dealing with non-economic in-equality would necessitate government interference in "private" matters, and that is in principle to be minimized. The answer thus is simply to make the system function smoothly, not to disturb it by artificially countering inequality.

It is a solution that has been sold effectively enough to become acceptable to a significant part of the population, and has substantial resources behind its propagation. It is a solution that will be strongly objected to by some, and consensus about it is not likely, but it must be imposed on those that disagree, for the greater benefit of all.

The Liberal Response
In the recent Democratic debates, as exemplified by Hillary Clinton, the exis-tence of economic inequalities of wealth and income is evident, but the focus is on non-economic inequalities. In addressing economic inequalities, the an-swers are to improve incomes and wealth at the bottom of the scale, leaving the top untouched. That response is based on a social morality which objects to gross inequality that relegates some to living in abject poverty for no fault of their own, and finds the answer in alleviating their poverty. This is the implicit

view of Piketty who would raise taxes on the rich to benefit the poor, but not really change the system. (Unrealistic in any event.) The causes of inequality are not dealt with, nor are the huge benefits gained through exploitation visible to those who profit from sustaining inequality without challenge, let alone face mobilized resistance which has historically won concessions. The argument is perhaps that there is no reason to object to inequality at the top if no one is hurt by it. If all at the bottom have enough for a decent standard of living, why shouldn't the rich be richer than they? The answer thus lies in anti-poverty programs, with a focus on who the poor are, how to help them get ahead with education for jobs and careers, if they are doing their best then to support them with subsidies up to the point where all, regardless of natural capabilities, achieve some minimum standard of living. Morally the rich should act charitably to help the poor, but the fault that creates poverty lies not in their riches, but in the stars, or in the incapacities of the poor, or in the important economic laws that produce prosperity but inevitably have unequal results for some, with results that should be countered by help from the general funds of society. The goal is not to reduce inequality *per se*, but to put a safety net under the poor, to end poverty. The whole society should agree to such a moral goal, in the liberal view.

The argument that quantitative inequality is unjust because it is unfair to the middle class is a different formulation of this approach, perhaps politically more appealing than a purely moral approach because more people identify as middle class than as poor. But that response rests on a usually unspoken distinction between the "deserving," hard-working, and law-abiding middle class who are typically white, often church goers, and the "undeserving" poor, who are typically people of color and or ethnic difference, as well as those who, in non-economic life style ways, are non-conformists and do not share "middle class values" or patterns of behavior, including, for instance gender relationships, LGBTs, and those most likely to be criminal and behave in anti-social ways.[7] The concern is that the middle class families are slipping out of the middle and into the bottom, and the answer is to help them with governmental support, perhaps low-interest loans to encourage their entrepreneurship, labor laws that prohibit unhealthy working conditions, mandatory sick leaves, rationalized and partially subsidized health care, and expanded skill-oriented

7   It is interesting to note that the conservatives of *National Review* have seen the working class Trump supporters, overwhelmingly white, in much the same pathological ways as were African Americans seen in the late sixties, lazy, hedonistic drug users that embraced pathological life styles, identities and values. See Charles Murray, *Coming Apart,* New York; Crown Forum Murray, 2012)

higher education, etc. Conformity to middle class values is demanded of recipients of such benefits, but those not conforming may be helped by carefully moderated measures to come into conformity. The response assumes an essentially normal and inevitable quantitative economic and qualitative non-economic inequality to be natural, and seeks to ameliorate it after it has occurred, in the distribution of the system, rather than dealing with the causes that produce it. Consistent with a liberal analysis, the wealth of the top is only gingerly addressed, by non-confiscatory taxes on the rich only to the level needed to pay for ameliorative support for the endangered members of the middle class and poor. They do not question whether the acquisition of wealth by the rich is a cause of the insufficient wealth of the middle and poor. And the taxes on the rich must also be kept moderate, because it is assumed that the rich are needed to provide jobs for the middle class and poor, and too high taxes would reduce their incentives to run the businesses that provide those jobs. Thus the liberal response to inequality is to address it only at the bottom and middle of the distribution of wealth, leaving both the political and the economic structures that have created the inequality at the top modified but essentially intact. But it is a solution that might find consensus support among a large part, if not a majority, of the population.

The Progressive Response

The Bernie Sanders campaign, he as a declared democratic socialist, might be called the progressive side of the liberal approach. Bernie Sanders' approach generally could then be seen as well short of something more radical (see below). The liberal and the progressive approaches share most of the same values, but differ in their politics, which I believe leads also to differences in the analysis used to undergird them. The Clinton liberal approach aims at forming a broad coalition that would move towards consensus by minimizing areas of disagreement and conflict, seeking a practical majoritarian compromise on the liberal side of key disputes. The Sanders progressive approach is more confrontational, speaking for a younger and more populist base, does not expect consensus, but accepts the necessity to confront sharp clashes of interest in achieving its objectives.

Strategically, the Clinton liberal position hopes to avoid direct and painful confrontation with the prevailing structures of power, and hopes to redress unjust inequalities in the system through progressively oriented accommodation with those in power. On the radical side of the progressive approach, the Sanders position is willing to directly attack the holders of power to achieve the goal of reducing inequality. The liberal view focuses on lifting the middle and lower parts of the 99%, seeing redistribution from the top 1% as a simply an unfortunate necessity to achieve that end. The progressive view also addresses the disparity between the 1% and the 99%, but sees the 1% as unjustly enriched, having accumulated obscene amounts of wealth-at the cost of unjustly "hollowing out the middle classes." Higher taxes on the rich are seen as a means to help the poor, in the liberal view; in the progressive view, they are also seen as a way of limiting the unjust wealth they take from the poor and middle, thus remedying a fundamental cause of unjust inequality. Whether the difference in political strategy leads to a difference in analysis, or *vice versa*, is not an easily resolvable or particularly useful debate.

Some progressives, including Sanders, call for revolution, but through the existing political process via electoral processes that mobilize the society to seek major reforms to temper the wealth and power of the "billionaire" classes and foster a more just system. But in the end, the measures called-for on the liberal and progressive sides differ more in language and in scope than in basic values in which the current levels of inequality, sustained by the political power of the elites are seen as fundamental unjust. A higher minimum wage is supported by both, although both implicitly agree that it cannot be so high as to interfere with a reasonable profitability for businesses or will dissuade entrepreneurship. Abolition of the wage relationship is not suggested by either, nor a fundamental recasting of the governmental role in the economy. Public regulation is seen on the liberal side as basically an undesirable necessity to be limited as far as possible; on the progressive side, it is accepted as inevitably needed, but its extent subject to reasonable negotiation. Redistribution is centrally involved in both; higher taxes are the conventional means to that end. Exploitation is inevitable, but can be moderated. Non-economic forms of unjust inequality are wrong, but a large part of that inequality will disappear if economic inequality is addressed. Everyone in society will not agree to that solution; the rich will object to supporting the poor at their expense. Liberals believe it can and should be reasonably compromised; progressives see consensus as thus not likely, unanimity not achievable, and conflict as inevitable. But stable compromises can be reached through social mobilization and the existing political processes.

To generalize, the liberal response seeks to address quantitatively measured inequality at the distribution end, after it has been created in the economy, and sees such change as feasible through the existing political processes. The progressive response to quantitatively measured inequality is to address its unjust production in the economy, but within the basic structures of the existing economy, and it sees the necessary changes as a "political revolution" on the necessary path to undermine that unjustly created inequality. A radical response would go even further, and seek fundamental changes in existing economic structures. Since such changes do not seem to be imminent in most of the world today, a transformative approach going-step wise in that direction might be a realistic way forward today.

The Radical Response

A traditional socialist view would approach inequality in a quite different way. It would define unjust inequality not in terms of the quantitative mal-distribution of the wealth of society, the difference between the 1% and the 99%, measured in monetary units, but in terms of the source of that mal-distribution, economically in the exploitation of labor by capital, which includes the maintenance of unemployment to create a "reserve army of the poor" at the bottom to buttress the power of employers, that is supported politically by the oppression of the ruled by the rulers. The injustice of inequality lies not simply in the quantitative dimensions of inequality, as Piketty suggested, or simply in the harm, indeed immiseration of those at the bottom, as in the liberal view, to be dealt with by anti-poverty programming. Nor does the injustice lie, as in the progressive view, simply in the differences in wealth and power *per se*, differences that are self-reinforcing and must be countered together. The radical view, by contrast, sees that the injustice stems from the source of those differences, not simply from their magnitude; it lies in the actions of those at the top which deprive those at the bottom of their share of the common wealth which in a just society they should have. David Harvey focuses as a major source of unjust inequality, in his radical view, on the dispossession of the 99% by the 1% to begin with.

Taking some of the wealth of the rich and using it for the poor is not enough; it does not address the source of that wealth, the conduct of the 1% who own and control capital created both the global/financial economy and used their wealth to control, if not buy the political power that led to the extreme inequality. Redistribution is a remedy that only ameliorates the consequences after the damage is done; it doesn't prevent the damage. That requires structural change. Ironically, it has parallels in the criminal justice system that punishes the guilty and compensates the victims, but it doesn't address the causes of crime. It is fair, or, indeed, by definition, produces an immediate just result, but it assumes the unjust structural arrangements of the society in which it exists, in which exploitation and oppression are legally permitted, which are essential parts of the system, if subject to some limits. In the radical view a revolution is needed to address the structures that support unjust inequality, including such aspects as the definition and enforcement of property rights in the economic system and the electoral arrangements in the political system that limit participatory democracy or render it ineffective. Radically, the argument goes,

a revolution is needed which continually seeks to end exploitation and oppression and regulate the conduct which creates them, going beyond simple
amelioration of the unjust inequality after it has been produced.

The radical response to quantitative inequality is thus to seek its sources in the structures of the *status quo*, and to pursue an economic as well as
political revolution to foster the changes that would limit inequality only to
just inequality. The kinds of goals a radical answer to inequality might lead
to, which in practice socialist theory and socialist practices have sought to address, might include (for suggestive purposes only!):

- A guaranteed annual income to all, at a standard commensurate with
  the real capacities of the productive system, set high enough to eliminate the pressure to sell one's labor on the profit-driven market simply
  to live a decent standard of living;
- Either direct government or non-profit voluntary private responsibility for the production of the goods and services minimally required for
  that standard of living;
- Nationalization of all major productive enterprises, with compensation limited to non-financialized values or less;
- Confinement of profit-motivated activities to minor production of
  goods and services over and above the necessary, and research and development above that level;
- A sharply progressive to confiscatory tax on incomes and wealth over
  some socially defined ceiling;
- Education at all necessary social levels public and guaranteed free;
- Cessation of productions of all munitions;
- Procedures for fully participatory and democratic decision-making at
  all levels of public action, with public support for the necessary informed implementation;
- Environmental standards set and implemented at levels to maintain
  fully sustainable levels of desired health for all;
- Recognition that the unjust inequalities produced by exploitation and
  oppression are linked together, and must be treated as a whole, and that
  the process of undoing them must be comprehensive in scope and depth;

And, most importantly:

- The issue of unjust inequality would then simply disappear, because,
  with all having enough for a really fulfilling life and with limits established on wasteful excesses of privatized wealth, the incentive to

exploit or oppress would imply disappear, and there would be no reason for concerns about comparative incomes or wealth that logically fuel current concerns about inequality.

These are obviously utopian goals, and practically relevant only in so far as they may provide a standard for evaluating the desirability of pursing specific realistically achievable goals. But to thinking through and visualizing alternatives to the existing along the above lines—playing with reality-based alternatives for an ideal society, as was common in critical parts of human history in the past but has virtually disappeared from today's intellectual or artistic life, might indeed be a generally welcome development.

In the context of the recent presidential electoral campaign in the United States, no major figure would espouse such goals, but neither would any explicitly defend the level of quantitative inequality that exists today. The more moderate wing of the Republican Party and the more conservative side of the Democratic Party espouse a liberal approach, differing from each other mostly in the extent of its implementation. The further left voices in the Democratic Party lay claim to a progressive response, in rhetoric sometimes similar to that of the radicals, but pragmatically toned down, so that revolution is spoken as reform of the political system, not in basic economic structures.

Politically, on the electoral campaign the view on the Republican side is conservative and the existing inequality, if acknowledged at all, is not seen as a major problem. On the Democratic side the liberal position is widely seen as desirable in principle but subject to a touchy debate to be resolved by compromise in realistic political terms. The progressive position is seen to have significant popular support, but unlikely to gather enough political momentum to be implementable to the extent necessary. The radical position is not seriously considered, however idealistically it may be discussed at the fringes of present realities, and espousing it may in fact weaken even serious liberal and progressive attempts at change. A different response is needed today. Might a blended mix of responses be feasible?

The Transformative Response

Might we combine and blend some of the strengths of each of the three critical positions in one approach that is politically feasible despite its conflictual character—a transformative position? The goal would be to maximize the immediate contribution to the reduction of the ills of poverty (the moderate position: placing some limits on the extremes of exploitation and oppression, with decent minimum wages, support for labor unions, anti-discrimination based on race, ethnicity, immigration status, limits on the role of money in elections) while addressing frontally the need to redistribute the wealth from the extreme rich to the rest of society (the progressive position: sophisticated and tough tax laws, protective labor legislation and support for labor unions and social movements, while the need to recognize the necessity for redistribution from the rich to the less rich) and keeping in awareness the causes of Unjust Inequality (the radical position: constantly illuminating the implications of the need to eliminate the those causes and address them directly). Is such a blended approach feasible? Perhaps.

Transformative might be the name of such blended proposals aimed at dealing with unjust inequality in a politically feasible fashion. It would characterize ideas, demands, program proposals, legislative actions, social movement demands, which would marshal political power behind immediate demands for moderate objectives with a consistent and open consideration of the political feasibility of achieving the goals of the progressive approach and building the foundation for struggles for more radical action. A transformative approach would add a recurring footnote, as explicit as the political situation will allow, to moderate and progressive demands to maintain awareness of the depth of the problem of Unjust Inequality and of the need for each individual program and proposal to recognize that the ultimate goal is actually the elimination of Unjust Inequality altogether. It would keep pressure on the arc of history to bend ever more towards social justice and true equality

One could list the systemic changes that would be needed before such models could become more than limited oases in a desert undercutting their ideals:

- Ownership or comprehensive contracts by industry segment, linking worker-owned businesses with the profit-driven businesses with which they must rely for supplies, subcontracts, presumably, e.g. common labor standards, environmental restraints, pricing. If competitors can undercut the worker-owned in such segments, they will win.
- Government role in setting such standards segment-wide is likely to be the only way to achieve and protect such standards.
- Nationalization, national level decision-making, would then be required to broaden the scope of worker power, e.g. to control marketing, what is produced, how it is distributed.
- Intersectoral linkages with other businesses on which any business, worker owned or not, must interact need to be established that will support the unique aspects of worker-owned businesses, e.g. relations with banks, sources of capital, patent holders, retailers or other distribution mechanisms, credit institutions, etc.

    – Central planning powers, e.g. environmental standards, health protec-
tions, safety regulations, protections against more powerful and better
capitalized competitors, decisions as to allocation of scarce goods, and
their uses, regulation of public goods, would have to be in place.

Conclusion: Equality and Its Limits

Equality is a goal in each of the responses to inequality outlined above. But
none of them are focused on what that response should produce—equality in
what? Economic and/or non-economic /goods and services, governmental or
legal rights, equality of whom, by race, ethnicity, gender, age, physical strength,
language, preferences, exactly how much equality is desired, based on what
criteria, quantitative, qualitative, need and to what extent does equality as a
goal over-ride or relate to other goals such as justice, growth, diversity, sustainability. Obviously the attempt to answer all these questions goes far beyond
what can be attempted here, but one point seems to me very important and
deserves specific consideration: Is "equality" really the goal that these various
responses to inequality are after? For equality is, after all, ultimately a very conservative goal.

    As the term "equality" is commonly used, it is simply the opposite of "in-
equality," as it is measured by the size of the difference in wealth and income
between the top and the bottom of the scale.. That is certainly the fundamental assumption of Thomas Piketty's *Capital*. For those whose wealth and
income is at the bottom of the scale, pointing to the size of the difference is
an immediate, understandable, indeed compelling when it ends below what
is needed for a socially acceptable standard of living, That could be defined
in a number of ways; John Rawls speaks of access to "primary goods," legislative drafting dealing with a right to housing defines the sought-after level
of income as the "AMI," the average metropolitan income of those in a given
residential area.

    Calling for increased equality by those below such levels is intuitively jus-
tified, should have a priority claim on the distribution of resources, and does
not need lengthy or complex definitions of its ultimate goals to be politically
effective. And nothing in this conclusion should be interpreted as criticizing
that call or diminishing its urgency. But in longer-term policy discussions, and
in political theory, providing that all persons have adequate access to primary
goods and allowing them to enjoy a minimally adequate standard of living,
would not be taken to be the ultimate of social policy. Having an adequate

safety net would not be considered in most contexts to be the definition of an equal society. It is too low a goal.

But raising the level of the safety net to meet some higher level of income and wealth does not work either. It would be a treacherous goal. Everyone having a six-digit annual income? A mansion to live in? The same ability to travel, eat at quality restaurants, have extensive personal services? Nor would many rejoice if everyone were equally poor. Equality, if used in its conventional sense as a goal of public policy, should not mean sameness, uniformity, even if at a high level. What is wanted is something not only more but also different. Susan Fainstein, for instance, makes a strong argument for diversity as the fundamental component of a just city, and for policies characterized by their democratic origins. Desiderata such as those cannot be measured in terms of equality of income and wealth.

Further, "equality" taken as a goal is ultimately conservative. It is a demand for a greater share of what already exits, a demand for more of what other people already have. It is a demand for fuller entry into the prevailing system. It does not challenge exploitation or oppression; it accepts the risks that go with prosperity as long as they are equally shared. It does not challenge the distribution of power, only its results. In fact, by focusing attention on the measures of differences in the distribution of wealth and income, it diverts attention from the causes of those differences.

Conservatives can be satisfied with a limited quantified goal and state it in terms of income and wealth. They adjust to the goal of equality if it is equality of opportunity to acquire wealth and income such as the rich already have that is asked for, if what is wanted is simply the hope to be able to climb the ladder at the top of which the rich are already located. They will tolerate safety net measures, while they hold back on their costs. But this obscures questions about the structure of that ladder. It is assimilationist to the *status quo*, no threat to conservatives.

Liberals by and large also regret extreme inequalities of wealth and income, but see the answer to the problems they reveal in social programs reducing inequality at the bottom and providing a safety net. But they tend to support regulating at the top only to the extent necessary to make available the resources for those programs. The quantitative measures of inequality as in Piketty are useful primarily to indicate the scope of the problem at the bottom. Progressives add to the social programs of the liberal response addressed to those at the lower end of the ladder direct regulation of the conduct of those at the top of the ladder. But they do not question the nature of the ladder itself, although they address inequality at both of its end.

Radicals agree both with the need for regulation at the top and social programs at the bottom, and use measures of inequality in income and wealth to buttress the need for dramatic change in the ladder, generally aware of the strategic necessity of not letting the even better, the seemingly utopian become the enemy of the good and the achievable better. A constituency for radical approaches, combining regulation at the top and safety measures at the bottom would address frontally the power issues that need to be faced to achieve the level of results needed. They would push for policies that both contribute to addressing inequality at both ends of the ladder, but would consistently point to the full extent of change needed to in fact end unjust inequalities, even when they seem at the moment utopian.

The careful quantitative measurement of equality defined in terms of distribution of income and wealth, as provided by Piketty and other careful and imaginative researchers, can be useful in moving ahead in all these efforts to reduce inequality and its impacts, but is of lesser help in analyzing the source of those inequalities and may even distract by its striking findings, from the effort to understand the processes of exploitation and oppression that are its underlying causes.

When inequality is addressed in public policy and political debates, it is really unjust inequality that is meant, not all inequality. Unjust inequality is really a major problem of our times. Perhaps emphasizing justice as an essential characteristic of what is desired is the answer, and recognizing that only justice can ultimately end the inequalities that plague society.

Conclusion: Capitalism, Contradiction, and Crisis

Lauren Langman and David A. Smith

The publication of *Capital in the 21st Century* catapulted French economist, Thomas Piketty, to the academic equivalent of a "rock star" as millions of people bought the book and discussed its themes (though whether they read it completely is another story). His extensive economic research and data from over 20 societies, covering about 200 years had a profound impact on discussions of inequality—a topic given little concern by most economists. The general public and the media were enthralled with the patterns described. And the sales of his book indicated, many people, experts and laymen alike are worried that increased inequality could have disastrous results. Growing inequality is increasingly seen as a threat to stability and profits of global capital. The concern with inequality may be "new" for economists, but for at least the last half century, every introductory sociology text has had a chapter, if not an even larger section on inequality, and in the last decade, that chapter has noted the growing economic inequality which was often discussed again in the social movement chapter of the text when examining the Arab Spring or Occupy Wall Street. But insofar as the impact of growing inequality has moved from academic debates to the broader society, it garners serious concerns, specially when seen as problem for White folks, and especially among working class men in small towns that have lost their industrial jobs, this "culture of despair" has seen poor health, rising mortality, opiod addiction and rising suicide rates. It has been suggested that the level if inequality in the US has become toxic.[1]

Indeed, many elites do see growing inequality as a problem. One of the major worries of the economic and political elites voiced at the 2017 Davos, Switzerland meeting of the WEF (World Economic Forum), was concern about the stability and/or profitability of global capitalism in face of growing reactionary, populist-nationalist movements like Brexit and the election of Trump, many of which are directed against globalization, in general, and the EU, in particular.[2] It is clearly evident that they fear major revolts as angry peasant brigades with their pitchforks, staves and torches might march to the castles:

---

1 Thomas M. Shapiro, *Toxic Inequality: How America's Wealth Gap Destroys Mobility, Deepens the Racial Divide, and Threatens Our Future*, (New York: Perseus Books, 2017).

2 See Rising Inequality threatens world economy. https://www.theguardian.com/business/2017/jan/11/inequality-world-economy-wef-brexit-donald-trump-world-economic-forum-risk-report. Accessed February 16, 2017.

aka, the country clubs, mansions, gated communities and mega-yachts of the elites. Various angry, if not reactionary/populist, movements are growing, including the rise of Marine Le Pen's National Front or Nigil Farage style UKIP nationalism that fueled the Brexit vote, and the reactionary ethno-nationalist Donald Trump was elected President of the United States

As a Frenchman, Piketty was surely aware of the fate of the *ancien regime* fostered inequality and hardship, critiques of dynastic rule abounded, supposedly Marie Antoinette suggested the "peasants eat cake" then came the Revolution, the guillotine and reign of terror.[3] Thus, he makes the classical liberal argument to ameliorate inequality through democratic control of the existing market economy along with more progressive taxation of global commerce and in turn, greater redistribution in order to "save the system." Piketty suggested ways of solving the problem of inequality, higher taxation and generous redistribution, that remained within the dominant frameworks and did not question the very nature of capitalism or imagine structural transformation, especially of ownership. But progressive scholars were not so sanguine, as they read the book, noting how a tome on capital fundamentally ignored Marx, and thus could not really offer either a comprehensive diagnosis of the basis of inequality, and nor offer a "solution." As Robinson notes (Chapter 13), it offered "solutions" to the problem that might appeal to elites since there was little critique, let alone challenge to capitalist neo liberal globalization.

Whatever else might be said, there is a great deal of appreciation for Piketty making class based inequality, heretofore ignored or minimized, a widely shared concern. Indeed contrary to the mainstreams of establishment economics, inequality is growing and addressing it, requires massive intervention, (for instance, see Wright, Chapter 1). Piketty is loud and clear that inequality has grown and provides a great deal of evidence to support his claim. When Occupy noted the 99% versus the 1%, the national conversations in the u.s. changed from debt to inequality. And there was more notice of the recent escalating growth in income and wealth at the top, which was due to the super salaries of elites that often included bonuses and stock options that counted as labor. Piketty sounded an alarm about growing inequality which has meant increasing immiseration for many given the waning of economic mobility as a legitimation of capitalism, especially via consumerism and the erosion of some of the central values of advanced democracies. Much like many more

---

3   The French economy had been bankrupted largely by its massive financial and material support for the American Revolution.

progressive thinkers, he did raise concerns about the growing inequality both within "developed," core economies and between developed and underdeveloped peripheral economies, recreating a feudal like, ossified class system of the very rich and very poor. As Krier and Amidon (Chapter 9) put it, "Piketty and his collaborators deserve the accolades they have received for making this laboriously constructed data set available on his website." His work has brought wider attention to the questions of inequality and for that we are indeed thankful. Nevertheless, many progressives would suggest, as have many of the authors herein, that Piketty fails to see that capital is not simply a quantity of wealth, but for Marx, an expression of value in monetary terms reflecting a relationship between competing classes in which one class, the capitalists, seek to maximize their capital by extracting "surplus value" from workers, reselling it at a higher price as the "exchange value" of commodities, and thus as labor creates more value that it receives, capitalists accumulate profits.[4] Given the vast profits they gain, they cannot consume it all and they can afford investments that further increase their wealth, while most wage-earning workers are barely given enough income to survive.[5] As Charles Reitz shows (Chapter 10), of the value created in the manufacturing sector, about ¾ went to the ownership classes and ¼ to the workers.[6]

Piketty did an exhaustive study of tax filings of over 200 years from a number of "core" capitalist countries and showed various trends of inequality. As many authors note, his fundamental insight that calculating capital/income ratio, β (the total stock of capital owned by a nation over income) enables tracing fluctuations of private wealth over time, within and between nations showing that investment income, often inherited, in the form of land, stocks, housing etc., is always greater than wages. Thus r>g, the rates of return on investments, grow more rapidly than overall national income growth and workers' wages. Buttressed by a vast and extensive database, with many graphs, this appears to be "natural law" of how markets operate. But some question just how "natural" are markets and resulting extremes of inequality. The authors in the present volume, many tied to Marxist, neo-Marxist and Critical Theory traditions are glad he's highlighted this issue—but we see the problems of inequality as basic

---

4   Thus for Marx, income and wealth, and inequality were based on the ownership of income producing private property and the exploitation [and alienation] of workers, it was no more a "natural law" than the divine right of kings.

5   It has been suggested that half of all families in America would be unable to come up with $1000 if it were necessary to meet some kind of emergency expenses.

6   For Marx, this meant that the "surplus value" added by labor that was going to the few, had 3x the value as "socially necessary" labor going to the many workers -as expressed in money.

and acknowledged by scholars for almost two hundred years. Surely inequality was addressed by Marx in the *1844 Economic and Philosophical Writings, the Communist Manifesto* of 1848, *The Grundrisse* and of course *Das Kapital.* That said, Piketty claims to have not read Marx, yet was dismissive of *Kapital* for not having data, while claiming Marx ignored technology and productivity that reduced the costs of labor. But, of course, this is exactly what Marx meant by the "organic composition of capital."[7]

There were important difference between the US and Europe given traditional patterns of land ownership, more likely inherited in Europe, while land was gained at low cost in the early USA. Europe was more prone to "U" shaped distributions of β-one reason that Europeans are more critical of capitalists. Investment incomes based on the wealth e.g. the ownership of property, stocks, bonds etc., rentier income (investment), almost always grows greater than incomes based on wages; workers rarely accumulate enough savings to make investments. This fosters inequality, oligarchy and rigid class barriers. Over time, the disparities grow, meaning that the incomes and wealth of the ownership classes increases over time and that indeed, today we might be seeing the emergence of a neo-feudal patrimonial class with increasingly rigid class barriers ever more distant from the lives of ordinary people. As Kus (Chapter 2) reminded us, following Piketty, education hard work, and even a relatively successful career rarely provide as much wealth as inheritance or marriage into inherited wealth. Bologh (Chapter 7) and Bakker, (Chapter 6) incorporating Weber's analysis of feudalism suggest the reconstitution of a patrimonial prebendialism of inherited wealth and an ossified class/status system.[8] Robinson (Chapter 13) argues this is a truly "global", process today (Piketty's focus is on various national inequalities "misses" this) and argues that a new TNC (transnational class) of the superrich, the new oligarchs and plutocrats, has emerged consisting of billionaires and multimillionaires who generally tend to be detached from any particular nation state, but whose wealth influences the political decisions of particular nation states and/or global agencies. Needless to say, this class of financial managers, CEOs of global corporations and investors, property owners and digital wunderkind generally embrace neoliberalism that eases regulations regarding labor/worker rights, pollution, and corporate profits; it seeks to reduce corporate taxation, privatize government services, retrench benefits and entitlements and generally regards democracy as uncomfortable nuisance, a relic of the past. But that said, many of the political

---

7 For a more complete discussion of Marx versus Piketty on this topic, see the analysis above in Daniel Krier and Kevin Amidon (Chapter 9).

8 Max Weber, *Economy and Society*, (Berkeley: University of California Press, [1922] 2013).

elites, especially those involved in global trade are themselves members of this transnational class while many of the "elected" leaders are easily bought off and/or incorporated into their ranks. As Oxfam recently noted, eight men, Bill Gates Mark Zuckerberg, Jeff Bezos, Carlos Slim, Michael Blumberg, Amancio Ortega, Warren Buffett, and Larry Ellison now have as much of the world's wealth as the bottom half of the of the world's people.[9] Otherwise said, while Piketty noted the "aberration" of growing wealth and greater equality during the 20th C, that was then and now, a new transnational class of the superrich has emerged, whom he calls hyper managers, along with growing number of unemployed, underemployed, migrants and refugees that Standing (2011) has called the precariat.

More recently, as Reitz (Chapter 10) shows, the explosion of mega million dollar salaries of top CEOs and upper managements, whom Piketty called "hyper managers" skewed "average" incomes, obscuring the growing inequality and "hollowing out "of the middle classes. As the old joke goes, Bill Gates walked into a bar and suddenly the average person was a multimillionaire. There were fluctuations of inequality along with the rise of the welfare state, or "shocks" such as wars. This was especially true in the post WWII period when a burst of prosperity, rising incomes and greater equality became the "new normal" while the subsequent return to the more typical patterns more recently generated many discussions, analyses and indeed, social movements.

The concerns with Piketty's work came from various critical, progressive, indeed Marxist and neo Marxist scholars (like those who wrote the essay in this volume) who were both highly appreciative of the fact that inequality had become a more widely discussed topic, and moreover, that massive state intervention would be required to ameliorate this growing inequality. At the same time, given the title, of his book, one might think his work was informed by Marx and more recent Marxist critiques of political economy. In fact, many of Marx's central ideas were ignored, e.g. just what he meant by capital which, of course, was not wealth/money *per se*, but a class relation generating value expressed as money. If rental/investment income grew, given the nature of capitalist accumulation, the exploitation/appropriation of "surplus value" created dysfunctions from alienation, immiseration, degradation and inequality, while at the same time, falling rates of profit, crisis tendencies, etc. As many of the contributors note, Piketty attempts to revive the traditions of political

---

9   We might note that 4 of them made their digital fortunes on the basis of computers and/or the Internet that were developed by the government.

See the Oxfam report: https://www.oxfam.org/en/pressroom/pressreleases/2017-01-16/ just-8-men-own-same-wealth-half-world. Accessed Feb 12, 2017.

economy ignored by the marginalists, but he seems to have overlooked the political part of political economy, namely how the power of wealth enabled capitalists to control the state and write its laws, the power to control the means of coercion, as well as production of consent of citizens.

Why do particular ideas and proponents of those ideas appear at particular times and places and resonate with particular actors? Borrowing a page from Thomas Kuhn, while noting that the ideas of every society are those of its ruling class, we would note how capitalism, especially its early industrial mode of production that created inequality and desperate poverty also gave rise to the conditions for a critique of capitalist ideologies and practices. Then came workers movements, socialist parties, and indeed revolutionary communist parties. Slowly but surely, there were three major responses by the capitalist classes, the State began to provide various benefits and entitlements, social security benefits and labor laws that mollified some of the discontents of workers. Nationalism "united" citizens into an "imagined community" and finally, by the early 20th C. rising incomes and the spread of consumerism again assuaged conditions and undermined the critiques of capitalism, at least till the Great Recession and the run up to WWII.[10]

From the viewpoint of the present day, the postwar period from roughly 1945 to sometime in the late1970s was the "Golden Age" of contemporary capitalism at least in the United States and some of the core or semi peripheral countries—especially those like Germany, Japan and Korea that received massive American aid.[11] Although Piketty attributes that postwar spurt to "accidental" factors, we would instead look at the intact manufacturing base of the US, pent up demand, Keynesian economics, and government policies and programs. Moreover, and often not recognized, some of technological innovations coming from the war effort had important civilian consequences and the burst of affluence and the decline of inequality. For example, the mass rapid and efficient production of bombers enabled the growth of passenger air travel, while the jet engines developed by Germany would eventually become the norm for passenger aircraft and explosion of tourism. And the mass production of radar created the facilities for the mass production of television.

---

10   A common theme of the many critiques of his work is his downplaying, if not ignoring the role of the political in political economy. State policies and practices, from military protection for merchants, wars, tariffs, taxes, entitlement programs, have always impacted the economy in general and inequality in particular.

11   As was noted by many of the authors, and will be mentioned again, it strikes many of us as incredulous that an economic analysis ignores so much of the economic realities since WWII, especially geopolitics and globalization.

Finally, computer technology rapidly advanced, and the legacy of Turing and cracking the German Enigma code was a major factor that facilitated the war effort.

As Tony Smith (Chapter 12), points out, during this era massive government programs enabled and supported consumerism, such as the G.I. Bill which provided higher education to millions, who then moved into the expanding corporations and the new middle classes; FHA mortgages fueled the explosion of suburban housing, aided by the massive construction of an interstate highway system. And let us not forget the legacy of strong union movements that existed at that time and supported such progressive legislation. Meanwhile small business loans encouraged a burst of entrepreneurship. The generally healthy economy of the USA, fostered a period of solid economic growth, investments in infrastructure, upward mobility and explosion of consumerism-especially when television became a household fixture.[12] Ultimately these programs led to rising incomes, growing prosperity and declining inequality that became the taken for granted "new normal": but that blip was an aberration.

"All good things must come to an end." And so too did the "Golden Age" of American capitalism begin to spurt, sputter and wane in the late 1960s, as low cost, high quality imports began to effectively compete with American made products and it became cheaper to import steel rolls and ingots from Japan than to produce them in either Pittsburgh or Gary. In order to deal with the competitive advantages of low-cost, skilled labor around the world, we began to see major changes in the American industrial system, more and more unionized factories of the Northeast and Midwest were shuttered and various facilities moved to the US South where not only was labor cheaper, but unions less prevalent (and increasingly that capital flight "kept going" all the way out of the country to the Global South). It was at this time that various critics began to talk about the "deindustrialization of America" and the growth of the Rust Belt. The fundamental reality was that the wages of most workers, especially industrial workers producing goods began to stagnate relative to the costs of living. Thus the Keynesian "solution" of pump priming, based on deficit spending via government debt, along with growing internationalization of commerce, created crises of over-accumulation, declining rates of profits based on manufacturing which a number of the papers in this volume highlight. The Keynesian moment waned. The falling rate of profits spurt in manufacturing prompted the advent of a "post-Fordist" regime (Smith Chapter 17).

---

12   We might also note the "military Keynesianism" in which vast sums of money were spent building up the industrial war machinery as well as mobilizing millions and millions of men and women into the military.

Manufacturing moved to a "race to the bottoms" of wages, sans benefits, including union busting, outsourcing, and the erosion worker's rights, coupled with a growing indifference to environmental concerns.

Between the quest for greater profits from global production and growing national debts, the Keynesian/Fordist moment was displaced by neoliberal economic theory inspired by Hayek and Freidman whose students, the "Chicago boys" advanced the "Washington consensus" that extolled free trade and de-regulation of businesses and markets, as well as outsourcing, import substitution and export of jobs, privatization and retrenchments of public services. And perhaps most important, global commerce expanded the role of financialization, especially the growing role of financial speculation, rightly called "casino capitalism" based on investment, currency speculations, the explosions of mergers and acquisitions, hedge funds, derivative markets etc. leading to the major transformation of industrial capitalism[13] (Strange, 1997). While early industrial capitalism depended on the appropriation of surplus value, congealed or crystallized labor within a commodity, more and more of the value created was subsequently used for financial investment. Today, more and more of that "investment" is "fictional" meaning that wages and wage laborers are now less necessary. Financialization thus became the major site and source of profits as shown by Saskia Sassen (Chapter 4) and Eoin Flaherty (Chapter 5). The "solutions" to the capitalist crises of one period, led to the current epoch of neoliberal globalization, financializaton and the crises of growing inequality for many. Governments retrenched providing social benefits and services, many were privatized, austerity budgets were introduced, and tariffs were cut, as were taxes for the rich. But once again, capitalists elites prospered, their incomes and wealth mushroomed, and the financial industries (including waves of mergers and acquisitions-often plants or units sold off and jobs lost, currency speculation, and new "instruments" like derivatives) produced vast wealth but few jobs. And many of those that have been created are low wage, contract jobs, gig jobs, hotel service, domestic service, fast food and various other forms of poorly paid, precarious labor. Much like the 1920's, in recent years capitalist contradictions have become more blatant, especially since we have seen a vast increase in wealth and its extreme concentration at the very top of the 1%,

Moreover, the emergence of newer forms of automation, coupled with artificial intelligence is such that many companies, even in low wage countries, seek to replace low-wage workers with no wage robots. Foxconn (a Taiwanese owned firm with electronics factories in mainland China), the world's largest

---

13   Susan Strange, *Casino Capitalism,* (Manchester: Manchester University Press, 1997).

manufacturer, is seeking to reduce its workforce by employing the newest generations of robots, which, joined with emerging artificial intelligence, promises to replace a large number of service workers. The staff of one new Japanese hotel consists entirely of robots. It is well possible that most work that tends to be menial, repetitive and alienating may disappear.

On the *way* to this growing wealth gap, there were a serious of crises, the Asian tiger crisis, the Thai real estate bubble, the dot com crisis, Enron, Countryside Bank, etc. Along with episodic crises, the past few decades have been times of growing numbers of precariat workers, many of whom had lost jobs to globalization, automation, etc. Then came the 2008 implosion and Great Recession, the worst crisis since 1929.[14] In the aftermath, the discontent was evident with Arab Spring, Southern Europe, and then the Occupy Movement. Surely the Obama administration bailed out the banks and financial industries and well as auto makers. Subsequent quantitative easing kept the economy afloat. But the crisis tendencies led to enduring uncertainty for many people and growing economic difficulties, which led to a reduction of consumerism and the diversions it offered. As a crucial moment of contemporary legitimation crises, there is been a slow but increasing withdrawal of legitimacy from the system and serious interrogation by both the left and the right.

Piketty's work, had a great deal of influence in making growing inequality visible, while raising serious issues for the lacunae of concerns in mainstream economics. At the same time, as has been seen in the current collection, his dismissal of Marx, notwithstanding his pretentious title and his attempt to suggest a "solution" via a global tax on trade, will not ameliorate the growing misery, suffering and discontents of many people in the advanced capitalist societies (never mind the immiserated masses elsewhere in the world). These hardships have engendered various reactionary movements as seen in the growing anger now evident with Brexit, Brazil and the ultimate tragedy, Trump President of the United States, etc.[15]

The 2008 crisis was a product of unregulated financialization, initiated by the massive collapse of the derivatives market that had been "secured" by the sale of "subprime" mortgages, mostly sold to largely unqualified buyers. Mortgage debt was magically collateralized, rendered assets to secure highly

---

14   Saskia Sassen, Chapter 4, explained how sub-prime mortgages were transformed in collateralized debt obligations, bundled, tranced and used in derivative markets. This house of cards was bound to fail, as NYU econ professor, Nouriel Roubini predicted in 2006.

15   To be sure, the election of Trump was not just based on growing inequalities, but demographic changes-growing immigrant populations that were visible, racism, mass media, the defense of traditional values etc.

speculative investments Sassen, (Chapter 4). But soon this house of cards faced an implosion and there was massive wave of bankruptcies, economic retrenchments and ultimately there was a major rise in unemployment and subsequent stagnation, if not decline for many that has endured till this day.[16] Although during the final days of the Bush administration the initial efforts to bail out the banking/financial organizations began, the completion of that task fell to the Obama administration. They would not only bail out the banks, AIG, and car manufacturers, but followed up with massive stimulus package and "quantitative easing" by the Federal Reserve that would slowly but surely turn the economy around. However, that "rebound" was primarily evident in a slow rise of the GNP, a threefold rebound of stock markets, and the explosions of incomes and even greater accumulation of wealth at the top levels of the financial/banking sector. Meanwhile, the stagnation, if not decline, of incomes for the majority, the "hollowing out" middle class incomes, and the demise of some well-paid working-class occupations became more and more evident. Although the unemployment figures seem to "improve," (US unemployment declining from over 10% to under 5%) such figures are often deceiving because more and more people had given up looking for jobs and many now work in either the "grey" economy, or many of the short term jobs of the "precariate" or the various "gig jobs," which became especially prevalent recently. None of these people are counted in official figures.

This is now a worldwide phenomenon. The conditions of global capital have reconfigured the contemporary class system: many nations now possess a new dangerous class, the "precariate" a term coined by Guy Standing to describe an emergent class, or perhaps a category, quite different than either the old working classes or even the *lumpenproletariat* at the very bottom of the class system, the expendables, people who may be homeless or living in substandard housing.[17] These are often the inhabitants of the burgeoning *favelas, barrios,* slums and tenements of the world.[18] Meanwhile most remaining jobs, lesser skilled service "McJobs" ranging from fast food workers to stocking shelves, and/or staffing various security services, if available at all, are likely to require less skill and are for the most part, poorly paid dead-end jobs. As a result of these changes large and growing numbers of workers now constitute the growing "precariat" that now consists of millions with insecure jobs, housing and (little or no)

---

16   Yes, there were 75 months of tepid economic growth, about 2% per year, for most people, incomes remained stagnant.

17   Guy Standing, *The Precariat: The New Dangerous Class.* (London and New York: Bloomsbury Academic, 2011).

18   Mike Davis, *Planet of Slums.* (New York: Verso, 2006).

social entitlements. Most have scant occupational identity, and do not belong to any occupational community with a long-established social memory providing an anchor for ethical and social norms. Being urged to be "flexible" and "employable," they act opportunistically. Politically, they tend to be denizens, not citizens, in that they have fewer rights than citizens. There are three 'varieties' of precariat, all detached from old political democracy and unable to relate to twentieth-century industrial democracy or economic democracy. The first variety consists of those drifting from working-class backgrounds into precariousness, the second consists of those emerging from a schooling system over-credentialized for the flexi-job life on offer, and the third are migrants and others, such as the criminalized, in a status denying them the full rights of citizens. Each has a distinctive view on life and society.

In some of the European countries like Spain or Greece that were hardest hit by austerity policies, close to half the youth are intermittently employed at best and permanently unemployed at worst. At the same time, there have been major cutbacks and retrenchments and privatizations of benefit programs as well as government services. In many cases, with the privatization of a number of government services and utilities, including electricity, phone services, waste collection and water, basic necessities now cost more and become unaffordable to many.

While surely much of the history of capitalism required the appropriation of the surplus value created by production workers, then service workers, with financialization less dependent on new sources of exploiting labor, many people become somewhat "expendable" and have seen stagnation or absolute decline in their incomes.[19] Moreover, the capitalist elites, of today, the TNC (transnational class), themselves relatively deterritorialized, rule the global economy by controlling individual nation-states in ways that makes democratization all but impossible. The limitations of mainstream economics, and even embracing marginal utility theories, limit Piketty's ability to explain the growing disparity of incomes, and even greater disparities of wealth. The only "solution" he can offer to growing disparities of income/wealth between and within nations, is by resurrecting the Keynesian solutions of taxation and re-distribution—and even he admits that is not likely to happen. In the unlikely

---

19   We do however see various forms of accumulation by dispossession and or dispossession
      that do not so much exploit labor, but appropriate few resources that enable the meager
      lifestyles in not lives of workers and the poor by reducing benefits and entitlements, or
      land seizures etc. See for example, David Harvey, *The New Imperialism*. (Oxford: Oxford
      University Press, 2003). See also Saskia Sassen, *Expulsions Brutality and Complexity in the
      Global Economy*, (Cambridge: Harvard University Press, 2014).

event these reforms did happen, small increases of redistributed taxes would actually have very little impact on the distributions of wealth in a system that remains capitalist with the persistence of private property. Given his own analysis, the rate of increased wealth of owners compared to workers would endure which would result in capital accumulated by the rich and alienation for the producers of wealth. Can neoliberal capital permit changes that might challenge profits of global corporations?

For Wright (Chapter 1), like many of the authors, especially progressives sociologists, class based inequality between workers and owners has been a central organizing principle of society since Marx's early writings, with further elaborations by Weber. Although there is no agreed consensus as to what needs to be done, most of the authors of this collection doubt that anything less than a major transformation of capitalism and its property relations can adequately address its problems, contradictions and crises. Real solutions would require massive transformations, changes in property relationships/ownership of capital in ways suggested by some of the progressive global justice movements that have embraced cooperatives, anarcho-syndicalist organizations, community owned enterprises and gift economies etc. For at least the last half century, every introductory sociology text has had a chapter, if not a section on inequality, and in the last decade, that chapter has noted the growing economic inequality which was often discussed again in the social movement chapter when examining the Arab Spring or Occupy Wall Street.

As was noted, we applaud Piketty's painstaking empirical research. But despite his sympathy to the plights of the impoverished, he is hamstrung by the narrow assumptions of mainstream economics, which limits his analysis, restricts his vision and narrows his range of imagined solutions. Again, the most comprehensive analysis of income inequality under capitalism remains the work of Marx. Perhaps the most salient point here, is that by looking at income as a variable—both its sources (wages/investments) and amounts of income, as Bologh (Chapter 7) argued—Piketty aligns himself with mainstream sociology where social class is conflated with quantitative differences along continua such as income, occupational prestige, and patterns of consumption, conflated into a politically neutral "socio-economic status", while power, domination and exploitation are little considered. But for Marx, class was a relationship, a struggle between workers who sold their labor power for wages, and owners who appropriated that labor power, including the surplus value added by labor and over time, so the inequality of owners grew. Thus classes were not just lifestyles, but fundamentally antagonistic groups engaged in struggle.

The political economy of the world-system is an important perspective, rooted in Marxist analysis and a long-term analysis of the rise and fall of great powers over the past 500 years. This approach provides a historical analysis of the rise of semi-peripheral powers emerging as cores, as well as the decline of the some core hegemons over the past centuries, from the Dutch to the British and now the USA (Christopher Chase-Dunn provides a brief overview in Chapter 14). This global dynamic and its impact on inequality is obviously critically important, but is ignored in Piketty's work, as well the recent dynamics of the nascent Transnational Capitalist Class, articulated by Robinson (see Chapter 13). Perhaps the crucial point here is that while Piketty based his analysis on historical data, he seems to little appreciate the qualitative changes of neoliberal globalizations in which a growth at all cost ethos is now the driving force of the global economy with its race to the bottom wages, repression of worker rights, and indifference to environment. The dynamics of these changes include population growth, commodified land use (agricultural and/or resource exploitation/expulsions) that displace peasants who move to growing cities with vast slums, *barrios* or *favelas* where crime is rampant, disease frequent and despair abundant. Piketty cannot account for this growing population: it is not a reserve army of unemployed, but a permanent underclass of the precariat. He can no more explain this than he can account for the *banlieues* of his Paris—where a mostly marginalized Muslim precariat are housed.[20] (And some feel a *ressentiment* that feeds terrorism.)

One of major critiques of Piketty has been the narrowness of his approach. It might be first noted of course that despite the title of his book he is not very familiar with Marx, nor other significant political economists such as Polanyi and/or Schumpeter. As several chapters noted, he ignores the insights of sociology. Perhaps this is especially clear in failing to consider any of the insights of Max Weber (2013) whose economic works remain essential readings in comparative historical sociology and political economy. In the essays by Rosalyn Bologh (Chapter 7) and Hans Bakker, (Chapter 6) Weber's *comments* on class, status and power provide us with a better picture of contemporary capitalism than does the narrow focus on the economic. One of the essential insights of their approaches, is to point out the growing tendency of global capital to foster a neo-feudal pattern in which contemporary classes take on the qualities of more or less permanent status groups, many of which remain consigned to living in abject poverty as incomes decline along with government provided social benefits.

---

20   See for example, Mike Davis, *Planet of Slums*, (New York: Verso, 2006).

The vast comparative historical study of political economy is little considered, especially the long period from the early empires of China, Persia or Rome; the transition from patrimonial feudalism to bureaucratic capitalism has been given little attention. Bakker (Chapter 6) and Bologh Chapter 7) note that this lacunae sharply limits his analysis, more specifically, in a book on capital, he sees capital as a quantitive entity, numerical wealth and as opposed to a historically specific form of power that structures society, he thus fails to see classes as groups defined by their relation to capital as owners or workers. As Reitz (Chapter 10) stated:

> Piketty does *not* see inequality as primarily a matter of the structural relationships in the economic arena between propertied and non-propertied segments of populations. Capitalism generates some extreme inequalities, but apparently not primarily through a system of appropriation embedded within the relationship of wage labor to capital in the distribution process. In his view U.S. capitalism is less a society dominated by a parasitic rentier class than by (non-parasitic?) supermanagers.[21]

By remaining within mainstream paradigms, and using rentier capital as his focus, he fails to look at various kinds of capital beside land ownership, namely mines, banks, factories etc. Thus, there is no interest in the exploitation and alienation of workers, just a focus on their incomes. Most unsettling is the fact that despite his historical concerns, he does not see the fundamental transformation brought by neoliberal globalization, especially financialization that is been so important in changing the distribution of wealth contemporary society.[22] Bologh (Chapter 7) argues for the importance of understanding this fundamental shift, especially the growing ratio of debt to income, which might be called "debt peonage," a situation of deep dependency and powerlessness for most people.

On the one hand the title of Piketty's book suggests a critique of political economy that has parallels to Marx's conception of capitalism—which is not simply an economic system of production, exchange and consumption, but also integrally politically-grounded by a state that generally serves to sustain and protect the economic system and encourage its profitability.[23] Although

---

21   See Chapter 10, p. 198.

22   See also Chapter 5 by Eoin Flaherty and also the discussion below.

23   The state serves an important role in production and dissemination of ruling class ideology, aka hegemony that engineers consent. It sustains legitimacy that either masks adversities such as inequality, or distracts people's attention from serious concerns by emphasizing popular culture such as gossip and love lives of celebrities.

Piketty noted the impact of war upon inequality, surprisingly enough, as Bakker (Chapter 6) notes, given the history of France and neighboring Great Britain, there is little concern with the role of imperialism/colonialism in earlier stages of capitalism. The quest for resources/markets highlights the earlier imperialism of the United States, as the prelude to the current domination of the United States of contemporary neoliberal globalization—the infamous "Washington consensus" which is however, now facing serious competition in a more multi polar world. While Piketty acknowledges that inequality is influenced by various political (e.g. wars/revolutions), social, and cultural factors that act as "shocks" to the system and might impact its current trend toward greater concentrations of wealth, his focus remains too narrowly recent and too narrowly economic, without sufficient attention to how these "extraneous" factors are contextualized in wider political economy. Bakker (Chapter 6) finds his focus on economic data (primarily tax returns) a very narrow constricted view of political economy. More specifically, Bakker (Chapter 6) argues, as does Dahms, (Chapter 8) that a Frankfurt School perspective on the dynamics of capitalism, along with Weber's insights on political economy, subjectively meaningful social action, and goal oriented rationality (along with later perspectives from thinkers like Horkheimer and Adorno) are needed correctives to Piketty's narrow views of Reason as a basis of legitimation of capitalism as well as its fostering dehumanization and entrapment within "iron cages" of bureaucracy.

Both Bakker (Chapter 6) and Bologh (Chapter 7) note the growing gulf between the billionaire classes of today and what is broadly called the "middle classes" of incomes averaging about $75,000 a year (with the latter seeing erosion of incomes as this class gets "hollowed out"). Even the upper middle-class professionals that generally average between $100,000 and $250,000 a year are rapidly falling away from the super-rich, the .01% at the top. The working classes are generally given little attention while the growing precariat remains ignored. But the 1% generally made 25 times as much as the 99%. This increasing inequality, suggests a society with income distributions more typical of a feudal society dominated by a patrimonial class whose income is derived primarily on the basis of the hereditary ownership of land typical of feudalism. Remember that at one time Peter the Great was the richest man in the world, shortly after George Washington became the richest man in America and in both cases such wealth was based on land ownership. Today the richest men in the world typically accrue wealth from various aspects of the digital economy and/or financialization, areas of the economy which increasingly limit the possibilities of mobility for most of the population. Moreover, whereas the traditional patrimonial elites legitimated their status/wealth on the basis of God's will, today, such elites justify their fortunes on the basis of personal abilities, skills and motivation while paying very little attention to cultural and financial capital of their families.[24] (And given their circumstances, most tend to be relatively oblivious to the living conditions of the majority of people.) While Piketty notes the emergence of this patrimonial elite, he fails to acknowledge the importance and indeed current relevance of Weber's analysis of the various forms of patrimonialism. Understanding contemporary inequality is not simply a matter of income from investment versus wages, but the extent to which class domination needs to consider the rapid rise of this neo-feudal patrimonial elite in a class analysis within a neo-Marxist/Neo-Weberian framework. As Bakker (Chapter 6) so clearly concluded,

> Piketty's use of the term patrimonialism is both heuristic and misleading. It is fruitful because it draws attention to the ways in which billionaire clans in the u.s. and elsewhere have a kind of "baronial" influence comparable in a metaphorical sense to the power of aristocratic classes like the British and French landed elites. Neo-patrimonialism is a reasonable way to think about the top one percent and especially the top one tenth of one percent or top one hundredth of one percent.

So since Piketty buys the idea of the "inevitability" of the persistence of capitalism, he cannot envision major changes beyond reformist measures such as taxation and redistribution. But a dialectical, comparative historical perspective, informed by the dynamics of pre-modern political economies, the foundations of which were in the writings of Marx and Weber, we can better grasp the various forms of patrimonial prebendalism, which are being reconstituted today-based not on the ownership of land, but capital.

If Piketty gave classical political economy/sociology too little attention, Walby argues (in Chapter 3) he also needs some contemporary sociology for a more comprehensive analysis of inequality. She is quite critical about his treating war as an exogenous "shock," and outside his theorization of societal dynamics. As Weber reminded us, the modern Sate monopolizes the means of violence, and thus violence and the economy are interconnected. Pikkety's

---

24   Many of the mega-rich of today owe their fortunes to the development of computers and the Internet. However, the computer research and Internet development were initiated during and after wwii by the Defense Department. The problem is that civilian use of computer and Internet technologies has not only made certain people extremely rich (think Bill Gates, Carlos Slim, Steve Jobs, Jeff Bezos) but these technologies have also eliminated millions of jobs.

work paid little attention to the nature of governance (e.g. monarchy or democracy), nor the impacts of political mobilizations on government's fiscal laws and policies. Moreover, a crucial problem is his lack of understanding of contemporary global political economy, especially the distinctiveness and significance of finance capital. Similarly, Walby Chapter 3) says he neglects considerations of gender, in particular, paying insufficient treatment to fertility and demographic changes concerning married/partnered women. Her criticisms were not only spot on, but many of the contributions to this collection specifically picked up these themes. As she notes, war and militarism play little role in his analysis. Yes, wars affected inequality, especially in Europe, between the world wars. Wars are important, not simply as forms of "chaos" (Piketty's argument) but as essential aspects of a society: especially modern industrial capitalist societies which have generally used imperialism as a means of gaining/defending markets and perhaps more important, securing resources such as oil and/or raw materials. War, military salaries, weapon construction and international sales, are now an essential aspect of national incomes. Moreover, modern warfare generally required large standing armies with trained recruits and expensive weapons—military spending both to support soldiers/sailors, the costs of military are paid through taxation, "military Keynesianism" and thus limit money spent elsewhere where it might produce more jobs and socially useful products and indeed, less inequality. Nevertheless, wars are often profitable. But none of this has any place in Piketty's argument. Similarly, the extent to which economic factors might precipitate nationalist/imperialist political mobilizations, leading to war, seems little addressed. Had not the Great Depression led to the rise of fascism/Hitler would World War II have happened? Would France have been invaded and the Vichy government installed? Moreover, a significant factor of many modern economies, not the least of which is the American case, vast revenues spent on the military, sometimes called "military Keynesianism," play a significant role in the economy-creating jobs in some sectors while draining resources for infrastructure, education, welfare, etc. This is especially the case when certain military technologies require relatively complex advanced skills they tend to be very well paid, while ever more jobs are quite poorly paid. Walby (Chapter 3) also reminds us of the importance of democracy—although the relationship is quite imperfect, there seems to be a relationship between more democratic politics and more progressive economic policies, perhaps beginning with rates of taxation. She also notes Piketty's inattention to considerations of gender, motherhood and demographics might also link to the way more egalitarian and democratic societies are more likely to have women legislators and/or leaders and typically, greater economic equality (compare Scandinavia to the Middle East). Thus she echoes a theme in the volume: Piketty presents us with an admirable piece of research, but we need to consider many factors he leaves out.

Krier and Amidon (Chapter 9) make a similar critique, observing that Piketty's location within academic economics tends to obscure a variety of political questions, especially those that might involve the role of politics and in turn, history and culture, in fostering inequality—or for that matter, parallel forces that might promote resistance to inequality. Like several other authors in this collection, they advocate for Frankfurt School Critical Theory, as offering a Marxist-grounded, informed, interdisciplinary perspective to link political economy, history, culture, subjectivity/identity/emotion, and what is especially important in the contemporary world, media including the Internet.[25]

Globalization

The financial institutions for rebuilding the postwar world were established in 1944 at Bretton Woods. Collectively this meant that a variety of natural resources from poor countries were relatively inexpensive for the United States while the manufactured products sold were quite expensive for purchasers in other countries. Bear in mind that this also meant the labor costs in other countries, including Germany and Japan, with many millions of highly trained industrial workers, were low in comparison to their American wages. With the rebuilding of various industrial economies (and the emergences of others such as the "Newly Industrialized Countries" of East Asia), many intermediate products and indeed finished imported products became much cheaper than what was produced in the United States and indeed often of high quality.[26] The legacies of Bretton Woods would eventually morph into the now deterritorialized, seamless world market with massive and rapid flows of goods, information and most of all, financial instruments dominated by a transnational capitalist class. And while Piketty does

---

25   One cannot imagine contemporary globalization without considering the importance of the Internet in the coordination and control of design, production, and inventory of the world's products, global finance, mass media, social media, conventional warfare as well as cyber warfare, especially hacking, whistleblowing and even as this volume was being completed, there are serious questions about Russian intervention into the election of Trump.

26   Japanese production was very influenced by Dunning, an American engineer, who advocated quality production, only to be ignored by American manufacturers until such time as Japanese goods were not only less expensive but of much higher quality than those made in the United States.

address globalization, from the perspectives of the editors and contributors of this volume, many of whom have long been scholars of "globalization," his work shows little attention to the considerable scholarship of WSA (World-Systems Analysis), the dominant role of the TNC (Transnational Class), the vast scholarship on globalization found in sociology, political science or philosophy for example, or the various now global political mobilizations left or right.

Tony Smith (Chapter 12) pointed out several of these shortcomings of Piketty's approach. He begins with its very limited concern with global markets and the worldwide flows of technology, goods and capital, as well as information (intellectual property) and people, all of which have had considerable impact on economic growth and inequality. These connections, whether direct investments, technologies or intellectual property/information coming from developed countries, do not automatically foster convergences of incomes and/or rising wages for the poor. More often, this leads lead to increased local inequalities, much as the earlier comprador economies benefited local elites rather than local workers. Indeed, such inequality can mobilize worker resistance and lead to reduced foreign investments. In fact, many of the most "successful" economies of Asia, Japan, Korea and China limited foreign investment.[27] And a great deal of investment that came from the United States, for example, the Marshall Plan—the massive investment in rebuilding European economies, the "frontline" allies—was designated to limit the spread of Russian style communism. This successfully promoted European economic growth, while encouraging limited political reforms, thus insuring that the fundamental capitalist nature of Western Europe was unchanged.

But for Piketty, much of the postwar economic growth was based on diffusion of knowledge and know how—as if these existed in a world apart from economic investments. But the most advanced technologies and associated intellectual properties, based on highly capital-intensive R&D, is often too expensive for developing countries, while the levels of older and outdated, albeit affordable technologies are unable to compete with products already available on world markets. This can lead to "technological dependence"[28] and ultimately lead poorer countries into "debt traps."

---

27   Ha Joon Chang, has clearly demolished the myth of free trade as fostering economic development especially in the Asian countries where strong family businesses, closely intertwined with political elites, limited any attempts at foreign investments. See Ha Joon Chang, *Bad Samaritans*. (London: Bloomsbury Press, 2008).

28   For a full discussion of this in reference to South Korea in the 1990s, see David A. Smith, "Technology, Commodity Chains and Global Inequality: The South Korean Case in the 1990s." *Review of International Political Economy*, vol. 4 (4), 1997, pp. 734–762.

As we have seen, for both Bologh (Chapter 7) and Bakker (Chapter 6) Picketty's analysis ignored a long history of pre-capitalist societies and indeed, while noting the impact of "shocks" such as wars, and how WWII was followed by a period of prosperity, his analysis paid little attention to the recent transformations of global capitalism which is qualitatively different from its earlier iterations. More specifically there were major transformations that followed the end of World War II, many of which were initiated by the Bretton Woods conference. While the Bretton Woods agreements established the US dollar as the basic currency for international transactions, and established the institutions that would make globalization possible, e.g. the IMF, WTO and World Bank, by the end of the 1970s, an extremely important transformation would take place in the global economy, namely the rapid growth of financialization. While much of the concern with globalization focuses on the Chinese production of clothes, toys or cell phones, Japanese cars or German machinery, for some scholars, the most important moment of contemporary globalization is the rapid growth of financialization, which depends on recent developments in digitalization. Of course, financialization was the major factor leading to the implosions of 2007—2008, and the subsequent stagnation that precipitated the various anti-systemic movements of the left or right discussed below.

The chapters by Flaherty (Chapter 5) and Sassen (Chapter 4) not only instantiate recent financializaton as qualitatively different from its earlier forms, but illustrate the extreme importance of financialization, which is a major shortcoming in the work of Piketty. One must not only look at distribution, but the different ways income can be garnered—profits made via the manufacturing and sales of goods; the classical M–C–M' circuit depended on exploiting workers to extract value. But falling rates of manufacturing profit encouraged the "casino capitalism" of speculation. This was clearly the case at the collapse of the derivatives market dependent on the bundling of collateralized, securitized, subprime mortgages, credit default swap. Flaherty (Chapter 5) suggests that the class based Marxian critiques of accumulation offer an understanding of financialization little considered in the work of Piketty.

As Sassen (Chapter 4) points out, Piketty does go beyond simple analyses of distributions of income, but says little about the "predatory logic" of financial capital—especially its role in the financial implosion of 2007–08 and subsequently fostering the Great Recession (Meltdown) of 2008 that adversely impacted businesses, workers, consumers and public institutions, pension funds etc. She explains "It is a distinct domain, with a distinct operational space that feeds into that distribution." Financializaton is quite distinct from traditional banking, it is based on the logic of extraction rather than consumption. Traditional banking paid depositors or the government interest while lending money to consumers to buy cars, appliances or houses repaying loans at higher interest rates. This "spread" was the basis of their profit. Financializaton however represents a logic of extraction based on the financializaton of certain domains, the most salient of which was the collateralization and securitization of mortgage debt, packaged and resold as speculative, income-producing assets that ultimately led to the subprime mortgage crisis. Financializaton involves a much wider assembly of organizations than traditional banks: think only of Goldman Sachs or AIG. The explosion of financialization depended on deregulation which was a central moment of neoliberalism. It is also depended on digitalization and the explosion of the derivatives market, derivatives being little more than bets on what may or may not happen in the future e.g. fluctuating exchange rates, commodity prices, stock market indices, etc. Moreover, and quite naturally, financializaton has been a major factor fostering inequality. Many elites with highly specialized and arcane knowledge of this field have become multi-millionaires and in some cases billionaires—all the while the majority faced stagnation if not decline. At the same time however, financializaton required various normative/ideological changes, especially the normalization of privatization which provides the financial sectors freedom from various regulatory constraints, public accountability or popular pressure for the redistribution of the vast profits they garner.[29] Of course this has benefited the elite few rather than the many. For Sassen this logic is the norm for economic policy today which is especially likely to freely cross borders, especially since the system is relatively invisible to the public, insofar as the system takes place in disembedded spaces with "distinct assemblage of bits of territory, authority, and rights that function as a new type of operational field" with little public awareness or scrutiny. The strategic actors [predators] prefer it that way while the critical academics and/or a few progressive activists are relatively ignored.[30]

Sassen (Chapter 4) shows, financializaton, especially the esoteric knowledge that enables securitization, the derivatives markets, and credit default swaps is not simply relevant as an academic topic, but far more important than the ability of the mortgagee to repay the loans when the teaser rates expired.

---

29   We might note that Piketty embraced a position quite similar to the French group ATTAC that would put a tax on global transactions. Given the absence of any sort of enforcement mechanisms, dependent on the "goodwill" of an extremely predatory class, such ideas are pure fancy.

30   It is of course interesting to note that the enormous power of global finance is little recognized, while many of the reactionary mobilizations of today, target blame, and quite often anger, if not aggression, toward relatively weak, powerless minorities, immigrants etc.

The massive defaults brought down the market, but also left vast numbers of people, 14 million households, perhaps 30 million people, homeless. But the blame was attributed to the "unqualified," "irresponsible," purchasers of such mortgages, typically Black or Hispanic minorities. For many Americans, this was the received wisdom, at least until the Occupy movements proclaimed that "the bankers got bailed out and the people got sold out." (As already noted, the anger toward the elite classes contributed to the support for both Donald Trump and Bernie Sanders.)

The fundamental point that Sassen (Chapter 4) detailed is the growth of financializaton that followed the neoliberalism of the global economy; along with that neoliberalism came deregulation of commercial practices, privatiza-tion, and digitalization in which the predatory logic that cumulatively led to the explosion of wealth—most of which went to the very top financial elites. This of course was little considered by Piketty who devoted almost no concern to the specifics of financialization—especially transformation of debt into se-curitized assets, the explosion of debt and the crises of that debt. Nevertheless, the implosion of 2008, from which many (perhaps most?) households never recovered, was based in large part on the implosions of the highly indebted fi-nancial sector. That collapse impacted a number of industries outside of bank-ing and real estate, including automobile manufacturers, small businesses, etc. From the vantage point of today, it is now evident that while financializaton led to an explosion of wealth and inequality, it is also led to a more fragile glob-al political economy.

Crisis

A major aspect of contemporary capitalism has been the explosion of debt that has fostered both crises and growing inequality. "Crisis theory," rooted in Marx's analyses of capital's inherent tendencies, joined with Critical Theory's critique of cultural crises and conflicts (*kulturkamp*) and Systems theory then informed Habermas' (1975) notion of legitimation crises.[31] Further influenced by Weber on legitimacy and Schutz's analyses of the life world, Habermas pointed out that in any society, its majors systems need to adequately attain their goals to insure their legitimacy, acceptance by most of the people. But failures of 1) the economy provide jobs, adequate goods and services, and/or 2), the political system to provide stable leadership, regulate the economy and provide for the

---

31   Jürgen Habermas, *Legitimation Crisis*, (Boston: Beacon Press, 1975).

common welfare, and/or 3), the cultural systems to sustain social cohesion and shared meanings and values, challenge legitimacy of the system. At such times there is discontent and a migration of the impact of crises from the level of system to life worlds of identities, emotions and motivations. At such times, there is a withdrawal of loyalty to the system that might create openings for social change. As many note, the nature of neoliberal capitalism has been an unending series of crises. As Bonanno (Chapter 15) notes, the Fordist-Keynesian moment regulated both the economy to offer the lower and middle classes a stable, managed period of growth and in turn fostered ideological consent (hegemony). But neoliberalism, and unbridled individualism and competition, is fundamentally at odds with any kind of intervention, except when its contradictions lead to massive implosions like in 2007/2008.[32] Today, there is a permanent state of crisis insofar as growing inequality promotes suffering and uncertainty and erodes consent and loyalty—conditions that lead to anti-systemic movements; today, the reactionary movements are ascendant. And most reactionary movements seek a restoration of an age that is now lost ... but that mythical imaginary cannot be restored. Nor does Bonanno (Chapter 15) see a revitalized neo-Keynesian agenda, "it is difficult to imagine a progressive redirection of state intervention that would overcome the contradictions that engendered the crisis of the Fordism regime." How long can we endure this state of permanent crisis?

Global Warming

A serious lacunae raised by Piketty's work, is a lack of concern of the impact of fossil fuels, and "externality" of production/transportation that has produced global warming and climate changes portending apocalyptic disaster. Will the human race survive? Chase Dunn and Nagy (Chapter 14) raised some important questions regarding the costs of energy in world economy; much of the growth of Britain and its ascent to world power was based on its relatively cheap coal for its industrialization, transportation and imperialist ascent as a core country then acquiring control of oil resources from the Middle East. (Most modern weapons like ships, planes, tanks, trucks, and jeeps depend on

---

32   And even with massive bailouts, Dodd-Frank, there was little actual regulation, the taxpayers bailed out banks and automakers, when they could have owned them. But there was no way a well bribed State would support a nationalization that would benefit the people. NB. Not one of the highly regulated Canadian banks lost a cent since they were not allowed to engage in speculative investments.

oil products). But in the last few decades we have become more aware of air, water and land pollution, CO_2 levels, CO levels, rising temperatures, melting glaciers, and more frequent, ever more volatile storms, draughts, hurricanes tsunamis etc. Antonio (Chapter 16) noted that it was only at the end of his book that Piketty addressed climate change and the depletion of resources as "ecological shocks that can change a system"- as some wise person put it, there are no jobs or social classes on a dead planet. Little addressed by Piketty in terms of growing inequality is the fundamental conflict between the growth imperative of neo liberalism—profits at all costs, and its impact, not just on inequality, on the environment and in turn social and physical health. More-over, as Antonio (Chapter 16) notes, while true that Piketty notes the problems of climate change, he sees it as a future, long term issue and not the immediate problem taking place now. Nevertheless, as Antonio (Chapter 16) points out, he does suggest that global warming may very well lead to system transfor-mation. Whether from GMOs, pesticides, antibiotics and growth hormones or high fats, salt and sugar in fast food, there are multiple dangers to health to secure profits. Between industrial wastes and consumerism, lands and water are polluted.

Morality

In this collection, whatever else the contributors may have in common, there is a sense of outrage, moral indignation over the injustices of inequality and the vast amounts of human suffering that accrues from neo-liberal globaliza-tion. The primary animus for Marx was the immoral nature of the radical dis-crepancy between the lifestyles of splendor enjoyed by the capitalists and the conditions of squalor, degradation and immiseration of those who sold their labor power—not the least of whom included women and children. As Peter Marcuse (Chapter 18) argues, there is a great deal of "justified" inequality in the world, few can become basketball stars or world class violinists. But the extent to which inequalities of income and wealth exist, most are more typ-ically based on the power of a few to exploit people and eschew democratic processes since the latter can promote progressive taxation to support social benefits. Perhaps the most salient critique of morality was found in Michael Thompson's essay (Chapter 11) where he points out that in a "good society," the fundamental moral principle must be justice, *and that such justice must include economic justice.* This is not the reality of today, in which vast numbers of marginalized groups, the precariat, the homeless, surplus populations beg for handouts, dumpster dive for food, and/or search garbage containers to find a few aluminum cans, while the elites live in luxurious condominiums, palatial estates, and quite often not only have residences in both, but may also have ski lodges and Caribbean or European villas and a mega yacht to boot. The six Walton heirs have about 30% of the wealth of the USA. Meanwhile about 2 billion people on the planet attempt to survive on less than a dollar a day; 65 million people have become homeless migrants due to expulsions, climate change, wars, etc. Here we might also mention how many refugees die trekking across deserts, drowning at sea, or simply starving while seeking better living conditions. As many of the contributors have noted, the analysis of Piketty, remaining narrowly in mainstream economics, fails to illuminate any of this with his myopic understanding of capital and the actual basis of inequality. Thus, if his diagnosis is limited, his prescription, taxation of global transactions, is not just unlikely, but even if it happened, would not really change matters much. Rather, as Peter Marcuse (Chapter 18) so clearly points out, what is needed is a fundamental transformation of national and global political economies such that workers are more likely to own the companies they work for, governments set equitable standards for work and income, a guaranteed annual income is needed, as are certain kinds of nationalization and central planning, etc. While envisioning such fundamental social transformations goes beyond the scope of this collection, the analyses of Piketty herein clearly show that the amelioration of current inequality cannot take place within the current form of neoliberal global capitalism.

Social Change and Social Movements

As we have seen, whatever else might be said about Piketty, his book brought wider attention to the growing inequality of the last few decades that has brought so much hardship anger, fear and/or humiliation to so many. The economics profession in general and its American versions in particular, extolling esoteric mathematical models to explain economics but not actual economies, have paid scant attention to inequality, implicitly assuming the growing wealth of the elites would promote spending, investment and ergo job creation and the "trickle-down effect" would raise all ships, though many ships had short anchor chains and sank. It would be more accurate to say it was a tinkle down phenomenon and the majority were peed upon, and many could not afford umbrellas. But as we have seen, broad sectors of the general population have felt onerous consequences from growing inequality as it skyrocketed in the last several decades; meanwhile, the wealth of the upper segments of the elites, especially those involved in financialization, also skyrocketed.

For Marx every hitherto economic system rested upon dialectical conflicts, contradictions between classes, within a class and/or contradictions
of ideological promises and realities. These contradictions eventually foster
negations, that trigger mass mobilizations and transformations until the fundamental contradictions of class conflict between haves and have-nots was
overcome. Piketty was clear that the growing levels of inequality might spell
unrest and social instability—and since his book came out the impact has been
especially clear in terms of mounting unrest, challenges, resistance and social
movements. We would argue that the increasing contradictions of global capital raise fundamental questions about crises of legitimation. As the bard put
it, when troubles come, they come not as single spies but as whole battalions.
Thus the critique of Piketty, as many of chapters claim, is not simply about
economic inequality and hardships, but leadership indifferent to the masses,
and/or changing cultural values. When people are denied the possibility of a
decent and secure quality of life that allows for social relationships and creative fulfillment the adverse consequences of those heightened moments of
system crisis lead to withdrawal of commitment to the system and spaces for
critique, resistance and change. It is clear that the various social movements
of recent times, are not motivated simply by economic factors, but indignation and resentment toward indifferent governments and the consequences
of neoliberalism, in general, followed by the 2008 implosion, in particular
and the enduring stagnation. Economic crises lead to tightfisted austerity programs, major retrenchments of government support and the privatization of
various resources and services from water and garbage collection to education
and healthcare. As we have seen, these factors, are not only crucial for understanding the conditions of our time, but are hardly broached by Piketty who
despite his "liberal" sympathies, has nevertheless remained within a relatively
constrained economic framework indifferent to morality and seemingly indifferent to the types of critiques raised in this volume. Nevertheless, as noted,
the current wave of anti-systemic movements may be coming as much from
the reactionary right and as the progressive left.

Anger

Thus we see a growing trend of anti-systemic movements that while somewhat
independent of each other, at the same time often linked to each other ideologically and sometimes virtually. With stagnation and/or decline, especially
following various crises, many people have become fearful, anxious and angry.
The responses most typical of the petit bourgeoisie, the classical bearers of

reactionary ideologies, have often been various populist-nationalisms, expressions of *ressentiment*, ranging from the Tea Party in the United States to the growth of various right wing movements in Europe (e.g., Geert Wilders in Holland, Marine Le Pen's National Front or the UKIP and the Brexit campaign). Great dissatisfaction with economic stagnation, coupled with highly visible migration and fear of Muslims, creates a patina of racism, nationalism and xenophobia to these mobilizations, along with targeting "enemies" and seeking revenge.[33] This was epitomized by the election campaign of Donald Trump in the U.S. This been a reaction to feelings of anger and despair in the face of the juggernaut of global neoliberalism that clearly has failed to "deliver" for so many ordinary citizens, but may appear to many as all powerful and impregnable.

One of the key elements of most conservative-reactionary movements is a promise to return to a Golden Age, the loss of which is generally attributed to various "enemies." As we earlier noted, the "Golden Age" of American capitalism in the post-war period was a time of growing prosperity at the national and personal levels. This era of career mobility, growing incomes and more affluent life styles of consumerism for many, is now long past. (We might note that it was not so golden for everyone, for instance, most African-Americans and other US minority groups.) But, of course, the "demise" of this "Golden Ages" has been largely due to structural factors tied to contemporary capitalism, not "enemies" such as immigrants, foreigners, Islamic terrorist etc. Nevertheless, the appeals of Geert Wilders, Nigil Farage, Marine LePen and Donald Trump, promise to restore a lost, pristine "past" that is often more mythical than actual.

The various right-wing populisms and nationalisms might well articulate anger, anxiety and the discontents of growing inequality, but economic nationalisms are no longer viable strategies for producing/distributing wealth and are thus quite unable to offer policies that might ameliorate the inequality and assuage the anger. Indeed, recalling Nietzsche's comments about *ressentiment* goes beyond anger and indignation to a need for revenge and harsh punishment of those deemed responsible for one's misfortunes suggests that given that the

---

33   The *petit bourgeoisie*, e.g. lower middle class, though some elements of blue collar workers, are prone to reactionary ideologies for social psychological as well as structural reasons. Their socialization tends to be rather strict, authoritarian and disposed to submit to authority, while dominating "subordinate" groups. Moreover, as small business owners, lower echelon state employees, their work demand submission and cordiality to those above, and need to differentiate themselves from the working class fosters an anxiety alleviated by submission to leaders, especially those who promise a "return" to a glorious era and who designate "enemies" who thwart the "people."

hardships that many face are structural, inevitable consequences of a capitalist political economy, there are no real "enemies" just personifications. This intense humiliation based rage shades into a nihilist destructiveness seen in various reactionary movements from fascism to Trumpism to Al Qaeda and ISIS. Quite often, individuals or groups become the scapegoats for this rage, so much easier to target "evil" or "bad" people than deal with more abstract structural forces. The fury of their anger—humiliation based—rage becomes self-destructive.

Hope

It is all too easy to feel hopeless, helpless and despairing given the present moment of global capital with its unprecedented wealth, ever growing inequality, environmental despoliation and almost universal legitimation of neoliberalism, even extolled by President Xi Jingping of PRC. The system and its ideological justifications might be seen as all powerful and impregnable. And meanwhile, we note the demise of democracy in face of an ascendant conservative-reactionary plutocracy of the uber rich who support, if not outright buy, politicians that disdain popular democracy and are indifferent to the plight of the masses. And beneath the surface of glittering consumerism, rising stock markets and declining unemployment—even if most job growth is at lower levels of skill and remuneration—as we have noted everything is not well. How might ameliorative change come about? Piketty's reformist framework, can little apprehend the nature of the problem and can only suggest a "band aid" solution, progressive tax, when a major transformation is required

Christopher Chase-Dunn and Nagy (Chapter 14) critically highlight the salience of social changes/world revolutions across the contemporary world-system which underlines how anti-systemic social movements have often challenged and impacted inequality. Indeed, in this year, 2017, we might recall that 100 years ago, a revolution in Russia ended the power of the Tsar and the Boyars, a landed gentry class of rentiers; communist Russia rapidly industrialized and changed the world. Counter hegemonic movements have a long history, often ignored, yet have led to major transformations and altered patterns of inequality. Following the 1929 crash in the US, various labor, progressive and indeed communist movements pressured for a more democratic "New Deal," in which FDR was forced to initiate a Keynesian agenda. And in Germany, similar forces led to an atavistic nationalism in which Hitler came to power, the German economy again prospered, rebuilt a military—and the rest is history.

Marx provided us with insights and tools for the critique of capitalism and its transcendence. His critique was not simply a demand for better wages/working conditions and/or unemployment/retirement benefits, but the overcoming of capitalism and its inherent forms of inequality, domination, alienation and exploitation, immiseration and injustice, in which selfhood was truncated, people were left without recognition and ultimately and bereft of dignity, devoid of their very humanity. Its fundamental contradictions and crises, its immiseration impelled change, resolution through transformation, or more likely, revolution. Marx created space for visions, if not exact blueprints, of what might be possible in an alternative, post-capitalist society where freedom would displace necessity, community would overcome atomization and creative, dignified human fulfillment was possible for all.[34] For Jacoby (2005) such a society needs to promote "peace, ease, plenty, equality, leisure and pleasure ... linked brotherhood and communal work." It is for this reason that Marx remains useful, not only in offering a systematic critique of capitalism and its dysfunctions, but instead, Marx and subsequent Marxists have provided us with alternative visions of a humanistic society; for example, what Erich Fromm (1967) called a "sane society" which encourages the creative fulfillment of everyone, privileges being" over "having," community over fragmentation, and grants recognition to every person's humanity, provides him or her dignity rather than degradation and promotes living in harmony with and in awe of nature.[35]

As many of the papers in this volume show, contra Piketty, global capitalism is far less formidable and inevitable than it seems. History tells us that all hegemons eventually collapse—and typically from within.[36] Crises of inequality are less likely to abate rendering the system more unstable, creating openings for change.[37] In our dialectical view, current contradictions of capitalism that that have fostered right wing, if not reactionary mobilizations, e.g. National

---

34   While he was critical of utopian socialism, his critique opened space for such visions.

35   Erich Fromm, *The Sane Society*. (New York: Holt, 1967).

36   More specifically see Chalmers Johnson's trilogy, especially, *The Sorrows of Empire: Militarism, Secrecy, and the End of the Republic*, (Henry Holt: New York, 2004), and Nemesis: *The Last Days of the American Empire* (New York: Henry Holt, 2006). The author has noted this recurrent pattern as the "sorrows of Empire" and the parallels between Rome's move from Republic to Empire, the growth of militarism and the expenses of "imperial overreach" is eerily similar to what is now happening in the United States today. And surely Donald Trump is playing the part of Nero all too well, tweeting while America decays and military budgets grow. Where is Cicero when we need him?

37   Moreover, as Piketty suggested and more fully elaborated by Bologh (Chapter 7) and Bakker (Chapter 6), we might be moving toward a more feudal like structure where mobility is quite rare.

Front, Brexit and Donald Trump, have given rise to a variety of progressive social counter reactions and movement movements, rarely covered by mainstream media. They have attracted and recruited large numbers of people, especially younger people, including many not previously connected to various NGOs or SMOs.[38] Since Trump's election, liberal organization have received huge contributions and a variety of protests and opposition mobilizations. In Germany, the SPD (Social Democratic Party gained while right wing AfD lost. Holland, the Left-Green party did well, Wilders, came in second.[39]

While many of these progressive movements may well be critical of neoliberal capital, these movements, from feminism to human rights, LGBT rights, ecology, animal rights or medical aid to the poor etc., tend to be focused on their particular goals rather than transformative movements when large segments of the population reject the existing system, discard the status quo and attempt to bring about another kind of social political life. But at the same time, as many of these movements advance their causes, they begin to connect the dots and align with each other, as they see that the underlying basis of their issues is the fundamental nature of global capitalism whether the massive expulsions of people from traditional lands, the exploitation of women workers, and/or sex trafficking as a profitable business, massive environmental despoliation aka "externalities" production based on fossil fuels, and/or the limited quantities of low-cost medicines available to poor countries lest the value of intellectual property is compromised. Thus, as has become evident in many of the social movements today, there is a clear progression from dealing with particular and often local manifestations to a more comprehensive, anti-systemic perspectives critical of capitalism in its global moment and more likely to see transformations and reform.

As Chase Dunn and Nagy (Chapter 14) argue, since the world revolution of 1789, there has been a growing world civil society, now facilitated by the Internet that has enabled "virtual public spheres." These facilitate a world civil society of "internetworked social movements" (Langman, 2005). Progressive activists in the North or South and their organizations and supporters can

---

38   There has been an explosion of new movements that have emerged to counter
      Trump's agendas. See: http://www.alternet.org/activism/trusted-resources-resistance
      -against-trump. Accessed March 15, 2017.

39   Some evidence suggests that the rightwing mobilization may have peaked given it could
      never deliver its promised prosperity nor ethno-national purity. A number of Brits regret
      having voted for Brexit-as the Pound's value dropped, just as a number of Trump support-
      ers now see that his promises of jobs, better/cheaper health insurance, were as worthless,
      as any of his other bizarre claims. Will this demise continue? Stay tuned.

now more easily communicate, establish connections, network, exchange views, share information and strategies, support each other and coordinate actions across the globe.[40] This can be currently seen as a "new global left" evident in a variety of global justice movements, especially evident with the rise of the rise of various expressions of "globalization from below", from the masses of people, not the elites. The Zapatistas of Chiapas went public in 1994 when NAFTA went into effect, soon followed by the anti-WTO movements that converged in Seattle in 1999. Then came the World Social Forums that emerged in Brazil, as a "movement of movements" in "the space of flows," a forum where various diverse, progressive movement activists from all over the world gather. The worldwide nature of these mobilizations was clearly evident when Arab Spring, erupted as mass movement that quickly spread from Tunisia to Egypt, to Syria and Libya, then to Southern European anti-austerity Indignado mobilizations, and Occupy Wall Street were harbingers of anti-systemic transnational movements that emerged in response to the adverse impacts of neo liberal globalization.[41] Perhaps what is most important, these mobilization have shown that change is possible and in turn, "another world [that] is possible."

Despite what we see as the current shift to the right, the progressive spirit of the global justice movements should be seen as a long drawn out process, in which as variety of mobilizations and movements form or grow as younger cohorts enter dismal job markets with few chances of upward mobility and/ or stable careers. Quite likely, many will join the growing ranks of the precariat. Here we see an articulation of growing rage, anger and indignation toward the elites who have prospered while youth are especially hard hit. Such mobilizations must of course consider the nature of the actors, their visions and consequences that may take generations to realize. Most progressive social activists tend to be relatively young, old enough to be impacted by oppressive social conditions, and sufficiently educated to be capable of understanding the

---

40   When activists occupied the Wisconsin capital, Egyptian activists had pizzas delivered, and in turn, the Arab Spring inspired Occupy—and all were prompted by neoliberalism and inequality.

41   See Lauren Langman; Tova Benski, et al., "From the streets and squares to social movement studies: What have we learned?" *Current Sociology*, vol. 61(4) 2013, pp. 541–561. Some suggest that a great deal of the conflicts in places like the MENA regions are due to corrupt leadership, neoliberalism, especially privatization aspects of climate change, droughts etc. See also Paul Mason, *Why It's Kicking Off Everywhere: The New Global Revolutions*, (London: Verso, 2012). Some of this material can be found in the Chase Dunn and Nagy Chapter 14.

complex nature and consequences of capitalism.[42] Thus under certain conditions, younger people especially those in the growing precariat classes, directly facing hardships, become especially sensitive to these factors. For Herbert Marcuse (1964), the "great refusals" of the 1960s, the massive mobilization for civil rights, free speech, antiwar, and in some cases feminism and environmentalism were spearheaded by young college students and marginalized minorities.[43] Now they are joined by a major segment of the precariat, the college graduates without decent job prospects.[44] Facing growing debt burdens, college students and other youth facing problematic careers, the Occupy movement tended to shift national discussions from austerity to growing inequality, especially the growing fortunes of the 1%.

While the Occupy movement was indeed short-lived, it nevertheless exposed longer standing discontents that have been growing. Moreover, as social movement research shows, participation in social mobilizations, does change one's values, identities and perspectives and disposes one to future participation. Occupy, itself inspired by both the occupation of Madison Wisconsin, the capital, and Arab Spring, planted the seeds for the Bernie Sanders campaign, Black Lives Matter, and of late, the Women's Marches. Furthermore and especially relevant to the question of ameliorating inequality, while a number of progressive movements had been growing, the election of Trump has rapidly mobilized millions of progressives, far more have joined and far more rapidly than did the elite funded Tea Party. While such movements, Our Revolution, or Indivisible, linked with MoveOn.org, are far more spontaneous and unstructured, democratic and participatory, than traditional hierarchical movements, and many of these activists do demand and advocate for major structural change, clearly overcoming capitalism, the only real way to deal with inequality, will be a long slow slog.[45] Thus under certain conditions, younger people become especially sensitive to various injustices and initiate and/or join the kinds of social mobilizations seeking

---

42   It is of course outside the scope of the current discussion, but level of education especially in social sciences and/or philosophy that encourage critical thought are typically associated with more progressive complex worldviews while lesser educated actors, typically more authoritarian, uncritically accept the "explanations" of leaders, embrace more simplistic understandings, quite often "blaming" particular personifications and actors rather than larger social forces. This often turns to scapegoating which often turns violent.

43   Herbert Marcuse, *One Dimensional Man*, (Boston: Beacon Press, 1984).

44   See Guy Standing, *The Precariat*, (London: Bloomsbury Academic, 2011).

45   Paul Rosenberg, *Stronger than Tea: The anti-Trump resistance is much bigger than the Tea Party*. See http://www.salon.com/2017/03/11/stronger-than-tea-the-anti-trump-resistance-is-much-bigger-than-the-tea-party-and-it-has-to-be/. Accessed March 13, 2017.

fundamental changes that require generational changes to be realized. This is a central principle for NSM (new social movement) theory that sees current social movements as initiating cultural or political changes to be realized in the future; such realization might depends upon generational base changes in values and identities, noting what Mannheim (1952) said about the generational mediation of social change. Every generation is shaped by the events of youth who age, mature and move through the life cycle, what he called "cohort flow." A number of factors now suggest that younger generations mobilizing for a more progressive, humanist future, disposes the ascent of alternative forms of ownership, different kinds of work, prioritizing dignity and meaning, and a more democratic social system without the central control of an authoritarian party of the rich, dedicated to the common good, yet one in which individual creativity, self-realization enable dignity, community and living in harmony with Nature.[46] Given the processes of cohort flow coinciding with "wars of position" (see below), transformative change is a long term process, how ironic it may be when future historians ascribe the progressive transformation of the United States if not the world to the reaction to the Trump administration where never before has mendacity joined with incompetence and self-aggrandizement.

Theorizing Social Transformation

How do we conceptualize transformative social movements today when the dominant frameworks 1) little address large scale transformation, 2) give little attention to emotions and, 3) the primary agents of change are unlikely to be either labor organizations or political parties? As some of the authors in this volume suggest, some hints might be found in the work of Gramsci and Critical Theory. While structural crises and dysfunctions may dispose transformative social movements, nevertheless, dedicated activists, reflecting wider sentiments, are needed to organize collective efforts to transform classes/groups from "in themselves" to "for themselves" to confront power and implement change Transformative movements require both dedicated activists and "organic intellectuals," Gramsci's term for scholar activists with roots in the popular classes, yet at the same time achieving the kinds of critical understandings of (capitalist) domination that enable its overcoming. For Gramsci,

---

46   After what happened in the 2016 election, we cannot make predictions of the future but
      many pundits nevertheless have suggested that the combination of reactionary policies
      and agendas, with the complete incompetence of the Trump administration will moti-
      vate vast numbers of youth to more actively participate in the politics of the future.

hegemony, the ideological control of culture, enabled elite classes to secure "spontaneous consent" to domination and social stability by rendering the historically arbitrary social arrangements as "natural, normal and in the best interests of all." Insofar as cultural understandings that are generally accepted as "normal" serve as the primary barriers against social movements/transformative change, ideologically shaped culture is the primary site of contestation and challenge where "organic intellectuals" who understand the salience of long "wars of position," engage in ideological critiques at the level of personal experience rather than academic lectures or political pamphlets. It is here were social activists/organic intellectuals must undermine the cultural understandings that sustain domination. Moreover to Gramsci's insights, we might note that the embrace of hegemonic understandings and "willing assent" to domination requires further understanding of motivation and identity. While NSM (New Social Movement Theory) paid attention to the issues of cultural values and the transformation of identity as a means of transforming society, for the most part, that tradition generally ignored both economic factors as well as emotional factors.[47]

For Harry Dahms (Chapter 8) the early foundations of Critical Theory as a critique of capitalist domination, considered the totality of political economy, its ideology/cultural values, mass media and subjectivity, which still offers us critical insights toward understanding contemporary capitalism and its inequality. One aspect of their classical studies in authoritarianism was seeing that the anxiety of social fragmentation and powerlessness at times of crisis fostered massive mobilizations, left and right. In this vein, as Bonanno (Chapter 15) noted, following Habermas (1975), crises at the level of system, namely of the economic system, the political system and cultural system migrate to the life words of identity, motivation and emotion. As the capitalist classes accumulated more and more profits, often based on the reduction of wages there was a massive expansion of credit in the form of credit cards in which standards of living for many people were maintained by growing levels of debt. The ingredients were set for number of legitimation crises, particularly since 2008 when many people lost jobs and could not repay what they owed

As Dahms (Chapter 8) argues, today we live in a global society characterized by growing economic inequality, political crises, resource depletion and/or environmental despoliation. These are truly planetary problems which, while we

---

47   See more specifically Manuel Castells, *Networks of Outrage and Hope; Social Movements in the Internet Age,* (Cambridge: Polity Press, 2012). In his recent book on Arab Spring, Castells incorporated concerns with the economic strains fostering emotions which in turn impelled resistance and mobilizations

may not really have the theoretical tools to fully understand, require approaches that will hasten the transformation of our contemporary world, which not only requires sensitivity to political economy, but to the identities, values and lifestyles of people who've been shaped by the conditions of our times.[48] Survival, not to speak of social peace and harmony, requires us to create alternative, democratic, egalitarian economic systems that enable people to realize their freedom, creative self-fulfillment and even dignity in various ways impossible under the current inegalitarian system of owners and workers.

Technology and Hope: As we have seen, Piketty was quite clear how advanced technologies along with quite sophisticated "know-how" increased productivity and often give advanced societies a comparative advantage that grew over time. (He suggested that Marx ignored technological innovation.) And surely as we noted, increased productivity through technology, from steam powered textile mills to Fordist production lines, and to contemporary CAD/CAM design and production, robotics and artificial intelligence have lowered labor costs, and reduced the numbers of workers in manufacturing and assembly jobs while vastly increasing output. Today, half as many automobile workers produce twice as many cars as they did three decades ago—and most often, at much lower wages Of late, it seems as if driverless trucks will displace close to 3 million long distance truckers while driverless cars displace taxicab drivers as well as drivers for Uber or Lyft. Even fast food workers will be replaced by robots. Some futurists suggest that within three or four decades, perhaps 30 or 40% of the current jobs will disappear.

As was previously noted, the advances in robotics/artificial intelligence, suggest a future of massive unemployment and even greater inequality and hardships than we face today. But there is another view, informed by the progressive vision of Marx; we can design and control technologies of manufacturing and/or transportation to enable the reduction, if not the very elimination of alienated labor that produces profits for the few, hardships for many, and environmental despoliation for all. Instead, while certain labor will always be socially necessary, a post capitalist, post-scarcity society that allows people greater time and freedom for community engagement, play, self-fulfillment, and above all, human dignity, is to be much preferred to the work in the

---

48   It has been clear to a number of social movement scholars, for example Touraine and Castells, that many of the contemporary global justice movements can be understood as mobilizations for dignity, while conversely, the various reactionary, populist, and nationalist movements have been fueled by *ressentiment* in which economic duress has been compounded by cultural changes ranging from growing immigration to challenges to traditional identities

contemporary global political economy. With rapidly changing technologies replacing more and more human labor, much of which is menial, mind numbing, repetitive and degrading we will need to find new ways for people to work far less, enjoy life far more and live in harmony with Nature. Informed by the progressive vision of Marx namely the reduction of the necessity of work that produces profits for the few, a technologically enabled post-scarcity society that allows people greater time and freedom for community, self-fulfillment, and above all, human dignity is to be much preferred to the contemporary system of alienated labor, and mindless, distracting consumerism/mass media. Many of disappearing jobs like mining and food processing are actually quite dangerous. Let robots do that work! It is clear that the interests of a capitalist society are to maximize profit by minimizing the costs of labor, reducing workplace (safety) regulations as well as cutting taxes and ignoring environmental externalities.

Every society rests upon an economic base that would ideally provide its members with meaningful work providing a sufficiently secure and decent standard of living such that they might pursue a variety of gratifying activities such as hunting, fishing, and writing social critique. Thus for many years, various dreamers, visionaries, utopians, futurists etc. have imagined a world in which "smart" robots not only do much of the "socially necessary" toil, but provide everyone with a decent standard of living, a better quality of life for all, in which greatly reduced standards of consumption provide for the collective good. But perhaps most important reality is that living in ecological harmony with Nature, lest as Dahms (Chapter 8) and Antonio (Chapter 16) warned us, our species may not survive. But such a vision of a "good society," a democratic, egalitarian, inclusive society, resting upon a post-capitalist society that benefits the majority of its people, grants them freedom, self-realization, dignity and meaningful communities, living in harmony with Nature, cannot be imagined in Piketty's framework, analysis and prescriptions. We would of course hope that a collection such as this might be a starting point for more people to imagine that "another world is possible."

Index